1876
YEAR OF THE GUN

THE YEAR BAT, WYATT, CUSTER, JESSE
AND THE TWO BILLS
(BUFFALO AND WILD)
CREATED THE WILD WEST, AND
WHY IT'S STILL WITH US

Steve Wiegand

1876: YEAR OF THE GUN

This book is an original publication of Bancroft Press.

978-1-61088-580-5 HC
978-1-61088-581-2 PB
978-1-61088-582-9 Ebook
978-1-61088-583-6 PDF
978-1-61088-584-3 Audio

FIRST EDITION: July 2022

Cover & Interior design: TracyCopesCreative.com
Index: Deborah E. Patton (dp@pattonindexing.com)

Published by Bancroft Press
"Books that Enlighten"
(818) 275-3061
4527 Glenwood Avenue
La Crescenta CA 91214
www.bancroftpress.com

PRINTED IN THE UNITED STATES OF AMERICA

To my wife Cecilia,

who is living proof that some human beings

can endure almost anything—or anyone.

TABLE OF CONTENTS

INTRODUCTION

"Contemporary man has rationalized his myths,
but he has not been able to destroy them."

– Nobel Prize laureate Octavio Paz

"Events themselves are unimportant:
it is the perception of events that is crucial."

-- American historian John E. Ferling

"I never seen anybody but lied one time or another."

—Huckleberry Finn

Growing up in the 1950s, there were three things I knew for sure about Wild Bill Hickok:

- He had a fat, sandpaper-voiced sidekick named Pete "Jingles" Jones.
- He loved Kellogg's Sugar Corn Pops for breakfast.
- He was a good guy.

I learned these things while watching the televised adventures of Mr. Hickok on a small black-and-white set, precariously perched on a wheeled stand in my grandparents' living room. At the time I'm thinking of, my mother, younger sister and I were living with my mother's parents in their tiny house in Seaside California, while my father was sailing around the Pacific Ocean with the United States Navy. Despite my father's occupation, and the fact my grandparents' house was only a few blocks from Monterey Bay, I had no aspirations toward a nautical life. I wanted to be a cowboy.

Every Saturday morning—or so the generally accepted family story goes—I would prepare for my hero's TV show by donning a red cowboy hat and a pair of brown cowboy boots. Strapped around the waist of my pajamas, which were decorated with cactuses, lassoes and bucking broncos, was a pair of Mattel "Fanner 50" revolvers.

These were the *crème de la crème* of toy pistols at the time. Their costliness reflected the high esteem in which I was then held by my parents. You could actually load the revolving cylinders with metal-clad bullets! You could stick caps on the metal shells so they would make a convincing bang! The one flaw was you could not stick them securely in the holsters with the handle butts facing toward your belly button, as Wild Bill wore them.

No matter. As soon as the corpulent fuss-budget Jingles yelled his plaintive "Hey Wild Bill, wait for me!" at the beginning of each episode, I was transfixed for the next 30 minutes. My grandfather, a diminutive man known to his friends as "Little Al" (and who seemed to always be dressed in a stiffly starched white dress shirt and in dire need of a shave), would sit behind me in his padded rocking chair and watch me watch Wild Bill.

Granddad knew something about the Old West. His grandfather and great uncles had ridden the Chisholm Trail as real cowboys. He had lived in Oklahoma before it was a state. Prior to it blowing away during the Dust Bowl storms of the 1930s, the family farm adjoined a real Cherokee reservation, and Granddad was a good friend to several of the Cherokee Nation's leaders. So, as the show progressed, and Wild Bill would shoot the pistol out of the bad guy's hand or fight his way across the saloon without losing his hat, my grandfather would snort "foolishness" or "ridiculous." But every once in a while, even Granddad would grunt approvingly at some action on the screen, particularly if it involved fancy horsemanship.

These idyllic mornings were made all the sweeter when I got to consume some of the Kellogg's Sugar Corn Pops endorsed by Wild Bill during every show. In hindsight, this may have been due less to Bill's endorsement and more to the fact they were "shot with sugar, through and through." If there was enough milk on the table and my mother and grandmother weren't looking, I would sneak a second bowl. Granddad would smile, and not say a word. He even dubbed me "Sugar Pops Pete," after the cereal's mischievous gun-toting prairie dog mascot, and rarely called me anything else.

At least that's the version of events most often recited when my family gathered over the years and someone dragged out a photo album, or began reminiscing with vivid detail about events only dimly recalled.

In this particular family legend, however, there are undeniable factual discrepancies, quickly revealed by a cursory internet search. The Wild Bill television show was not on Saturday mornings in the Monterey area when I lived there, but on weekday evenings. The "Sugar Pops Pete" character didn't debut until 1959, the year after the television series ended. And it's possible I didn't get the costly Mattel revolvers until we moved to San Diego in 1960. But the legend's *essence* is true: I loved Fanner 50s, Sugar Corn Pops, Bill Hickok, and the Wild West.

There was plenty of fuel to feed my fever. In the 1950s, Hollywood churned out more than 650 Western movies, an average comfortably more than one per week for the entire decade. They ranged from *Abilene Trail* (starring Whip Wilson, who in actuality was an Illinois-born singer named Roland Meyers and was renamed in hopes of emulating the success of the already-established cowboy star Lash Larue), to *Yukon Vengeance*, (starring Kirby Grant, who would become TV's *Sky King*, the only Western star to employ a Cessna T-50 instead of a horse.)

There were Academy Award-winning films, such as *High Noon*, featuring Gary Cooper and Grace Kelly, and somewhat less-heralded efforts, such as *The Beast of Hollow Mountain*. This film featured a stop-motion dinosaur and Guy Madison, the very actor who played Wild Bill on my favorite show. Madison apparently squeezed in making the movie between Wild Bill episodes. As an actor, he probably regretted having done so after seeing how cheesy Hollow Mountain's beast was. But at the age of seven, I much preferred the movie with the dinosaur to the one with Grace Kelly.

The movies were abetted in fanning the flames of Wild West Fever by their rival, television. The 1950s saw at least 90 TV Westerns debut, many in prime time. They were followed by 82 more in the 1960s and 1970s. The small-screen shows ranged from the beloved and durable *Gunsmoke*, which ran for 20 years and 635 episodes, to *Wrangler*, which lasted only six episodes but was notable for being the first Western to be videotaped rather than filmed. For what that's worth.

Eventually, the Navy moved us to San Diego. I succumbed to the lure of the sea, and became a surfer/snorkeler/fisherman. But my love for the Wild West remained unabated, even as I grew older and learned that guns can be dangerous, (at least in the hands of people like me); sugar is bad for you, and Wild Bill was not exactly as Guy Madison portrayed him.

For one thing, the real Wild Bill's sidekick was not a garrulous fat guy named Jingles. At the time of Hickok's death in August, 1876, his partner was a short, fastidiously groomed hunter, guide and freight service operator named Colorado Charlie Utter. And if there was any grain in the real Wild Bill's breakfast, it was far more likely to have been distilled and poured into a shot glass than infused with sugar and poured into a cereal bowl.

As for Hickok's character, a Wyoming newspaper opined two weeks after his demise—which occurred from being shot in the back of the head while playing poker in a saloon—that "Bill Hickok was a desperado, and had a fair share of faults, but he also had good qualities, such are seldom met in a man of his stamp." To buttress their point, the paper's editors added a line from Shakespeare's *Julius Caesar*: "The evil that men do lives after them. The good is oft interred with their bones."

But the Bard and the Cheyenne *Daily Leader* missed the mark when it comes to America's Wild West. It's not the evil or the good that lives on. It's the legend. And 1876, the year of Hickok's death was a big one for Wild West legends:

- Six months before Hickok was blasted into history, a 22-year-old buffalo hunter and freight hauler shot and killed a U.S. Army corporal, in a flyspeck of a Texas Panhandle town.The gunfight left Bat Masterson with a severe wound, a lifelong limp, and a reputation as a dangerous man that lasted well into his later career as a rotund New York City sportswriter.

- A few months after Masterson's gunfight, a tall, handsome former brothel bouncer and horse thief became a cop in a Kansas cow town. The citizens of Dodge City would eventually name one of their principal streets after Wyatt Earp.

- About six weeks before Bill Hickok cashed in his chips, a loose confederation of Plains Indian tribes in southeastern Montana rubbed out a flamboyant Civil War hero and military bad boy, George Armstrong Custer, along with much of his command.

- A few weeks after Custer's demise, a sometime Army scout, William F. Cody, killed and scalped a Cheyenne warrior near a small creek in northwestern Nebraska. Later in the year, "Buffalo Bill" would proudly display his trophy for the entertainment of Eastern audiences as "the first scalp for Custer."

- And in September, a gang led by Jesse James and Cole Younger would rob a bank in Northfield, Minnesota. When it was over, four people would be dead, six wounded, $26.70 stolen, and the greatest manhunt in American history would begin.

By the end of 1876, Masterson, Earp, Custer, Cody, Hickok and the James-Younger gang had all planted seeds that would sprout into legends, or participated in events that would elevate them from already-well-known figures to American icons. The events themselves would become archetypes for thousands of written, spoken or filmed stories of America's Wild West: the saloon gunfight, the poker game killing, battles between cavalry and Indians, the bank holdup—and the arrival of a new marshal in town.

All this legend-building occurred against the backdrop of America's 100th birthday. After a tumultuous birth and childhood, and a painful adolescence, the country was facing young adulthood with tremendous potential—and serious problems.

In the nation's capital, a festering swamp of political scandal culminated in the most corrupt presidential election in U.S. history. The country was plagued with a moribund economy marked by bank failures and the collapse of thousands of businesses. The ever-present chasm between society's haves and have-nots deepened, leading to widespread labor and political unrest. Several million Americans newly freed from slavery struggled to adjust to freedom while at the same time fighting efforts to take it away again. American women increasingly questioned why 100 years after a nation had been founded on the principles of justice and equality for all, they were denied the basic right to vote.

But with all that, there were reasons to be optimistic about the country's second century. Spurred by its first truly big business—railroads—America was beginning to capitalize on the possibilities inherent in its vast resources. Waves of Americans and immigrants from around the world mined, ranched and farmed their way across the continent. There were manufacturing and technological advances, big and small. Steel and oil production, under the leadership of "robber barons" like Andrew Carnegie and John D. Rockefeller, became much more efficient and began to push Americans from farms to factories.

In America's centennial year, Alexander Graham Bell gave the world the first practical telephone. In Indianapolis, a Civil War veteran and failed cotton plantation owner, Eli Lilly, opened a pharmaceutical company that would become the largest drug producer in the world. In Pittsburgh, Henry J. Heinz, who had just gone broke selling horseradish, began selling tomato "catsup" in clear glass bottles. It caught on.

There were cultural strides as well. Americans in 1876 were introduced to the banana, the nation's first cooking school, and the *Adventures of Tom Sawyer*.In Chicago, businessman William Hulbert and athlete/

entrepreneur Albert G. Spalding spearheaded formation of the National League of Professional Base Ball Clubs, the country's first major professional sports organization. Overshadowing everything during the year was America's first world fair. A staggering 10 million people—equivalent to almost 20 percent of the nation's population—attended the Centennial Exposition in Philadelphia. And at 100 years old, America busied itself with inventing—or at least reshaping—some of its past.

Humans seem to have an innate need to blend historical fact with exaggeration—or outright fantasy—and create legends. Perhaps the need springs from wanting to build a cultural commonality, or to provide sources of inspiration and associative pride. Or maybe we just like good stories.

But America lacked the centuries of home-grown history and folklore that Old World countries could draw on in creating their legends. And Americans are generally an impatient bunch. So we created instant legends, embracing and embellishing events from the exploration and settlement of the West, even as the events were occurring. In the years after the American Revolution, for example, there were the "Leatherstocking Tales" concocted by James Fenimore Cooper. Books about Daniel Boone, and plays and biographies of David (he disliked being called "Davy") Crockett turned the men into legendary figures even while they were still breathing.

As America expanded—through the Louisiana Purchase, the acquisition of Texas and the Oregon Territory, and the vast geographical spoils from the war with Mexico—so did the potential pool of source material for creating a national mythos in a relatively short time. It also afforded those moving west to reinvent themselves, an opportunity reflected in a verse of a popular song at the time: *"Oh, what was your name in the States? / Was it Johnson or Thompson or Bates? / Did you murder your wife and fly for your life? / Oh, what was your name in the States?"*

The lure of reinvention wasn't lost on the subjects of legend themselves, none of whom were shy about embellishing their own images. As Bat Masterson put it, "I don't mind all of the lies told about me; just some of them." In the former category, presumably, were the ones he told about himself and his contemporaries.

This is a bifurcated book, which means it's like you're getting two books for the price of one, or one book that is worth twice as much. Your choice. The first part recounts the events that in 1876 laid the foundations for the legends that surround some of the most recognizable figures and events of the Wild West. Interspersed among these chapters are interludes designed to give you a feel for what was going on in the rest of 1876 America, while the Western icons were pushing themselves—or being pushed—into the nation's treasury of legends.

The second part of the book explores the aftermaths of the 1876 events, and how the protagonists' lives were turned into legend and came to form the foundations of the mythos of America's Wild West. It looks at how written accounts, movies, and finally television created a "reality" that persists, no matter how far removed it is from the facts.

In the 1962 film *The Man Who Shot Liberty Valance*, a newspaper reporter explains why he is declining the chance to print the facts about who really shot the movie's title character. "This is the West, sir," the reporter says. "When the legend becomes fact, print the legend."

But sometimes the legend and the fact are inextricably intertwined. Sometimes, what squeezes out is the truth.

PART I

THE YEAR

CHAPTER 1

"He was a good shot, and not afraid"

Bat Masterson and the Sweetwater Shootout

JANUARY

There was very little sweet about Sweetwater. Few of its inhabitants washed with any regularity, either themselves or their clothes. Dental hygiene was as novel as vermin-free bedding. In the streets, the odorof horse manure competed with the aroma of buffalo hides, only recently removed from their former occupants. In fact, the original name of the 18-month-old settlement was "Hidetown," because buffalo skins had been used to form walls for the first structures.

The town was located in the Panhandle, that part of Texas that squeezes itself in between New Mexico and Oklahoma and almost but not quite keeps those two states from touching each other. Its nearest neighbor was Dodge City, Kansas, 200 miles away. A creek called the Sweetwater flowed through the area, eventually hooking up with the Red River. Early on, the town's denizens decided "Sweetwater" was a better name than "Hidetown."

(In 1879, in bid to get a post office, the town would change its name again, after residents discovered there was already a Sweetwater, Texas. They chose "Mobeetie," which a couple of local Cheyenne told them meant "sweet water." It was later learned the word in Comanche could be translated as "buffalo dung." They kept the name anyway.)

"Dishwater, laundry water, leftover foods were merely tossed out the back door into the yard," an early resident recalled. "Dead chickens, bones and other rubbish littered the ground. Personal hygiene left much to be desired, as bathing was seldom resorted to...and 'privy vaults' were conspicuously unsanitary." The privies were small sheds over holes in the ground. When people were done relieving themselves, they used a bucket of dirt to cover the product of their efforts. When its hole was full, a shed was moved over a newly excavated depression.

In fairness to Sweetwater, it should be pointed out that the rest of America in 1876 was no bed of roses: In the nation's largest city, New York, it was still common practice to dump bedpans out of apartment building windows onto pedestrian-populated sidewalks. Horses that dropped dead in the streets were allowed to rot to pieces before they were disposed of, since it made them easier to move.

And like New York City, what Sweetwater lacked in sound sanitation practices it made up for with saloons, and lots of them: The Pink Pussycat Paradise, Cattlemen's Exchange, Lady Gay, Buffalo Chip, Mint, Cabinet and White Elephant, to name a few.

By the beginning of 1876, Sweetwater had a population of maybe 100 to 150, not counting a fluctuating number of soldiers from nearby Fort Elliott. African-American troops comprised part of the fort's detachment. The Native American dubbed them "buffalo soldiers" because it was thought their tightly curled hair resembled the manes of bison. The Buffalo Soldiers did their drinking at the Ring Town Saloon, about two miles from Sweetwater.

The population ballooned during the first part of the year, with as many as 400 buffalo hunters congregating for the whiskey, gambling and female companionship the town offered. At Charlie Rath's store and trading post, the hunters could trade or sell their buffalo hides and buy supplies. It was estimated Rath, an entrepreneur from Dodge City who had helped establish Sweetwater, bought or traded for 100,000 hides in the winter of 1875-76 alone. He bought the hides for $2.50 to $4.00—and sold goods for what a clerk in the store later described as "high, and sometimes fantastic, prices:" $10 for a 100-lb. barrel of flour and 25 cents for a cigar or a spool of thread. Nothing could be purchased for less than a quarter—and an 1876 quarter was roughly equivalent to $6 in 2022.

Sweetwater's other establishments included a laundry operated by Chinese immigrant Charlie Sing; a dance hall co-owned by Billy Thompson, who was wanted in Kansas for killing a sheriff and was the brother of the notorious gunfighter Ben Thompson, and a restaurant and hotel run by Tom and Ellen O'Loughlin. Ellen was said to be "the only virtuous woman in town."

Most of Sweetwater's two or three dozen other women performed various, and sometimes-unvirtuous, tasks in the saloons and dance hall. One of these, according to her tombstone, was "a young blue-eyed, black-haired beauty Lady Gay saloon girl" named Mollie Brennan. More about her later.

The town's male population was represented, in the words of Miles O'Loughlin, the son of Sweetwater's aforementioned "only virtuous woman," by "soldiers, saloon keepers, buffalo hunters, freight haulers, gamblers and for a time the refugee criminals who would head west...to escape the law of the east."

Charlie Goodnight's description of Sweetwater's inhabitants was a bit harsher. Goodnight—legendary Texas Ranger, cattle rancher, inventor of the chuckwagon and model for novelist Larry McMurtry's iconic *Lonesome Dove* character Woodrow F. Call—declared Sweetwater was "patronized by outlaws, thieves, cut-throats and buffalo hunters, with a large percentage of prostitutes. Taking it all, I think it was the hardest place I ever saw on the frontier, except Cheyenne, Wyoming."

Among the youngest male residents was a Canadian-born 22-year-old who was nominally the town surveyor, but spent most of his time in early 1876 dealing faro and playing poker. His given name was Bartholomew Masterson. Everyone called him Bat.

He loved to laugh. "I do not believe it would have been possible to find a man who loved practical joking more than Bat Masterson," said Billy Dixon, a sharpshooting buffalo hunter who as an Army scout won the

Medal of Honor. "He was in his glory in that sort of thing, and was forever pulling off something."

(One of those "somethings" occurred in 1879, when a minister came to Dodge City to raise funds for construction of a church. The local Ladies Aid Society, made up of the town's female upper crust, decided to stage a "beautiful baby contest," in which mothers would solicit votes for their babies, selling ballots at six for 25 cents. Inspired by Masterson, the town's gamblers poured money into the contest, scooping up $20 or $30 worth of tickets at a time. One gambler promised $100 in gold to the mother who won. When the votes were tallied, however, the winner turned out to be a prostitute for whom all the gamblers had voted. Dodge's "proper" mothers were outraged, the prostitute bewildered (but happy about the $100 prize), and the town's gambling element doubled over with laughter. The minister, meanwhile, was placated by the fact Masterson's practical joke raised $2,000.)

A Denver newspaper once referred to Masterson as "the man who smiles." The famed vaudevillian Eddie Foy described him as "a trim, good-looking young man with a pleasant face and carefully barbered mustache, well-tailored clothes, hat with a rakish tilt, and two big silver-mounted pistols in a heavy belt." Wyatt Earp, with whom Masterson had a deep and lasting friendship, recalled that as a young man, Masterson was "something of a dandy...but before all else, a man...Bat Masterson had a wealth of saving graces which shone from the honest fullness of his face."

Earp's description of his friend as "something of a dandy" was a reference to Masterson's fondness for attire that sometimes bordered on the outlandish. One such outfit reportedly included a sombrero with a rattlesnake skin band, a scarlet silk neckerchief and waist sash, silver-plated pistols in silver-studded holsters and pair of gold-mounted spurs. An observer joked that in a gunfight, the outfit might help blind the opponent. In his later years, as a saloon manager in a Colorado mining town, his wardrobe included a lavender corduroy suit.

Masterson's about-average-for-the-time height (5'9") belied his strength.At 170 pounds, he was solidly built, with well-muscled arms and shoulders. One biographer claimed, quite possibly with more admiration than accuracy, that Masterson once pulled so hard on an obstreperous mounted cowboy that he pulled down the cowboy's pony as well. His large head—his trademark derby hat was a size 7-3/8—was topped with thick dark hair and decorated with equally thick dark eyebrows and mustache. Below the eyebrows were a pair of slate-blue eyes. Throw in a ready smile, and it was easy to see why women generally found him worth a second or third look.

But his genial personality and peacockish wardrobe also concealed a steely side. The eyes that could twinkle with devilish merriment could go cold as glaciers, depending on what the situation required. "He is absolutely devoid of fear, has a cool steady nerve, excellent judgement and an aim that has never been known to fail when his life depended on it," a Montana newspaper observed. "He was a chunk of steel," said the sharpshooting Medal of Honor winner Billy Dixon, "and anything that struck him in those days always drew fire."

The aim of which the Montana paper spoke referred to Masterson's dexterity with firearms. This was widely admired—and usually respected. "He would fire with the hand in any position, seldom higher than his hip or belt," recalled one witness to Masterson's shooting. "I saw him kill many a rabbit by simply pointing, without sighting, the six-shooter no higher than his hip." Bill Tilghman, a Masterson contemporary who himself gained fame as a Western lawman, said he had "seen Bat shoot at a tin cup thrown in the air, with his six-shooter, at twenty-five cents a shot, and make money at it."

Of course shooting rabbits and tin cups was one thing; shooting men was quite another. As Masterson himself noted later in life, "I have known men in the West whose courage could not be questioned and whose expertness with the pistol was simply marvelous, who fell easy victims before men who added deliberation to the other two qualities." Before the first month of 1876 was over, the little burg of Sweetwater, and the rest of the West, would find out how many of those three qualities Bat Masterson had.

Bartholomew Masterson arrived in Henryville, Quebec, on Nov. 26,1853, the second of seven children born to Thomas and Catherine Masterson. Henryville was a tiny town 30 miles southeast of Montreal and only a few miles from the Vermont border. That apparently wasn't close enough to the United States for Thomas. He moved the family to upstate New York when Bat was about 8. Over the next 10 years, the family moved several more times, mostly in and around Illinois, before settling on an 80-acre tract in Sedgewick County Kansas, about 15 miles northeast of Wichita. There the Mastersons stayed put. At least some of them did. Thomas Masterson would remain on his farm for 50 years, or until his death in 1921 at the age of 96.

But Bat was a restless youth, restless enough to at some point to change his name from Bartholomew to William Barclay. (It's not clear why, and it didn't much matter to history, since the colorful nickname "Bat" was what identified him anyway.) The family's moving around during his formative years got into his blood, as well as that of his slightly older brother Ed. A future built on farming looked bleak and boring to both of them.

After one season helping to get the Mastersons family's new home on a firm footing, Bat and Ed headed for the perils and promise offered by the American frontier. They didn't have to go far. It was only a few miles from the family farm to the Arkansas River, and as Bat recalled 50 years later, "it was only a few miles west of the Arkansas River to the buffalo range." In the fall of 1871, not long before Bat's 18th birthday, the brothers traveled west. They stopped when they got to the Salt Fork of the Arkansas River, in a region that is now southern Kansas and northern Oklahoma. There the Masterson brothers joined the dangerous, bloody, exhausting and pitiless industry known as buffalo hunting.

While the precise approach to killing and processing buffalo varied somewhat from group to group, the basics were similar. The hunter was usually the boss, and owned the two to five wagons, oxen, horses and other gear (including hundreds of pounds of lead to make bullets.) His crew of three to five men included someone to cook, guard the camp during the day and look after the livestock. All of them doubled in other jobs or switched off duties.

The shooter generally carried two .50-caliber Sharps rifles. That let him keep firing one as the other cooled down. The guns were about four feet long, weighed about 16 pounds and fired three-inch-long cartridges that held 110 grains of black powder. A competent shooter could get off eight to 10 rounds per minute and hit targets from 500 to 800 yards away.

"You would try to get within 300 yards of them on foot, then shoot one through the lungs," hunter Richard "Uncle Dick" Bussell recalled in a 1926 interview. "If they began to bolt, you put a shot in front of the leaders, and again, until they milled around. By this time they were distracted, and you could kill all you wanted to without any further trouble. This was called a 'stand.'"

When the shooting stopped, usually after 20 to 40 buffalo were down, it was the skinners' turn. Armed with specially designed razor-sharp knives, they sliced the carcass down the belly, along the insides of the legs and around the neck, loosening the hide from the body. A rope was tied around the neck, with the other end fastened to the saddle on a horse. The horse moved away, and the hide was stripped intact off the buffalo. The tongue and sometimes the hump were removed, and the rest left for the immediate enjoyment of the ever-present hordes of flies.

"After skinning," Bussell, said, "we staked the hides out in rows sometimes 200 yards long, where we would leave them four or five days, then take them and crimp (fold) them. We would cross-pile them up and then pile logs or something on them to mash them flat. We put about 700 on two wagons. The cow hides were supposed to weight about 30 pounds, the bulls 40. It was an awful heavy load."

It could be a profitable business, but it was also highly speculative. Investment in equipment was expensive. A wagon could cost from $450 to $600, roughly $10,000 to $16,000 in 2022 dollars. And as the number of hunters increased and the market flooded with product, prices dropped. In 1870, the average hide sold for $4.20. By 1880, it was $3.40.

As lowly skinners, the Masterson boys were not getting rich in the buffalo trade. When their first season ended in Spring 1872, Bat and Ed found jobs in the Plains' other big industry—railroads. In early 1869, Congress had granted a charter for construction of a rail line from the eastern Kansas towns of Atchison and Topeka to the New Mexico capital of Santa Fe. By 1872, the rails had reached an army outpost called Fort Dodge. The Mastersons were hired to grade a five-mile section between the fort and Buffalo City, a speck-sized town on the Arkansas River. The town was fortuitously located. It was against federal law to sell liquor within five miles of an army outpost, and Buffalo City—which was renamed Dodge City when the railroad arrived—was just a bit more than five miles away—or enough to legally sell spirits to both buffalo hunters and soldiers.

Bat and Ed dutifully fulfilled their grading task. By September, the first train rolled into Dodge. But the man who hired them, a contractor named Raymond Ritter, paid them only a small part of what he owed them. Ritter promised to make good on the rest after a quick trip east. Only the quick trip stretched into months. The Mastersons—broke, furious and more than a little embarrassed at being slickered—returned to buffalo hunting.

For the next year or so, Bat seems to have split his time between hanging around Dodge and small-scale buffalo hunting with Ed, younger brother Jim Masterson, and a family friend, Henry Raymond. During long nights in the buffalo camps, Bat had learned to drink and gamble. He was good at the former, and excellent at the latter. In a terse-but-fascinating diary kept by Raymond in 1872-73, Bat's name appears only infrequently as 1873 progressed, indicating he was spending less time hunting and more time in Dodge's entertainment establishments.

There was no shortage of efficient and colorful drinkers and gamblers in town. But two events during this period helped distinguish Bat Masterson as a young man to be reckoned with among Dodge's citizenry. The first involved Ritter, the railroad contractor who had cheated Bat and Ed out of their pay.

In April, 1873, Masterson got word that Ritter would be on a train passing east from Colorado through Dodge—and that he was flush with cash. Armed, and accompanied by a crowd of curious citizens who figured the situation had potential for a lively show, Masterson was waiting when the train rolled in. The 19-year-old entered the passenger car and soon emerged with Ritter—at gunpoint. To a cheering crowd, Masterson collected the money he and Ed were owed. Bat bought drinks for the onlookers. His bravura performance—and the free drinks—favorably impressed the citizenry.

The second event that burnished Masterson's local reputation earned him both cash and a gash on the noggin. While skinning a buffalo alone one day in late December, 1873, about a half-mile from camp, Masterson was surprised by five Cheyenne warriors. The warriors relieved him of his weapons, confiscated his horse and bopped him in the forehead with the butt of his own rifle. They then instructed him to scram. He did. When he made it back to camp, most of his colleagues decided to head back to Dodge, about 60 miles away.

But Masterson stayed behind. On Christmas night, he and another hunter, Jim Harvey, snuck into the Cheyenne camp and ran off about 150 Indian ponies. They took the herd to Dodge, where they sold them, according to Masterson, for $1,200 (about $30,000 in 2021.) Coupled with the Ritter incident, the raid added to Bat's building celebrity in a town replete with outlandish and dangerous characters. His next adventure would put him close to the top of the heap.

* * *

"Myriads of Carcasses"

Biologically speaking, an American bison is not a buffalo. Among the differences are that bison have beards, humps and short sharp horns, while buffalo (native to Africa and Southeast Asia,) are beardless, hump-less and have horns than can span six feet from tip to tip. European explorers, who knew about African and Asian buffalo but had never seen American bison, mis-named them. Most biologists have long since given up trying to correct people.

Whatever they were called, there were a lot of them. It's estimated that in the late 18th century, as many as 40 million buffalo (I'm yielding to convention on the name) populated a range that covered two-thirds of the North American continent. As late as 1871, there were still a lot of them. In a letter to his sweetheart, soldier George Anderson described a Kansas herd he saw. "I am safe in calling this a single herd," he wrote, "but it is impossible to approximate the millions that composed it. It took me six days on horseback to ride through it."

Prior to the arrival of horses, brought by Spanish explorers in the mid-16th century, Plains Indians relied mainly on luck and ambush to bring down a buffalo. Armed with bows, it was a formidable task: an adult male buffalo can stand 6 feet high at the shoulder, weigh up to a ton, reach speeds of 35 mph, swim well, leap surprisingly high and when cornered easily stomp a human into a puddle of unrecognizable goo. Horseback hunting made it easier, but not easy.

When Indians did down a buffalo, however, it amounted to finding a walking Walmart. There was meat to eat; hides to make clothes, shoes, blankets, water bags and shelter; bones to fashion into knives, jewelry and other accessories; horns for spoons and cups, sinews for bow strings; hair for thread and rope; fat for soap; tails for fly-swatters; scrotums for bags, and dung (aka "prairie coal") for fire fuel.

While the Plains tribes made use of almost all of the buffalo and often felt a spiritual connection to an animal that provided them with a lot of useful things, they sometimes, if not often, killed more animals than they could use. This was particularly true when stampeding a herd over a cliff, or when they took only the choicest parts such as the tongue and left the rest for the coyotes and buzzards. But there were relatively few Indians, and lots of buffalo.

Even the earliest forays of Caucasians didn't seem a particular threat. Explorers, sport hunters and those who supplied meat to the railroad workers, or shipped buffalo tongues to fancy Eastern restaurants and thick, warm "coach" robes to wealthy Europeans, didn't seem to significantly threaten the animals' future. But by the early 1870s, a convergence of factors added up to doom for North America's largest mammal. These included:

- A deep, widespread and lasting economic recession that made any kind of work—even the unappetizing and grueling task of buffalo hunting—appealing.
- A shortage of cow hides from South America on which American and European industry had heavily relied.
- The development of new tanning techniques that made buffalo leather a useful, and in some ways superior, substitute for cow leather.
- A mushrooming demand for buffalo leather to make shoes for the multitude of immigrants pouring into the country, and for machinery belts as America became increasingly industrialized.
- An oft-stated desire by both military leaders and politicians to subdue the Plains tribes by eliminating their main food supply.

"If I could learn that every buffalo in the northern herd were killed, I would be glad," wrote Gen. Phillip Sheridan, the Union Civil War hero who was in charge of efforts to "pacify" the Plains tribes. "The destruction of this herd would do more to keep Indians quiet than anything else that could happen, except the death of all the Indians."

In the early 1870s, buffalo hunters flocked to the Plains. The resulting carnage was staggering. An estimated 30 million buffalo still roamed America at the end of the Civil War in 1865. By 1884, the government's official count was 325. Using those figures, that means every single day for 20 years, 4,000 buffalo were killed—167 per hour, not quite 3 per minute.

Individual hunters became celebrities for their bloody efficiency. George Simpson claimed to have delivered 3,600 hides in 1876 and another

2,500 in 1877. Dick Bussell was said to have killed as many as 150 buffalo in an hour. C.E. "Ed" Jones acknowledged "the biggest killing I ever made was 106 before breakfast."

The slaughter was as wasteful as it was vast. William Temple Hornaday, a zoologist, conservationist and first director of the Smithsonian Institute's National Zoo, produced an exhaustive study in 1889 on the demise of the buffalo. Hornaday reported that in 1873, just one railroad had carried the hides of 251,443 animals, and 1,617,600 pounds of meat. That figures to about 6.4 pounds of meat per 1,000-to-2,000-lb. buffalo. The rest was left to rot.

"Where there were myriads of buffalo the year before," Lt. Col. Richard I. Dodge observed in 1873, "there were now myriads of carcasses. The air was foul with a sickening stench, and the vast plain...was a dead, solitary, putrid desert."

There were some protests to the slaughter. Even William F. Cody, who had earned his fabled nickname "Buffalo Bill" by killing an estimated 4,280 animals in one 18-month stretch to feed railroad workers, urged that restrictions be imposed to prevent extinction.

In 1875, after four years of dithering, Congress sent a bill to President U.S. Grant's desk that imposed relatively small fines for anyone killing a buffalo for any reason other than to eat it. The bill exempted Indians. But because of the Indian exemption, Grant refused to sign it, and congressional efforts on the subject ceased in 1876.

"This was the country of the buffalo and the hostile Sioux only last year," an exultant General Sheridan wrote in early 1877. "There are no signs of either now, but in their place, we find prospectors, emigrants and farmers."

Plains tribes recognized their way of life had gone the way of the vast herds. "A cold wind blew across the prairie when the last buffalo fell," said the Lakota leader Sitting Bull, "a death wind for my people."

By the spring of 1874, buffalo anywhere near Dodge were few and far between. The mass of Great Plains buffalo had effectively been split in two by the encroachment of civilization that paralleled the railroad. The herd north of the tracks was almost gone. In March, a group of buffalo hunters began planning a major expedition into the Texas Panhandle, where a sizeable southern herd still roamed.

The area was legally off-limits to white men, under terms of an 1867 treaty that ceded the right to hunt buffalo south of the Arkansas River to Native Americans. It was also devoid of any place the hunters could get supplies or sell their hides. Several Dodge City entrepreneurs offered to solve that problem by building and stocking a couple of stores, a saloon and a restaurant at a still-unselected site. The treaty problem was solved by ignoring it.

"We were leaving such protection as there was," recalled Billy Dixon, one of the expedition's organizers, "and plunging into a solitude through which we would have to fight our way, if attacked by hostile Indians... there would be no be no getting away by making a fast run to Fort Dodge or Fort Hays; it meant fighting to the last ditch, and victory to the strong." Dixon was the second-youngest of the hunters who agreed to chance it. The youngest was Bat Masterson.

The site chosen for the Kansas buffalo hunters' foray into forbidden territory was already well-known for violent confrontations with the locals. Situated in a small valley near the Canadian River, about 175 miles south of Dodge, Adobe Walls was established in 1845 as an outpost to trade with the area's Indians. Within a few years, however, the traders, who had constructed their buildings of thick adobe bricks, grew tired of periodic raids by various tribes and abandoned the post.

In late 1864, the area hosted a battle between 350 Union Army troops, led by famed frontier scout Kit Carson, and more than 1,000 Comanche and Kiowa warriors. Vastly outnumbered, Carson adroitly used two howitzers to hold off the Indians while he made an orderly retreat. But a decade later, the tribes still maintained control of the area.

Adobe Walls' location near both water supplies and the southern buffalo herd, however, was irresistible to the Dodge hunters. Two stores, a saloon, restaurant and blacksmith shop were erected about a mile from the original site, and served as a center for hunters that followed the original Dodge group into the area. "A little town was sprouting in the wilderness," Billy Dixon recalled, "a place where we could buy something to eat and wear, something to drink, ammunition for our guns, and a place where our wagons, so necessary in expeditions like ours, could be repaired."

Not everyone in the region was enamored with the "little town." In June 1874, Kiowa, Comanche and Cheyenne tribes gathered together. They united under the command of the legendary Comanche war leader Quanah Parker in an effort to rub out the Adobe Walls encampment. The warriors were encouraged by the promises of Isa-Tai, a chubby Cheyenne mystic who claimed he could ensure the white men's bullets would pass harmlessly through the warriors' bodies. Moreover, he said, he would vomit sufficient ammunition for them to win the fight.

Just after dawn on the morning of June 27, the Indians poured down the bluff above the settlement. "There was never a more splendidly barbaric sight," Dixon said. "In after years I was glad I had seen it. Hundreds of warriors, the flower of the fighting men of the southeastern Plains tribes, mounted upon their finest horses, armed with guns and lances, and carrying heavy shields of thick buffalo hide, were coming like the wind."

Providentially for the 28 hunters and one woman (the wife of the restaurant owner) in the settlement, many of them had been awakened during the night by a sharp cracking sound. The noise was caused by either the cracking of a ridge pole supporting the saloon's roof—or a rifle shot secretly fired by Jim Hanrahan, who owned the saloon. Some of the defenders later suspected Hanrahan had fired the shot because he had received advance warning of the looming attack. They figured he had told no one out of fear the hunters would flee and leave his establishment with no defense. The suspicion arose because nothing was found wrong with the ridgepole.Either way, most of the hunters were awake and dressed when the attack began.

The fighting was furious. The Indians tried everything to get into the buildings, from charging on foot directly into fire from the hunters' big buffalo rifles, to climbing onto the roofs and firing through them, to backing their horses into the doors in an effort to break them down. "The Indians were very brave," said Jimmy Langton, who ran one of the settlement's stores and had all his canned goods shot off the shelves. "For hours they kept in range and died like men."

The hunters fought from within the two stores and the saloon. Masterson was in the saloon with eight others, including Dixon. "Bat Masterson should be remembered for the valor that marked his conduct," Dixon said. "He was a good shot, and not afraid."

In later years, Masterson said little about the battle, at least for the record. But in 1908 he did tell a magazine writer that during the battle, a fellow hunter named Shepherd had fruitlessly fired several times at an attacker hiding behind a small sod outbuilding. Shepherd suggested Bat try his luck. "I commenced getting a bead on him," Masterson said. "As he backed an inch or two more, I let fly, and Mr. Indian bounced in the air about three feet, dropped his rifle and fell dead. I turned around to Shepherd and said 'Shep, I got him on the first try.'"

On the third day of what had become a tense siege, a group of 15 warriors appeared on the edge of a bluff. "Some of the boys suggested I try the big '50' on them," Dixon recalled. "The distance was not far from seven-eighths of a mile." Dixon aimed, squeezed the trigger, and a few seconds later, one of the Indians fell from his horse, either dead, wounded or just faint with wonder at where the heck that bullet came from, it isn't certain. Dixon called it a lucky shot. Army surveyors that later measured the distance at 1,538 yards, called it "the shot of the century."

Dixon's shot helped sink the Indians' morale. It was already ebbing because of their failure to overwhelm the hunters; the fact their leader Quanah Parker had been wounded, and the discovery that the mystic Isa-Tai was full of baloney. (He did not, however, lack chutzpah. When his own pony was shot, Isa-Tai explained that in covering the animal with magic paint, he had missed a spot.)

More hunters from surrounding areas broke through the Indians to reinforce the settlement. By the fifth day, the warriors moved off. The Adobe Walls defenders lost four men. Two brothers had been sleeping in a wagon when the attack began and were killed almost immediately on the first day. A third hunter was shot while standing in a doorway. The fourth—the husband of the only woman there—shot himself accidentally while descending a ladder. The Indians lost at least 13.

Despite their retreat, the Indians succeeded in ending buffalo hunting in the region for the time being. With many of the other hunters, Masterson returned to Dodge. He was glad to be alive, proud to be hailed as a hero—and out of a job.

He soon found one, as an Army scout in what would be called the Red River War. The "war," which lasted less than a year, resulted in most of the Southern Plains tribes being harassed into surrender and relocated to the Indian Territory, in what is now Oklahoma. Masterson was involved in some skirmishes, but nothing came close to the Adobe Walls battle. He became a teamster for a while, driving freight wagons and performing other mundane tasks. His friend Henry Raymond noted in a December, 1874 letter that "Bat has got a job at Camp Supply counting mules night and morning."

By March, 1875, Masterson was back in Dodge. For the rest of the year, he appears to have drifted between buffalo hunting, hauling freight, and gambling. But as 1876 began and America entered its second century as a nation, he was in the stinky little town of Sweetwater—and a few weeks from cementing his status as a Western legend.

Melvin King was a decent soldier and a nasty drunk. "He was a general favorite throughout the regiment," his sergeant wrote to King's sister, "both with officers and enlisted men, and especially with his commanding officer, General (Ranald) Mackenzie ...". But his army record was also pock-marked with courts-martial and other disciplinary measures for everything from shooting a dog to attacking an officer. Many of his troubles were directly attributable to a serious drinking problem.

King's real name was Anthony Cook. He was born in October,1845, in Quebec (like Bat Masterson), and as a youngster moved to upstate New York (like Bat). At the age of 18, he enlisted in the Union Army and served through the end of the Civil War. He re-enlisted in 1866, reaching the rank of sergeant. But a series of charges for drunkenness, brawling and insubordination led to a dishonorable discharge in 1869.

Undaunted, he enlisted again, this time in the 4th Cavalry as Melvin A. King. He also apparently straightened himself out, rising to the rank of corporal, becoming known as a competent horse wrangler and even being assigned as Gen. Mackenzie's orderly. He served in the Red River War against the Southeastern Plains tribes (again, like Bat.) In October 1875, he was assigned to Fort Elliott, the new outpost near the lively town of Sweetwater.

Another resident of Sweetwater at the time was a young woman with a whole lot of miles on her. Mollie Brennan had been a prostitute in Dennison, Texas; Ellsworth, Kansas, and possibly other towns before alighting in Sweetwater. She was apparently quite popular. One of her paramours, in fact, was Billy Thompson, a gunman who had killed at least three men, including a Kansas sheriff. In Sweetwater, he was co-owner of the town's dance hall.

Brennan was also friendly with Bat Masterson, although just how friendly has not been precisely determined. Of course, a lot of people in Sweetwater were friendly with Bat. He was handsome, polite, funny and one of the heroes of the Battle of Adobe Walls. While he was nominally employed by the Army as a freight hauler and inactive scout, he was also reportedly the town surveyor, possibly because of the four or five months he had spent grading the railroad into Dodge. Sweetwater's first postmaster, George A. Montgomery, contended in a 1934 newspaper piece that Bat's real job was as "the faro dealer for Henry Fleming (at the Lady Gay Saloon.) But he would also play poker at times. That got him into trouble."

The trouble to which Montgomery referred took place in the Lady Gay on the evening of January 24. Melvin King, Mollie Brennan and Bat Masterson were all in attendance. By January 25, two of them would be dead and the third grievously wounded. Just why and how isn't clear.

The chief trouble in recounting legends like the Sweetwater Shootout is in picking the right trail to follow among the various versions that spring up in the retelling. That King and Bat shot it out is generally accepted as fact, as is that at the time of the shooting King was drunk. But did they quarrel over: A) a card game; B) Mollie; C) both A and B; or D) it was part of a general fight between Bat and the buffalo hunters on one side and King and the soldiers on the other?

The answer, based on the accounts of various witnesses, is mostly A, with some B and a bit of C. And possibly D. According to Montgomery, Bat and King were in a poker game with two other men. King lost several hands, accused Bat of "robbing" him and stormed out. "Big Nose" Kate Elder, a prostitute who was there, and who was later the notorious Doc Holliday's consort and knew Bat well, also said the trouble started over a deck of cards.

But George Curry, who was then a 14-year-old clerk in Charlie Rath's Sweetwater store and would become a Teddy Roosevelt Rough Rider and territorial governor of New Mexico, told a different story. Curry wrote in his autobiography that the shooting was part of a fight "between Bat Masterson and several buffalo hunters on one side, and King and other soldiers on one side," and that two other soldiers besides King were shot during the shootout. A quarter-century after the fight, Masterson himself hinted at a rumble between the hunters and the soldiers, when he told a reporter that he had been in Sweetwater "along with government employees and soldiers. There were 400 buffalo hunters. Everything was quiet... and then things went lickety-bang."

Romantically inclined narrators of the shootout claim it was rooted in the fact Molly and Bat were lovers, and King was jealous. Even postmaster Montgomery, who contended the cause was cards, recalled Molly and Bat were living together and she "had stayed up all night as his mascot" during the poker game.

What happened next is generally, but by no means unanimously, agreed upon. After King left the Lady Gay, Bat, Mollie and dance hall co-owner Charlie Norton went to have a drink at the dance hall, which was closed that night. There was a pounding on the door. Bat opened it, and a raging King entered with his Army Colt .45 in hand.

Then it gets murky again. One version, inscribed on Molly's granite tombstone in the town cemetery, is that "she jumped in front of Bat Masterson and saved his life in the fight ...". It's a nice sentiment to think she took a bullet for her lover, but if so, it didn't help Bat a whole lot since he got shot anyway. It's more likely King fired twice. One shot hit Bat somewhere south of his navel (groin, stomach, thigh and pelvis have all been mentioned.) King's other shot hit Molly. From the floor, Masterson pulled his own Colt and shot King in the chest.

In all versions, Molly died almost instantly. King lingered for about an hour before he expired. One account has him asking to have his boots removed and his body moved out of the building, to somehow make his mother feel better about the whole thing. Bat, bleeding profusely, was written off as a goner. It was said a doctor maneuvered a silk handkerchief through Masterson's intestines to determine if he had recently eaten anything. If he had, the doctor concluded, he would die. Apparently he hadn't, and he didn't.

In the immediate aftermath of the shooting a crowd quickly gathered. With no civilian law enforcement anywhere within at least a hundred miles, several of Bat's friends moved to prevent King's fellow soldiers from finishing Masterson off. Henry Fleming, the Lady Gay's owner, sent young George Curry to the fort to summon the commanding officer. Billy Thompson (or in some versions, his brother Ben) was said to have jumped atop a faro table with guns drawn and promised to ventilate the first person who threatened Bat.

Curry brought the troops, who halted at the edge of town. "After a brief parley," Curry wrote, "he (Fleming) agreed that the soldiers could come in to remove the body of the soldier, the woman and the wounded soldiers." The next day, a hearing was held at the fort "after which officers and civilians agreed that the killing of King was justified." Nonetheless, the fort's commanding officer prudently prohibited his troops from visiting the town for several months after the shooting to prevent further trouble.

By that time, Masterson had recovered, although he would require a cane to get around for some months, and would walk with a slight limp the rest of his life. In later years, he seldom mentioned the shootout. In an 1881 interview, he was described as being "quite reticent" to discuss the episode. "I had a little difficulty with some soldiers down there," he said, "but never mind, I dislike to talk about it."

But other people loved to talk about it. Various writers would later claim King was well-known throughout the West at the time as a burly, swaggering bully and bonafide killer, who spent his leaves carousing with Texas cowboys and terrorizing towns. Wyatt Earp claimed to have once disarmed King on a Wichita street a few months before King's fight with Masterson, slapping him in the face and tossing him out of town. But Wyatt Earp claimed a lot of things, and there is no evidence the 5'5" soldier had ever killed anyone or terrorized anything. King's after-the-fact reputation, however, helped swell the shootout's dramatic status: the loveable 22-year kid against the mad-dog murderer, the dashing young lover against a raving jealous rival.

By the time he was up and around, Bat Masterson, buffalo hunter and Indian fighter, was also Bat Masterson, gunfighter and killer. The foundation of legend was poured. Solid blocks of true adventures– and lots of flimsy nonsense—would be added.

After some weeks in Sweetwater, Masterson returned to the family home near Wichita for a while, then drifted into Dodge City in the late spring of 1876. There he renewed acquaintance with an old friend, who was dabbling in law enforcement.

Chapter 1 Notes

(In 1879 *Sioux City (Iowa) Journal*, Jan. 18, 1888, p. 2.

"Dishwater, laundry water" Sallie B. Harris, *Hidetown in the Texas Panhandle: 100 Years in Wheeler County and Panhandle of Texas,* 1968, p. 22.

The town's male population Ibid., p. 56.

Charles Goodnight—*Frontier Times*, Dec. 1929, p. 17.

He loved to laugh Olive Dixon, *Life of "Billy" Dixon,* p. 124.

But Bat was a Robert K. DeArment, *Bat Masterson: The Man and the Legend,* p. 14. DeArment's 1979 biography, along with his 2005 follow-up, *Gunfighter in Gotham: Bat Masterson's New York City Years,* are considered the definitive works on Masterson's life, although more recent research has superseded some of DeArment's findings and conclusions.

A Denver newspaper *Denver Tribune*, May 16 1882, p. 4; Eddie Foy and Alvin F. Harlow, *Clowning Through Life*, p. 98; *San Francisco Examiner*, Aug. 16 1896, p. 28.

Earp's description of his Paul Trachtman, *The Gunfighters,* p. 119.

Masterson's genial personality *Omaha Sunday Bee,* Dec. 8 1907, p. 5.

But his genial*Anaconda (Mt.) Standard*, Dec. 19, 1897, p. 14; Dixon, op. cit., p. 115.

The aim of which DeArment, op. cit., p. 78.

Of course shooting rabbits W.B (Bat) Masterson, *Famous Gunfighters of the Western Frontier,* p. 25. This is a reprint of a series of five articles Masterson wrote in 1907 for a magazine called *Human Life*. Each of the articles featured a gunfighter Masterson had known, including Wyatt Earp, Doc Holliday and Luke Short.

"You would try" Transcript of July 19, 1926 interview with Richard Bussell, Panhandle-Plains Historical Museum Archives.

"After skinning" Bussell, op. cit.

"We were leaving" Dixon, op. cit., pp. 111-12.

Whatever they were David Hugh Bunnell, *Good Friday on the Rez*, p. 172.

"If I could learn" David D. Smits, "The Frontier Army and the Destruction of the Buffalo, 1865-1883," *Western History Quarterly*, Autumn 1994, p. 336.

The slaughter was, William T. Hornaday, *The Extermination of the American Bison.*

"Where there were" Ibid., p. 327

"This was the country" Ron Chernow, *Grant*, p. 836.

Plains tribes Smits, op. cit., p. 338.

Adobe Walls' location Dixon, op. cit., p. 155.

Early on the morning Ibid., p. 158.

The fighting was Edward Campbell Little, "The Battle of Adobe Walls." *Pearson's Magazine,* January 1908, p. 79.

The hunters fought Dixon, op. cit., p. 178.

In later years Little, op. cit., p. 81.

On the third day Dixon, op. cit., pp. 180-81

He soon found Nyle H. Miller and Joseph W. Snell, *Why the West Was Wild*, p. 321.

Melvin King was Gary L. Roberts, "Bat Masterson and the Sweetwater Shootout," *Wild West Magazine,* Oct. 2000, p. 49. This is a highly informative and entertaining summary of the fight.

She was also *Pampa (Tx) Daily News*, Aug. 5 1934, p. 22.

The answer H.B. Hening (ed.), *George Curry, 1861-1947, An Autobiography*, p. 10.

A quarter century, *Butte (Mt.) Weekly Miner*, March 10 1892, p. 2.

Curry brought the troops Hening, op. cit., pp. 10-11.

By that time *Winfield (Ks.) Courier*, Nov. 24 1881, p. 1.

CHAPTER 2

"I never heard him laugh"

Wyatt Earp comes to Dodge City

MAY

It was an embarrassing way for any law enforcement officer to start a new year, especially a legendary lawman. That's not to suggest that Wyatt Earp was a legendary lawman in January, 1876. In fact, at that point in his adult life, he had probably spent more time as a criminal than as a cop.

But as a member of the Wichita, Kansas, police force, he was at least a lawman on the evening of January 9. It was a Sunday, and Wyatt was hanging out with a few of the boys in the back room of the Custom House Saloon. At some point, he leaned back in his chair—and his six-gun fell out of his holster. The gun's hammer was resting on a loaded cylinder, and when it hit the floor, the gun went off. "The ball passed through his (Wyatt's) coat, struck the north wall, then glanced off and passed through the ceiling," the local newspaper dutifully—and a bit mirthfully—reported. "It was a narrow escape, and the occurrence got up a lively stampede from the room."

In later years, Earp lectured his biographer, Stuart Lake, that "top notch" gunfighters always left the chamber under the hammer of their revolvers empty to prevent such accidents. "It was only (with) tyros and would-bes," he said, "that you heard of accidental discharges or didn't-know-it-was-loaded injuries ...". While Lake dutifully included Earp's mini-lecture on gun safety in Wyatt's biography, he tactfully omitted any mention of the "The Gun Drop at the Custom House Saloon."

As embarrassing as his accidental discharge was, what happened three months later to Wyatt would for most men have been even more humbling, if not downright humiliating. Earp's boss, city marshal Mike Meagher, was running for re-election against a former marshal, William Smith. In the course of the campaign, Smith claimed that if Meagher won, he planned to add one or two of Wyatt's brothers to the police force. For some reason this angered Wyatt, perhaps because it implied his brothers wouldn't be worthy deputies. Earp expressed his ire by beating Smith to a bloody pulp on the eve of the election. "It is well known that in periods of excitement, people do not always act as they would when perfectly collected and unexcited," the *Wichita Weekly Beacon* philosophized in reporting the beating.

Marshal Meagher (who won re-election) reluctantly arrested his deputy. Earp was fined $30—the equivalent of two weeks' pay—and fired. The city council briefly reconsidered Wyatt's dismissal, because, in the words of the *Beacon*, "he has made an excellent officer and hitherto his conduct has been unexceptionable." But after voting 2-6 and then 4-4 to reinstate him, the council let the firing stand. To rub salt in the wound, it also withheld Wyatt's back pay until he forked over some fines he had collected but neglected to turn in. Then, on May 10, the council declared Wyatt a vagrant and invited him to leave Wichita. He did, moving on to a town 150 miles west.

On May 24, the *Beacon*, which had consistently misspelled Wyatt's name as "Erp," finally got it right: "Wyatt Earp," the paper reported, "has been put on the police force at Dodge City."

An oft-repeated story on the Great Plains in the 1870s concerned a railroad conductor's confrontation with a drunken cowboy. It seems the wrangler was on the train without a ticket. The conductor asked the ticketless passenger where he was going. "To Hell I reckon," the cowboy snorted. "Alright," the conductor replied, "give me a dollar and get off in Dodge City."

It was that kind of town—or at least it had that kind of reputation. "Her incorporate limits are the rendezvous of all the unemployed scalawagism of seven states," thundered an editor from the rival Kansas town of Hays City. "...Decency she knows not...seventeen saloons furnish inspiration, and many people are inspired...the town is full of prostitutes and every other house is a brothel." Other titles bestowed on Dodge by newspapers around the country included "the beautiful bibulous Babylon of the frontier," "Hell on the Plains" and "the Wickedest Little Town in America."

Buffalo hunter Winton Wilson, who passed through Dodge in 1876, noted "all kinds of gambling going on; hundreds of dollars changing hands every hour. The women are out on the streets smoking cigars. This is the hardest place I ever saw in my life." It's possible Wilson may have been more upset at the price of cigars than at the sight of women smoking them: a stogie went for 25 cents ($6 in 2022) in Dodge while they cost only a nickel in, say, Chicago. "Twenty-five cents for a shave," he complained, "75 cents for a haircut, whisky 25 and 50 cents!"

The town had its apologists. "In extenuation of the conduct of her early inhabitants," wrote Robert M. Wright, one of the town's founders, "I plead the newness of the territory, the conditions of life, the dangers and associations of a Western frontier, and the daring and reckless spirit that such conditions engender."

Wright knew whereof he spoke. While running for the state legislature, Wright was sharply criticized by a Dodge newspaper editor. The enraged candidate beat the stuffing out of the editor. The editor promptly sued for $10,000. After a brief trial, a jury awarded the editor $4.50—and only because the judge ordered them to cover the editor's medical bill.

Dodge City began life in May, 1872, as the Atchison, Topeka and Santa Fe railroad built itself west across Kansas toward Colorado and New Mexico. Two liquor dealers set up tents on a small incline above the usually placid and shallow Arkansas River. Within a month, several other merchants opened businesses, mostly trading with buffalo hunters and selling booze to soldiers from nearby Fort Dodge. In July, a group of entrepreneurs and Army officers bought 87 acres from the federal government for $108.75 (about $2,600 in 2022) and divided it into town lots. The Santa Fe tracks reached the settlement in September, and Dodge was soon hurtling through its childhood.

The town was at first dependent on the buffalo industry. Wright, who became Dodge's most prosperous citizen, estimated he bought more than 200,000 hides in the winter of 1872-73. As the region's buffalo were all but exterminated, immense mounds of their bones—25 feet high and stretching for hundreds of yards—piled up around the town. Starving Indians and struggling settlers eventually collected and sold the bones—for a few dollars per ton—for use in fertilizer, bone china, as a carbonizing element in sugar refining, and to reduce acid in wines and vinegars.

Even as the buffalo boom waned, Dodge's fortunes rose to new heights on the backs of two very different animals—the Texas longhorn and the fever tick. The former roamed the plains of post-Civil War Texas in the tens of thousands. The latter roamed the bodies of the former. As America's population soared in the 1870s (an increase of more than 30 percent between 1870 and 1880) and railroads made it increasingly easier to move products, demand for Texas beef intensified. Vast herds were thus headed north to waiting trains in Kansas, to be shipped to meat-packing centers in the east.

But there was a problem. The Texas cattle's ticks sometimes carried splenic fever (known as "Spanish Fever" in Texas and "Texas Fever" everywhere else.) The longhorns generally tolerated the disease, but the livestock of Kansas farmers did not. As the number of farmers increased, so did their political clout. They voted in Kansas elections; the Texas cattlemen didn't.In 1867, the state legislature established a north-south quarantine line in Kansas. East of the line, the longhorns were banned. The ban was initially ignored by cattle drovers and towns alike. But as the farmers gained more influence, the line was pushed west. By 1876, Dodge was the only sizeable Kansas city still out of the quarantine zone. It now had another title: "Queen of the Cattle Towns."

The "queen" had a "permanent" population of around 1,000, which was routinely doubled by transients of all sorts, especially during the cattle season from May to September. That didn't count an estimated 200,000 head of cattle sometimes grazing on the town's outskirts.

Dodge had a drug store, run by Philadelphia-trained physician Thomas I. McCarty, who would periodically convert his pharmacy into a medical clinic for a day or two. The town barber, George Dieter, billed himself as "the eminent tonsorial artist of the Arkansas (River) Valley." The 38-room Dodge House hotel offered a restaurant and billiard hall. The town's first newspaper, the *Dodge City Times*, began publication in 1876. There was even an ice house, which meant the beer was occasionally cold, or at least cool.

Wright operated one of the largest retail establishments on the Plains, a handsome two-story brick building that offered everything from plum preserves and long johns to wagons manufactured by the Studebaker Brothers in South Bend, Indiana. The store also served as a bank, lending money to cowboys and businessmen alike at fair interest rates.

But it was still a rough place. Wright calculated, with a fair degree of accuracy, that 25 men were killed during Dodge's first two years, "and more than double that wounded." The town's first jail was a 15-foot-deep hole, into which rowdy drunks were lowered by ropes to sleep it off. Lumber was too scarce for use as coffins, so the violently departed were buried without caskets—but with their footwear still on—at the town's "Boot Hill" cemetery.

Wright wrote that in Dodge's early days, the nearest legal system was 95 miles away in Hays City. Few of Dodge's citizens bothered with the trip: "Most differences were settled by rifle or six-shooter on the spot." The earliest attempt at more local law and order came in the form of a "vigilance committee" of about 40 locals. But the vigilantes proved to be a cure worse than the disease. After several committee members committed a few murders themselves, an incensed Major Richard I. Dodge led troops from Fort Dodge into Dodge City and broke up the vigilante group. (By the way, the fort took its name from a Gen. Grenville Dodge, not the major. The town took its name from the fort.)

The vigilantes were followed by Dodge's first "marshal" in 1873. The city wasn't formally incorporated until late 1875 and thus had no official officials, but Bill "Bully" Brooks was hired as unofficial enforcer. Brooks was an ex-buffalo hunter and experienced killer. But his nickname too accurately described his law enforcement methods. The citizenry shed few tears when he slunk out of town after a confrontation with an even tougher ex-buffalo hunter. In the same year, the level-headed and highly competent Charlie Bassett was elected the first sheriff of Ford County, in which Dodge resided. Bassett's main jurisdiction, however, was outside the city limits. Inside there was still little law and less order.

"There are law-abiding and clever people in Dodge," a reporter from the *Atchison (Kan.) Daily Champion* noted in April 1876, "but they look awful lonesome...the town is infested with gamblers, horse thieves, prostitutes and murderers, who look upon law as a huge joke...the arm of the law is palsied and hangs powerless by the side of Justice, who stands away in the background like the statue of a forlorn and helpless exile."

But in the same month the Atchison newspaper story appeared, Dodge elected a new mayor. George Hoover, a German immigrant who had opened one of the first saloons in Dodge, decided it was time to give the town's law enforcement some teeth. Hoover appointed saloon owner Larry Deger as city marshal. Deger's resume included working as a wagon boss for the U.S. Army and as a square dance caller in Hays City. Deger was considered a tough enough fellow, but at 307 pounds, he wasn't exactly blessed with cat-like reflexes, and was not an accomplished gun-slinger. So the mayor also appointed Wyatt Earp, an experienced lawman with a generally good reputation, as Deger's chief deputy. The appointment forever linked a legendary Western lawman with a legendary Western town.

In later years, Earp claimed Hoover wanted to name him to the top job, but couldn't for political reasons. He also claimed he received a higher salary than Deger to take the No. 2 job. And Earp sometimes told people he had been marshal of Dodge for several years. In actuality, his salary was lower than Deger's; he was never marshal, and he only stayed in Dodge for a few months before leaving, coming back, leaving, coming back, and then leaving for good.

Then again, there was a lot about Wyatt Earp's life that was more than a little convoluted. In fact, the man was a bundle of contradictions:

- He is inarguably one of the most famous lawmen in American history. But he was thrown in jail or fled prosecution in a half-dozen states, for offenses—real and alleged—that ranged from pilfering public funds and working in a brothel (as a bouncer), to horse theft and murder.
- He was widely praised as an honest lawman nearly everywhere he worked, with a rigid code of honor and unshakeable sense of justice. But he was also an occasional con man who bribed public officials, and routinely ignored laws that interfered with his business enterprises.
- He was fiercely loyal to his friends, and maintained friendships for decades. But many people, if not most, considered him moody, taciturn and generally unlikeable.
- He hated publicity, and the plethora of silly and often scurrilous stories that plagued him wherever he went. But he sometimes resorted to exaggeration and outright lies himself, particularly in his old age, in hopes of polishing his public image and leaving behind a more admirable legacy.

More recently, some serious—and/or seriously fixated—Earp scholars have used terms like "complicated" or "conflicted" or "a product of his times" to describe the convolutions of his life. But a friend of Earp's, who had known him at the height of his notoriety in Tombstone Arizona, may have best summed up the contradiction that was Wyatt Earp. "He was not an angel," wrote George Parsons in 1928, the year before Earp died, "but his faults were minor ones, and he never killed a man who did not richly deserve it."

There were four things about Wyatt Earp that those who knew him generally agreed on. The first was that he was a good-looking guy. Jimmy Cairns, who was Earp's roommate and partner on the Wichita police force, recalled in a 1929 interview that Wyatt in the 1870s "was in the prime of his young manhood, a little over six feet tall, well-proportioned, an athlete, quick as a cat on his feet; erect, (ash blonde) hair a bit long but well-combed, a large moustache that dropped down over his mouth, almost hiding it, a big strong chin." A female resident of Wichita at the time of Earp's residency there told Earp biographer Lake that Wyatt "was the handsomest, best-mannered young man in Wichita." Others remarked on Earp's eyes, their descriptions ranging from "ice blue" to "cold as a dead fish."While generally well-groomed, his customary attire was plain: black trousers, black hats, black boots, white shirts. He often went coatless, and often without a gun, relying on his fists in case of trouble.

Second, he exuded courage. "I think it was the distinguishing trait of Wyatt Earp...that more than any man I have ever known he was devoid of physical fear," Bat Masterson said of his close friend. "He feared the opinion of no one but himself and his self-respect was his creed." William Hunsaker, a one-time mayor of San Diego who was co-defense attorney for Earp after the epic Gunfight at the O.K. Corral, recalled his former client "was quiet, but absolutely fearless in the discharge of his duties...he never stirred up trouble, but he never ran away from it." Arthur M. King, a former Los Angeles police detective who worked with Earp as a bounty hunter when Earp was in his 60s, called him "one of the coolest I've ever seen. He was afraid of nothing."

The third aspect of Wyatt Earp was that he defined—and dispensed—justice in highly personal terms. "Wyatt is a man that can forget his badge, make his own law and rule and enforce them," noted famed lawman Bill Tilghman. Earp himself was unapologetic about having killed men without bothering with the legal system. "The men we killed, they had to be killed," he told a visiting writer a few months before his death. "They were bad, and if any part of the country lets itself be stampeded by bad men, it will infect the whole shebang before it's through...it takes a resolute man not to make mistakes when he gets to acting as his own law."

The fourth thing that people noticed about Wyatt Earp was that he had almost no discernable sense of humor. "Earp is a man who never smiled or laughed," recalled Dick Cogdell, who knew Earp in Wichita in the mid-1870s and was that city's police chief. Thirty years later, a young Mojave Indian named Merritt Laffoon was sent by his father to work for Earp "to learn discipline." By this time Wyatt was a 60-year-old gold miner with claims in the desert that straddles the Colorado River, where it separates southern California and Arizona. Laffoon recalled two things that set Earp apart. One was that he always carried a gun, apparently from a sense there were people with a grudge still out to get him. The other was "he never laughed out loud. In all the time I knew him, I never heard him laugh."

Wyatt Berry Stapp Earp was born on March 19, 1848, in Monmouth Illinois. His middle names were bestowed to honor his father's commanding officer in the just-concluded war with Mexico. Wyatt was the fourth of eight children born to Nicholas and Virginia Ann Earp. He also had two half-siblings from his father's first marriage.

Nicholas Earp was a peripatetic fellow. By the time Wyatt was 21, the Earps had moved from Illinois to Iowa, back to Illinois, back to Iowa, then to California and then to Missouri. At the time of Wyatt's birth, his father had recently been discharged from the army after being kicked in the groin by a mule. It was among the most impressive things on his resume. In addition to briefly (six months) being a soldier, Nicholas was also a farmer, grocer/restaurateur, harness maker, wagon master, constable, justice of the peace and convicted bootlegger.

Wyatt apparently told only two stories about his youth. One was how he tried to enlist in the Union Army at the age of 14, only to be thwarted by his father showing up at the recruiting station. The second was how he saved the family's wagon train to California by stampeding livestock into attacking Indians. The first tale was possibly true, the second almost certainly not.

In his late teens, Wyatt joined his older brother Virgil in grading for railroad tracks in Colorado and Wyoming, and hauling freight between California and Utah and Arizona. As a freight hauler, he learned how to fight with his fists, a talent he later routinely employed as a law enforcement officer. "There were few men in the West who could whip Earp in a rough-and-tumble fight thirty years ago," Bat Masterson wrote in 1907, "and I suspect he could give a tough youngster a hard tussle right now, even if he is sixty-one years of age."

At the age of 21, Wyatt took part in his first gunfight, in a Beardstown Illinois hotel/brothel. A railroad worker taunted Earp as "a California boy;" Earp tossed the fellow into the street; the worker drew his gun and fired; Wyatt returned the compliment, hitting his antagonist in the hip. The wound apparently wasn't serious, as no one was arrested, and Earp moved on to the hamlet of Lamar Missouri, where his father had become a constable.

While he could fight and shoot, however, Wyatt failed at another frontier rite of passage: drinking. In her memoirs, his younger sister Adelia recounted that Wyatt took his first drink of whisky in Prescott Arizona, and promptly passed out. When he came to, brother Virgil suggested a "hair of the dog" remedy for his hangover, in the form of another drink. That also knocked him flat. Until he was well into his 50s, the gunfighter who spent much of his time in saloons seems to have much preferred ice cream to liquor.

In Lamar, Wyatt was appointed to replace his father as a constable when Nicholas became the local justice of the peace. Lacking a jail, or very much crime, Lamar's constables spent most of their time rattling door knobs, killing stray dogs and impounding wayward hogs. Their small salaries covered the door-knob checks, but there were 75-cent bonuses for each dead dog and 25-cent payoffs for each penned pig. Wyatt liked the job enough to run for election to the post in 1870. He won, and soon thereafter got married and bought a small house for his new family. Then things went south.

Ten months into his marriage, Wyatt's wife died, probably of typhoid fever, and possibly pregnant. Soon after, Earp left Lamar, but only after engaging, for unknown reasons, in a bloody street brawl with some of his late wife's relatives. His departure also coincided with accusations he had absconded with $200 in bond funds he had collected for construction of a new school, and another $20 by falsifying the amount he collected for a court fee.

Earp's downward spiral continued when he was accused of horse theft in early 1871 in what was then Indian Territory and is now Oklahoma. Plunked into a federal jail in Arkansas, Wyatt decided not to wait around for a trial. He escaped with five other prisoners by prying rafters from the ceiling and shimmying down the wall on a rope made of bedsheets. There is some evidence Wyatt might have fled as far as the buffalo hunting fields of Kansas, where he later said he met Bat and Ed Masterson for the first time. If so, he didn't linger long. By early 1872 he was in Peoria, Illinois, where he joined older brother Virgil and younger brother Morgan in the brothel business, as a bouncer and possibly a pimp.

Court records show Wyatt was arrested at least three times and fined or jailed during Peoria police's periodic prostitution crackdowns. Records also hint that he might have married a Sally Haspel, one of the "good looking" but "terribly depraved" hookers. If not, Wyatt didn't object to her listing her name as "Sally Earp."

By his third arrest, Wyatt was being described in the local press as "the Peoria Bummer," a pejorative term of German derivation that meant "loafer" or "low-life." Wyatt Earp clearly needed a fresh start. In the fall of 1872, at the age of 24, he headed west.

"Just Plain Ordinary Men"

There is no more romanticized figure of the Wild West than the lawman. In thousands of books, movies and television shows, marshals/sheriffs/deputies/rangers strode purposefully down dusty sunbaked streets or into smokey saloons. Wearing a five-or-six-pointed star pinned to their vests, revolvers poised in holsters rakishly low on their hips and white Stetsons pulled low over their foreheads, they confronted the forces of evil, no matter the odds.

But who were they in real life? According to Bat Masterson, who "lawed" in several towns himself, "they were just plain ordinary men, who could shoot straight and had the most utter courage and perfect nerve—and for the most part, a keen sense of right and wrong."

Masterson's characterization is contradictory in the extreme, since an ordinary man with "utter courage," "perfect nerve" and "a keen sense of right and wrong" is hardly ordinary, then or now. And however keen their sense of right and wrong, like most people, Wild West lawmen were generally neither purely heroes nor villains, but something in between.

Take Bill Tilghman. During a law enforcement career that spanned 50 years, Tilghman was a deputy sheriff, a sheriff, a city marshal, a deputy federal marshal and a chief of police. In dozens of gunfights, he killed a half-dozen men, He gained fame for supposedly, and single-handedly, capturing Bill Doolin, "king of the Oklahoma outlaws," by disguising himself as a minister and getting the drop on Doolin while the bad guy was lounging in an Arkansas bathhouse. (There is some evidence there was a deal made between Tilghman and Doolin to trade a staged "capture" for an easy escape, which Doolin made not long after his arrest.) As Oklahoma City's chief of police, Tilghman was credited with cleaning up the town. "It would take a volume the size of an encyclopedia to record the many daring exploits and adventures of this remarkable man," Bat Masterson wrote about Tilghman.

But there is also evidence that Tilghman was also a horse thief who sold whisky to Indians, took bribes and ran gambling houses and brothels. In 1924, at the age of 70, he was shot and killed by a Prohibition agent. An on-the-take Tilghman was either trying to prevent a speakeasy from being raided, or the Prohibition agent was drunk, corrupt and itching for a chance to gun down the marshal. Both versions have their adherents; take your pick.

Tilghman's resume, although quite a bit longer than most, was not unusual among Wild West lawmen. Law enforcement then, as now, was a multi-layered profession, and lawmen often served in more than one capacity. At the top of the pyramid was the U.S. marshal. Marshals were (and still are) appointed by the president and confirmed by the Senate, one for each of the (now 94) federal judicial districts. Created in 1789, the marshal's office was originally charged mainly with serving court papers and acting as assistants to the federal judiciary.

On the frontier, however, U.S. marshals were often the only law of any kind for hundreds of miles, and were pressed into the role of catching criminals. Even so, most marshals were men with political connections rather than experienced lawmen, and functioned mainly as administrators. The heavy lifting was left to deputy U.S. marshals, who could be appointed by marshals, territorial governors and sometimes by another deputy marshal, and served at the pleasure of their appointers. Wyatt, Virgil and Morgan Earp, Bat Masterson and Wild Bill Hickok all briefly served as deputy U.S. marshals. Until 1896, deputies were paid fees and expenses rather than salaries, and as a result, it was often regarded as a part-time job.

County sheriffs were usually elected, and often had jurisdictions that covered thousands of square miles. Within the limits of cities and towns, there were marshals who were elected by a popular vote or selected by the mayor or town council. County sheriffs and town marshals usually had at least one or two deputies or police officers, and sometimes pooled their forces.

In addition to keeping the peace, frontier lawmen earned their pay performing other civic tasks. Sheriffs often served as tax collectors. Deputy marshals and police repaired wooden sidewalks, removed animal carcasses, inspected chimneys and ensured old whisky barrels, placed on corners around the town, were kept filled with water for use in fighting fires.

While the job could be unglamorous as well as dangerous, it paid reasonably well. A city marshal might earn $150 a month ($3,600 in 2022), which was six times an average cowboy's salary. Town police could make $60 to $75 a month, and were often paid a bounty of $2 to $2.50 for every person they arrested who was convicted. (To add insult to the arrest, the bounty was paid in the form of a fine imposed on the convicted party.)

County sheriffs could fare even better. Johnny Behan, sheriff in the early 1880s of Cochise County, Arizona, bragged of making $40,000 in a year, equivalent to nearly $1 million in 2022. The reason was that sheriffs who doubled as tax collectors often got to pocket a percentage of what they collected. In Sacramento, California, Irish immigrant James McClatchy picked up nearly $50,000 in his two-year term as sheriff. That was enough to buy an interest in one of the local newspapers, which planted the seed for what would become the McClatchy Company, once one of America's largest newspaper chains.

Needless to say, Wild West law enforcement wasn't without its risks. Tom "Bear River" Smith had been on the job as police chief in Abilene, Kansas, for five months in 1870 when he attempted to serve an arrest warrant on a murder suspect. He was shot in the chest for his troubles. Returning fire and wounding his assailant, he was wrestling with the suspect when the suspect's confederate hit him from behind with a pistol then picked up an axe and "chopped Smith's head nearly from his body."

"The sad event has cast a gloom over the town," a local newspaper noted, but apparently the gloom wasn't deep enough to give him more than a $2 funeral in an unmarked grave. Thirty-four years later, Abilene officials decided to reinter Smith in a place of honor, with a bronze plaque that any

Wild West lawman would have been proud to lie under: "A fearless hero of frontier days who in cowboy chaos established the supremacy of law."

Just where Wyatt went after he left the bordello business in Peoria, and what he did when he got there, is a bit murky. He may have spent some time hunting buffalo, as well as riding herd on cattle ranches. In mid-1873, he probably drifted into the lively cattle town of Ellsworth, Kansas. How lively it was can be deduced from a note in a competing town's newspaper: "As we go to press, Hell is still in session in Ellsworth."

On Aug. 15, 1873, an event occurred in Ellsworth that initiated the foundation-pouring for the legend of Wyatt Earp—whether he was actually there or not. It concerned the Thompson brothers, Ben and Billy, who had also figured in the Sweetwater Shootout, which launched Bat Masterson on his voyage to legendary status. If you wanted to be a Wild West legend, it was apparently a big help to have the Thompson brothers around.

The Thompsons were born in England in the 1840s, and immigrated to Austin, Texas, while still in their teens. By 1873, both had widespread and well-deserved reputations as killers. In Ellsworth, the brothers had spent the summer gambling, and feuding with some of the local police. Things came to a head when after a quarrel with other gamblers over a card game, Billy Thompson killed the Ellsworth County sheriff, Chauncey B. Whitney. The unarmed lawman had been trying to mediate the dispute. "For God's sake Billy," Ben Thompson was reported to have cried, "you have shot our best friend!"

According to newspaper accounts at the time, Ben kept any would-be posse at bay with a shotgun while Billy escaped. Now, here's where Wyatt Earp comes in—maybe. Frustrated by the town's police officers' refusal to confront Ben Thompson and a mob of Texas cowboys who were backing him up, the Ellsworth mayor fired the entire force on the spot. That much is fact.

Then, according to Earp, who said he was watching events as a disinterested bystander, the mayor appointed Wyatt as the new marshal. With a pair of borrowed pistols, Earp strode up to Ben and cajoled him into giving up his guns and marching off to jail. "People have a right to live in peace," Wyatt's third wife recalled him telling her, "and he (Ben) was protecting the getaway of his brother, who for pure meanness had killed a good man."

According to Stuart Lake, Earp's first biographer, Wyatt was disgusted when Ben Thompson was only fined $25 for disturbing the peace, and immediately freed. Turning in his badge after a half-day on the job, Wyatt supposedly snorted that "Ellsworth figures sheriffs at $25 a head. I don't figure the town's my size."

How much truth there is to Earp's account is highly debatable. Town records and contemporary newspaper accounts not only don't mention him having anything to do with the incident, but credit Ben Thompson's arrest to Ed Hogue, the dead sheriff's deputy. But somehow the idea that Wyatt Earp had stood alone against a mob and arrested the notorious Ben Thompson began to circulate among Texas cowboys. Billy Thompson would eventually be arrested and tried for the killing, but acquitted after witnesses testified the dying sheriff had insisted it was an accident. Ben Thompson would go on to be the beaver top hat-wearing city marshal of Austin, Texas, before being gunned down in an ambush in a San Antonio vaudeville theater. As for Wyatt Earp, he pushed on to Wichita, the next stop on his way to immortality.

Aside from nearly shooting himself by dropping his gun, and being fired for beating up his boss' political rival, Wyatt was by almost all accounts a praiseworthy cop in Wichita. "Wyatt Earp was a good and efficient officer, and well-known for his honesty and integrity," a cadre of leading Wichita citizens wrote in an 1881 affidavit. The document was meant to bolster Earp's reputation, since at the time he was facing murder charges as a result of the legendary-if-slightly-misnamed Gunfight at the O.K. Corral (it was actually near the corral, not at it). "...His character while here was of the best," the Wichita citizens said, "and no fault was ever found in him as an officer or a man."

Wichita was still Kansas' top cattle town in 1874, where Texas cowboys loaded their bovine charges into train cars and unloaded their money into saloons, gambling houses and brothels. The four-year-old town's vice industry was mainly located on the east bank of the Arkansas River, the "respectable" part of town on the west. A resident noted that along with cattle buyers, merchants and professional people, the town's population of about 1,200 included "transient cowboys, gamblers, horse-thieves, whores and land swindlers."

In addition to that assortment, there were three other Earps in Wichita besides Wyatt. James, Wyatt's older brother, was a bartender and pimp in Wichita. James' wife Bessie ran a brothel, and Sally Earp, who may or may not have been legally married to Wyatt, apparently worked for Bessie.

Wichita was a tough town. In the first 10 months after it incorporated as a municipality, its first three marshals either formally quit or fled without telling anyone. Wichita officials sometimes hired temporary police to support the regular force, which ranged in size from two to seven. For much of 1874, Wyatt apparently supplemented his income as a gambler by signing on as a rent-a-cop. In late October, he and a regular officer were credited with riding 75 miles to collect an unpaid debt—at gunpoint—from some swindlers. "These boys fear nothing and nobody," a local newspaper crowed. "...They just leveled a shotgun and six-shooter upon the scalawags...and told them to 'dough over,' which they did." Even so, the "fearless" Wyatt was not exactly a well-known figure: The paper spelled his name "Wiatt Erp."

Wyatt officially joined the police force on April 21, 1875, for $60 a month ($1,400 in 2022). As the new guy on the force, he was generally assigned to menial tasks. But he evidently performed them adequately, and occasionally got to do something more exciting than repairing hitching posts and scraping up animal carcasses. Less than three weeks into the job, Earp was making his rounds when he spotted a man who answered the description of a wanted horse thief. When the suspect made a break for it, "Erp (sic) fired one shot across his poop deck to bring him to...the man cast anchor near a clothes line, hauled down his colors and surrendered without firing a gun."

In December, "Policeman Erp" was praised in print after he found a man lying near a bridge "in a drunken stupor." The fellow had $500 in cash on him, which he still had after sobering up the next morning and paying a small fine. "He may congratulate himself that his lines, while he was drunk, were cast in such a pleasant place as Wichita," the *Beacon* noted, "as there are but few other places where that roll would ever have been heard from. The integrity of our police force has never been seriously questioned."

Wyatt's presence on the force might also have been something of a bonus for his "wife" and sister-in-law. Court records show that Sally and Bessie Earp were routinely fined $10 every month or so for violating anti-prostitution ordinances from May 1874 through March 1875. Such fines were a tacit way for the town to make some money while allowing the technically illegal bordellos to stay in business. The fines for the Earp women stopped, however, when Wyatt became a full-time cop. Of course, it might have been just a coincidence.

But any protection Sally and Bessie enjoyed ended abruptly when Wyatt was fired after beating up the man running against his boss in April, 1876. Like Wyatt, James and Bessie Earp left Wichita for Dodge City. Sally Earp did not. Either she was abandoned by Wyatt, or left him. In any event, Wyatt Earp was a single man when he rode into Dodge.

Wyatt Earp was not the first choice to be top assistant to Dodge Marshal Larry Deger in 1876, the year of the town's first major cattle drives. That honor fell to Jack Allen, a gambler who had a reputation as a fast gun. He was also fast on his feet, which he proved when he hurriedly got out of Dodge rather than face a bunch of drunk cowboys who were hurrahing the town. (Allen later shot a man in the back, felt bad about it, and became a minister.)

Allen's hasty departure made room for Wyatt, who signed on for $75 a month, or $15 more than he had been making in Wichita. Under his deal with Mayor George Hoover, Wyatt, not Deger, was allowed to choose the rest of the police force. He decided to retain Joe Mason, who was already a deputy marshal. Mason was known for sporting two ivory-handled Colts, and was enough of a ladies' man to be dubbed the "Apollo of Dodge." Earp's next choice was James Masterson, Bat's 21-year-old brother who had no law enforcement experience but was a seasoned buffalo hunter. Earp's third choice hobbled into town sometime in late spring.

Wyatt told his biographer Stuart Lake that Bat Masterson was still limping from the wound he received in his shootout with Melvin King at the beginning of the year. "Bat's gun hand was in working order, so I made him a deputy," Earp was said to have said. "...Even as a cripple, he was a first-class peace officer."

The Dodge cops' primary duty was to keep potential trouble "south of the Dead Line," which meant confining the drinking, whoring and gambling of cattle drovers to the part of town south of an east-west line roughly defined by the railroad tracks. The idea was to let Dodge's merchants, saloon owners and brothel operators soak up as much of the cowboys' money as possible without exposing the "good" citizens of the town to the perils of such activities.

To accomplish that, the police force had strategically hidden shotguns around town so deputies could grab extra firepower to supplement their six-shooters. But shooting was frowned upon: It tended to rile up the rest of the cowboys when one of their number was shot, and thus interrupted the flow of commerce. Instead, deputies were instructed to initially try to cajole would-be troublemakers into calming down. If that didn't work, they were to "buffalo" the miscreant.

"Buffaloing," as Wyatt explained to biographer Lake, consisted of whacking a man over the head with the barrel of a revolver. "With the proper method, you had your man covered until you hit him," Wyatt said, "and moreover, the barrel of a three-pound Colt's forty-five applied full-length to a man's head would stun without killing...". There was an added incentive to buffaloing over shooting: Deputies got $2.50 bonuses (about $60 in 2022 currency), which they pooled and divided evenly, for each arrest and conviction. There was no bonus for killing a man.

Earp was particularly adept at the "buffaloing" approach, which he had learned in Wichita. "It takes more guts to arrest a desperate man peaceably than to shoot him and discuss the case later," Bat Masterson observed. "No other man I ever heard of did (that) day after day as Wyatt did. It often seems he had a charmed life."

How well Wyatt's methods worked in 1876 isn't clear, since there are almost no copies of Dodge City newspapers still around for the year. But a visiting reporter from Atchison Kansas noted that while the various vice enterprises were running full-tilt, "Dodge has the benefit of being under a good city marshal, Larry Deger by name, who has with Wyatt Earp managed the wild and wooly gentlemen...in fact, I think there has never been a single shooting scrape even."

However effective it was, there wasn't a whole lot for the town's police force to do when the cattle season ended in the fall. So sometime late in the year, lured by the glittering promise of the Dakota Territory gold-strike town of Deadwood, both Bat and Wyatt pulled out of Dodge. Bat got as far as Cheyenne, Wyoming, where he ran into a lucky streak at the gaming tables that lasted several weeks. By then his enthusiasm for Deadwood had waned. Flush with cash, he drifted back to Dodge, where some friends talked him into embarking on one last buffalo hunt.

Wyatt made it to Deadwood. Instead of mining, however, he showed a business acumen he would rarely demonstrate in later life. Horses were scarce in Deadwood because feeding them was expensive. But firewood was also scarce—and a dire necessity in the bitter Black Hills winter. Wyatt had a team of horses, and learned where to get an ample supply of firewood. So he launched a business that used his horses to haul wood. The result was a very tidy profit. He also may have ridden as a shotgun guard on the region's stagecoach lines.

By the end of 1876, Wyatt Earp had yet to kill his first man. In fact, he had been in only one gunfight, which was memorable to no one but the two participants. But he had money in his pocket, had established a solid reputation as a lawman, and had demonstrated enterprise to go with his unquestioned nerve. It seemed he was headed for success—maybe greatness.

Chapter 2 Notes

Still, he was Wichita *Wichita Weekly Beacon*, Jan. 12 1876, p. 8.

In later years, Stuart N. Lake, *Wyatt Earp: Frontier Marshal*, pp. 42-43.

As embarrassing as, *Wichita Weekly Beacon*, April 5 1876, p. 5.

On May 24, *Wichita Weekly Beacon*, May 24 1876, p. 5.

It was that kind *Hays City Sentinel*, Sept. 14 1877, p. 4.

Buffalo hunter Winton Andrew Isenberg, *Wyatt Earp: A Vigilante Life*, p. 91; Andrew Isenberg, *The Destruction of the Bison*, p. 157.

Of course Dodge Robert M. Wright, *Dodge City, The Cowboy Capital and the Great Southwest*, pp. 6-7.

Dodge had a There are numerous and varied books on the history of Dodge City, from Robert Wright's highly personal account in the above footnote to Stanley Vestal's anecdote-laden *Dodge City, Queen of Cowtowns* (1952) to Tom Clavin's*Dodge City: Wyatt Earp, Bat Masterson and the Wickedest Town in the American West* (2017). All have their merits.

Wright wrote that Wright, op. cit., p. 10.

"There are law-abiding" *Atchison (Ks.) Daily Champion*, April 6 1876, p. 2.

More recently, some Casey Tefertiller, *Wyatt Earp: The Life Behind the Legend*, p. 1.

There were four *Wichita Eagle*, Jan. 21 1979, p. xx; Lake, op. cit., p. 103.

Second, he exuded *Salt Lake Tribune*, July 17 1910, p. 4; Stephens, op. cit., p. 46; ibid., p. 128.

The third aspect Stephens, op. cit., p. 232; *Pittsburgh Post-Gazette*, May 22, 1960, p. 114.

The fourth thing *Los Angeles Herald*, Dec. 5 1896, p. 2; *Arizona Highways*, April 2005 (Vol. 81, No. 4), p. 47.

In his late teens Masterson, op. cit., p. 57.

Court records show *Peoria Daily National Democrat*, Sept. 10 1872, p. 3.

But who were they Chicago *Inter-Ocean*, July 3, 1910, p. 27.

Take Bill Tilghman Masterson, op. cit., pp. 52-53.

"The sad event" *Abilene Chronicle*, Nov. 3, 1870, p. 3; *Topeka Daily Capital*, May 31, 1904, p. 3.

Just where Wyatt, Lake, op. cit., p. 74.

According to newspaper Tefertiller, Op. Cit., p. 8.

According to Stuart, Lake, op. cit., p. 92

Aside from nearly, Dale T. Schoenberger, *The Gunfighters*, p. 28.

Wichita was a *Wichita City Eagle*, Oct. 29 1874, p. 3.

Wyatt officially joined *Wichita Weekly Beacon*, May 12 1875, p. 5

In December *Wichita Weekly Beacon*, Dec. 12 1875, p. 5

Wyatt purportedly told Lake, op. cit., p. 142.

"Buffaloing," as Wyatt Ibid., p. 143.

Earp was particularly *Arizona Highways*, (Vol. 81, No. 4), April 2005, p. 47.

How well Earp's *Atchison Daily Champion*, Nov. 8 1876, p. 2.

CHAPTER 3

"Rascality so shameless"

Money, politics, and other entertainments

INTERLUDE

In the same month that Bat Masterson was shooting a soldier and Wyatt Earp was almost shooting himself, the mayor of Bridgeport, Connecticut, was shooting off his mouth—and getting handsomely paid for it. And while it's not out of the ordinary for politicians to earn their living talking, Phineas Taylor Barnum was certainly no ordinary politician.

Born into a poor Connecticut family in 1810, P.T. Barnum spent the first 25 years of his life treading water as a shop clerk, grocer and boarding house owner, while searching for a way to make a lot of money in a hurry. "I had long fancied that I could succeed if I could only get hold of a public exhibition," Barnum wrote in his autobiography, which he first published in 1855 and updated every year thereafter.

In 1835, he found his "exhibition." Scraping together $1,000 by selling everything he had and cadging a loan from an associate, Barnum "leased" Joice Heth, an African American woman slave. Heth was supposedly 161 years old, and claimed to have served as nanny for the infant George Washington. She died after only six months of being exhibited by Barnum. But the experience sparked a flame of flim-flam in her exploiter. "I had," he wrote, "at last found my true vocation."

His career veered periodically into politics—he was a state legislator in Connecticut, an unsuccessful U.S. Senate candidate and a surprisingly capable mayor of Bridgeport for a year. But P.T. Barnum truly immortalized himself by becoming America's undisputed master showman. He owned and operated museums, circuses and "hippodromes," which were part zoo, part aquarium, part circus and part ridiculous. Whatever the setting, he gave the country fakes it delighted in, such as the "Fejee Mermaid" and the "Cardiff Giant"—and real curiosities it seemingly couldn't get enough of, such as singer Jenny Lind, (aka the "Swedish Nightingale") and three-feet-tall Charles Stratton, (aka "General Tom Thumb.")

But in the fall of 1875, Barnum decided to take a break from the more sensational aspects of show business. He sold most of his properties—he got $25,000 ($600,000 in 2022) for the sole hippopotamus in the entirety of America, but only $600 ($14,400) each for his lions and tigers.He peddled a vast wardrobe of costumes, from tutus to suits of armor, for a pittance, and said goodbye to his clowns, orchestra and peanut vendors.

By the time the country's centennial year dawned, P.T. Barnum was on the lecture circuit. In the years before movies, radio, television and podcasts, lectures by well-known personalities were popular with the public. They could also be quite profitable for the lecturer, since there was much less overhead involved in delivering monologues than in feeding elephants and bearded ladies. Barnum, for example, earned as much as $10,000 ($240,000 in 2022 currency) in a single year for speaking, plus expenses.

One of his favorite talks was titled "The Art of Money-Getting." It was filled mostly with time-worn bromides, many filched from Benjamin Franklin, about pennies saved being pennies earned, avoiding debt and trying and trying again. But in his introduction, Barnum struck a chord that resonated with Americans everywhere.

"In the United States," Barnum declared, "...it is not at all difficult for persons in good health to make money...there are so many opportunities... that those who really desire to obtain (financial) independence have only to set their minds to it." He concluded his remarks with praise for those who pursued wealth: "Money getters are the benefactors of our race."

If America had a collective mantra in its 100th year as an independent nation, it was "MONEY." It was chanted, at least internally, by both the

Baltimore blacksmith making an average of $1.99 a day (about $48 in 2022) in wages, and by the Rhode Island socialite who at a birthday party gave the guest of honor a necklace valued at $15,000—roughly equivalent to the *annual* wages of 24 Baltimore blacksmiths. The guest of honor was her dog.

The fixation on finances was by no means a new aspect of the American character. As early as 1836, the writer Washington Irving had coined the term "almighty dollar" to designate what he called "the great object of universal devotion throughout our land." But the dollar's devotees had honed their worship to a particularly fine edge by 1876.

Americans, observed John Leng, a Scottish newspaper editor and politician who toured the country from coast to coast in 1876, "are more restless (than Europeans), less willing to be satisfied with moderate (compensation), more intent on rapidly amassing wealth...the speculative element enters largely into American life, and wherever there is much speculation there is all the excitement, and often much of the desperation, of gambling."

The country's pecuniary preoccupation was visible as far away as Australia. In June, the *Melbourne Age* noted the recent death of Alexander T. Stewart, an Irish immigrant to New York who at the time of his demise was the world's most prominent retailer. The *Age* predicted that Stewart's rags-to-riches saga "will make many an American lad yet unborn run after wealth as the only thing worth striving for."

But running after wealth and catching it are two different things. And despite Barnum's assertion that desire and determination were all you needed to get rich in 1876 America, the reality was that for most people times were hard, and getting harder. In fact, the nation was squarely in the middle of what became known as "the Great Depression," at least until an even greater one debuted in 1929.

America's post-Civil War economy was driven by a boom in railroad construction, with a staggering 35,000 miles of new track laid between 1866 and 1873. But it ran off the rails when the train boom busted. As in all economic upheavals, it wasn't that simple. While overbuilding systems, duplicating routes, wildly optimistic speculation and outright thievery helped lead to the collapse of the railroad industry, Congress also played its customary role in screwing things up. In January 1873, Congress passed the Mint Act, which called for backing U.S. currency with gold only. Silver coin production was halted and the Treasury quit buying silver; the money supply shrank as a result; lending sputtered to a crawl, and the nation's economic outlook wandered into uncertainty.

On September 18, uncertainty turned to panic when a major New York bank headed by "the financier of the Civil War," Jay Cooke, collapsed. The collapse was so stunning, a disbelieving Philadelphia policeman arrested a newsboy for "slandering" the banker by shouting "All about the failure of Jay Cooke!" while hawking his newspapers. The failure of Cooke's bank and the subsequent run on other banks caused the New York Stock Exchange to close for 10 days.

In the aftermath, about a quarter of U.S. railroad companies went belly up. More than 18,000 other businesses closed, and unemployment doubled, to 14 percent. Of those who still had jobs, few were full-time, and most were working for reduced wages. More than 90,000 families lost their homes in New York City alone. Basements of police stations and jails became de facto homeless shelters. Parents begged authorities to allow their children entrance to the lower Manhattan jail, appropriately nicknamed "The Tombs," where they would at least have some food and a roof over their heads.

A *New York Daily Herald* reporter described the plight of the Parkers, a family of six "huddled in a small dark room," who had not eaten in two days. "The children are young and quite unable to provide for themselves. With the sickness of father and mother, and requiring sustenance, the future of these young folks seems sad indeed."

Hard times were not solely the province of the big Eastern cities. In Pittsburgh, half the banks closed, and while wages in "working trades" were cut by 40 percent or more, a newspaper noted, "there has been no corresponding reduction in the necessaries of life, and at the present rates workingmen have to content themselves with a bare livelihood." In a California mining camp called Lake City, an unemployed laborer complained "there seems to be about fifteen hunting work where one gets it."

While there were plenty of have-nots in 1876 America, however, there were also a handful of haves. Slightly more than one-half mile from where the starving Parker family was huddled in their small dark room in New York City, the richest man in the country lived in a four-story mansion with two parlors, a dining room, library, six bedrooms "and rooms for the domestics." Cornelius "Commodore" Vanderbilt was in his 83rd, and last, year. In fact, the same edition of the *Daily Herald* that recounted the plight of the Parkers also reported that Vanderbilt "was not quite so well...that he is growing weaker day by day there can be no doubt ...".

When he died a few weeks after the paper's story appeared, Vanderbilt—who made his fortune in the steamship and railroad industries, and once said "I have been insane on the subject of moneymaking all my life"—left an estimated fortune of about $105 million, the modern equivalent of which would be roughly $2.5 billion. He epitomized the period's "robber barons:" men who were ruthless with competitors, pitiless with employees and for the most part parsimonious with charities.

The barons, whose drive and rapacity saw them accumulate a sizeable share of the country's post-Civil War wealth, were aided and abetted by a number of factors. Rampant political corruption resulted in a subsequent lack of government oversight or regulation. "What do I care about law?" Vanderbilt rhetorically asked. "Hain't I got the power?" A justification for ends-trump-the-means avarice developed around a term coined by English philosopher Herbert Spencer: "Survival of the Fittest." Spencer molded Charles Darwin's nascent theories on the evolution of species to account for human interaction. Capitalism, it was argued, naturally separated the weak from the strong. It assumed the best-equipped by Nature to lead society would do so, and would rightfully profit the most from it.

Rightfully or not, they did. It's estimated that about 10 percent of Americans controlled 70 percent of the nation's wealth in the mid-1870s—about the same ratio as in 2020. And while they certainly envied, and quite probably hated, the economic elite, many "average" Americans also looked on the wealthy's wealth—and their ostentatious displays of it—with something akin to admiration. "In any average assembly of Americans," notes a character in William Dean Howells' novel *A Traveler from Altruria*, "the great millionaire would take the eyes of all away from the greatest statesman, the greatest poet or the greatest soldier."

Most of the "top 10 percent" were only too happy to publicly roll around in their riches. Vanderbilt, for example, once took his family on vacation to Europe—via a 270-foot steam-powered yacht he had specially built. Including the costs of employing a doctor and clergyman as part of the crew, the trip was estimated to cost the 2022 equivalent of $15 million. Jay Gould, who was so audacious a crook he once tried to corner the nation's gold supply by bribing President U.S. Grant's brother-in-law, paid $50,000 ($1.2 million in 2022) for an 88-foot-long, four-bedroom private railroad car. James "Gentleman Jim" Fisk, who rose from tin peddler to railroad mogul, scratched his itch for going to the theater by spending $850,000 ($20.4 million in 2022) to buy an opera house.

It was indeed America's "Gilded Age." That sobriquet came from the country's most popular humorist and author, Mark Twain, and was the title of an 1873 novel written by Twain and Connecticut newspaper editor Charles Dudley Warner.Twain borrowed the term from a phrase in Shakespeare's *Life and Death of King John:* "To gild refined gold/ to paint the lily...is wasteful and ridiculous excess." In case anyone missed the point that it was meant to mirror 1870s America, the authors sub-titled it *"A Tale of Today."*

The shambling plot of the Twain-Warner satire involves ludicrous get-rich-quick schemes and salacious scandals. It also takes pains to point out that when it came to lusting for wealth, politicians were like most other Americans—only more so. At one point, for example, a businessman explains that bills are moved through Congress only by greasing lots of palms: "A majority of the House Committee, say $10,000 apiece...a majority of the Senate Committee, the same...a little extra to chairmen of one or two such committees...then a lot of small-fry country members who won't vote for anything whatever without pay, say $500 each; a lot of gimcracks for Congressmen's wives and children—those go a long way—you can't spend too much money in that line ...".

The same year *The Gilded Age* was published, Twain wrote to a New York newspaper to comment on a controversial murder trial. In acidly suggesting the defendant's lawyers could have just as ably defended Judas Iscariot, Twain noted that "to my mind, Judas Iscariot was nothing but a low, mean, premature congressman." By 1876, most Americans might have thought Twain was being overly harsh and unfair to compare the traitorous disciple of Christ to a congressman. Unfair, that is, to Judas.

The 44th Congress of the United States began the second year of its two-year session on Jan. 5, 1876. Among the 363 House and Senate members, representing 37 states (Colorado would become the 38th in mid-year), there quite probably were some decent, well-intentioned and responsible men. But the most distinctive feature of the 44th Congress was not the possible presence of some honest men (there would be no women of any kind for another 40 years.) What was unique was that for the first time since the beginning of the Civil War 15 years before, the House of Representatives was in the hands of Democrats.

The Democrats' ascension in the House was due to several factors. One was the fact the nation's economy was in the dumpster, a condition that has always made American voters nervous and fickle. A second factor was weariness with the violence and divisiveness rooted in the country's post-war racial strife. Then there was the assortment of scandals that involved both members of Congress and the administration of President Ulysses S. Grant.

One such scandal was named "Crédit Mobilier." This was a scheme by which a phony construction company, named after a major French financial institution that had nothing to do with it, was created to submit fake bills to the Union Pacific Railroad Company. The Union Pacific, in turn, was heavily subsidized by the federal government. Payments for the fake bills—which totaled an estimated $44 million (a hefty $1.1 billion in 2022 currency)—were divvied up among railroad executives and about a dozen members of Congress. The scheme was exposed by the *New York Sun* in 1872, while Grant was running for re-election. As a result, Vice President Schuyler Colfax, who had been one of the congressional members involved, was booted off the ticket. But none of the other miscreants received more than a rhetorical rap on the wrist.

The Crédit Mobilier scandal was rivaled in its ability to anger voters only by what became widely known as the "Salary Grab Act"—a political blunder that has to rank among Congress' Top 10 Miscalculations of all time.

It started in late February, 1873, when Rep. Benjamin Butler, R-Massachusetts, attached an amendment to a bill whose main purpose was to grant a long-overdue pay raise to all federal employees. Butler broadened the bill to also give members of Congress a 50 percent annual pay raise, from $5,000 to $7,500 ($180,000 in 2022 dollars). Even more cheeky was the fact that the lawmakers' pay raise was to be retroactive to the beginning of the congressional session in 1871. That amounted to a bonus of $5,000 for each congressman. The proposal also increased the annual salaries of Supreme Court justices from $8,000 to $10,000, and doubled the salary of the president to $50,000. The average American worker at the time, if he was lucky enough to have a job, would be doing well to bring home $700 a year.

In defense of the measure, supporters argued that congressional salaries had not been raised since 1852, and the president's salary had been frozen since George Washington held the job back in 1789. Moreover, it was pointed out, congressmen and senators had to pay for their own staffs, if they had one. The cost of living in Washington D.C. had soared since the

Civil War. And a pay raise, the bill's supporters contended with mostly straight faces, would enable "ordinary" citizens without outside fortunes to afford to serve in Congress. After some fierce back-and-forth, the measure was approved on a bipartisan basis, just before Congress recessed for the year. President Grant signed it the day before he began his second term.

Much of the nation's press howled in protest. "This is bold, defiant, flagrant robbery, particularly that portion of the law that is retroactive," thundered the *Defiance Democrat* in Ohio. Even normally pro-Grant, pro-Republican newspapers such as the *New York Times* weighed in: "The public will not readily forget a piece of rascality so shameless, so despicable and so conspicuous. It has wrought a deep impression on the people, which will make itself felt sooner or later."

Realizing its lapse in judgement, Congress hastily rescinded the raise for itself when it reconvened in January 1874. But the political damage was done. Voters generally blamed the Republicans, since they were the party in power. In the elections that fall, the GOP lost 96 House seats—and its majority control. (Rep. Butler, who was the chief architect of the plan and had brazenly spent his "bonus" money on a family cruise to Europe, not only lost his house seat, but also a gubernatorial race he had been favored to win in Massachusetts.)

In the Senate, Republicans retained control despite losing 20 seats. But the two-house split assured a fierce partisan gridlock in the federal government's legislative branch as the nation's centennial year began. In fact, congressional control would remain split for seven of the succeeding nine sessions.

The executive branch, meanwhile, had copious problems of its own. Generally hailed as second only to Abraham Lincoln in preserving the country during the Civil War, Ulysses S. Grant in 1876 was entering his eighth and last year in the White House. As the man who led Union forces to victory, Grant was personally still a hero to millions of Americans, at least outside the South. But his administration had been plagued by an assembly line of corruption and scandal, perpetrated by those around the president—including close advisers and even relatives.

The chicanery was breathtaking in both its breadth and audacity. Customs collectors gave preferential treatment to some importers in return for hefty fees; postal officials awarded huge contracts to private firms for delivery of mail in rural areas, in exchange for kickbacks; treasury agents were lavishly paid by whiskey distillers to underreport how much hooch was being produced, thus allowing the distillers to evade stiff federal liquor taxes.

Individual members of Grant's cabinet and staff also distinguished themselves as first-class villains. Attorney General George H. Williams was forced to resign after it was revealed he and his extravagantly spending wife had extorted $30,000 from a company in return for the Justice Department dropping a pending case against the firm. Interior Secretary Columbus Delano resigned amid accusations that he and his son had blackmailed speculators seeking illegal land grants. Even the president's brother Orvil was accused of obtaining valuable licenses for operating Indian trading posts, then clandestinely selling half-interests in them to agents who subsequently swindled their Native American clients.

There's little to no evidence to suggest Grant himself was directly involved in any of the shady dealings. As eminent Grant biographer Ron Chernow put it, the president "was an honest man in a corrupt age." But Grant stubbornly stood by those he mistakenly trusted, even in cases where their guilt was apparent. This was particularly true in the case of Orville Babcock, who was Grant's private secretary—the equivalent of a modern White House chief of staff. West Point-educated, the handlebar-mustached, pointy-goateed Babcock possessed polished manners and a decided dearth of loyalty, ethics and morality.

Babcock became a key operative in the "Whiskey Ring," a cabal of distillers and federal agents that pocketed millions by falsifying whiskey production data to avoid the hefty 70 cents-a-gallon federal tax. In doing so, he succumbed to the wiles of former Union Gen. John McDonald, a trusted friend of the president who ran the biggest part of the multi-state scheme. In addition to money, McDonald even fixed up Babcock with a beautiful blonde mistress. In return, Babcock tipped off the ring's leaders when honest agents, under the direction of Treasury Secretary Benjamin Bristow, were set to stage inspections or raids.

Babcock was eventually found out and indicted, along with McDonald and 236 others. But Grant refused to believe his trusted confidant was guilty. After being dissuaded by advisers from testifying in person at Babcock's trial in St. Louis, the president gave a deposition in February, 1876, on Babcock's behalf. "I have always had great faith in him," Grant said, "...and as yet, my confidence in him is unshaken."

Swayed by Grant's words, and due to a lack of indisputable evidence (as well as the distinct possibility they were bribed), jurors acquitted Babcock. (McDonald was convicted and served 3-1/2 years.) But Grant's confidence in his top aide was shattered, and he fired him. Fans of poetic justice may be delighted to learn that Babcock wound up a federal lighthouse inspector and drowned in 1884 while on the job at Mosquito Inlet, Florida.

The unceasing controversies and personal betrayals thoroughly soured Grant on a job he had only reluctantly sought in the first place. Despite his still-sizeable personal popularity, he wavered a bit, then declined to seek a third term in 1876. "I do not want to be here another four years," he told his wife Julia. "I do not think I could stand it."

Grant's decision meant a wide-open race for the White House. On the Democratic side, the early favorite for the party's nomination was New York Gov. Samuel Tilden. Wealthy, well-educated and politically wily, Tilden created an efficient organization that would rather easily deliver him the nomination on the second ballot when the Democrats convened in St. Louis in June. Given the depressed economy and the swarm of scandals, Democrats liked their chances to win the White House for the first time since 1856.

The Republican side was decidedly murkier. The GOP was split into three factions: Reform-minded party members, known as "Mugwumps;" those who favored the status quo, known as "Stalwarts," and the "Half-Breeds," whose main interest was in electing James G. Blaine of Maine.

Blaine had been Speaker of the House before the Democrats took over. He was considered a master at "waving the bloody shirt," a reference to Republicans who stirred up animosity against Democrats by reminding voters the GOP had been the party of Lincoln and the Union during the Civil War. Blaine's principal opponents were considered to be Sen. Roscoe Conkling of New York, backed by the Stalwarts, and former U.S. Treasury Secretary Benjamin Bristow, who was credited with breaking up the Whiskey Ring and was the Mugwumps' choice.

There was also a long-shot whose name was sometimes mentioned, if only because he had just been inaugurated to begin his third term as governor of Ohio, and the GOP nominating convention was scheduled for June in the Ohio city of Cincinnati. His name was Rutherford B. Hayes. A handsome and distinguished Union general who had been severely wounded at the Battle of Antietam, Hayes was wealthy, and had served in Congress without being sullied by his colleagues. That was about all anyone who was interested in national politics and didn't live in Ohio knew about him. In the early part of 1876, that seemed enough.

Despite having 12 fewer states and 280 million fewer people than 2022 America, 1876 America was still a big place. The Scottish newspaperman and centennial visitor John Leng pointed out to his readers that the distance he traveled throughout the United States in 1876 was the equivalent of someone going from Edinburgh to China, via India. "Few persons on this (European) side of the Atlantic have any conception of American distances," Leng wrote. "...The sense of greatness—the mere physical greatness of this country—is strong upon every American."

So was the sense of nostalgia. Despite its relative youth as a nation, America in 1876 had already faced a formidable heap of crises in its first 100 years: Four wars (one against itself); the complex creation of a form of government unique in human history; four serious economic calamities;

the scourge of slavery, and the assassination of perhaps its greatest leader. Most had been surmounted with a mix of pluck and luck. As Leng observed, "America has already had not a few pages in its history of which the Americans may be justly proud."

The centennial was thus the perfect opportunity for the country to suspend its collective dismay with corrupt politics and a sagging economy, and pat itself on the back. Americans could revel a bit in what one hyperbolic congressman proclaimed was a celebration of the year "upon which our Great Republic was born, and, baptized in the fire of battle and the blood of patriots, took its place in the great family of nations...".

One way Americans celebrated was to raid Grandma's attic. The centennial set off a craze for collecting and displaying "antiques," from the real things found in cobweb-shrouded hay lofts to new furniture that was purposely chipped, stained and scratched to look like it came over on the *Mayflower*. The art critic Clarence Cook noted approvingly that in saving pieces of the nation's past—or at least replicating them—"we are bringing ourselves a little nearer in spirit to the old time."

The nostalgia bug extended to popular art as well. Folksy plaster sculptures by New York artist John Rogers decorated middle-class parlors around the country. One was even lugged around by Lt. Col. George Armstrong Custer during his various military campaigns in the West. Rogers' sculptural groups, with names like "Weighing the Baby," and "The Village Schoolmaster," foreshadowed the nostalgic work that Norman Rockwell would produce 75 years later.

The literary event of the year didn't arrive until December, when *The Adventures of Tom Sawyer* was published. Mark Twain's classic ode to boyhood transported readers back to an idyllic time before the nation ripped itself apart with a war that pitted brother against brother. While waiting for Twain's book, American readers perused hundreds of newspapers and magazines full of stories about the Founding Fathers, particularly George Washington. There were also yarns that bordered on the mythical about other historical figures, such as Daniel Boone. And contemporary characters—and the roots of legends—were created out of men still alive in 1876, or for at least parts of it. These included Buffalo Bill Cody, Jesse James, Wild Bill Hickok and the plaster sculpture-toting Col. Custer.

This latter group, or more accurately, characters based very loosely on them, were often the subjects of the age's ubiquitous "dime novels." Created in 1860 by a New York publisher with the Dickensian name of Erastus Flavel Beadle, dime novels were flimsy paperbacks of about 100 pages. The books' subjects varied, from big-city detectives to pirates. But among the most popular were those set in the Wild West. Sometimes the heroes bore the names of real-life figures such as Buffalo Bill or Jesse James, but often even the names were made up—"Deadwood Dick" or "Denver Dan."

While some of the real-life "heroes" depicted by the dime novelists basked in the limelight the books afforded, others were less appreciative. Ned Buntline, one of the most prolific of the dime novel writers, is said to have once approached Wild Bill Hickok in a Wyoming saloon and told him he was "in search of a real, live Indian-fighting hero" to write about. "I'll give you just twenty-four hours to leave the community," Hickok replied. "I don't care what your business is, but I don't like your looks nohow."

But America's most significant paean to its past in 1876 came in the form of what amounted to its first world's fair. The formal title was the "International Exhibition of Arts, Manufactures and Products of Soil and Mine." It was more generally referred to, however, as "the Centennial" or "the Centennial Exposition."

The expo was the brainchild of John L. Campbell, an Indiana college math professor. In 1866, the year after the Civil War ended, Campbell proposed that the country stage a mammoth fair to celebrate America's 100th anniversary, and invite the rest of the world. Philadelphia, as the nation's second-largest metropolis (behind New York City) and the birthplace of both the Declaration of Independence and the U.S. Constitution, was the logical host. The city's leaders enthusiastically embraced the idea, as did most of America.

"It promises to be the most magnificent national and inter-national exposition ever known," enthused a California newspaper. "...Many of the exhibits will be upon the greatest scale...doubtless the visitors at Philadelphia during the six months of the exhibition will be numbered by millions."

It also promised to be a mountain of logistical headaches for the commission created by Congress to oversee the exposition. Each state and territory had one representative, all of them male. As a sop to female Americans, an auxiliary women's committee was established, headed by a great-granddaughter of Benjamin Franklin. The group would raise $30,000 ($720,000 in 2022) for a women's exhibition building.

At the tip of the iceberg of problems the expo commission faced was, well, ice. It was a vital resource for a fair being held during the sticky, sweltering days of a Philadelphia summer. And the higher-than-normal winter temperatures in the normally ice-bound Northeast did not augur well for America's 1876 ice crop. In fact, the *New York Times* dolefully reported in late January, "The present prospect of an ice crop is exceedingly poor." But commission members ferreted out an unclaimed ice field in Maine's Penobscot Bay and secured the rights to it.

They also busied themselves selling concession rights to supply the centennial with other needed goods and amenities. One company paid $50,000 ($1.2 million in 2022) for the exclusive right to provide janitorial services to the hundreds of vendors at the fair. Another paid $30,000 to sell all the expo's soda water. "A popcorn capitalist has given $7,000 for the sole privilege of impairing the digestion of the world at the great fair," a newspaper observed, adding that a peanut purveyor offered $8,000 for a similar monopoly. "But the committee thought...that all the world crunching peanuts at once would make too many shells...the application was rejected and the applicant is dejected."

Fair organizers, however, were well aware that revenue raised from selling concession rights and admission tickets wouldn't cover the centennial's costs. They also sold stock shares, with buyers to get a piece of any profits the expo turned. The city of Philadelphia and state of Pennsylvania kicked in a total of $2.5 million. Even Congress agreed the federal government should loan the centennial $1.5 million—and Congress agreeing on anything in 1876 was something of a minor miracle.

While setting up the finances, the commission also basically had create an entire city: More than 200 buildings on 286 acres of Philadelphia's Fairmount Park, with the largest structure covering more than 21 acres by itself. Temporary hotels and boarding houses were constructed near the fairgrounds, and extra train and streetcar lines added. A 500-man "Centennial Guard" was established to keep order, corral lost children and operate the lost-and-found department. There was even a new bank chartered specifically to handle the expo's mini-economy.

The rest of the country got into the spirit of '76 by selling and buying everything from centennial hats to centennial buckwheat cake mix, and/or saving up to get to the Expo when it opened on May 10."Come at all events," urged the *Chicago Tribune*, "(even) if you have to live six months on bread and water to make up the expense." While waiting for the great fair to begin, Americans were diverted by a base ball pitcher who was selling recreation and a former shoe salesman who was pitching salvation.

Humans have played games involving sticks and balls for thousands of years. Hieroglyphs on ancient Egyptian tombs describe a game called "seker-herat," or "batting the ball." More recently, pre-Revolutionary War American kids, including a tall-for-his-age Virginia lad named George Washington, played stick-and-ball games with various names: "cricket," "wicket," and "one-old-cat" through "four-old-cat."

In the 1840s, varieties of "base ball" began to more closely resemble the modern version of the game. Young adult males organized clubs and agreed on a set of rules, although these changed with some regularity. During lulls in the hostilities of the Civil War, Northern and Southern soldiers would sometimes engage in competition with each other on a ballfield rather than a battlefield. By 1876, base ball had become, in the words of a *Boston Globe* headline, "Our Great Game."

"Human society on the North American continent can now be distinctly ranged into two classes," the *Globe* noted in a Page 1 story. "They are composed on the one hand of those who take an interest in our great and glorious national game, and on the other hand, of those who think it all 'bosh and rubbish.' "...The latter class is largely made up of the portion of the population that does not vote, namely 'idiots and women.'"

The *Globe's* enthusiasm was doubtless fueled by the fact Boston had the best team in the country at the time. But parochialism and chauvinism aside, base ball was indeed a national passion. "We are in a whirlpool of excitement," enthused a correspondent for the *Abilene (Kansas) Gazette*, in reporting about an upcoming game between the home team and a rival squad from Salina, 27 miles away. "Base ball (is) all the talk...can't hear anything but base ball wherever we go." Salina won, 42-36. The *Gazette* was nonetheless a good sport about it, even acknowledging that the umpire, a Salina resident, favored "our boys as much as his own club."

If the game itself was popular, however, its professional version reeked with almost as much corruption as the federal government. In 1871, the nine-team National Association of Professional Base Ball Players had formed to become America's first professional sports league. The league's star players, such as Albert Goodwill Spalding and Adrian "Cap" Anson, both of the Boston club, could make more than $1,000 ($24,000 in 2021) for a six-month season, almost triple the average workingman's salary for a full year. But most players made much less, and many were happy to take a few bucks from gamblers to "heave" or "hippodrome" a game, meaning they played as badly as necessary to ensure the outcome would be in their benefactor's favor.

Spalding, a tall, handsome and luxuriantly mustached 25-year-old Illinois native, was the game's best pitcher and, with Anson, the league's biggest star. He hated the rampant cheating. But true to his time, he did like money. So in mid-1875, Spalding began secretly meeting with William Hulbert, a Chicago coal tycoon who was a director, and soon to be owner, of the National Association's Chicago White Stockings. By the beginning of 1876, Spalding had formally jumped ship in Boston and joined the Chicago club, bringing Anson and two other good Boston players with him. Because National Association rules would almost certainly nullify the Boston players changing teams, Hulbert decided to put together a new professional base ball organization: The National League of Professional Base Ball Clubs.

Consisting of eight teams, the new league promised to be much better organized than its predecessor, with standardized 50-cent admission fees, paid umpires for every game, and a formal schedule. It would also be far less tolerant of drunken players, gambling and "heaved" contests. On April 22, 1876, a Philadelphia crowd estimated at about 3,000 watched the hometown team lose 6-5 to Boston. "The contest was very exciting," the *Boston Post* reported.

Despite a rocky start—two of the original teams, in Philadelphia and New York, were kicked out by the end of the first season for violating various rules—the National League would endure, establishing itself as America's first successful professional team sports organization, and becoming a model for those that followed.

Spalding, meanwhile, prospered. On the field, he managed and pitched the Chicago team to the league's first championship, winning 46 games as a pitcher and compiling a 52-14 record as manager. Off the field, he did even better. With $800 borrowed from his mother, Spalding announced in February "his intention to open a large emporium in Chicago where he will sell all kinds of base ball goods and turn his place into the headquarters for the Western ball clubs."

Thanks to his star power and persistent lobbying, Spalding base balls, which sold for $16 a dozen ($384 in 2022), were designated the National League's official ball, to be used in all games. To further nudge sales, a new rule was instituted that if during a game a ball was lost for more than three minutes in the crowd or somewhere on the field, a new ball had to be put in play. Spalding's company tripled its original investment in its first year. It was the beginning of a sporting goods empire, and exemplified both the country's entrepreneurial spirit and the eyebrow-raising ethics of the Gilded Age.

While Spalding's business tactics were raising some folks' eyebrows, another Chicago figure was raising many folks' hopes of eternal salvation. Dwight Lyman Moody was a 17-year-old unemployed farmhand in 1854, when he made a deal with an uncle. In return for room, board and a job in his uncle's shoe store, the short and very stout teenager agreed to attend church services every Sunday. By the time he was 23, Moody had parlayed selling footwear into a prosperous career as a Chicago real estate investor.

But his uncle's compulsory church attendance had an unforeseen impact. Moody gradually gave up selling land on Earth and began peddling parcels in Heaven. He became an evangelist, with the stated goal of "reducing the population of Hell by one million souls." His career switch earned him the nickname "Crazy Moody."

And then in 1871, he met Ira D. Sankey at a YMCA convention in Indianapolis. It was the late-19th century equivalent of John Lennon meeting Paul McCartney and forming the Beatles. Sankey was a fat, mutton-chop whiskered former bank clerk from Pennsylvania. He wrote and sang ecclesiastical music, in a voice that some critics decried as painful to hear, but caused tens of thousands of fans to soulfully swoon and sway.

America had always had religious celebrities. In the 1740s, for example, an English evangelist, George Whitefield, used a mixture of drama and soaring oratory to enthrall audiences that often numbered in the thousands. Whitefield's outdoor revivals were copied in the century that followed by scores of "camp meeting" revivalists. Less emotional and more intellectual were preachers such as Henry Ward Beecher.

In 1876, Beecher, the brother of Harriet Beecher Stowe, the woman who wrote *Uncle Tom's Cabin*, was among the most widely known people in the country. A leading abolitionist before and during the Civil War, Beecher was recognized as a leading theologian, a champion of women's rights—and the defendant in an 1875 adultery case that was among the most highly publicized legal proceedings of the 19th century. Despite substantial evidence that the clergyman was a serial philanderer, a hung jury let Beecher off the hook, as did the religious organizations with which he was associated. And if anything, the scandal increased his drawing power when he toured America's churches or appeared on the lecture circuit. The day after the National League debuted, for example, Beecher drew an overflow crowd of hundreds to a Boston church.

But Beecher was an old-school preacher, whose sermons were basically just sermons. Moody and Sankey offered a new kind of evangelism that mixed God, music and show-business savvy into a spiritual show unlike any Americans had ever seen. And millions of Americans saw it. On New Year's Day 1876, three shows in Philadelphia attracted a total audience of about 36,000, In New York City, people were trampled in the rush to fill a 10,000-seat auditorium. In Brooklyn, they appeared night after night before crowds of 15,000.

Attired in a baggy business suit, Moody delivered a simple message: Heaven was a much nicer place to spend eternity than Hell. Moody's heaven had pearly gates and streets of gold, but otherwise was pretty much like Atlanta or London or Chicago, only "without smoking (tobacco) chewing, drinking, horse-racing, dancing (and) card playing." His simple message was liberally sprinkled with "aint's" and "you wasn'ts," which audiences loved because it sounded like he was talking directly to them over the backyard fence, rather than at them from a lofty pulpit.

Interspersed within the sermon were songs from Sankey, who accompanied himself on a small organ and was often backed by a choir of hundreds of voices. His vocal range was limited, but his tone was often described by his numerous fans as "sincere" or "sweet," and he sometimes talked the lyrics more than sang them anyway.

Somewhat surprisingly for Gilded Age America, Moody and Sankey weren't crooks or con men. They charged no admission, and while they accepted donations, they weren't pushy about it. Although their revivals raked in hundreds of thousands of dollars, almost all the net proceeds went to the YMCA, Sunday schools and other social service organizations. Moreover, Moody took great pains to point out he neither profited from, nor approved of, the numerous cottage industries that sprang up selling his photographs and other Moody-Sankey memorabilia.

Still, not everyone was enamored of the duo's religious crusade, particularly because it was accompanied everywhere it went by a blizzard of publicity generated by Moody's full-time press agent. "P.T. Barnum never had a more zealous (PR) clerk in his employ," sniffed one newspaper editorialist. "If this is true Godliness, it is very strange that this (kind of) effort was not discovered two thousand years ago."

As for Barnum himself, the great showman's retirement from the spotlight was short-lived. Unable to resist the lure of staging a spectacle during the country's 100th birthday celebration, Barnum announced his comeback in late January. He repurchased his hippopotamus, obtained a bad-tempered sea lion along with an estimated 510 other animals, bought 120 railroad cars to move his show from town to town, put together a payroll of more than 1,000 workers, and retained the services of "Captain Georges Costentenus," who was said to have no fewer than 386 tattoos from his head to his toes.

Barnum's new spectacle, the *New York Times* reported, will comprise "the most colossal show ever collected...he says he is about to produce the culminating show combination of his lifetime and will exhibit it in the Centennial year to the greatest multitude of citizens and strangers that has ever upon any one great occasion of celebration been drawn together in the world's history."

Of course, as both a politician and a showman, the legendary Barnum was known to sometimes exaggerate.

Chapter 3 Notes

Born into a *P.T. Barnum, Life of P.T. Barnum, Written by Himself,* (1888 edition), p. 35.

In 1835, he Ibid., p. 39.

"In the United States" *Leavenworth (Ks.) Times*, Oct. 31, 1875, p. 4; Neal Harris, *Humbug: The Art of P.T. Barnum*, p. 156.

The fixation on Washington Irving, "The Creole Village," *Knickerbocker Magazine*, Nov. 12 1836.

Americans, noted John Leng John Leng, *America in 1876: Pencillings During a Tour in the Centennial Year*, pp. 319-320.

The country's pecuniary *The Melbourne Age*, June 27 1876, p. 3.

A New York Daily Herald *New York Daily Herald*, Dec. 11 1876, p. 8.

Hard times were *Pittsburgh Weekly Gazette*, Feb. 28 1876, p. 4; *Junction City (Ks.) Weekly Union*, May 20 1876, p. 2.

While there were *New York Daily Herald*, Dec. 11 1876, p. 5.

The shambling plot Mark Twain and Charles Dudley Warner, *The Gilded Age*, pp. 209-210.

The same year *Buffalo (N.Y.) Weekly Courier*, March 19 1873, p. 6.

Much of the nation's *Defiance (Ohio) Democrat*, March 27 1873, p. 1; *New York Times*, March 8 1873, p. 6.

There's little to Ron Chernow, *Grant*, p. 800.

Babcock was eventually Ibid., p. 806.

The unceasing controversies Ibid., p. 810.

Despite having 12 Leng, op. cit., p. 308.

So was the sense Ibid., p. 389.

The centennial was Dee Brown, *The Year of the Century: 1876*, p. 20.

One way Americans J.C. Furnas, *The Americans: A Social History of the United States, 1587—1914*, p. 600.

While some of Joseph G. Rosa, *They Called Him Wild Bill*, p. 243.

"It promises to be" *(Sacramento) Daily Bee*, April 26 1876, p. 2.

At the tip *New York Times*, Jan. 30, 1876, p. 12.

They also busied *Chattanooga (Tn.) Daily Commercial*, Feb. 26 1876, p. 4.

The rest of *Chicago Tribune*, May 22 1876, p. 1.

Humans have played John Thorn, *Base Ball in the Garden of Eden*, p. 57.

"Human society" *Boston Daily Globe*, June 3, 1876, p. 1.

Chauvinism aside *Abilene (Ks.) Gazette*, July 28 1876, p. 5; August 4 1876, p. 6.

Spalding, meanwhile, *Chicago Tribune*, Feb. 13 1876, p. 12.

Attired in a Brown, op. cit., p. 38.

Still, not everyone was *Clearfield (Pa.) Republican*, Jan. 12 1876, p. 2.

Barnum's new spectacle *New York Times*, Jan. 21 1876, p. 8.

CHAPTER 4

"Thou of the sunny flowing hair"

The end of George Armstrong Custer

JUNE

It was unclear how much George Custer's body had been mutilated. The first newspaper reports indicated that "Chief Rain-In-The Face, after shooting Custer through the head, took his heart out and put it on a pole, and the Indians held a grand war dance around it." It was whispered that an arrow had been shoved up Custer's penis, but this was kept out of the press so as not to offend his widow. And it was said Lakota women jammed bone awls into his eardrums, "so he would listen better in the next world." A fingertip might also have been snipped off.

As it turned out, Custer's heart wasn't torn out, and no one danced around it. Some historians, however, believe that the arrow-in-the-penis, awl-in-the-eardrums procedures were indeed performed. Possibly also the fingertip snip. On the other hand, a lot of contemporary witnesses insisted Custer's body was untouched except for the wounds that killed him. "I stood six feet away," said Pvt. Charles Windolph, a survivor of the battle. "(and) he looked almost as if he had been peacefully sleeping." So, who knows?

General Custer (he was actually a lieutenant colonel in the U.S. Army at the time, but everyone still called him "General,") died on the sweltering Sunday afternoon of June 25, 1876, on a hill above the Little Bighorn River, in what is now southeastern Montana. His death occurred during what white Americans called the Battle of the Little Bighorn. The winners, a loose confederation of Lakota and Dakota Sioux, Northern Cheyenne (and a few Arapaho who just happened to be in the area), called it the Battle of the Greasy Grass.

Custer expired from one or both of two bullet wounds, one in the left temple and one in the left breast. His body was stripped, but he had not been scalped. This latter bit of information must have surprised most newspaper readers at the time. Custer was famous for his long golden locks. The poet Walt Whitman would eulogize him (in a poem Whitman sold to the *New York Tribune* for $10 and which was subsequently reprinted across the country) as "thou of the sunny flowing hair." The Indian leader Sitting Bull called Custer's hair "the color of grass when the frost comes." That famous a scalp would seem to have made it a highly coveted post-battle souvenir.

But unbeknownst to the reading public, Custer had cut his wavy mane short just before embarking on the campaign to conquer the Plains tribes. He may have done so because the notoriously vain Custer knew it would be hard to keep clean on the trail. Or it may have been that his wife Libbie entreated him to trim it so he would not be so easily identified by the enemy. As a result, the Indians may have deemed it too short to bother with removing. Or it may have been that Cheyenne women intervened, out of deference to a beautiful young Cheyenne woman with whom Custer was said to have had a romantic dalliance.

In any event, Custer still had his hair when his body was found. The 50 or so dead soldiers close to his corpse—and the 160 more scattered or bunched in the hills and ravines that composed the battlefield—did not.

"All of them were scalped and otherwise horribly mutilated," recalled Thomas Coleman, a 7th Cavalry private who survived the battle, only to then undergo the horrors of burying his comrades' remains. "Some had their heads cut off, others, arms and legs. Their (Indians') hatred extended even to the poor horses, as they cut and slashed them before they were dead."

William W. Cooke, a Canadian-born officer who was serving as Custer's adjutant, was scalped twice. The hair on top of his head was removed, as was one of the massive shaggy sideburns that hung down to his neck. One soldier's body reportedly had 105 arrows in it. The glass eye of another soldier had been shattered while still in the eye socket. The head of Captain Tom Custer, George's younger brother and a two-time winner of the Medal of Honor during the Civil War, was so thoroughly mashed, his remains were identified only because someone recognized the tattoos on his arms. His abdomen had also been sliced open and his genitals hacked off. His heart was also reported to have been torn out, but that was an exaggeration.

There were grisly oddities among the gore. The body of Mark Kellogg, a *Bismarck (N.D.) Tribune* correspondent, and the only newsman at the battle, wasn't stripped at all, although it was scalped and missing an ear. The body of Captain Myles Keogh, a seductively handsome Irishman, was unmarked by mutilation, but stripped of everything but his socks—and a leather pouch around his neck. The pouch contained a medal Keogh had received from Pope Pius IX for his service in the Papal Army during the Italian Unification war of 1860. Historians have speculated Native Americans, who sometimes wore talismans of their own in similar pouches, left the post-mortem Keogh intact as a sign of respect. It's also speculated Keogh may have been the individual Indians later said was the bravest fighter of Custer's men, and the last to fall.

The pillaging of the dead did not please Sitting Bull. The Lakota holy man had no formal title, but he was generally regarded as the spiritual and political leader of the tribes. Coveting the white man's shirts, shoes and other belongings, Sitting Bull warned, was a weakness that would come back to haunt the Indian.

The mutilations were a different matter. They were mostly carried out by women, and men too old to fight, and there were several motivations. One was anger. The soldiers had attacked the encampment without warning, and as far as the Indians were concerned, without reason. Among the first killed, albeit accidentally, were as many as 20 women and children. They included most of the family of Gall, who along with Crazy Horse was the Indians' chief battle leader. The Indians also harbored the belief that injuries inflicted on the enemy in this world would carry over to the next. Decapitation would certainly make it harder for soldiers to fight in the afterlife. Finally, the disfigurements and desecrations may have been a sign of contempt for what seemed a rash and arrogant attack of a few hundred soldiers on a few thousand Native Americans—the equivalent of a prairie dog attacking a buffalo.

The various tribes had removed the bodies of their own dead, estimated at anywhere from 35 to 150, as soon as the battle was over. But it was two days before survivors of Custer's command, from a besieged site a few miles away, along with members of a relief column, began burying what amounted to about 40 percent of the 7th Cavalry. It was a grim business.

Sickened by the overpowering stench of corpses exposed to relentless sun and 90-plus-degree heat, and hampered by a lack of shovels, soldiers scraped shallow trenches and nudged the bodies into them. Dead officers had their names placed in spent cartridges and hammered onto stakes to mark their burial sites. Enlisted graves went unmarked. It didn't matter much, since coyotes and other prairie scavengers ensured no body stayed buried for long.

The wounded, numbering about 50, were dragged on Indian-style travois or strapped between two mules—there were no wagons—and moved 15 miles to the steamboat *Far West*, which had brought supplies for the campaign up the Missouri, Yellowstone and Bighorn rivers. Under the command of the remarkably skilled captain, Frank Marsh, the *Far West* raced 710 miles down the rivers to Fort Lincoln, near Bismarck, North Dakota, in just 54 hours. It carried not only the wounded, but the first confirmed news of what would be reckoned one of the most significant defeats ever suffered by a U.S. military force.

Before the boat left, General Alfred Terry, who was in overall command of the expedition against "the hostiles," and who had arrived too late at the battle site to save Custer, told Marsh to take extra care with the wounded. "Every soldier here who is suffering with wounds is the victim of a terrible blunder," Terry said. "A sad and terrible blunder."

George Armstrong Custer was a brigadier general at the tender age of 23. He didn't remain a general for the last 13 years of his life, but in many ways, he did remain 23: impetuous to the point of rashness; romantic to the point of sentimentality, oblivious to his own mortality. The artist and journalist Theodore Davis, who in 1867 accompanied Custer on his first foray against the Plains tribes, described him as "endowed by Nature with confidence in himself...and a believer that the future would surely unfold as a continuation of the successful past."

He was indisputably brave. By his own count, no fewer than eight horses were shot out from under him during various battles of the Civil War. (He billed the Army for several of the dead horses that he had paid for himself.) He constantly volunteered for dangerous assignments. At the pivotal Battle of Gettysburg, Custer's performance against a Confederate cavalry force four times the size of his might well have preserved the Union's victory, in a battle it desperately had to win. "He was not afraid to fight like a private soldier," one of his subordinates wrote after the battle. "...He was ever in front and would never ask them to go where he would not lead."

In addition to his valor, Custer also had a reputation—deserved or not—as having a warrior's instinct, an ability to simultaneously survey myriad factors on the battlefield and make swift, decisive and correct decisions. "Gen. Custer always sees 'the vantage of the ground' at a glance," the eminent journalist Horace Greeley wrote, "and like the eagle watching his prey from some mountain crag, sweeps down upon his adversary, and seldom fails in achieving a signal success."

His mountainous ego ensured his courage would not go unnoticed. During the Gettysburg fight, Custer sported a black velvet uniform he had designed himself, festooned with coils of gold lace. He insisted the costuming wasn't out of vanity, but to ensure his men always knew where he was on the battlefield. But it was mostly vanity. After a battle in Virginia, he crowed in a letter to his wife Elizabeth ("Libbie") that his exploits were soon to be written up in the *New York Times*. "Your Bo has won new laurels," he wrote, referring to himself by her nickname for him. "Never have I witnessed such enthusiasm...I thought they—men and officers—would throw themselves under my horse's feet."

A bit under 6 feet tall and weighing a muscular 175 pounds, Custer's athletic build complemented his blue eyes, prominent cheekbones, curly hair and abundant mustache. An aide to President Grant described Custer's appearance in a post-war victory parade: "His long golden locks flowing in the wind...his crimson necktie, and his buckskin breeches presented a combination which made him look half general and half scout, and gave him a daredevil appearance which singled him out for general remark and applause."

At times, Custer seemed impervious to physical discomfort, with a penchant for such long hours in the saddle that his nicknames included "Hard Ass" and "Old Iron Butt." But he also loved his creature comforts: On at least two long expeditions he insisted on bringing an absurdly heavy cast-iron stove on which "suitable" meals could be prepared by his personal cook.

Despite cheating on her from time to time, Custer leaned heavily on Libbie for emotional support. In an 1873 letter to "my darling sunbeam," he assured her he had shaken his once-overwhelming ardor for gambling. "...It no longer possesses the slightest power over me," he wrote, "and I never feel tempted to take a hand. You often said I could never give it up. But I have always said I could give up anything—except you." One vice Libbie need not have worried about was drinking. After some experimentation with liquor in his late teens and early 20s, Custer became a teetotaler. That alone made him an unusual specimen in a profession crawling with serious drinkers. He also eschewed tobacco products, and despite having a volcanic temper, he rarely cursed more than an occasional "damn."

In addition to his wife, Custer also doted on his relatives and kept them close whenever possible. This turned out to be unfortunate for two brothers, a brother-in-law and a nephew, all of whom died with him at the Little Bighorn. He treated the horses and dozens of dogs he owned with concern and kindness. He once crawled on his belly under a cavalry post house to retrieve puppies so they could be nursed in a nicer location.

But his treatment of the enlisted men under him ranged from callous indifference about the state of their rations or health, to disciplinary measures that were barbaric even by 19th century military standards. Despite an Army prohibition against flogging, Custer routinely ordered men lashed and their heads shaved, for infractions as trivial as stealing a piece of fruit. Among the charges brought against him at a court martial was an illegal order he gave to shoot deserters. Such practices, an officer in another regiment wrote, "won for Custer the lasting hatred of every decent man in the command."

However much his men may have hated him, his superiors generally doted on him. "Custer is the ablest man in the cavalry," noted General Phil Sheridan, the Union Army's cavalry chief. In presenting Libbie Custer with the small writing desk on which Confederate commander Robert E. Lee had signed the surrender document at Appomattox Court House in Virginia, Sheridan wrote "there is scarcely an individual in our service who has contributed more to bring this (victory) about than your very gallant husband."

Finally, there was the matter of "Custer's Luck." It was a term that throughout the U.S. military came to mean the ability to escape an untenable situation—often of one's own making—at the last minute. It was also a trademark of Custer's life—at least up until that Sunday afternoon in Montana.

A classic example occurred in 1867, when Custer saw his first buffalo. Despite the fact it was known there were angry Indians in the area, Custer had galloped off alone onto the prairie to exercise some of his greyhounds by having them chase antelope. "That such a course was rashly imprudent I am ready to admit," Custer wrote in his 1874 memoir. Determined to bag the lone bison, Custer spurred his thoroughbred mount and closed in on his quarry. He cocked his revolver, took aim—and shot his horse in the head.

Now lost, alone and on foot, Custer wandered around for several hours and a number of miles. Finally, a detachment of his troops found him. With a mixture of nonchalance and bravado, Custer shrugged off the harrowing incident as something of a wash: "plus a valuable experience, and minus a valuable horse."

"Custer's Luck" began almost as soon as he did, which was on Dec. 5, 1839, in the almost invisible village of New Rumley Ohio, about 100 miles southeast of Cleveland. His father, Emanuel Custer, was a Maryland-born blacksmith who was successful enough at his trade to eventually settle the family on a tidy and moderately prosperous 80-acre farm.

The Custers were known locally for three things: They were staunch Democrats; they loved playing practical jokes, and there were lots of them. Due to previous marriages by both parents, George had five half-siblings and five full ones. In terms of age, he was right in the middle. The family nicknamed him "Autie," a derivative of the way he pronounced his own middle name as a toddler. It stuck.

As a boy, Custer exhibited traits he would maintain throughout his life. One was impetuosity. Irked by a school chum making faces at him through a window, Custer smashed his fist through the glass in what turned out to be a bloody, painful and fruitless effort to strike his tormentor. Another was a love for the pomp and glory promised by a military life. At the age of four, "Autie" would dress in a uniform sewn by his mother and accompany his father to meetings of the local militia. A third trait was chutzpah.

Desperate to escape a looming career as a small-town schoolteacher, the 17-year-old Custer petitioned his local congressman, John A. Bingham, for an appointment to the U.S. Military Academy at West Point, New York. In his letter, Custer freely admitted his family's Democratic predilections, even while knowing Bingham was a rock-ribbed Republican.

But Custer's luck paid off. The congressman was impressed with the applicant's candor. In addition, the father of a young girl Custer had been wooing was a good friend of Bingham. Since the dad didn't like Custer's attentions to his daughter, he was glad to recommend him for an appointment that would send him 450 miles away. "Mr. C. is a young man of more than ordinary ability," a local newspaper noted, "and we believe he will make a creditable military officer."

During his four years at West Point, Custer skated on the thinnest of ice. He assiduously avoided any academic effort, graduating 34th in a class of 34. He compiled 726 of a possible 800 demerits for disciplinary infractions, mostly for pranks, sloppiness and minor rule-breaking. In one instance, he asked the Spanish language instructor at the beginning of a class how to say "class dismissed." When the instructor complied, Custer promptly led his classmates out the door.

"West Point had many a character to deal with," a classmate recalled, "but it may be a question whether it ever had a cadet so exuberant, one who cared so little for its serious attempts to elevate and burnish, or one on whom its tactical officers kept their eyes so constantly and unsympathetically searching as upon Custer. And yet how we loved him."

Custer's academic record seemed certain to precede a low-level and lackluster military career, if any. But he got lucky, again. Two months before he graduated, the Civil War began. The Army needed trained officers, no matter how undisciplined and irresponsible they seemed.

Custer reported for duty just in time to take part in some of the earliest fighting, including the initial Battle of Bull Run, the first major fight of the war. And as poorly as he had performed learning to be a soldier, he excelled at actually being one. A fellow officer noted Custer "was the first to cross the stream, the first to open fire, and one of the last to leave the field." A subordinate wrote "he is a glorious fellow, full of energy, quick to plan and bold to execute, and with us has never failed in any attempt he has yet made."

His rise through the ranks was meteoric. The Union Army desperately needed officers who were not afraid of a fight. Custer was both charismatic and courageous, traits that quickly brought him to the attention of his superiors. So it was that on June 28, 1863, George Custer was a mere 23-year-old captain, and on June 29 he was a "brevet," or temporary, brigadier general, in command of the Michigan Cavalry Brigade, also known as "The Wolverines."

A week after that, the "boy general," as the newspapers dubbed him, was pitted against the fabled Confederate cavalryman Jeb Stuart at Gettysburg. Stuart's plan was to get behind the Union forces and slash through their infantry. Heavily outnumbered and leading men he did not know well, Custer outmaneuvered and outfought his rival. After the battle, Custer's immediate boss, Gen. Alfred Pleasanton, publicly praised him as "the best cavalry general in the world."

Gettysburg was followed by an almost-unbroken series of battles, raids into enemy territory and promotions, to the rank of brevet major general. Custer reveled through it all. "Darling little one," he wrote his wife in October 1864, "yesterday...was a glorious day for your Boy. He signalized his accession to his new command by a brilliant victory...I attacked...and gained the most glorious victory."

And then the war ended. The country no longer needed a mammoth military machine, nor an abundance of youthful and relatively high-salaried generals. After nine months mopping up sporadic rebel resistance in Texas, the romance and glory of Army life had lost much of its romance and glory.At 26, Custer began to explore other job opportunities, which included a possible run for a Michigan congressional seat, or joining the insurgent army of Benito Juarez and the struggle to overthrow Maximillian I, France's puppet dictator in Mexico.

Ultimately, he decided to stick with the U.S. Army. He accepted a drop in rank to lieutenant colonel and took command of the newly created 7th Cavalry Regiment. Among the 7th's tasks was to help the federal government deal with its "Indian Problem."

The ingredients comprising the "Indian Problem" stew were many and varied. Its base stock was the widespread belief among many European-descended Americans that Native Americans were biologically and culturally inferior. That somehow was supposed to justify dealing with them as something analogous to mosquitos, floods and other nuisances that Nature had put in the white man's way. More specific ingredients included the post-Civil War restlessness of thousands of former soldiers; the mass arrival of land-hungry immigrants, and the explosive development of a railroad system that enabled the restless and land-hungry to move west.

The Plains Indian tribes—Blackfoot, Cheyenne, Comanche, Kiowa, Lakota, Dakota, Arapaho, Crow and others—were in the way. They had in their time shoved aside other Native American groups. Now, the argument went, it was their turn to be shoved. George Armstrong Custer seemed a great choice to help do the shoving. Custer "is precisely the man for that job," wrote the well-known journalist Henry M. Stanley, who in 1867 accompanied the 7th Cavalry on its first prolonged, and as it turned out, fruitless, effort to find and fight Indians. "A certain impetuosity and undoubted courage are his principal characteristics."

But Stanley omitted another of Custer's principal characteristics—an appalling lack of self-discipline and common sense. In mid-July 1867, he abruptly and inexplicably left his command at Fort Wallace Kansas, and with an escort of 75 troopers dashed 150 miles in 57 hours to visit his wife at another fort. His motivation may have been rumors that Libbie was fooling around with another officer. Custer's impulse resulted in a court-martial on several charges, from leaving his post without permission to illegally ordering that deserters—of which there were many under Custer's command—be shot on sight.

Custer received a relatively lenient sentence of one year's suspension without pay. Then there was more of "Custer's Luck." A rash of deadly raids by Southern Cheyenne in Kansas and what is now Oklahoma convinced

Generals William Tecumseh Sherman and Philip Henry Sheridan, Custer's commanders, that they needed Custer back in command of the 7th. He was restored to duty two months before his suspension was up. "I breakfasted with General Sheridan and staff," he wrote Libbie in October 1868. "He (Sheridan) said 'Custer, I rely on you in everything, and shall send you on this expedition without orders, leaving you to act entirely on your judgement.'"

On the bitterly cold, snow-choked morning of Nov. 27, 1868, Custer's "judgement" found the 7th Cavalry on the banks of the Washita River, in what is now west-central Oklahoma. A detachment of troops led by Major Joel Elliott had tracked an Indian raiding party that had passed through a village of Southern Cheyenne, who, as it turned out, had nothing to do with the raids. Undeterred, Custer divided his force of about 700 troops into four groups and swooped down on the village.

The Cheyenne were led by Black Kettle, a prominent 65-year-old Indian patriarch with a reputation as a peacemaker. Within 10 minutes of the attack's start, Black Kettle and his wife were dead, shot in the back while fleeing. The troopers killed or wounded anywhere from 40 to 100 other Indians (the number is still disputed.) They also killed about 800 Indian ponies; a common army tactic designed to hamper the Indians' mobility. The 7th lost one man in the initial attack. To prevent a counterattack, Custer seized women and children as human shields. Then he withdrew with his hostages after realizing there were as many as several thousand Indians from other tribes camped nearby along the river.

Custer's withdrawal was as unfortunate for Major Elliott as Custer's attack had been for Black Kettle. With 17 troops, Elliott, a 28-year-old Civil War veteran who was considered both brave and brilliant, had pursued what he thought was a small group of retreating Cheyenne. It turned out to be a large group of Cheyenne, Kiowa and Arapaho, who promptly wiped out Elliott's entire force.

Custer's decision to leave without searching for or attempting to reinforce Elliott engendered bitter resentment among Elliott's friends.

One of those was Captain Frederick Benteen, a regimental commander in the 7th who considered Custer a windbag and a showboat. "But surely some search will be made for our missing comrades," Benteen acidly wrote to an associate in a letter that made its way into the newspapers. "No, they are forgotten...that, my dear friend, is the *true* story of the 'battle of the Washita.'"

The "battle" was also harshly criticized in some quarters as "simply a massacre" of peaceable Indians who were legally encamped and in fact on their way to a reservation. One federal Indian agent, Col. Edward Wynkoop, angrily resigned in protest. "I must certainly refuse to again be the instrument of the murder of innocent women and children," Wynkoop wrote. But most newspapers trumpeted the fight as a decisive blow against the Plains tribes and hailed Custer as a hero. "If followed up by one or two more equally decisive (victories)," the *Minneapolis Tribune* declared, "the savage marauders will become convinced their only safety lies in making peace and submitting to reasonable terms."

The battle at the Washita thrust Custer back into the limelight, and for the next six-plus years, he reveled in it. During extended leaves, which were not particularly uncommon in the army at the time, he hobnobbed in New York City with robber barons such as John Jacob Astor, August Belmont and Jay Gould. He indulged his passion for the theater, openly weeping at performances by noted Shakespearean actor Lawrence Barrett, a close friend. And he escorted luminaries such as the Grand Duke Alexis of Russia and showman P.T. Barnum on buffalo hunts.

"He (Custer) received us like princes," Barnum recalled in his memoirs. "He fitted out a company of fifty cavalry, furnishing us with horses, arms and ammunition. We were taken to an immense herd of buffaloes, quietly browsing on the open plain. We charged on them, and during an exciting chase of a couple of hours, we slew twenty immense bull buffaloes."

Custer added writing to his repertoire of interests, which also included taxidermy. He penned a series of articles about his exploits in the West for a New York magazine, *The Galaxy*. The pieces were collected in 1874 into a poorly written but brisk-selling memoir, *My Life on the Plains.* Like seemingly every other American in the Gilded Age, he also tried to get rich. He failed. An 1871 scheme involving a Colorado silver mine went nowhere. In 1875, he lost $8,500 (about $204,000 in 2022 dollars, and more than twice his annual Army salary,) in a stock speculation that soured.

He did manage to squeeze in some military duties. After a posting at a small Kentucky base, where he bought a farm, Custer was assigned command of forts nearer the frontier. The first was at Fort Hays in Kansas, the second at the newly constructed Fort Abraham Lincoln, on the Missouri River near Bismarck, North Dakota.

In June, 1873, the 7th was dispatched from Fort Lincoln to guard a survey party striving to find a route west for the Northern Pacific Railroad. The expedition was impressively large: 1,540 soldiers, 350 civilian employees, 275 wagons and a herd of beef cattle. Custer was second in command to General D.S. Stanley, a disagreeable drunk who loathed Custer. "He is a coldblooded, untruthful and unprincipled man," Stanley wrote his wife. "He is universally despised by all the officers of his regiment, excepting his relatives and one or two sycophants."

The journey introduced Custer and the 7th to a new adversary, the Lakota Sioux. The Indians and the cavalry engaged in two relatively minor battles. In one of them, Custer narrowly avoided being lured into what might have been a disastrous ambush by a force that greatly outnumbered his. Pinned down along a river and in danger of being surrounded, he ordered a charge. The audacious maneuver surprised the Sioux into retreating. "What a history and reputation this 7th Cavalry has achieved for itself!" Custer bragged in a letter to his wife. "Although a new and young regiment...it is the best and most widely known of any in the service."

Other than enhancing Custer's popularity with both himself and the public, however, the expedition accomplished little in practical terms.

The 7th returned to Fort Lincoln on September 18, 1873. That happened to be the same day the first of the New York bank failures signaled the beginning of the worst economic recession America had yet known. Any thought of building a railroad along the route the expedition had followed was shelved.

But the recession did whet the country's appetite for exploiting whatever resources could be found in the spectacular Black Hills region of the Dakotas that Custer and the 7th had traversed. The United States government had pledged in a six-year-old treaty with Plains tribes to respect the tribes' claims to the area, not only as sacred ground, but as a reliable and valuable source of food. But the federal government, as Native Americans had learned, was reliably consistent when it came to breaking treaties. "They made us many promises, more than I can remember, " the Ogallala Lakota leader Red Cloud is said to have said, "but they never kept but one; they promised to take our land, and they took it."

In July, 1874, the 7th undertook another expedition into the region. This time, along with a cannon and three Gatling guns, the manifest included journalists, a handful of scientists, President Grant's son Frederick—and two miners. Custer took advantage of the journalists' presence to pose for a photograph with an aged grizzly bear he had shot. Copies of the picture became a favorite item in the nation's stationery stores. The miners, meanwhile, found gold. "...It is the belief of those who are giving their attention to the subject that it will be found in paying quantities," Custer casually mentioned to General Sheridan in a letter that quickly became public.

The expedition returned to Fort Lincoln at the end of August, having covered 883 miles in 60 days. The Custers settled into a life of relative luxury in a handsome home built especially for them on the post. From it, they hosted a steady stream of parties, dances, hunting jaunts and base ball games. "In the evenings," an 1875 visitor wrote, "the house is crowded with company...the general has got a beautiful house with five servants, and they live in a high state."

The 7th's excursion into the Black Hills, however, had ignited a powder keg. Gold-seekers began trickling, then pouring, into the area, despite the fact it was legally off-limits to white men—and a very dangerous place. By the beginning of 1876, primitive mining camps had sprung up: Deadwood, Spearfish, and the appropriately named Custer City. "One hundred houses have been erected in Custer City," a newspaper reported in February, "and building operations are being pushed forward night and day...Custer City has three stores, two saloons and one saw mill...other business houses will be opened within a week."

The thought of a town named after him doubtlessly further inflated Custer's outsized ego. His vaunted luck however, was about to run out.

A Soldier's Story

In 1876, Charles A. Windolph was a 24-year-old bootmaker who had fled his native Germany to avoid fighting in the Franco-Prussian War, joined the U.S. Army because he couldn't find a job in recession-ravaged America; deserted; and then re-enlisted, this time in the 7th Cavalry.

About half of the 7th was foreign-born. "Always struck me as funny," Windolph recalled years later. "Here we'd run away from Germany to escape military service, and now, because most of us couldn't get a job anywhere else, we were forced to go into the army here."

Except for winning a Medal of Honor at the Battle of the Little Bighorn, Windolph's story wasn't much different from many of the men who served in the cavalry during the 1870s. Actually, even winning the nation's highest award for military valor didn't distinguish him from all his comrades: Medals of Honor were awarded to two dozen of Custer's command. But Windolph did have one unique distinction, which we'll get to in a minute.

Being a U.S. cavalryman was a job only slightly better than no job at all. The pay was miniscule—$13 a month ($312 in 2022 currency) for an enlisted man. Many of the troops were worth every penny—and no more. One officer observed that "the enlisted personnel consisted largely of either the dregs from the Union and Confederate armies, or recent emigrants from Europe."

Few recruits had any experience with the cavalry's standard-issue arms—Springfield single-shot, breech-loading carbines and Colt revolvers—and little chance to get any. Enlisted men were issued a paltry 15 rounds of ammunition a month for target practice. Even fewer enlistees were accomplished riders, and many knew nothing about horses other than they stank and could be dangerous. In one "skirmish" that turned out to be a false alarm, a company of the 7th mounted up to chase a presumed Indian band. A dozen of the troopers fell off their horses, and two broke their legs.

In truth, chasing after Indians and shooting at anything were only a tiny part of the job. Prior to the Little Bighorn battle, the 7th had not been in a fight of any sort for three years. The daily routine was mostly tedious, hard physical labor, with leisure time so boring that excessive drinking became a favorite hobby. It was interspersed with long treks through winter blizzards and broiling summer days, marked by little water and scant rations that were often maggot-infested or otherwise spoiled. Unsurprisingly, desertion rates often topped 30 percent.

The forensic archeologist Douglas D. Scott has noted that studies of troopers' bones found over the decades on the Little Bighorn battlefield "clearly show evidence of hard sustained horseback riding:" damaged shoulders, compressed vertebrae, degenerative disks. "While our prevailing view is that the Army enlisted boys and made men of them" Scott wrote, "the bones suggest it took young men and turned them into physical wrecks before their time."

But somewhat amazingly, poor training, paltry pay, acute physical discomfort and the very real possibility of being killed in nasty ways wasn't enough to prevent Charles A. Windolph from spending 12 years of his long life as a member of the 7th Cavalry.

"You felt like you were somebody when you were on a good horse," said Windolph, who was decorated for holding off Lakota and Cheyenne warriors during the Little Bighorn battle while other soldiers gathered water from the river. "You were a cavalryman of the Seventh Regiment. You were part of a proud outfit."

And Windolph's distinction? He was the last member of Custer's command to die, in 1950, at the age of 98. "We all fought the grand fight that June day in 1876," he said 70 years after the battle. "I lost a lot of good friends."

The last year of George Custer's life started quietly enough. He and Libbie were cozily ensconced at Fort Lincoln, comforted by the knowledge that Plains tribes, quite sensibly, did not like to fight during the harsh Midwest winters. The Custers' financial problems were somewhat assuaged when a New York agency offered George a deal in which he would tour the country, giving up to five lectures a week, at $200 ($4,800 in 2022) per lecture. Unable to secure yet another leave from the army, Custer decided to postpone the tour until the end of the year or early 1877. In the meantime, he mulled the prospects for a Spring 1876 campaign against the Plains tribes.

There was no doubt there would be one. In November, 1875, President Grant had ordered the tribes that had not already done so to report to government-designated reservations by the end of January, or face the U.S. Army's wrath. Most of the non-reservation Indian groups either never heard about Grant's order, or ignored it.

By late 19th-century standards, Grant was relatively sympathetic to the Indians' situation. While stationed in Oregon after the war with Mexico, he had a front-row view of how Native Americans were routinely cheated, abused and sickened by federal Indian agents, white settlers, and diseases such as smallpox. "It is really my opinion that the whole race would be harmless and peaceable if they were not put upon by the whites," he wrote his wife in 1848.

Twenty years later, in his first inaugural address, the new president cautioned the tribes that they could not expect to continue their nomadic way of life, but would have to adapt "civilization, Christianization and ultimate citizenship." But in his first State of the Union address, he also told Congress that to consider any policy "which looks to the extinction of a race is too abhorrent for a Nation to indulge in."

There were plenty of people who disagreed. "The more (Indians) we kill this year," General Sherman wrote General Sheridan, "the less we would have to kill next year." A Nevada congressman bluntly called for "extinction, and I say that with a full sense of the meaning conveyed by that word."

Custer was a shade more ambivalent. Like most whites, he made little effort to distinguish among individuals, bands, tribes or nations of Native Americans. An Indian was "a savage in every sense of the word...one whose cruel and ferocious nature far exceeds that of any wild beast of the desert." On the other hand, he supposed an Indian was "no worse, perhaps, than his white brother would be, similarly born and bred." And he admitted that if he were a Native American and facing a choice between resistance or a reservation, he would choose the warpath every time.

To avoid what would amount to genocide, Grant tried various tactics. He met with tribal leaders, both in Washington D.C. and in the West, attempting to persuade them to adopt white ways. He appointed a former Union general and full-blooded Seneca, Ely Parker, as commissioner of Indian Affairs. He canvassed various religious groups, particularly Quakers, to suggest honest men to serve as federal Indian agents. He even offered to buy the Black Hills region from the tribes (who refused the offer) after Custer's 1874 expedition incited a gold rush to the area.

In the end, however, the president caved in to those who, like General Sheridan, believed "the only good Indians I ever met were dead." The Jan. 31 deadline was issued; the non-reservation Indian groups did not comply, and George Armstrong Custer's fate was sealed.

But this being America's Gilded Age, it was seemingly inevitable that an episode ripe with melodramatic partisan politics and government corruption must occur first. It began in March, when Custer was summoned from Fort Lincoln to testify before Congress on the long-standing, systemic and unabashedly larcenous practices of government-licensed traders at many military posts and Indian reservations.

The crooked traders paid hefty bribes or provided kickbacks to government officials for the licenses, which gave them virtual monopolies on remote outposts or reservations. "Since 1874," the *Brooklyn Daily Eagle* reported in March, "not a single important post tradership has been secured without the payment of large sums of money." Having secured the posts, the traders were thus free to lie, cheat, steal, swindle and con both Indians and soldiers, to their hearts' content.

The corruption touched high places. President Grant's ne'er-do-well brother Orvil was implicated—in part by Custer—for having bought and sold four licenses. William Belknap, Grant's secretary of war, was also hip-deep in corruption. Belknap was a slippery character whose two wives were in on the scheme (he married his sister-in-law after his first wife died, keeping the chicanery in the family.) Facing impeachment and a messy trial in Congress, Belknap resigned his post, after falling to his knees before Grant at the White House and sobbingly confessing his transgressions.

For his part, Custer had long, loudly and publicly complained about the slimy underpinnings of the trading post system. Particularly galling was the fact that while the army equipped its soldiers with breech-loading single-shot rifles that often jammed after being fired two or three times, Indians were frequently sold new repeating rifles by post traders. In two appearances over five days, Custer told a congressional committee about payoffs to various officials; how Belknap had schemed to increase profits for his trader buddies by illegally moving whiskey across state lines to avoid taxes, and how grain shipments meant for the cavalry had been diverted to crooked traders. And on a Washington street he confronted an Indian agent who had publicly called Custer a liar, "and gave him a severe caning."

His performance was front-page news across the country, and he naturally basked in the limelight. dining out almost every night as guest of admiring politicians and other capital luminaries. "I am overrun with invitations," he wrote Libbie in one letter. In another he noted "I have been recipient of kindest attention from all newspapers except a few radicals. Leading papers throughout the country commend my courage."

The president, however, was less commendatory. Grant did not like Custer. While conceding Custer's "personal gallantry and valor," Grant thought he "was not a very level-headed man." He was also furious that Custer in his testimony before Congress had singled out Orvil Grant, and had even broadly hinted that Grant himself was involved in the scandal. The president privately told General Sherman that Custer had tried "to besmirch his administration and he proposed to put a stop to it." Grant ordered that the brash and showy commander of the 7th Cavalry be banned from the upcoming campaign against the Plains tribes.

Custer was devastated by the news. He went to the White House to plead his case. But Grant, after keeping Custer waiting for five hours, refused to see him. Desperate, Custer resorted to the pen. "I appeal to you as a soldier," he wrote Grant, "to spare me the humiliation of seeing my regiment march to meet the enemy and I not share in its danger." Other officers, including Sheridan, interceded. And sympathetic newspapers unleashed a barrage of criticism at the president, labeling his decision as petty and politically motivated.

Grant eventually relented, on the condition that Custer understand he was to be a subordinate to General Alfred Terry, a calm and kindly former lawyer, and an experienced Civil War officer who nonetheless had never fought Indians. Never one to worry too much about chains of command, Custer was elated. He reportedly told a colleague that he could easily "cut loose" from Terry's oversight. Earlier, at a lunch given in his honor in New

York, Custer had boasted "that his regiment could whip and defeat all the Indians on the plains."

On May 12, Custer arrived back at Fort Lincoln. On May 17, while the regimental band played a lively Irish quick-step tune called "Garry Owen" (Gaelic for "Owen's Garden,") George Armstrong Custer and all 12 companies of the 7th Cavalry rode west, toward immortality.

No battle in U.S. history, with the possible exceptions of Gettysburg, the Battle of the Bulge and the Battle of Midway, has been more thoroughly, exhaustively—and often tediously—analyzed, dissected and argued over than the Battle of the Little Bighorn. I will thus preemptively concede and stipulate to all of the numerous shortcomings, both real and perceived, in the following brief synopsis.

The Army's plan was simple, and brimming with optimism. It would be a three-pronged campaign. Colonel John Gibbon led a force of 450 cavalry and infantry troops out of Fort Ellis, near Bozeman, Montana. A second force of about 1,000 was commanded by Gen. George Crook, out of Fort Fetterman, in what is now central Wyoming. Custer and the 7th, led at least nominally by Gen. Terry, were part of slightly less than a 900-man group that started from Fort Lincoln. Any or all of the three columns would locate the recalcitrant tribes, defeat them, and force the survivors onto reservations.

Sounded easy, proved difficult. Just finding an enemy who constantly moved around a country that was virtually unknown to the Army was hard enough. Then there was the almost complete lack of communication among the three columns. General Crook's command did manage to find a group of Lakota and Cheyenne warriors led by Crazy Horse—much to Crook's regret. At the Battle of Rosebud Creek on June 17, the general's bacon was probably saved only by the fierce efforts of his Shoshone and Crow scouts. Although Crook declared victory, the fight's outcome was at best a draw. Crook's column withdrew to a camp from which it would not move for the next seven weeks, until reinforcements arrived.

In the meantime, Gen. Terry, who had no inkling of Crook's troubles, decided to send out Custer and the 7th to see if they could find and flank the Indians while the rest of Terry's troops and Col. Gibbon's column closed in from the opposite direction.

"My darling," Custer wrote Libbie on June 22, in the last letter she would get from him, "...Do not be anxious about me. You would be surprised how closely I obey your instructions about keeping with the column. I hope to have a good report to send you by the next mail. A success will start us all toward Lincoln."

Libbie's "dear Bo" also attached an extract of Gen. Terry's orders, to demonstrate Terry's confidence in Custer. Basically, the orders consisted of some general instructions, accompanied with the broad caveat that Terry placed "too much confidence in your zeal, energy and ability to impose on you precise orders which might hamper your actions when nearly in contact with the enemy." In other words, Custer could do what he wanted—as long as he succeeded.

A huge group of Indians, meanwhile, had come together near the Little Bighorn River. The tribes, totaling maybe 1,500 to 2,000 warriors and another 6,000-plus women, children and men too old to fight, had gathered for reasons both pragmatic and spiritual. The region, fed by the Powder, Rosebud and Yellowstone rivers as well as the Bighorn, teemed with game. The tribes also celebrated their annual sun dance ceremony. Sitting Bull, who was recognized by the entire Sioux nation as its leader when it came to matters of war and peace, had a vision—after some pretty excruciating self-torture—during the ceremony. In it, he saw soldiers falling upside down from the sky into the village. He predicted a great victory would occur soon for his people.

On the sunbaked afternoon of June 25, they got it. "Custer's luck," and his scouts, had led the 7th to the Indian encampment, although the element of surprise had been lost the day before when their presence became known to the settlement. Fearing the Indians would slip away, Custer decided to attack without waiting for the other columns. He divided his attack force into three groups. Major Marcus Reno and about 140 men would charge into the village from the east; Capt. Frederick Benteen and 125 men would swing to the southwest and the prevent the Indians' escape, and Custer and 210 men would sneak into position to the north and swoop down as soon as the warriors reacted to Reno's attack. The remainder of the troops stayed with the supply wagons.

The plan didn't work. Reno, due either to prudence, cowardice or drunkenness (historians and armchair generals heatedly differ on the subject), charged as ordered, and then beat a hasty retreat to high ground on the other side of the river. There he dug in. Benteen, who had openly questioned Custer's decision to divide his command, dawdled a fair way from the fight. He eventually joined Reno's besieged troops on what would become known as Reno Hill. Custer, who had no clue where the rest of his regiment was, charged anyway; retreated; was surrounded, and killed, along with all the men with him. In one warrior's estimate, it took about as long as it does to eat lunch.

With Custer's force wiped out, the Indians then turned their attention to Reno and Benteen. Despite being greatly outnumbered, with little water and low on ammunition, the remnants of the 7th held off the Indians until the next afternoon. Aware of the looming arrival of the now-combined forces of Terry and Gibbon, and of the vulnerability of their women and children, the Indians pulled up stakes and moved their entire village that evening.

On the morning of June 27, scouts from the Terry-Gibbon column found Custer and his command. Stripped naked, mutilated, and bloated from long hours in the sun, the bodies "from a distance resembled white boulders," according to one officer. An enlisted man later insisted that Custer's corpse seemed to be smiling.

Libbie Custer got the news at Fort Lincoln, five days after the battle. "None wounded, none missing, all dead," an officer tersely told her. It was another week before most of the rest of America, which was celebrating the 4th of July and the nation's 100th birthday, learned the fate of Custer and the 7th, under headlines like "General Custer's Terrible Defeat." "It appears that his command and Reno's attacked the camp at different moments, losing the morale effect of a simultaneous attack," one newspaper theorized. "Major Reno lost 95 killed and wounded. General Custer's (force) was annihilated."

The finger-pointing and rear-end-covering began almost immediately. In a confidential letter that was leaked to the press, Gen. Terry self-servedly and disingenuously noted that Custer had disobeyed the purposely vague orders Terry had given him, and would probably have been court-martialed if he had survived. Captain Benteen wrote his wife that Custer got what was coming to him "from the fact of not wanting any other command to have a finger in the pie." Even President Grant piled on, telling the *New York Daily Herald* "I regard Custer's massacre as a sacrifice of troops, brought on by Custer himself."

For the Plains Tribes, the fruits of victory were bitter in the extreme. Any pretense of a just and thoughtful accommodation with the federal government was obliterated by howls for revenge. Congress hastily approved the Army's request for more troops and better equipment. Rations and other aid to non-hostile tribes were stopped. Proposals to reform the corrupt administration and oversight of Indian affairs were forgotten. Within a year, Sitting Bull would lead his band into near-starvation in Canada. Crazy Horse would surrender, and eventually be bayoneted to death by a soldier while unarmed and under arrest.

And three weeks after Custer's demise, a 30-year-old Army scout, wearing a gaudy black-and-scarlet velvet costume and a sombrero from a forgettable stage play, would take part in a skirmish with Indians that, much-embellished, would help make him the most famous American in the world.

Chapter 4 Notes

It was unclear *Chicago Inter Ocean,* July 18 1876, p. 1.

As it turned Frazier Hunt and Robert Hunt (eds.), *I Fought with Custer*, p. 110.

Custer expired from *Minneapolis Tribune*, July 14 1876, p. 3; *New York Daily Herald*, Nov. 16, 1877, p. 3.

"...All of them" Bruce Liddic (ed.) *I Buried Custer: The Diary of Pvt. Thomas Coleman, 7th U.S. Cavalry.* I have cleaned up Pvt. Coleman's original spelling and grammar for clarity.

Before the boat James Donovan, *A Terrible Glory: Custer and the Little Bighorn*, p. 313.

George Armstrong Custer Evan Connell, *Son of the Morning Star*, p. 276.

He was indisputably Thom Hatch, *The Last Days of George Armstrong Custer*, p. 22.

In addition to ibid., p. 30.

His mountainous ego Marguerite Merrington, *The Custer Story*, pp. 140-41.

A bit under Chernow, op. cit., p. 541.

Despite cheating on Merrington, op. cit., p. 250.

But his treatment Connell, op. cit., p. 122.

A classic example, George A. Custer, *My Life on the Plains*, p. 146.

Now lost, alone Ibid., p. 150.

But Custer's luck *The Cadiz (Oh.) Sentinel*, June 4 1857, p. 3.

"West Point had" Hatch, op. cit., p. 10.

Custer's academic record Ibid., pp. 16-23.

His rise through Ibid., pp. 20-25.

Gettysburg was followed, Merrington, op. cit., p. 122.

The Plains Indians Hatch, op. cit., p. 25.

Custer received a Merrington, op. cit., p. 217.

Custer's decision to *New York Times*, Feb. 14 1869, p. 6.

The battle was *New York Times*, Dec. 13 1868, p. 1;*Minneapolis Tribune*, Dec. 16 1868, p. 1.

The journey introduced Ibid., p. 248.

In July 1874 Hatch, op. cit., p. 97.

The expedition returned Donovan, op. cit., p. 87.

But the 7th's excursion, *Leavenworth (Ks.) Times*, Feb. 19 1876, p. 3.

About half of, Hunt and Hunt, op. cit., p. 4.

Being a U.S. Donovan, op. cit., p. 122.

The eminent forensic Douglas Scott, "The Case of the Men who Died with Custer," *Armchair General magazine*, January 2015, p. 26.

"You felt like" Hunt, op. cit., p. 53.

By late 19th-century, Chernow, op. cit., p. 78.

Twenty years later, Ibid., pp. 631-32; p. 658.

There were plenty, Ibid., p. 658.

Custer was a George A. Custer, op. cit., p. 14.

In many cases *Brooklyn Daily Eagle*, March 4 1876, p. 2.

Custer had long *St. Louis Post-Dispatch*, April 1 1876, p. 1

His performance was Merrington, op. cit., p. 281, p. 283.

The president, however Chernow, op. cit., p. 833; *New York World*, May 2 1876, p. 4.

Custer was devastated Donovan, op. cit., p. 114.

Grant eventually relented Van de Water, op. cit., p. 281.

"My darling," Custer Merrington, op. cit., p. 307.

Libbie's "dear Bo" Ibid., pp. 307-08.

On the morning Connell, op. cit., p. 285.

Libbie Custer got, *Bethlehem (Pa.) Daily Times*, July 8 1876, p. 1.

The finger-pointing Hatch, op. cit., p. 272; Chernow, op. cit., p. 835.

CHAPTER 5

"First scalp for Custer!"

Buffalo Bill and the Duel at Warbonnet Creek

JULY

The plan was to ambush the ambushers. It was Will Cody's idea. Col. Wesley Merritt, newly in command of the U.S. Army's vaunted 5th Cavalry, approved it. Captain Charles King and trooper Chris Madsen watched it unfold from their vantage points on grassy knolls above the dry creek bed.

The war against the Plains tribes of Sioux and Cheyenne in 1876 had not been going well for the U.S. Army. There had been two major battles since the beginning of the year, and so far, the Army was 0-2. On June 17, a force of about 1,000 men led by Gen. George Crook had met an Indian force of about the same size led by the Lakota Sioux warrior Crazy Horse, at Rosebud Creek in southern Montana. While Crook later claimed victory, the reality was he retreated after the battle to a base camp in Wyoming and licked his wounds for the next seven weeks.

Eight days after the Battle of the Rosebud, about 40 percent of Lt. Col. George Armstrong Custer's 7th Cavalry was killed after encountering a much larger force of Lakota and Cheyenne at the Little Bighorn River, about 50 miles northwest of the Rosebud fight. Unlike Crook, Custer did not live to claim a "victory."

Now it was just after dawn on July 17, in the grasslands and low undulating hills of what is now northwestern Nebraska. For more than seven weeks, the 330 or so members of the 5th Cavalry had been striving to find some Indians to fight. Instead, in the words of one officer, the regiment "was principally occupied in fighting flies."

Rations were short; dust was thick; the sun roasted skin, and the occasional thunderstorm soaked to the bone. News of the Crook and Custer defeats, when it finally reached the 5th, further lowered morale. One officer was so rattled he faked a lung hemorrhage by inducing a nose bleed, swallowing the blood and then coughing it up. Regimental surgeons were not impressed, but his resignation was approved anyway.

The 5th had been cheered somewhat on June 9 by the appearance of a tall, long-haired 30-year-old fellow who had hurriedly left his previous job as a touring stage actor to become the regiment's chief of scouts. Will Cody had scouted for the regiment seven years before in a successful campaign against Lakota and Cheyenne. He was well-liked and well-respected by the men of the 5th.

"There is very little change in his appearance since I saw him last in '69," a trooper wrote to a Kansas newspaper in late June, "except that he looks a little worn, probably caused by his (acting) vocation in the East not agreeing with him. All the old boys in the regiment, on seeing General (Eugene) Carr (whom Merritt relieved in early July) and Cody together, exchanged confidences, and expressed themselves to the effect that with such a leader and scout they could (handle) all the Sitting Bulls and Crazy Horses in the Sioux tribe."

But if Cody looked much the same to the trooper-correspondent in late June, he sure didn't on July 17. He showed up for work that morning wearing a red silk shirt with puffy sleeves, decorated with silver buttons. His trousers were black velvet, with a silver braid crisscrossing the thighs. He sported an extra-wide leather belt with a large silver buckle, and an oversized beaver-felt hat with a floppy brim. A colleague suggested he looked more like a fiesta-bound Mexican vaquero than a battle-bound U.S. Army scout.

Cody's attire accomplished two things, whether he intended it to or not. The first was it made him particularly conspicuous in any fight that might develop. This was a good way to ensure credit for his deeds on the battlefield—assuming it didn't get him killed. The second thing was a shrewd career move. Assuming he lived, Cody could don his costume again when he resumed his stage performances, thereby adding an extra layer of authenticity by wearing the very clothes in which he had fought Indians.

But there had to be a fight for that to work, and on July 17, at a place now generally designated as Warbonnet Creek, there was a fight. Not a big fight, compared with Rosebud Creek or Little Bighorn, but still, a fight.

A few days before, Col. Merritt had received word that as many as 800 Cheyenne warriors from the Red Cloud Indian Agency, near Fort Robinson, Nebraska, were planning to leave the reservation and join the large group of Sioux and Cheyenne in Montana that had defeated Crook and Custer. The report was mostly true. A group of Cheyenne led by a chief named Dull Knife were headed toward the vast Indian assemblage that had whipped Crook and Custer. But the total was actually about 200, and that included women and children.

Merritt planned to cut them off, and the 5th rode most of the night to be in a position to do so. As the sun rose on the 17th, regimental lookouts spotted Indians on a ridge to the southeast. The warriors were apparently readying an attack on the regiment's supply wagons, which had lagged slightly behind the mounted troops. The Cheyenne didn't realize the rest of the regiment was waiting behind a line of low hills. Before Merritt's trap could be sprung, however, two couriers from the supply wagons began riding toward the hidden troops. Seven of the Cheyenne began a stealthy approach toward the unsuspecting couriers.

What happened next was to engender over the succeeding decades more exaggeration than a congressman's accomplishments. One actual witness was Capt. Charles King. King had a remarkable pedigree. His great-grandfather helped draft the United States Constitution. His grandfather was a president of Columbia University. His father was a Union Army general and U.S. ambassador to the Papal States. King's own military career would see him serve not only in the Plains Indian Wars, but the Spanish-American and Philippine-American wars, as well as train troops in World War I, before retiring as a major general. King was also a prolific and successful writer, churning out more than 70 novels and memoirs.

In his 1890 book *Campaigning with Crook, and Stories of Army Life*, King recalled Will Cody's suggestion to Col. Merritt, as they watched the layers of planned ambushes unfold: "'By Jove!" says Buffalo Bill, '... now's our chance. Let our party mount here out of sight, and we'll cut those fellows off.'" Col. Merritt assented, ordering Cody and a half-dozen other scouts and troopers to wait until Capt. King gave the signal from his observation post. "Five seconds too soon," King wrote, "and (the Indians) can wheel about and escape us; one second too late, and my blue-coated couriers are dead men."

King evidently had pretty good timing. But his written observations from this point wander deep into hyperbole and melodrama. So let's turn instead to an account by trooper Chris Madsen, who watched from a lookout post through a field telescope. Like King's, Madsen's own biography was the stuff of novels. Born in Denmark, Madsen had fought in the Franco-Prussian War and professed to have belonged to the French Foreign Legion. He immigrated to America, and like many young male immigrants, joined the U.S. Army after being unable to find any other job. In later years, he would become a legendary U.S. deputy marshal in the Oklahoma Territory, and serve with Teddy Roosevelt's Rough Riders in the Spanish-American War.

In a 1938 letter to Cody's most prominent early biographer, Don Russell, Madsen wrote that the two groups seemed to surprise each other. "Cody and the leading Indian appeared to be the only ones who did not become excited."

The "leading Indian," who was in his mid-20s, turned out to be the son of Cut Nose, a Cheyenne leader. The son's name was Hay-O-Wei, which translated to Yellow Hair but for years was mistranslated to Yellow Hand. His name referenced the fact that he carried with his battle gear a scalp that was thought, probably erroneously, to have belonged to a blonde woman. Like Cody, Yellow Hair was no slouch when it came to dressing up for war. In addition to a long, eagle-feathered headdress, he wore silver bracelets, beaded leggings, vermillion war paint and a breechcloth fashioned from a cotton American flag.

"The instant they were face to face, their guns fired," Madsen recalled. "It seemed like almost one shot...Cody's bullet went through the Indian's leg and killed his pinto pony. The Indian's bullet went wild. Cody's horse stepped into a prairie dog hole and stumbled, but (Cody) was up in a moment. Kneeling, he took deliberate aim and fired the second shot. An instant before Cody fired the second shot, the Indian fired at him (again) but missed. Cody's bullet went through the Indian's head and ended the battle. Cody went over to the fallen Indian and neatly removed his scalp while the other soldiers gave chase to the Indian's companions."

As it turned out, Yellow Hair was the sole casualty on either side. Stunned by the presence of a cavalry regiment he had not detected, Dull Knife beat a hasty retreat back to the Red Cloud Agency. Merritt and the 5th followed them closely, but there was no more fighting. At the reservation, according to Cody's sister, Yellow Hair's father, Cut Nose, "offered Will four mules if he would return the war-bonnet and accoutrements worn by the young warrior and captured in the fight, but Will did not grant the request, much as he pitied Cut Nose in his grief."

In fact, Cody had other plans for the scalp and other "trophies" he had collected. "We have had a fight," he wrote to his wife Louisa the day after the skirmish. "I killed Yellow Hand a Cheyenne chief in a single-handed fight. You will no doubt hear of it through the papers." To ensure the newspapers had it, Cody persuaded Capt. King to write up an account and send it to the *New York Daily Herald*, which was owned by James Gordon Bennett Jr., a good friend of Cody's.

Cody sent Yellow Hair's scalp—a hank of hair 15 inches long and still attached to a three-inch piece of skin—along with the warrior's war bonnet, shield, bridle, whip, lance and other weapons to a close pal, Moses Kerngood. A grateful Kerngood proudly displayed them in a window of his Pickwick Cigar Store in Rochester New York. (At the time, Rochester was as close to a home town as Will Cody had.) The newspapers noted "the scalp is not yet dry, but has been sprinkled with some chemical to preserve it."

"I will write Kerngood to bring it (the scalp) up to the house so you can show it to the neighbors," Cody told his wife (who later wrote it smelled so bad she almost fainted.)"I have only one scalp I can call my own, that fellow I fought single-handed in sight of our command, and the cheers that went up when he fell was deafening." And if there was one thing for which Will Cody had an inordinate fondness, it was deafening cheers.

During his lifetime, William Frederick Cody appeared on stages, under tents and in arenas, before millions of people. But he never claimed to be an actor. "I'm a star," he would explain. "All actors can become stars, but not all stars can become actors."

He was being overly modest, a trait of which he was seldom accused. Will Cody was a star. But he was also a brilliant actor. A bonafide hunter, guide, scout and Indian fighter, Cody was also "Buffalo Bill," a highly romanticized, outrageously exaggerated and yet consistently believable version of himself; a character who somehow avoided becoming a caricature.

"Everybody has heard of 'Buffalo Bill,' the daring scout of the Plains," a reporter wrote in September, 1876, "but William F. Cody is by no means so widely known, although they are one and the same person." In Cody's 1917 obituary, the *New York Times* noted "it was not as an impersonator, but as himself, that Buffalo Bill delighted millions...and (became) the idol of generations of young boys the world over."

More accurate than either "star" or "actor," Cody was a showman. He seemed destined to it, through choice as well as fate. In his autobiography, he described his birth as his "debut" on the world's stage. In her biography of him, Cody's sister recounted a quite possibly apocryphal story about a young Will organizing his siblings into endless and elaborate settlers-versus-Indians games. "'I believe I'll run a show when I get to be a man,'" she recalled him saying. When it was pointed out that a fortune teller had once predicted he would be U.S. president, Cody is said to have retorted "I'll tell you right now girls, I don't propose to be president, but I do mean to have a show!"

He certainly looked the part of Wild West matinee idol. In his memoirs, Gen. Nelson Miles described Cody as "one of the handsomest men I have ever seen: very tall (6'1") and straight; an abundance of golden brown hair falling to his shoulders, like a cavalier of old; brilliant brown eyes, auburn mustache and goatee, and features as perfect as if they had been chiseled out of marble." The admiring wife of an Army officer remembered "his fine figure, as he stood by the sutler's store, straight and slender, with his scarlet shirt belted in, and his long hair distinguishing him as the well-known character."

The long hair could also be a distinguishing nuisance: Once, in a North Platte, Nebraska,saloon, a bartender noticed Cody fussily trying to stuff his hair under his hat. When the barkeep asked why he didn't just cut it off, Cody replied "if I did, I'd starve to death."

But Cody was astute enough not to overplay the role of rough, uncouth frontier scout. Asked in 1871 by Gen. Philip Sheridan to guide a hunting party of military brass, newspaper editors and Eastern businessmen on a hunting trip, Cody donned his buckskin coat and pants, crimson shirt and oversized sombrero. But he dazzled the group even more by his demeanor. The generals and city slickers found Cody to be "a mild, agreeable, well-mannered man, quiet and retiring in his disposition, though well-informed and always ready to talk earnestly upon any subject of interest, and in all respects the reverse of the person we had expected to meet."

And befitting a consummate showman, he was a prodigious liar. He frequently and adroitly blurred the line between his real deeds and heavily embroidered versions of them. He sometimes borrowed colorful events that had happened to others, and was not averse to trotting out several versions of the same story, depending on the audience. It was a habit to which he occasionally confessed.

"I am sorry to have to lie so outrageously in this yarn," he once wrote to a publisher of one of the books he wrote. "My hero has killed more Indians on one war-trail than I have killed in all my life. But I understand what is expected in border tales. If you think the revolver and Bowie knife are used too frequently, you may cut out a fatal shot or stab wherever you deem it wise."

He was exceedingly generous, to those he knew and those he didn't. For most of his life, he was the main, or sole, support for both his immediate and extended family. He routinely handed out hundreds of free tickets to his shows to poor boys he met on the streets. Annie Oakley, the iconic female sharpshooter who for years starred in Cody's Wild West shows, recalled a snowy night in New York City where she, Cody and her husband, the sharpshooter Frank Butler, were on their way to dinner after a performance at Madison Square Garden. Business had been poor, and the trio had barely $30 among them. Outside the restaurant door, they encountered what Oakley described as "20 to 30 of the most tattered and hopeless mendicant down-and-outs I have ever seen anywhere." Cody promptly pooled his money with Oakley's and Butler's, and gave a dollar each to the homeless men. "That left us just enough for frugal fare," Oakley wrote, "... but that was Cody's way."

He was as careless with money, however, as he was generous. Or as one of his sisters put it, "financially, his shortcomings were deplorable." He drove a hotel into insolvency by doling out free rooms and meals to the down and out. With a partner, he once built a town, called it Rome, and then watched it literally pick up and move to land he didn't own, so the townsfolk could be closer to a railroad line. And despite making millions of dollars over his long show business career, he died with a relatively modest estate, in large part because of an over-fondness for flashy jewelry and shaky investments.

Another of the contributing factors to his lack of financial acumen was that Will Cody loved to have a good time. The colorful cowboy/author E.C. "Teddy Blue" Abbott recounted how Cody was once hired, at a handsome salary, by a group of Nebraska cattle ranchers to supervise a massive roundup. "Mostly he raised hell," Abbott wrote. "He had everyone running horse races and shooting at marks instead of gathering beef. He offered $100 to the first man who could rope a jack rabbit...pretty soon he sent to North Platte for more whiskey, and we did not do any more work for a week." The cattle owners were not amused; Cody was fired.

Finally, it should be pointed out that Will Cody was as inconsistent as any other human being. A merciless slaughterer of thousands of buffalo, he became an ardent, though largely unsuccessful, advocate for bison conservation. Having built a legend as a fearless Indian fighter and having unhesitatingly portrayed Native Americans as ludicrous stereotypes on stage, he became an outspoken defender of them as a people who had been severely wronged by European Americans and who were entitled to respect and fair treatment.

"Every individual's character is a work in progress," reads a placard at the Buffalo Bill Center of the West, in Cody, Wyoming. "William F. Cody's was no exception. Paired opposites framed his character: rich vs. poor, success vs. failure, freedom vs. responsibility, vice vs. virtue, "untamed" West vs. "civilized" East. Throughout his life, he navigated between them, charting a course that would define his destiny."

The confusion surrounding Will Cody's early life begins almost as soon as he was born. In fact, it begins with exactly when he was born. In the first of the two autobiographies Cody wrote, he put his birth year as 1845. In actuality, he was born Feb. 2, 1846. Cody scholars differ as to whether Will just goofed, or deliberately added a year to his age, so the later adventures he made up would have a greater degree of believability by making him older than he was at the time they supposedly took place.

In any event, all accounts put his birthplace in Le Claire Iowa, a small town on a bend of the Mississippi River, about 175 miles east of Des Moines.

His father, Isaac Cody, was a Canadian immigrant whose family settled in Ohio. In 1840, Isaac married Mary Laycock, a widow with one daughter. The newlyweds would eventually produce three sons and three daughters. Will was the third-oldest of the siblings.

Like so many Americans of the mid-19th century, Isaac Cody had itchy feet. After having moved the family from Ohio to Iowa, where he managed large farms for absentee owners and owned and operated a stagecoach line, Isaac began looking farther west. In 1854, he uprooted the Codys from a moderately prosperous life in Iowa and moved to the newly formed territory of Kansas. It was a momentous move.

As part of ongoing and ultimately failed efforts to head off a civil war over slavery, Congress in 1854 decided to let residents in the new territories of Kansas and Nebraska decide for themselves if slavery would be allowed within their boundaries. Nebraska was too far north to grow labor-intensive crops like cotton, so the slavery issue was largely moot. But Kansas wasn't. Congress' pass-the-buck "compromise" set the stage for a protracted and violent struggle—sort of a Civil War preview—between pro- and anti-slavery forces. "Bleeding Kansas" became an everyday catchphrase.

Although labeled an abolitionist, Isaac was in truth a "Free Soiler," meaning he opposed the presence of any blacks at all in Kansas, slave or free. He was also vocal about it, which got him elected to the territorial legislature. It also got him stabbed in the back during a community meeting in the Salt Creek Valley where the Codys had settled. "Cody is severely hurt," a local pro-slavery newspaper crowed. "...the (pro-slavery) settlers on Salt Creek regret that his wound is not more dangerous."

But it was. Isaac Cody never fully recovered from the wound, and for the next three years he alternated between working for the Free-Soiler cause and dodging attempts to finish him off. In the meantime, his family endured a constant stream of threats and vandalism of their farm. In the spring of 1857, Isaac fell ill and died. Since the eldest Cody son had been killed in a riding accident, that left 11-year-old Will as the man of the family.

Separating fact from fiction over the next decade of Will's life is a somewhat daunting task. Events as recounted first by Cody himself, and then by his paid publicists and reverential biographers, range from the plausible to the eyebrow-raising. While his mother eked out a living from the family farm and renting out rooms to boarders, young Will took work where he could find it. He drove a wagon delivering hay, and rode a horse delivering messages from the town of Leavenworth to the telegraph office at the nearby Army fort. At the age of 12, he was hired on by the mammoth freight-hauling firm of Russell, Majors and Waddell. The company was said to have a payroll of 6,000 wagon-driving men and a herd of 45,000 wagon-pulling oxen.

The work was physically exhausting and inherently dangerous for a grown man, let alone a pre-teen. But Cody undertook at least one, and possibly as many as three, 1,200-mile roundtrips between Leavenworth and Denver. He quite probably tried his hand at gold prospecting in the Rocky Mountains and beaver trapping along the North Platte River too, breaking his leg in a misadventure while setting traps in mid-winter. He also sporadically attended school, and was recalled by one teacher as "being a particularly determined ballplayer."

Despite claims by himself and others, however, Will almost certainly did not kill an Indian chief at the age of 13; probably did not ride for the fabled Pony Express mail delivery service at the age of 14, and may or may not have killed a desperado while escaping from an outlaw gang he stumbled upon at the age of 15.

At some point in his youth, he did meet a man whose appearance he would eventually emulate, and whose experiences he would occasionally borrow for his own public persona. The man was nine years older than Cody. Like Cody, he had been caught up in the pre-Civil War violence that engulfed "Bleeding Kansas." And like Cody, who would become far better known by a nickname, James Butler Hickok would become a legend as "Wild Bill." The two Bills would share adventures both real and theatrical. But first came the Civil War. While Hickok would earn some distinction as a Union scout, spy and sniper, the much younger Cody would begin his wartime "exploits" as basically a horse thief.

Will Cody was 15 when the Civil War began. Pro-slavery thugs had hounded his family for years, and as far as he was concerned, had killed his father. So choosing a side was not nearly as big a problem as figuring out how to participate while helping to support his struggling family. Will's solution was to join a local group whose chief military strategy was to steal horses and other useful things from pro-slavery families.

Will's mother, however, disapproved, and Cody eventually "graduated" to a somewhat more organized paramilitary operation. Its distinguishing feature was the wearing of scarlet garters or leggings—hence the name "Red Legs." As an unofficial group, there were no records kept of the Red Legs' activities. But Cody claimed to have been in "many a lively skirmish" against Missouri guerilla raiders that included the Younger Brothers, who would achieve post-war notoriety as part of the outlaw gang that rode with Frank and Jesse James. The Red Legs themselves were hardly heroes. "They are a band of Land Pirates who infest the Missouri border," a Missouri newspaper fumed, "...(and) go forth to steal themselves rich in the name of liberty."

Will's connection to the Red Legs ended in late 1863, when his mother died. Disconsolate and restless, he began to drink heavily, and woke up one morning to find he had enlisted in the 7th Kansas Volunteer Cavalry. Despite his later contentions that he was a Union scout and spy, sometimes in the company of Wild Bill Hickok, there is nothing substantive to back the stories. At war's end he was a hospital orderly and messenger in St. Louis. He was not quite 20, and like many 20-year-olds, prone to compulsive behavior. So he got married.

Will Cody's bride was Louisa Maude Frederici. Nicknamed "Lulu," she was two years older than Will, moderately pretty, and something of a shrew. The couple would be married for 51 years, although Will was rarely if ever home for more than six months in a row. Louisa wanted a quiet, staid middle-to-upper class life. Will wanted to roam, pursuing the spotlight. They settled on a lengthy, if often uneasy and sometimes tempestuous, domestic armistice.

The youthful and newlywed Cody tried his hand at several ventures—speculating in real estate, running whiskey, operating a store, owning and hotel and saloon—but none of them fit. By 1867, his main income source was hunting buffalo to supply meat for workers building the railroad across Kansas. He was very good at it, and it paid very well: For providing 12 bison a day, Cody received $500 a month (about $8,700 in 2022.)

He also earned a lifelong nickname. And while there were plenty of other men throughout the West also referred to as "Buffalo Bill," Will Cody was the only one who had his own jingle. It was jokingly—and perhaps more than a little bitterly—sung by the dollar-a-day-earning railroad workers:

"Buffalo Bill, Buffalo Bill,

Never missed and never will.

Always aims and shoots to kill;

And the company pays his buffalo bill."

By the time his contract ran out in 1868, Cody estimated he had killed at least 4,000 buffalo. The real number was probably higher. He then took up work as a guide and scout for the U.S. Army. It was an occupation already being pursued by his friend and mentor Bill Hickok.

Army scouts were generally not considered an admirable group, at least not by Army officers. As civilian contractors, they generally could say what they thought, behave as they wanted and come and go as they pleased. "As a class, these men have a rather bad reputation," an officer wrote in 1876, "most of them being dangerous and good-for-nothing rascals who take their risky business because it pays well." In fact, it did pay well, at least by Army standards. Cody's salary as a scout ranged from $75 to $125 a month ($1,800 to $3,000 in 2022), five times what an Army private made.

But it was often exhausting and dangerous work, and Cody quickly distinguished himself as both tireless and fearless. In his memoirs, Gen. Philip Sheridan wrote about an 1868 assignment for which Cody volunteered. It required him to ride a triangular route carrying messages back and forth to three forts, through wild and dangerous country. Sheridan estimated Cody covered 350 miles in 60 hours, riding mostly at night to avoid Indians.

"Such an exhibition of endurance and courage was more than enough to convince me that his (Cody's) services would be extremely valuable in the campaign," Sheridan wrote. "So I retained him at Fort Hays until the battalion of the 5th Cavalry arrived, and then made him chief of scouts for the regiment."

For his part, Cody wryly recalled of his epic trek that he walked the last 10 miles because his mule had run away from him. (Scouts sometimes used mules on long rides because they were better suited than horses to the forage provided by the Great Plains.) Exhausted and furious at the animal, Cody confessed to shooting the mule when he finally caught up with it in sight of a fort. "Like the great majority of government mules," he wrote, "he was a tough one to kill."

As a scout, Cody was involved in at least 16 skirmishes and battles. In one, a bullet grazed his forehead, plowing a shallow but bloody gash just below his hairline. In another, he claimed to have killed two warriors with one bullet. The warriors, he said, were riding double, and he shot the rear rider through the back and into the lead rider. He was awarded the Medal of Honor for his role in what was actually a minor fight, and the award was more for his overall valor than the fight itself. (The medal was rescinded in 1917 on the grounds that Cody was a civilian at the time and thus ineligible to win what is a military award, and then restored in 1989.)

And on July 11 1869, he was involved in a battle that would result in his first taste of widespread and possibly undeserved fame. The Battle of Summit Springs, near the present-day town of Sterling in northeastern Colorado, pitted the 5th Cavalry under Col. Eugene Carr against Cheyenne

"Dog Men" led by Tall Bull. "Dog Men" was a term denoting a society of warriors who reputedly would tie themselves to stakes in the ground and refuse to yield their positions.

It was more rout than battle. Carr launched a surprise attack from three sides on the Indian encampment. Only one soldier was wounded, while about 50 warriors were killed or captured. Among the dead was Tall Bull. Despite conflicting accounts and contradictory evidence, Will Cody was widely credited—by himself as well as others—for having killed Tall Bull. When the regiment returned to Fort Sedgewick, Colorado, after the battle, Cody encountered a short, pudgy fellow who just happened to be passing through—and was looking for a hero.

The man sometimes credited with "inventing" Buffalo Bill actually invented a character far more outrageous and outlandish—himself.

During his 65-year life, Edward Zane Carroll Judson served in the U.S. Navy; fought Indians in the Seminole War and Confederates in the Civil War, and served a year in jail for inciting a deadly riot in New York City to protest a British actor "stealing" a role from an American actor. He incited another riot in St. Louis, this one to protest German immigrants voting. He established—and bankrupted—three newspapers. In Nashville, he was hanged by a mob for seducing a man's teenaged bride and then killing her husband in a graveyard shootout. He escaped when the rope broke.

He was once whipped and beaten on New York City's Broadway by an outraged brothel madam for libeling her in his newspaper, despite the fact Judson himself was an occasional customer at her establishment. A judge who was clearly mindful of Judson's checkered past found the madam guilty of assault and battery—and fined her six cents. And he toured the country giving passionate and inflammatory temperance lectures whenever he was sober—and sometimes when he wasn't—and had eight wives, several at the same time.

When not otherwise engaged, Edward Judson also wrote. A lot. Under the pen name "Ned Buntline," Judson churned out an estimated 600-plus "dime novels," cheaply produced paperbacks with lurid covers and subjects that ranged from pirates to big-city detectives to—most significantly for our purposes—the Wild West. As literature, the books stunk. But quality seldom plays a prominent role in popular culture, and Buntline's ludicrous prose sold well. At his peak, it was said his literary income exceeded $20,000 a year, or nearly $500,000 in 2022 dollars.

In July 1869, Buntline (we'll stick with his better-known pseudonym) happened to stop over at Fort Sedgewick on his way home to New York City, after having delivered temperance lectures in California and other parts of the West. At the fort, he met Will Cody, fresh from the Battle of Summit Springs. Cody thought Buntline was odd but likeable; Buntline thought Cody was a dime novelist's dream come true.

In December, *Street & Smith's New York Weekly* published a Ned Buntline serial entitled "Buffalo Bill: The King of the Border Men." It had nothing to do with the Summit Springs battle, and little to do with Will Cody. Instead, Buntline very loosely adapted some incidents that involved Wild Bill Hickok (who was also a character in the story,) and made up the rest. The widely advertised book was touted as "the wildest, truest story Ned Buntline ever wrote." For whatever that was worth.

Cody was so appreciative of his newfound fame, he proposed naming his first-born son Elmo Judson Cody, in honor of his "biographer." Cooler heads prevailed, however, and when the baby arrived in November, 1870, he was named Kit Carson Cody, after the famous scout.

Now something of a celebrity, Cody was invited to guide two highly publicized hunting trips for various VIPs. The first, in September, 1871, was a group of high-ranking Army officers and newspaper bigwigs, including *New York Daily Herald* publisher James Gordon Bennett Jr. The second, in January, 1872, was even more glittering. The guest of honor was Grand Duke Alexis of Russia, whose 19th century visit to America was akin to the 20th century visit of the Beatles. The duke, with the help of Cody and another participant, George Custer, bagged eight buffalo on the five-day trip. Alexis was so pleased he presented Cody with a handsome full-length Russian fur coat, a bag of gold coins and several pieces of jewelry.

In New York, meanwhile, playwright Fred G. Maeder had written a play based on Buntline's Buffalo Bill story. It ran successfully in 1871, then reopened on Feb. 19, 1872, at the venerable Bowery Theatre in Manhattan. John B. Studley, a proficient and popular actor, played Buffalo Bill. Among the mass of humanity who packed opening night was another fellow who had played the role of Buffalo Bill, albeit not yet on stage: Will Cody.

Cody had been invited to New York by newspaper publisher Bennett and others who were intrigued and/or enthralled with this real-life "hero of the Plains." The next day, the *Herald* called the play—which featured "hair-breadth escapes, burning prairies, trappers' last shots, guerilla raids (and) Indian war dances"—"one of the most exciting and thrilling melodramas that was ever played upon the Bowery boards." The *Herald* also reported that when the audience learned the real Buffalo Bill was among them, they clamored for an onstage appearance. "I made a desperate effort" to address the crowd, Cody recalled in his autobiography, "and a few words escaped me, but what they were I could not for the life of me tell...bowing to the audience, I beat a hasty retreat."

While Cody retreated to his scouting duties with the Army, Ned Buntline cranked out another Buffalo Bill novel. He also began lobbying Cody to undertake a new, and what Buntline promised would almost assuredly be a profitable, profession—acting. The profession had no immediate appeal to the scout, but the lure of money did.It also sounded good to John B. Omohundro, one of Cody's scouting buddies. Omohundro was a 27-year-old former Confederate cavalry scout from Virginia, who was better known as "Texas Jack." In mid-December 1872, the two friends somewhat uncertainly stepped down from a train in Chicago and into a career in show business.

"'Blood and Thunder' will draw..."

In 1876, most Americans had about as much actual knowledge of the American West as they did of Tehran, Tokyo or Timbuktu. That is to say, none. Despite the huge numbers of Americans and newly arrived immigrants who moved west in the mid-19th century, millions more *did not.* In 1880, nearly eight of every 10 residents of the United States still resided east of the Mississippi River.

The Wild West thus existed for them mainly as a tableau concocted mainly by sensationalistic journalists and semi-literate dime novelists. Occasionally mixed in was a well-written but still wildly exaggerated contribution from a first-class story teller such as Mark Twain or Bret Harte. But there was another medium, often overlooked by Wild West historians, which shaped visions of the frontier—the American theater.

Stage plays gave Eastern audiences a multi-sensory experience the printed word could not: the actual smell of gunpowder smoke; the sound of Indian war whoops (sometimes from bonafide Indians); the sight of real horses, mules and even a bear or two. Theater-goers could cheer the hero, boo the villain, laugh at the shamelessly stereotyped Irish/Chinese/African-American comic-relief character, and gasp at the last-minute rescue of the fair maiden, spared a not-so-subtly implied "fate worse than death."

Although the American Frontier was a theatrical subject as early as the 1840s, it blossomed as a topic after the Civil War. By 1871, plays such as *Across the Continent*, *Horizon* and *Kit, the Arkansas Traveler* played for weeks on New York stages. Frank M. Mayo, a respected actor who had actually honed his craft in the West, played the title role in *Davy Crockett: Be Sure You're Right, Then Go Ahead* for more than 22 years and 3,000-plus performances.

As the nation's population soared, many new arrivals and restless residents viewed the Wild West dramas as a sort of potential travel guide.

The popularity of Wild West magazine stories and dime novels whetted their appetites for their three-dimensional counterparts on stage. And it was relatively affordable, if not exactly cheap. The best seats in the house in a medium-sized city might run 50 cents, or about $12 in 2021 currency.

What audiences got for their money varied widely. The best-produced shows featured clever effects, such as using red-tinted gas flames to mimic prairie fires. Performers pulled off dangerous stunts, such as leaping horses through the windows of faux buildings. There was trick-roping and sharp shooting, dancing and singing. And sometimes a bear.

Critics generally despised them. The most charitable among reviewers dismissed the frontier-themed plays as pablum for the masses. "All of these plays are bad in an intellectual sense, and some of them are bad in a moral sense," a New York critic wrote. "They come no more in the sphere of dramatic art than a picture of pound cake on the door of a Broadway stage comes within the sphere of the art of painting."

However good or bad the performances were, the plays themselves were remarkably consistent. Violence was the generally accepted solution for nearly every situation that confronted the protagonist. When it was aimed at Indians, as it often was, it reflected what historian Richard Slotkin has called America's "contradictory impulses of ambition and nostalgia, racialism and sympathy for the victims of injustice." Nineteenth-century dramatists, in other words, wanted audiences to feel at least a little wistful about the "necessity" of killing off the Native Americans to make room for the New Americans.

While earlier plays fairly dripped with simulated gore and spectacularly high body counts, the "Westerns" gradually evolved to include more sentimentality and romance, and heroes and villains who were more nuanced as characters. But violence remained a key element. Reviewing an 1881 Buffalo Bill melodrama, a Brooklyn critic noted there was less violence than usual, and that "when someone is shot to the death, or wounded, there always seems to be some reason for it."

Troupes like Cody's were known as "combinations," groups of actors who traveled from city to city supporting the show's star or stars. It saved the star from having to repeatedly break in a new cast; solidified performances since they could be fine-tuned as the troupe traveled, and helped assure the star wouldn't be upstaged by some upstart local actor. But it was also more expensive because of the costs of moving a group from town to town as opposed to one or two people. So costs were often cut by eschewing the transportation of scenery and backdrops, and using whatever the local theater had on hand. This could prove problematical.

"A company of scouts fighting a battle among a forest of trees which are a fair representation of vegetation supposed to exist in prehistoric ages is an anomaly, to say the least," a Vermont critic observed. "The audience was not critical, however, and applauded the last war whoop to its final echo. Blood and thunder will draw in Rutland...".

By the end of the 19th century, the Western as a dramatic genre had become entrenched as a mainstay of the American Theater. The plays, acting and production values improved to the point that they were no longer knee-jerkingly panned by critics. By 1905, only five American-written plays ran for more than 200 performances in New York City that year—and all five were Westerns. It was a distinction not lost on the pioneers of a new form of entertainment that was cutting its first teeth as the 20th century began: the movies.

Ned Buntline liked to boast that he wrote *Scouts of the Prairie*, the play in which Cody and Omohundro were to appear, in just four hours. Critics were mystified as to why it took him that long. "Everything is so wonderfully bad that it was almost good," a New York scribe sarcastically marveled. "The whole performance was so far outside the human experience, so wonderful in its daring feebleness, that no ordinary intelligence is capable of comprehending it."

The show opened at Chicago's Amphitheatre on Dec. 16, 1872, four days after Will and Texas Jack hit town. Buntline, who proved to be an even worse actor than he was a writer, penned a meaty—make that hammy—role for himself into the play. The lead female role was filled by Giuseppina Morlacchi, a beautiful 26-year-old Italian professional actress and dancer who was credited with introducing America to a popular high-kicking French dance called the cancan. (She and Texas Jack would eventually get married and start their own theatrical combination.)

The initial performance was marked mainly by a long and seemingly extemporaneous temperance lecture by Buntline in the middle of a scene, and a leading man paralyzed with stage fright. To goad Cody into saying something—anything—Buntline began asking him questions about his recent activities. That brought Will around, although not to the script, which was probably just as well. Somehow the company staggered through three acts crammed with evil Mormons, a drunken Irishman, heroic Indian maidens with romantic notions toward Will and Jack, and 40 or so "Plains Indians," few of whom had ever been west of Peoria. Even with that large a "tribe," Buntline's play killed so many Indians that some of the warriors had to die several times in each act.

Critics were appalled. "Such a combination of incongruous drama (and) execrable acting...is not likely to be vouchsafed to a city a second time," one huffed, "even Chicago." But he was wrong. The play took in $2,800 the first night (about $59,000 in 2022), 40 percent of which went to the theater manager. It sold out for the rest of the week. The troupe moved on to enthusiastic audiences in St. Louis, Indianapolis, Cincinnati, and across Pennsylvania into New York. Reviewers continued to rip it, and Cody agreed with them. Spotting his wife in the audience in St. Louis, Will called to her "Oh Mamma, I'm a bad actor. Does this look as awful out there as it feels up here?"

But the public cared little for the quality of the play or the acting—they came to see the stars. Some reviewers began to get the point. "Whatever may be Buffalo Bill's merits as an actor," a critic wrote, "he is certainly a splendid specimen of physical manhood; and considering the credibility he has gained by actual service and exploits on the Plains...he is of himself no small attraction." Another noted that "it is something to see genuine scouts act as scouts."

Despite the show's success, Cody was disappointed that when the season ended in June 1873, he had netted "only" $6,000 ($129,000 in 2022). Still, he and Texas Jack decided it was easier money than shooting buffalo or being shot at by real Indians. So, they agreed to try it again for the 1873-74 theatrical season.

This time, the play was *Buffalo Bill, King of the Border Men*, the very play that Cody had watched from the audience in New York in early 1872. They also decided to cut ties with Buntline, in a split that was apparently amicable. Instead, Cody and Omohundro hired an old friend. Bill Hickok was living in Missouri, where his main occupation was gambling. He warily accepted the offer to tread the boards after a large salary was dangled in front of him. As we will see in Chapter 7, he wasn't good at it, and didn't like it. Hickok, who joined the company in September 1873, was gone by March, 1874.

About the same time Wild Bill left acting, Buffalo Bill moved his family to what was supposed to be a permanent home in Rochester, New York. He sometimes visited them, in between theatrical tours and summertime scouting gigs with the Army. Cody also occasionally led hunting trips, and even led fossil hunts for the esteemed paleontologist O. C. Marsh.

But in April 1876, just before a performance in Springfield Massachusetts, Cody received word that his only son, 5-year-old Kit Carson—"Kitty"—was gravely ill with scarlet fever. He rushed home and arrived just in time to have the boy die in his arms. "God has taken from us our little boy," Will wrote his sister Julia that night. "I got home only a few hours before Kitty died, he could not speak, but he put his little arms around my neck, as much to say Papa has come."

Grief-stricken, Cody returned to the stage a few weeks later. But his heart wasn't in it. It was quite probably a relief when the Army summoned him in early June for what would turn out to be his "duel" with Yellow Hair, and his last true adventures in the Wild West.

After the skirmish at Warbonnet Creek, Cody and the 5th Cavalry moved west, to join the combined forces of Generals Crook and Terry, who were in pursuit of the Sioux and Cheyenne forces that had beaten the Army at the battles of Rosebud Creek and Little Bighorn.

Scantily supplied and timidly led, the campaign was a lengthy and expensive mess. In disgust, Cody quit on Aug. 22, although he hung around unofficially for several more weeks as a favor to General Sheridan. On his way home, Cody wasn't shy about venting his disappointment at the Army's inability to decisively avenge Custer.

He told one reporter "that the soldiers did not want or intend to fight; that he had worn himself out finding Indians; and that when he did discover their whereabouts, there was no one ready to 'go for them.'" To another, he said "it has been more like a big picnic party than a campaign. As a general thing, instead of sending their cavalry out 'light' to fight the Indians until the infantry came up, the commanding officers have used the cavalry to prevent the Indians from attacking the infantry." Cody was particularly critical of General Terry, who he said had traveled with a full-sized bed, a cooking range and a dining table. "We could not travel fast enough to catch the Indians as we would break the dishes," he fumed.

Notwithstanding his ire at missing the chance at one more big battle, the showman in Will Cody shrewdly recognized an opportunity to cash in on his Warbonnet Creek fight. He commissioned a new play, titled *Red Right Hand; or, Buffalo Bill's First Scalp for Custer*. It was written by a longtime acting colleague, J.V. Arlington, from a story by the prolific dime novelist Prentiss Ingraham, and it took generous liberties with the facts.

Instead of a rifle fight, the play had Cody and Yellow Hair locked in hand-to-hand combat before Buffalo Bill plunges his Bowie knife into the warrior's stout heart, scalps him and triumphantly waves it over his head proclaiming "first scalp for Custer!" Even more far-fetched was the addition of having Yellow Hair challenging Cody by name to a duel to the death, since the real Yellow Hair had no idea who Cody was and Cody did not speak Cheyenne. But at least the costume was authentic—Will wore the same outfit on stage he had worn at Warbonnet Creek.

The role of Yellow Hair was played by yet another scouting acquaintance of Cody's. John Wallace Crawford, better known as "Captain Jack, the Poet Scout," was an Irish-born teetotaler whose colorful career included writing seven books of verse and more than 100 short stories; working as a special agent for the U.S. Department of Justice, and becoming a popular figure on the lecture circuit. His relationship with Cody, however, proved stormy, and after accidentally shooting himself in the groin during a performance in Nevada, he quit the show in mid-1877.

In addition to the "Poet Scout," Cody initially employed the "trophies" he had taken from the real Yellow Hair—including the scalp. The items were displayed outside the theater in which the show was currently performing. It doubtless enticed some potential customers, but it horrified and angered others. "It was hardly possible to believe that the public streets... would be a place for the exhibition of human scalps," one newspaper scolded. America was hosting thousands of foreign tourists who had come for the Centennial Exhibition in Philadelphia. When they went home, "and publish their volumes about the manners and customs of the Americans, we can imagine the horror and disgust with which the people will read that the scalps of our enemies are hung up over places of amusement."

Cody got the message, and the scalp was quietly returned to the window of Moses Kerngood's cigar store in Rochester. Even without the scalp, or a coherent script, the play did well. As Cody himself pointed out, the plot was so disjointed "it made no difference at which act we commenced the performance. It afforded us, however, ample opportunity to give a noisy, rattling gunpowder entertainment, and to present a succession of scenes in the late Indian War, all of which seemed to give general satisfaction."

Through the rest of 1876 and well into 1877, Will Cody's theatrical troupe continued to traverse the country. But in October 1877, a theater column in the *Boston Globe* carried an unattributed item announcing Buffalo Bill was retiring, once he completed a long final tour of the Far West. "Buffalo Bill (is) going to his (Nebraska) ranch to remain there as a cattle dealer and gentleman farmer," the item read. "He now has 4,500 head of cattle and hopes to have 10,000 by the close of next year. He will therefore retire from the stage with an ample competency."

The *Globe's* announcement was about 35 years premature.

Chapter 5 Notes

Now it was just Charles King, *Campaigning with Crook*, p. 12.

Rations were short, Paul Hedren, *First Scalp for Custer*, pp. 53-54.

"There is very little" *Ellis County (Ks.) Star*, June 29 1876, p. 4.

But if Will Paul Hedren, "The Contradictory Legacies of Buffalo Bill's First Scalp for Custer," *Montana: The Magazine of Western History*, Spring 2005, p. 18.

In his 1890 Charles King, *Campaigning with Crook, and Stories of Army Life*, pp. 17-18.

In a 1938 letter Don Russell, *The Lives and Legends of Buffalo Bill*, p. 226.

"The instant they" Ibid.

At the reservation, Helen Cody Westmore, *Buffalo Bill, Last of the Great Scouts*, p, 218.

In fact, Cody William F. Cody to Louisa Frederici Cody, July 18 1876, Buffalo Bill Center of the West Digital Archives.

He also sent *Buffalo (NY) Weekly Courier*, Aug. 2 1876, p. 3.

"I will write" William F. Cody to Louisa F. Cody, July 18 1876, op. cit.

During his lifetime Louis S. Warren, *Buffalo Bill's America*, p. 178.

"Everybody has heard" *Memphis Public Leader*, Sept. 19, 1876, p. 1; *New York Times*, Jan. 11 1917, p. 4.

More accurate than Westmore, op. cit., p. 44.

He certainly looked Nelson A. Miles, *Personal Recollections and Observations of General Nelson A. Miles*, p. 131; Hedren, First Scalp, op. cit., p. 37.

The long hair E.C. Abbott and Helena H. Smith, *We Pointed Them North*, p. 87.

But Cody was Henry E. Davis, *Ten Days on the Plains*, p. 18.

"I am sorry" Westmore, op. cit., p. 223.

He was exceedingly *Los Angeles Evening Express*, Feb. 2 1917, p. 7.

Another of the contributing Abbott, op. cit., p. 84

Although labeled an *Liberty (Mo.) Democratic Platform*, Sept. 28 1854, p. 3.

The work was Warren, op. cit., p. 20.

Will's mother, however, Ibid., p. 34; Palmyra *(Mo.) Spectator*, Nov. 11 1863, p. 1.

He also earned Russell, op. cit., p. 9.

Army scouts were *Wilmington (Del.) Daily Gazette*, Aug. 22 1876, p. 4.

"Such an exhibition" Phillip Sheridan, *Memoirs, Vol. II*, pp. 299-301.

For his part, William F. Cody, *Life of Buffalo Bill*, p. 197.

The man sometimes Two entertaining biographies of Edward Judson are Jay Monaghan's *The Great Rascal: The Life and adventures of Ned Buntline* (1952), and Julia Bricklin's *The Notorious Life of Ned Buntline* (2020.)

In December *Buffalo (NY) Commercial*, Dec. 15 1869, p. 4.

Cody had been *New York Daily Herald*, Feb. 21 1872, p. 2; Cody, op. cit., pp. 276-277

Critics generally despised *New York Daily Herald*, Jan. 13 1874, p. 7.

However good or bad, Richard Slotkin, *The Fatal Environment*, p. 502.

While earlier plays Sandra K. Sagala, *Buffalo Bill on Stage*, p. 149.

"A company of" *Rutland (Vt.) Daily Herald*, Jan. 24, 1876, p. 3.

Ned Buntline liked *New York Daily Herald*, April 1 1873, p. 12.

Critics were appalled *Chicago Times*, Dec. 18 1872, p. 4; Roger G. Hall, *Performing the American Frontier, 1879-1906*, p. 57.

But the public *Buffalo (NY) Commercial*, April 5 1876, p. 3; *Rock Island (Il.) Argus*, Jan. 12 1876, p. 4.

But in April Will Cody to Julia Cody Goodman, April 22 1876, Buffalo Bill Center of the West digital archive.

He told one reporter *Chicago Tribune*, Sept. 22 1876, p. 5; *Memphis (Tn.) Public Ledger*, Sept. 19 1876, p. 4; *Rochester (NY) Democrat and Chronicle*, Sept. 18 1876, p. 4.

In addition to *Fall River (Ma.) Daily Evening News*, Nov. 24 1876, p. 2.

Cody got the message Cody, op. cit., p. 360.

Through the rest of *Boston Globe*, Oct. 14 1877, p. 3.

CHAPTER 6

"My God, it talks!"

Inventions, innovations, and the Philadelphia Fair

INTERLUDE

On the cool, clear morning of May 10, 1876, a dark-eyed, dark-mustached former Union Army officer stopped before a modest two-story red-brick building in downtown Indianapolis, and opened the door to a business empire.

Or at least it would be eventually. On this particular Wednesday morning, it was still just a 720-square-foot empty space that the man later said "was not big enough to swing a cat in." The man's name was Eli Lilly. Fortunately for him, he had leased the building on West Pearl Street not to swing cats, but to make medicine.

In 1876 America, making medicine was neither art nor science. It was in large measure a combination of guesswork, folklore and flim-flam. On the day Lilly opened his door, for example, a single page in the *Indianapolis News* carried ads that promised "Dr. Morris's Syrup of Tar, Wild Cherry and Horehound" would cure "any diseases of the circulatory organs;" "Bethesda Water" would cure "any diseases of the kidneys or bladder," and "Humphrey's Homeopathic Specifics" would cure pretty much anything, from seasickness to "worm fever."

There were no federal laws to prevent such claims, and very few state or local rules. Passage of the nation's first substantive consumer protection law, the Pure Food and Drug Act, was still 30 years away. Medicines generously laced with opium were perfectly legal. The importation of "eating opium" from China wasn't banned until 1881, and opium itself, while heavily taxed, wasn't outlawed until 1909. Such "medicines" were widely available, and widely used.

"Not only in the great cities are opium eaters to be found," a newspaper reported, "but throughout the whole country, in the towns and villages and rural districts. Druggists and apothecaries have their regular customers, and the insidious poison is sometimes to be found for sale in the village grocery. So profitable has the sale of the narcotic become that the cultivation of the poppy is steadily increasing" in the United States.

There were non-narcotic remedies that were as ridiculous, if less addictive. These included curing depression in young women by having them drink the tears of other depressed young women; treating colic with a mixture that included mouse poop, and gargling with one's own urine to prevent tooth decay. All of this quite possibly contributed to the fact that in 1876, the average life expectancy of an American was 41 years.

"I firmly believe," observed the physician and poet Oliver Wendell Holmes Sr., "that if the whole *Materia medica* ("knowledge of medicines") as now used, could be sunk to the bottom of the sea, it would be all the better for mankind, and worse for the fishes."

While clearly not having to meet any exacting legal or industry standards, Lilly faced other obstacles in launching his business. One was that the nation was in the midst of a deep and painful economic recession. Another was a decided paucity of assets: about $1,400 in credit and inventory ($33,600 in 2022,) and a payroll of only three, including his 14-year-old son. And he was already 38, which in 1876 put him deep into middle age.

But Eli Lilly had faced obstacles before. Born in Baltimore, he was the eldest of 11 children. His father, a carpenter and builder, eventually moved the family to Indiana. After developing a keen interest in pharmacy, Lilly dropped out of college and earned a "certificate of competency" as a druggist. Then came the Civil War. It turned out Lilly was also keenly interested in big guns. He convinced the governor of Indiana to let him form an artillery battery, with Lilly as its commanding officer. The six-cannon unit fought with distinction in a number of significant battles, and Lilly eventually reached the rank of lieutenant colonel.

Toward the end of the war, however, Lilly was captured, and narrowly escaped execution before being released in a prisoner-exchange program. At war's end, he bought into a 1,200-acre Mississippi cotton plantation. It was, to put it mildly, a disaster. A two-year drought wiped out the plantation's crop and cash reserves. His wife died in childbirth, and the baby died too. Then his business partner skipped out, forcing Lilly into bankruptcy.

In 1869, "Colonel" Lilly moved to Illinois and found work again in the drug store business. But in 1875, a friend in the drug wholesaling business had a suggestion: Why not make pills instead of peddling them? That sounded good to Lilly, which leads us back to the small building on West Pearl Street in Indianapolis.

Working 72-hour weeks and paying his employees with gold coins he kept in his derby hat, Lilly produced tablets, as well as "fluid extracts" that included "bear's foot," "camp bark" and "worm seed." As with many 19th century medicines, some of them included up to 69 percent alcohol. But Lilly steered clear of opioids in his medicines, and also began innovating. One such innovation was encapsulating medicine in gelatinous capsules, flavored with sugar, cinnamon or chocolate to make them more palatable.

Another was to truthfully label the products' ingredients, an idea that was appreciated by both wholesalers and consumers. Lilly's firm quickly gained a reputation for consistency, reliability—and almost unique in the pharmaceutical industry—for ethical business practices. Within the industry, Lilly became a leading advocate for professionalizing and standardizing medicine making.

By the time of his death in 1898, Lilly's company had a product line of more than 2,000 items and annual sales of nearly $8 million in 2022 dollars. And by 2022, Eli Lilly and Company was selling products in 125 countries, had more than 35,000 employees, and held assets of nearly $44 billion. But in 1876, Eli Lilly, like a lot of other Americans, was just searching for better ways to do things.

On the very same day Eli Lilly was beginning to innovate the drug business, Wyatt Earp was being declared a vagrant in Wichita, Kansas; Bat Masterson was at his parents' house, still recovering from the wound he received in his January gunfight; George Custer was a week away from embarking on his ill-fated march into U.S. history books, and Will Cody was touring New England with his "dramatic combination." He was also vigorously denying a widely reported story that he had recently shot and killed a Texas sheriff. "He says the blood of no white man is upon his hands," the *Chicago Tribune* noted.

On the same day in Philadelphia, meanwhile, a massive group of Americans had gathered for the most anticipated event of the year: the opening of the Centennial Exposition. The crowd, which included President Grant, was estimated at 186,272. The *New York Daily Herald* declared it was the largest assemblage of humanity ever assembled on the North American continent. Despite the size of the audience, few were moved—or even heard—the president's 436-word welcome. Grant was a poor speaker, and it was a loud crowd. Still, there were other diversions.

One was the weather. It had poured rain the night before and into the early morning. But by the beginning of the festivities at 10:15 a.m., the sky was cloudless, and the mass of umbrellas were being employed as welcome sunshades. Besides Grant's speech, there were new compositions by the Southern poet Sidney Lanier and the Northern poet John Greenleaf Whittier. There was a version of Handel's "Hallelujah Chorus." There was even a "Centennial March," performed by a 150-piece orchestra and specially composed for the occasion—for the hefty fee of $5,000 ($120,000)—by the great German composer Richard Wagner. Critics sniffed that it didn't sound very American.

Before the Expo closed six months later, almost 10 million people would travel by train, ship, wagon, horseback and on foot to the 286-acre spectacle beside the Schuylkill River. The total attendance roughly equated to 20 percent of the entire U.S. population. Buffalo Bill was said to have attended, as did Jesse James. The latter did so incognito. Over the 159 days it was open (the grounds were closed on Sundays,) it averaged about 62,000 visitors a day. By comparison, California's Disneyland drew an average of about 50,000 per day in 2019.

The scale was grand enough that someone thought to keep meticulous statistics. There were four deaths among the 6,463 people treated for medical problems. Of the 504 children reported lost, all were eventually found, although it took overnight to reunite five of them with their parents or guardians. The fire department responded to 36 blazes, none of them significant. And the Expo's police squad made 675 arrests during the six-month run, including one for "fornication."

Making the attendance numbers even more impressive was the fact that most Americans with jobs had to work 5-1/2 to 6 days a week, and had no paid vacations. That meant they had to take unpaid time off to attend. Even so, there were few complaints about the admission price of 50 cents ($12 in 2022.) "When we perceive the immense display of all that is interesting and valuable," a magazine writer opined, "the fifty cents charged for admission seems too puny...people gladly pay this fee for shows not a thousandth part in extent." Which was easy for him or her to say, since like an estimated two million other VIPs, journalists and other freeloaders, he or she most probably got in free.

Naturally not all of the attendees were Americans. Thirty-eight other countries contributed exhibits or pavilions, and foreign tourists flocked to the fair. Not all of them had a good time. "The first day, crowds come like sheep, run here, run there, run everywhere," Fuki Makoto, the Japanese commissioner to the Expo, complained to a reporter. "One man start, one thousand follow. Nobody can see anything, do anything. All rush, push, tear, shout, make plenty noise, say 'damn' great many times, get very tired and go home."

The most celebrated foreign visitor was a stout, ginger-bearded 50-year-old who sported a white hat and "a plain suit...as devoid of ornament as a freight car." As emperor of Brazil, Dom Pedro II was just the second reigning monarch to set foot in the United States. (He lost out by a year to King Kalakua of Hawaii, who in 1875 also earned the distinction of being guest of honor at the first official White House state dinner.)

Dom Pedro was immensely popular in America as well as in Brazil. He had ascended the throne at the age of 16, and would occupy it for 58 years, before being overthrown in a military coup. He had abolished slavery in Brazil in 1871, and guided the country from backwater status to South American powerhouse. Plus, he was a nice guy, and according to *Harper's Weekly*, "a close and intelligent observer...whose enlightened views of government are so well-known that popular demonstrations of respect can scarcely be avoided."

His curiosity about the United States was insatiable, from wanting to obtain all the verses of the Star-Spangled Banner so he could translate them into Portuguese, to a desire to see wild buffalo, Native Americans, and San Francisco. The emperor, a New York paper noted approvingly, "keeps right down to useful work. When he goes home, he will know more about the United States than two-thirds of the members of Congress."

Given his curious nature, Dom Pedro must have found the Exposition heavenly. It was a vast and eclectic collection of nostalgia, nature, knick-knacks and new gadgets. There was a suit of clothes and a set of false teeth that had belonged to George Washington; a gigantic grapevine from California said to produce six tons of fruit annually, and a Tiffany diamond necklace containing 27 huge diamonds from India and valued at $80,000 ($1.9 million in 2022). This was at a time when most Americans had never even seen a single diamond of any kind. There was even a rubberized cloth suitcase that could be converted into a bathtub, "to afford travelers in places where such conveniences are wanting the luxury or comfort of bodily ablutions."

One could view "Old Abe," the celebrated bald eagle mascot from a Wisconsin Civil War regiment, while he ate live chickens, or watch 6,000 silkworms from China do whatever interesting it is 6,000 silkworms do. There were 72 vintners from Germany's Rhine River Valley, and 100 samples of various Iowa farm soil in tall glass cylinders. There was even a giant bronze hand holding a giant bronze torch, a gift from the people of France.

A decade later, it would form the uppermost piece of the Statue of Liberty.

There was so much to see, an imaginative reporter calculated that if a visitor spent five minutes at each item on display, it would take 60 years to see everything. Making that task even more difficult was the fact that the Expo grounds closed at 6 p.m. each day, to reduce the danger of a fire caused by the gas lamp lighting.

To get around the sprawling grounds, there were various conveyances that included a double-decked, steam-powered monorail running 170 yards between the horticultural and agricultural halls; a mini-train that for 5 cents allowed visitors to hop on and off at various stops around the grounds, and "rolling chairs," pushed by attendants, for the extravagant fee of 50 cents ($12) an hour. The chairs allowed semi-invalid poet Walt Whitman to take in the expo.

The Expo's comestibles were almost as varied as its exhibits. Food was available at dozens of restaurants and specialty food stands. Some of the fare was familiar to 19th century American palettes: tomato soup, roast chicken, baked lobster, pork and beans and of course pickled lamb's tongue. After a meal, gentlemen could avail themselves of cigars at six different stands. Soda water was the most widely available drink, although beer and wine were grudgingly allowed after an initial ban. Ice cream parlors abounded.

But there were new edibles as well. Sugared popcorn was a big hit, especially with urban dwellers who were not nearly as familiar with any kind of popped corn as their rural counterparts. On June 5, an enterprising vendor began selling a delicious fruit unfamiliar to many urban and rural fairgoers alike, although not entirely unknown in the United States. Ten cents ($2.40) got you a banana, wrapped in tinfoil and most often consumed using a knife and fork.

The Expo was also a launching pad for several food products with which 21st century Americans are familiar. Two Hungarian-born brothers who had emigrated to Cincinnati found a way to efficiently dehydrate baker's yeast so it would last for months on the shelf and eliminate the need for bakers to obtain fresh yeast each day. Charles and Max Fleischmann exhibited their product at the Expo via a "Vienna Bakery," where an exorbitant 25 cents ($6) was charged for a cup of "Austrian Coffee." The yeast caught on, and the brothers subsequently made a lot of dough. (Sorry.)

A Philadelphia pharmacist concocted a mixture of two dozen herbs, berries and other ingredients, and added the mix to carbonated water. Charles Elmer Hires then offered free samples of his drink to fairgoers. By 1891, he was annually selling more than two million 25-cent packets of his product, which turned five gallons of plain soda water into five gallons of root beer.

And a 32-year-old Pittsburgh condiment maker, who had gone broke the year before selling horseradish and vinegar pickles, operated a small Expo booth that offered a ketchup made of tomatoes and walnuts, based on his mother's recipe. By the end of the year, Henry J. Heinz added sweet pickles to the company's product line. By the mid-1890s, Heinz would oversee the largest food products company in America.

While fairgoers were sampling new foods, America's efforts in the fine arts were for the most part not exactly feasts for the eyes. Among the efforts was "a high-relief bust of a beautiful girl," sculpted by using "only paddles, cedar sticks, broom straws and camel's hair brushes"—and made out of butter. Then there was a large and laughable plaster figure of George Washington, from the waist up, sitting atop a much smaller eagle with outstretched wings and a countenance that suggested the first president was pretty heavy. If nothing else, it was an inviting target for kids with an itch to climb on something.

But if the country's contributions to the fine arts were lacking, it only served to reemphasize the Expo's overriding lesson: On its 100th birthday, America was a nation of doers. If we didn't think deep thoughts, paint great paintings or blaze new trails in medicine or physics, we did make lots of useful things. "The superior elegance, aptness and ingenuity of our machinery is observable at a glance," noted William Dean Howells, the eminent editor, novelist and all-around man of letters. "Yes, it is still in these things of iron and steel that the national genius most speaks."

In terms of both volume and variety, Howells was understating the case. In Machinery Hall, which sprawled over 14 acres, fairgoers marveled at American-made machines that churned out everything from wallpaper and pre-gummed envelopes to roof shingles and rifled gun barrels. There was a "threading" machine that increased production of screws and bolts from 8,000 a day to 100,000. The line of different sewing machine models stretched for a half-mile.

One device that caught the fancy of Expo visitors was described by a reporter as "a small sewing machine-shaped and piano-constructed affair called the Type Writer, at which you can sit down as at a piano and Lo! out comes your letter or sermon, all printed and ready for circulation." The machine was actually just the latest iteration of a contraption that the Remington Arms Company (which was diversifying from its firearms manufacturing) had been making for three years to almost no public interest. The 1876 metal-and-porcelain model, designed by Wisconsinites Christopher Latham Sholes and Carlos Glidden, weighed 30 pounds. It featured a keyboard with the letters arranged so that the letter-bearing arms striking the paper would be less likely to jam. The arrangement, with a top row of QWERTYUIOP, is still in use.

The model had a few drawbacks. It conveyed only capital letters, required daily cleaning with an oily cloth, and cost a whopping $125 ($3,000 in 2022.) But publicity from the Exposition—fairgoers could dictate a typed letter home for 25 cents—greatly boosted sales. By the following year, more than 4,000 machines had been sold. The machine's growing popularity also had an unanticipated impact on America's workforce. Because it was believed a woman's smaller hands were better suited to typewriters than a man's, females' employability became more desirable in business offices. In 1874, women filled just 4 percent of clerical jobs. By 1900, they comprised 75 percent.

Not far away were two machines that were less entrancing to the average visitor. Both were the children of George B. Grant, a Boston mechanical engineer whom the *Chicago Tribune* described as "a quiet, unobtrusive fellow, unlike in many respects the average inventor, who is always boring you with long-winded technical descriptions of his pet invention."

One of Grant's machines, called the "Difference Engine," occupied 40 square feet, weighed more than a ton, and performed as many as 20 logarithmic functions per minute. The other device, the "Calculating Machine," was considerably smaller. It took up only 72 square inches and weighed 20 pounds. To multiply 526 by 4,932, an impressed reporter explained, "you just adjust by a touch of a finger the numerals indicated, turn a crank, and Lo! there is your result before your astonished eyes! *(Author's Note: 2,594,232. I think.)* Almost before you have time to draw a breath. And there is no mistake. The iron creature is as accurate as mathematics itself." Both inventions were important steps on the road to the pocket calculator, with which I just deduced the product of 526 times 4,932. *(I think.)*

Inventors who were far more self-promoting than George Grant were also represented.A 29-year-old Thomas Edison demonstrated his "Automatic Telegraph," in which a telegraph receiver used a metal stylus to rapidly mark paper specially treated with chemicals. The paper could then be fed through a device capable of recording up to 1,000 words per minute. That was 25 times faster than the fastest human operator could take down messages.

Edison also showed off his newly patented "Electric Pen," which used a battery to operate a metal stylus. The stylus rapidly punched holes in special paper as the user wrote in his or her normal fashion. The paper could then be used as a stencil to make duplicate copies of the document—the forerunner of the mimeograph machine. "This invention of Mr. Edison is a wonderful step forward," a Missouri paper enthused. "In any case where duplicate copies are required, it makes every man his own printer."

The pen is often cited as the first American tool to be powered by an electrical device. But despite extensive advertising by Edison, it proved to be something of a financial flop. The battery used to power it was messy and required constant maintenance, and non-battery mechanical pens proved more efficient. Edison's pen, however, did bear one interesting child. In 1891, New Yorker Samuel F. O'Reilly came up with a variation of Edison's device that greatly improved the speed and precision of injecting ink into human skin. For a while at the end of the 19th century, tattoos became fashionable among trend-following Americans, in part because O'Reilly's pen made them more arty and less painful, and in part because tattoos for some reason had become a status symbol among European royalty.

The Expo's emphasis on mechanical marvels extended from Machinery Hall to the Women's Pavilion. Initially ignored in the Exposition's planning, a 13-member female committee led by Elizabeth Duane Gillespie, a great-granddaughter of Benjamin Franklin, raised $30,000 ($720,000) to erect a building to promote the accomplishments of the country's "second class" sex. The committee then raised another $150,000 ($3.6 million) from women all over the country to stock and operate it, as well as paying for "extras" such as composer Wagner's fee.

The pavilion was, in the words of the *Sacramento Bee*, "the first attempt ever made to systematically present the entire range of women's achievement." Its exhibits featured 80 patented inventions by women, including a dishwasher, iron with removable wooden handle and bricks that interlocked without mortar. The pavilion's six-horsepower steam engine powered dozens of looms, spinning frames, and the printing press that produced an eight-page weekly magazine called *The New Century for Women*. It was operated by Emma Allison, a 29-year-old schoolteacher and copy clerk who had emigrated from Canada and who had grown up around the machinery that ran her father's mills.

Allison not only ran the steam engine, she understood its workings, much to the surprise of the male-dominated press. "The ease with which she accomplishes the management of her busy machine, the care of which has hitherto been deemed to lie essentially within man's province, marks a decided epoch in female labor," said the *Saturday Evening Post.* Other periodicals praised her with pitch-perfect condescension. "Like most of her sex, she is a good talker and is continually explaining to visitors the peculiar charms of her iron pet," one paper noted. "Her dress is neat, and she makes it a point to keep both engine and room in the perfection of tidiness."

The jaw-dropping mechanical star of the entire Expo, however, was the offspring of George Henry Corliss, an unassuming, brilliant and wealthy 59-year-old mechanical engineer from Rhode Island. Appointed by his state to serve on the Centennial Commission, Corliss used his engineering skills, and personal fortune, to create the heart of the Exposition.

The 1,400-horsepower Corliss Engine cost a staggering $100,000 ($2.4 million in 2022), and Corliss not only designed it, he footed the bill to install it. It was a monstrous contraption, several stories high, a towering steam-powered mass of pulleys, belts, cogs, wheels and bars atop a massive concrete base. Connected to various machines by shafts totaling one mile in length, the engine simultaneously provided power to print newspapers, lithographs and wallpaper; spin wool into cloth; comb seeds from cotton; saw logs; make shoes, and pump water, among other tasks. More stunning, it took just a single operator to run it.

"The first idea which comes into the mind of the spectator as he approaches the huge piece of skillful mechanism," marveled a Canadian journalist, "is that of man's utter insignificance in comparison with the product of his own constructive faculty...it is impossible to gaze at the evolutions of the gigantic flywheel without admiration for the skill which has so nicely adapted all the parts to each other that neither the noise nor the jar is sufficient to attract attention at the distance of a few yards."

The Corliss Engine purred along without serious incident throughout the Exposition. At 3:40 p.m. on the rainy afternoon of Nov. 10, President Grant ordered the mammoth machine shut down. America's first hosted world's fair ended. The *Philadelphia Times* called it "the greatest source of instruction and amusement ever afforded by an exhibition of the industries, arts and sciences of the world, and perhaps that ever will be such again."

"Whatever else may be said of the American people," pronounced the Kansas City, Missouri *Daily Journal of Commerce*, "we have achieved wonders in those arts and sciences that are directly connected with the wants of civilized life, and our progress is as steady onward as the course of the sun."

About two hours after the American president and the Brazilian emperor pushed buttons and pulled levers on the Corliss Engine to kick off the Centennial Exposition in Philadelphia on May 10, a Scottish-born college teacher walked into a venerable library building on Boston's equally venerable Beacon Street.

Alexander Graham Bell, a 29-year-old professor of vocal physiology and elocution at Boston University, was about to demonstrate his "electric speech machine" to the distinguished members of the prestigious American Academy of Arts and Sciences. He had been working on variations of the device for years. This was its most crucial test so far.

Bell briefly explained the apparatus. Then the mutton-chopped, mustachioed young inventor sent a signal to Willie Hubbard, his fiancée's brother, who was waiting in Bell's university office a few buildings away. The two locations had been connected with wires strung between them. At Bell's signal, Hubbard began playing a hymn in Bell's office. The Academy's assembly hall filled with music, and the startled audience filled with wonder.

"I feel myself borne up by a rising tide," an exultant Bell wrote his parents two days later. "...Everything was most successful, and when I sat down, I was somewhat surprised to be greeted by a hearty round of applause—which, I am informed, is such an unusual thing at the Academy."

Then again, Bell was an unusual fellow, from an unusual family. He was born in Edinburgh. His grandfather and father made themselves experts on the mechanics of the human voice. His mother was deaf, and yet became an accomplished pianist. Bell—his family called him Aleck—was a mediocre student with a knack for finding practical solutions to difficult problems. At the age of 12, for example, he devised a machine for a friend's family that efficiently removed wheat kernels from their husks.

In 1870, the Bell family moved to Canada. There, Bell studied vocal anatomy, came up with innovative ways to teach the deaf, and worked on various machines designed to enable communications using electric signals. At first, he focused on developing an "harmonic telegraph" that could send multiple messages over a single wire. But his interest eventually veered toward trying to electrically transmit the human voice.

Working with a skilled and enthusiastic electrician, Thomas A. Watson, Bell decided in February, 1876, that his machine was close enough to completion to apply for a patent. He did so within hours of a similar application by an Illinois electrical engineer, Elisha Gray. A dispute as to which of the two was first and who stole what from whom erupted, and is still being waged by fans of both men. But the patent office—and more importantly, the courts—ultimately chose Bell.

On March 7, Bell was informed his patent application had been approved. Three days later he was working in his Boston lab when he was compelled to seek his assistant's assistance."Mr. Watson," he said to an empty room, "come here, I want to see you." Watson heard the request over a receiver in the room in which he was working, and rushed to Bell's side. For the first time, a human voice had been transmitted over a telephone. "To my delight," Bell wrote in his journal, "he came and declared that he had heard and understood what I said."

Despite his success at the Academy of Arts and Sciences, Bell decided he was too busy and too broke to attend the Centennial Exposition, although he did send a model of his machine. But by early summer, Bell's fiancée, and her father had badgered Bell into going in person. (Bell's future father-in-law, Gardiner Hubbard, was also his chief financial backer.) On June 25—the same day and at almost the same time that George Custer and much of the U.S. 7th Cavalry were being wiped out 1,900 miles to the west—Bell arrived at the Centennial just in time to demonstrate his machine to an audience of about 50, as well as a panel of judges who were determining which inventions warranted special recognition. The panel included Emperor Dom Pedro and Sir William Thompson, a brilliant British mathematician.

Elisha Gray was also there with his device, but had problems getting it to operate. When it was his turn, Bell went into another room and sang into the transmitter, recited a bit of Shakespeare's *Hamlet*, then said "do you understand what I say?" A startled Sir William replied "yes, do you understand what I say?" Then he exclaimed "where is Mr. Bell? I must see Mr. Bell," and raced into the other room. The emperor then listened and, according to some of the witnesses, said with amazement "I have heard, I have heard...my God, it talks!"

"Just returned from Philadelphia," Bell informed his parents in a letter two days later, "where I met with glorious success (which included winning a gold medal.)" He also said that he and Gray had a long talk "in which we have explained away all matters in dispute...this is probably the end of the lawsuit between Gray and myself. Union of interests probably means fortune and fame to both of us. Separation of interests will lead to protracted lawsuits and the ultimate result will be that the Western Union (Telegraph Co.) can step in and buy up whatever they choose."

Bell couldn't have been more wrong. His legal fights with Gray continued. In fact, Bell, and eventually his companies, fought more than 500 legal challenges before the dust finally settled. All of the challenges were unsuccessful. Moreover, when Bell and his financial backers offered the invention to Western Union the following month, the company's officials rejected the offer and dismissed the telephone as "a useless toy."

But the press was generally intrigued by it. "The development of the telephone, or a machine for telegraphed vocalization, has been rapid and striking," a Vermont newspaper noted in November. "(Bell) and Thomas A. Watson have transmitted vocalism over a two-mile wire between Boston and Cambridge-Port; it is not, of course, assured that the same force can be operated for an unlimited distance, but it is safe to presume that it can, for the principal would seem to have no limitations."

Of all the devices displayed at the Centennial, the *New York Tribune* opined, "the telephone is a new instrument of electrical science more likely than the rest to find immediate use...it is a curious device that might fairly find place in the magic of Arabian Tales. Of what use is such an invention? Well, there may be occasion when it is necessary for officials who are far apart to talk without the interference of an (telegraph) operator. Or some lover may wish to pop the question directly into the ear of a lady and hear from herself her reply, though miles away; it is not for us to guess how courtship will be carried out in the twentieth century."

Throughout the rest of the year and into the next decade, Bell and others continued to make improvements on the telephone. Thomas Edison, for example, came up with a microphone that eliminated the need to shout into the phone to be heard. By 1886, more than 150,000 Americans had telephones in their homes and workplaces. By the time of Bell's death in 1922, there were more than 20 million telephones around the world. More than half were connected to the Bell Telephone System. And despite persistent press reports that he had come to hate his invention because of its intrusiveness in people's lives, Bell was, according to his wife, "really tremendously proud of it and all it was accomplishing."

But Bell was less proud of the greeting most people used when answering his invention. That word was "hello," which was introduced into the English language in the early 19th century and was initially used to try and command someone's attention, as in "hello, look at this over here." Bell favored "ahoy hoy." It did not catch on.

Americans weren't just making new things in 1876. They were also figuring out betterways to do things. Take Julius Wolff and the fish that doesn't really exist. Wolff was a New York-based food wholesaler, whose primary distinction prior to 1876 was having been successfully sued by the Lea & Perrins Co. for fraudulently marketing a cheap imitation of the English firm's famous Worcestershire Sauce. But what Wolff didn't know about meat condiments he did know about fish, particularly sardines.

He knew that the U.S. market was dominated by sardines from France; that French sardines were really expensive, and that they were sometimes unavailable at any price. He knew there was a hefty developing market for sardines, particularly among the flood of European immigrants arriving in America, especially if the fish were packed in oil rather than salted.

And he knew it didn't matter much what kind of "sardine" you used, since there was no such specific species. The name came from the Italian island Sardinia, which had originated the canning of little fish in the early 19th century. In fact, modern international trade law recognizes 21 different small fish that can be legally called sardines, from pilchard to herring.

So in late 1875, Wolff went to Lubec, Maine, off the coast of which were plenty of small herring. He partnered with a local fellow, Moses Lawrence, and on Feb. 17, 1876, the pair opened America's first sardine canning company. The fish sold like hotcakes. By the end of the year, Wolff and Lawrence had peddled a million cans of "American Sardines," at a hefty $12 ($288 in 2022) for a 100-can case. Even at that price, they cost about half what the French were getting for their variety. Eventually, Wolff even patented an improved "leak-proof" can that keptair out and oil in. By the end of the century, an entire industry had sprung up in New England.

While Julius Wolff was sticking little fish in tin cans, a 24-year-old graduate student in Massachusetts was revolutionizing American libraries. Melville Louis Kossuth Dewey was by common measure an odd duck. As a child, he saved his pennies and walked 10 miles to purchase a massive Webster's Unabridged Dictionary, which he then lugged home. As an adult, he earned a well-deserved reputation as a sexual predator and unabashed anti-Semite. Along the way, he became "the father of the modern library."

In 1876, American had slightly more than 3,600 libraries with at least 300 volumes in their collections. They were organized about as well as a soup sandwich. Books were numbered as they were added to the collection, and stacked in that order. Or they were shelved by size. A book on birds might be nested next to one on the Peloponnesian Wars. Dewey, who was an assistant librarian at Amherst College while working on his master's degree, had a better idea.

In March, he released a 42-page copyrighted booklet entitled *A Classification and Subject Index for Cataloguing and Arranging the Books and Pamphlets of a Library*. Dewey proposed dividing collections into nine "special libraries." Within each would be nine divisions, and within each division nine sections. Books would be catalogued by subject, and each would have a file card noting its presence within the collection. A "444" on a book's card meant it was in the fourth section of the fourth division of the fourth "special library." The Dewey Decimal System came to dominate not just American libraries, but book depositories the world over.

But Dewey wasn't done. Also in 1876, he helped establish the American Library Association, co-founded and edited the *Library Journal*, and started a company called the Library Bureau, which sold supplies and equipment to libraries around the country, as well as services such as helping to recover un-returned books. Like Albert Spalding was doing with base ball equipment, Dewey strove to standardize the way libraries operated, from vertical filing to establishing uniformly sized catalogue index cards.

In later years, Dewey became director of the New York State Library, executive officer of the State University of New York, and founder of a posh—and highly discriminatory—resort at Lake Placid in upstate New York. He also became notorious for sexually harassing female employees and colleagues. Neither odious predilection was mentioned in his obituaries when he died in 1931 at the age of 80. But in 2019, the American Library Association removed his name from one of its top leadership awards in recognition of his transgressions.

While Dewey was bringing order to the nation's libraries, a U.S. Army engineer was attempting to bring order to, well, order. Henry Martyn Robert was a West Point graduate. His estimable career saw him build fortifications at Washington D.C. and Philadelphia during the Civil War; develop and improve harbors in New York and Wisconsin, and build dams in Tennessee and Virginia. When he died in 1923, he was buried at Arlington National Cemetery with the rank of brigadier general.

But he's most remembered for building a system of civility, in the form of *The Pocket Manual of Rules of Order for Deliberative Assemblies*—better known as "Robert's Rules of Order." Robert's book sprang from an 1862 Massachusetts church meeting, over which he had been asked to preside. Failing miserably at keeping things orderly, he determined to do better next time. But he couldn't find a decent manual on parliamentary procedure, so he decided to write his own. What with building dams and dredging harbors, it took a while.

Finally, in February, 1876, Robert published a 176-page how-to on meeting procedures and collective decision-making. He had to pay for publication of the first 4,000 copies himself. But the book caught on. Through 2020, its 12 editions had sold more than six million copies, and settled countless disputes at meetings of PTAs, fraternal organizations and stamp clubs.

And while Robert was making civic events more civilized, John Wanamaker was revolutionizing retail sales. Born in Philadelphia in 1838, Wanamaker was too sickly to enlist when the Civil War began in 1861. Instead, he opened a men's clothing store with his brother-in-law. The store, called Oak Hall, prospered. After his brother-in-law died in 1868, Wanamaker opened a second store. But he wanted something bigger, grander, and unique.

In late 1875, Wanamaker plunked down $500,000 ($12 million in 2022) for the gigantic former Pennsylvania Railroad terminal at 13th and Market streets. On May 6, 1876, four days before the Centennial Exposition began, bringing millions of people to Philadelphia, Wanamaker's new store opened. The building's ornate Moroccan-style exterior caused many to think it was part of the Exposition. Inside, its 130,500 square feet caused many to, in the words of the *Philadelphia Times*, "be struck dumb with astonishment." There was a huge central counter, from which radiated 129 other counters, bulging with clothing and accessories for men and boys.

But Wanamaker's offered something more than suits, shoes and suspenders: It specialized in customer service. "When a customer enters my store," Wanamaker told his employees, "forget me. He is king...a customer has the right to some guarantee that his purchase shall prove exactly as represented."

To that end, the store offered money-back, no-questions-asked guarantees on its merchandise; dozens of sales clerks to assist customers, and most innovative of all, a price tag on each item. The tags eliminated haggling and favored-customer deals that dominated other retail stores at the time. They also greatly reduced the potential for embarrassing a customer trying to buy something he couldn't afford.

Wanamaker knew the value of publicity. He sponsored elaborate parades down Philadelphia streets. He launched hot-air balloons with the store's logo on them, and anyone who returned one received a free suit. He advertised heavily, not just in Philadelphia but in the city's adjacent environs. "Half the money I spend on advertising is wasted," he is said to have acknowledged; "the trouble is, I don't know which half." But the half that wasn't greatly wasted served to reassure his customers. "That we may permit no possible cause of dissatisfaction to remain with anyone," a typical ad read, "we agree to return the purchase money rather than have a customer feel disappointed in his bargain."

Wanamaker, who was a prominent philanthropist and civic leader—and eventually a highly controversial U.S. postmaster general under President Benjamin Harrison—took other steps to modernize his establishment. The store was the first of its kind to offer an in-house restaurant. A pneumatic tube system made moving money and paperwork more efficient. Women's clothing and electric lighting were added in 1877, a telephone system in 1878. And although there were a few big retail emporiums in large American cities before Wanamaker's, the store's opening spurred a wave of similar establishments elsewhere in the following decade, including Marshall Field's in Chicago and Macy's in New York City.

As Eli Lilly was opening his pharmaceutical empire, President Grant was opening the Centennial Exposition and John Wanamaker was opening a new kind of shopping experience, America was generally optimistic that its second century would see it prosper.

In St. Louis, meanwhile, a 39-year-old just-married man who enjoyed a nationwide celebrity but faced a highly uncertain economic future, was rather haphazardly making plans to go west, in search of a fresh start for he and his new wife. Sometime in late May or early June, James Butler Hickok, better known far and wide as "Wild Bill," headed toward Deadwood.

Chapter 6 Notes

Or at least John W. Rowell, *Yankee Artillerymen: Through the Civil War with Eli Lilly's Indiana Battery*, p. 267.

In 1876 America, *Indianapolis News*, May 10, 1876, p. 4.

"Not only in" Dee Brown, *The Year of the Century*: 1876, p. 312.

"I firmly believe," Wilson Sullivan, *New England Men of Letters*, p. 238.

But Eli Lilly E.J. Khan Jr., *All in a Century: The First 100 Years of Eli Lilly and Company*, pp. 15-35.

On the very same *Chicago Tribune*, May 12, 1876, p. 5.

Making the attendance Brown, op. cit., pp. 133-34.

Naturally not all *Harper's Weekly*, July 15, 1876, p. 579.

The most celebrated *Chicago Tribune*, May 11, 1876, p. 1.

The emperor was Lally Weymouth, *The Way We Were: America in 1876*, p. 20.

His curiosity about *New York Daily Herald*, April 21, 1876, p. 7.

One could view J.C. Furnas, *The Americans: A Social History of the United States*, p. 637.

But if the country's William Dean Howells, "A Sennight of the Centennial," *Atlantic Monthly*, July 1876, p. 96.

One device that (Montpelier) *Vermont Christian Messenger*, Oct. 26, 1876, p. 1.

In another corner *Chicago Tribune*, May 20, 1876, p. 9.

Edison also showed (Kansas City, Mo.) *Daily Journal of Commerce*, Sept. 24, 1876, p. 2.

The pavilion was Sacramento Daily Bee, Feb. 2, 1876, p. 1

Allison not only, *Saturday Evening Post*, July 8, 1876, p. 44; *Lancaster (Pa.) Intelligencer Journal*, June 13, 1876, p. 2.

The Corliss Engine *Philadelphia Times*, Nov. 11, 1876, p. 2.

"Whatever else may" (Kansas City, Mo.) *Daily Journal of Commerce*, Sept. 24, 1876, p. 2.

"I feel myself" Alexander G. Bell to A.M. Bell and E.G. Bell, May 12, 1876,

Alexander Graham Bell Family Papers Collection, Library of Congress.

On March 7 Alexander G. Bell journal entry, March 8, 1876, *Alexander Graham Bell Family Papers Collection*, Library of Congress.

"Just returned from" Alexander G. Bell to A.M. Bell and E.G. Bell, June 27, 1876, *Alexander Graham Bell Family Papers Collection*, Library of Congress.

The press was *The (Burlington) Vermont Gazette*, Nov. 3, 1876, p. 1.

Of all the *New York Tribune*, Nov. 9, 1876, p. 4.

Throughout the rest "Dr. Bell's Appreciation of the Telephone Service," *Bell Telephone Quarterly*, Vol. I, No. 3, October 1922, pp. 65-66.

Wolff was a "Historical Outline of the Canning of Fishery Products," U.S. Dept. of the Interior, Fish and Wildlife Service, 1944; *Bangor (Me.) Daily News*, July 20, 1939, p. 13; *Nashville Union and American*, May 24, 1874, p. 4.

While Julius was The best look at Dewey's life is 1996's *Irrepressible Reformer: A Biography of Melvill Dewey*, by Wayne Wiegand (no relation.)

While Dewey was "An Army Engineer Brought Order to Church Meetings and Revolutionized Parliamentary Procedure," *Historical Vignette No. 38*, U.S. Army Corps of Engineers website (USACE.Army.mil/history), Nov. 2001.

So in late *Philadelphia Times*, May 8, 1876, p. 1.

But Wanamaker's offered, John Wanamaker, *Maxims of Life & Business*, p. 36.

Wanamaker knew the *Ocean Grove (NJ) Record*, May 6, 1876, p. 8.

CHAPTER 7

"Damn you, take that!"

Wild Bill's last hand

AUGUST

Leander Pease Richardson reached Deadwood on a Sunday. He was amused, bemused, and quite possibly a bit terrified by what he saw:

> "The long street was crowded with men in every conceivable garb. Taken as a whole, I never in my life saw so many hardened and brutal-looking men together...every alternate house was a gambling saloon, and each of them was carrying on a brisk business. In the middle of the street, a little knot of men had gathered, and were holding a prayer-meeting, which showed in sharp contrast to the bustling activity of wickedness surrounding it."

Nestled in the spectacularly scenic Black Hills of what is now South Dakota, Deadwood was born in late 1875, when a fellow out hunting elk in the narrow gorge formed by Whitewood Creek found gold instead. By April, 1876, a hastily constructed town of wooden-framed, canvas-walled structures had sprung into being. Its name derived from the scraggly cadavers of trees that clung to the hills above the gorge. By July 30, the date of Richardson's arrival, an impromptu census had found the town was home to 27 saloons, 21 groceries, 14 gambling houses, 11 haberdashers, five peanut-roasting companies and one soda-water plant, all serving a population of well over 5,000. Brothels were not listed as a separate category.

"The streets present a lively, bustling appearance day and night," a visiting St. Louis reporter wrote, "and gambling halls, dance-houses, bagnios, bar-rooms and dens and dives of every description are in full blast, and are well-patronized." "We have also a large number of very bad, hard characters among us who openly commit murder without provocation," a young Montanan wrote to the folks back home. "Neither law nor order prevails; we have no organized system to punish criminals ...".

Richardson had been born about 20 years before Deadwood sprang into being. He was an energetic and ambitious young journalist, who had finagled an assignment from the *Springfield (Ma.) Republican* to cover one of the biggest news events of 1876—the Black Hills Gold Rush. The stampede to the sacred lands of the Lakota people, Richardson later wrote, was "the subject of more newspaper discussion than any other discovery in America, if we except the excitement of 1849 over California."

Better yet, he had finagled a way to meet up with one of Deadwood's more colorful citizens—and that was saying something. The citizen in question was a short, thick-set 34-year-old fellow with "long hair which falls to his shoulders, a mustache and goatee, strong features (and) a mild, pleasant eye." Charles H. Utter, much more familiarly known in the region as "Colorado Charlie," had come to Deadwood to mine the miners. With his brother Steve, Charlie planned to operate a Pony Express-type mail delivery service, as well as a freight line.

Besides being a noted guide and hunter, Charlie Utter was well-known in Deadwood for two other things. The first was his peculiar habit of bathing on a daily basis. According to Richardson—who had a letter of introduction from Steve Utter to Charlie and was thus invited to share Utter's camp—the dapper and diminutive Colorado Charlie's bathing ritual was often observed by curious spectators "with interest not wholly unmixed with wonder." Consistent with his keen sense of personal hygiene, Utter's tent was also immaculately kept, and woe to anyone who dared to cross its threshold. That included Utter's "pardner," who was the other reason Charlie was regarded with both interest and respect. His partner was James Butler Hickok, better known as "Wild Bill." The young reporter Richardson was in awe:

> "Of course I had heard of him, the greatest scout in the West, but I was not prepared to find such a man as he

> proved to be. Most of the Western scouts do not amount to much...In 'Wild Bill,' I found a man who talked little and had done a good deal...his voice was low and musical, but through its hesitation I could catch a ring of self-reliance and consciousness of strength. Yet he was the most courteous man I had met on the Plains."

Wild Bill was also a troubled man. Like an aging sports star facing the day when the skills of youth could no longer be counted on, Hickok was seeking to transition from a reflex-reliant gunfighter to a financially comfortable gentleman of leisure. At the age of 39, he had recently married Agnes Lake, a former circus star. The bride had remained at her home in Cincinnati, with the intention to settle with Hickok in the West as soon as he had made some money.

Just how he planned to do that is uncertain. In a letter to his new wife shortly after he arrived in Deadwood, Hickok wrote he was well, "but you would laugh to see me now—just got in from prospecting. Will go away (again) tomorrow...I am almost sure I will do well here." It's doubtful, however, that he did much looking for gold outside of Deadwood's saloons and gambling joints, which he visited with regularity. He played poker with avidity, but not much skill. According to Richardson, Wild Bill "could not have cheated a blind baby. Almost every day his partner (Utter) used to 'stake' him to card money. If he ever won, nobody knew it."

It's just as well his new wife wasn't in Deadwood, since Hickok's living quarters at the time were not exactly conducive to domestic bliss. While Utter had his tidy tent, Wild Bill slept in the back of a canvas-covered wagon, often without bothering to undress. "Utter usually did the cooking," Richardson wrote, "while Bill sat around and smoked, and indulged with his partner in that kind of repartee which abounds in the frontier and consists chiefly of bold and ingenious profanity." At night, Hickok told stories about things he had seen in the East. Richardson prudently agreed with his descriptions: "They were great stories Wild Bill told, and as his other hearers knew nothing about them, and I didn't contradict him, he had a very fair margin for the play of his imagination."

But Hickok's musings apparently also included an unshakeable sense of imminent doom. "Charlie," he reportedly told Utter while they were riding into the gorge one day, "I feel this is going to be my last camp, and I won't leave it alive." In another letter to his wife, Hickok wrote "Agnes darling: If such should be we never meet again, while firing my last shot, I will gently breathe the name of my wife—Agnes—and with wishes even for my enemies I will make the plunge and try to swim to the other shore."

The letter was dated August 1, 1876. Sometime on the afternoon of August 2, Wild Bill tidied himself up and strolled toward Nutall & Mann's No. 10 Saloon, a favorite haunt. He had it in mind to have a few drinks, and maybe play a little poker.

The precise origin of James Butler Hickok's nickname is a mystery. There are several theories. One is that for some reason, his older brother Lorenzo became known as "Bill Barnes," and because of his even temperament, picked up the nickname "Mild Bill." As the more excitable younger brother, James Hickok became "Wild Bill." It's possible, but pretty lame as Wild West legends go. Another is that "Bill Barnes" was an alias Hickok used while serving as a Union Army spy, and "Wild Bill" was bestowed on him for his adventures during the Civil War. Yet another is that it was a derivation of "Duck Bill," which was a derogatory reference to his prominent nose and thin lips. Other nicknames included "Dutch Bill" and "Shanghai Bill."

More plausible—and certainly more heroic—is the story that Hickok himself told. At the age of 26, he said, he came to the rescue of a bartender in Independence, Missouri, who was being threatened by a rope-bearing mob of angry teamsters. Hickok reportedly yanked out two pistols, fired two shots in the air, and told the crowd to disperse, "or there will be more dead men around here than the town can bury." A woman cheered out "Ain't he wild! and/or "Good for you, Wild Bill!". The crowd cleared out, according to the story, and the *nom de pistol* stuck.

Whatever its origin, "Wild Bill" was not a particularly good fit for James Butler Hickok. True, he seemed to be a magnet for violence, from at least a half-dozen authenticated gunfights to a possibly apocryphal Bowie knife battle with an enraged bear. But if he invariably attracted trouble, he rarely sought it. "He was a man with a whole world of nerve and one of the kindest, best-hearted fellows on earth," recalled William F. Cody, a Hickok protégé—and briefly his employer. "He seemed to be unfortunate in getting into scrapes, but he always 'got' his man when he went for him." George Custer, who met Hickok when the latter was an Army scout in Kansas, declared that while Hickok was a deadly shot and unquestionably brave, his character was "entirely free from any bluster or bravado."

Or at least it was free of "bluster and bravado" by Custer's standards. It's true Hickok was sometimes described as being quiet and introspective by those who knew and liked him, and moody and arrogant by those who didn't. And while Cody reveled in being on stage performing in overwrought "Westerns," Hickok hated it, even when the money was good.

But acting aversion aside, James B. Hickok was still egotistical enough to enjoy being "Wild Bill." His deserved reputation as a dangerous man earned him the adulation of young boys, the sometimes-grudging respect of their uncles and fathers, and the admiration of their aunts, mothers and big sisters. He basked in the attention he received while hanging around various Kansas train stations. "He is a picture, the most striking object in camp," one traveler noted. As fascinating as Hickok's takes were, the tourist added, "we do not, however, feel under any obligation to believe them all." Hickok himself once acknowledged "I'm sort of public property," and he both looked and dressed the part.

"He was about six feet one in height," Custer wrote, "broad shoulders, well-formed chest and limbs, and a face strikingly handsome; a sharp clear blue eye, which stared you straight in the eye when in conversation; a finely shaped nose, inclined to be aquiline; a well-turned mouth, with lips only partially concealed by a handsome mustache." Custer described Hickok's hair—"worn in uncut ringlets falling carelessly over his powerfully formed shoulders"—as blonde, while others termed it black, brown, auburn and/or chestnut. It was most probably light brown.

"Whether on foot or on horseback," the notoriously vain Custer acknowledged, Hickok "was one of the most perfect types of physical manhood I ever saw." Mrs. Custer thought so too. "Physically, he was a delight to look upon," she recalled. "Tall, lithe and free in every motion, he rode and walked as if every muscle was perfection."

While not nearly as fastidious as his pal Colorado Charlie Utter, Wild Bill was generally well-groomed, and often strikingly clothed. "His attire was generally that of the Mississippi steamboat gambler," an associate wrote: "A long-tailed cutaway coat of dark cloth; wide blue trousers; high-heeled boots...a leather belt with two white-handled 'cap-and-ball' Colts; a white shirt and string tie ...". In Deadwood, the journalist Richardson reported Hickok's attire "was a curiously blended union of the habiliments of the border man and the drapery of the fashionable dandy," and included an "elaborately embroidered buckskin coat."

As befitting a gunfighter, Hickok quite literally dressed to kill. In addition to a pair of ivory-handled Colt's Navy pistols that he carried handle butt-first in his belt (or sometimes tucked in a scarlet sash), Wild Bill was also said to have routinely carried two .41 caliber single-shot Derringers on his person, a backup handgun in his coat and often a seriously large knife. Carrying his revolvers with the back of the handles facing forward allowed him to "cross draw," his right hand yanking the gun on his left hip, and vice versa. Unlike many pistoleers, he cocked the pistols as he drew them, and by the time they were leveled at his waist, they were ready to fire. Less than a second later, his opponent was wondering where the extra hole in his head or stomach had come from.

Being quick was only one element in Hickok's success at shooting people. Perhaps more important was the willingness to pull the trigger in the first place. He told a friend "I hope you never have to shoot any man, but if you do, shoot him in the guts near the navel. You may not make a fatal shot, but he will get a shock that will paralyze his brain and arm so much the fight is over."

That advice assumed the ability to hit what one aimed at, and Hickok's reported ability to do that bordered on the supernatural. Along the feats witnesses swore to have seen Wild Bill accomplish were drawing and placing six shots into a target the size of a human heart from 50 yards away; hitting a dime, placed on edge, at 20 paces; simultaneously firing pistols with both hands and hitting fence posts 16 feet apart, and making a tin can skip along the ground by shooting it until his two guns were empty. After seeing the latter feat, a witness wrote "I am prepared to believe any story of his skill or prowess that does not conflict with the laws of gravitation and physics."

As exaggerated as many of his accuracy exploits undoubtedly were, so too were tabulations of Wild Bill's victims—and not all of it was due to reporters or dime novelists. Hickok hugely enjoyed pulling journalistic legs. He told one gullible scribe that as a Union Army sniper, he once shot 50 enemy soldiers with 50 bullets during a single battle. In his book *My Early Travels and Adventures,* the journalist Henry M. Stanley said he asked Hickok in 1866 how many men he had killed. "I suppose I have killed considerably over 100," Hickok replied, adding that his first victim fell when Wild Bill was 28. Had Stanley paused to do a little math, he would have realized Hickok would have had to average about one killing every three days for a year, since he was only 29 at the time of the interview.

Wild Bill's sense of humor could also range to the self-deprecating. Surrounded by an admiring crowd around a campfire or in a saloon, he would describe a hopelessly desperate situation he had once found himself in, then pause for effect. When one of his listeners would breathlessly ask "then what happened, Bill?" Hickok would reply, "Why, by God boys, they killed me!"

But such levity didn't imply Hickok was cavalier about killing—or dying. In the summer of 1875, Annie D. Tallant, the first white woman known to have visited the Black Hills of Dakota, was walking down a Cheyenne, Wyoming, street when she encountered a tall, handsome man with long wavy hair. The stranger said he understood that Tallant had visited the Black Hills, and wondered if he might ask her a few questions about the region.

"'My name is Hickok,'" Tallant wrote in her journal. "'I am called Wild Bill,' he continued, 'and you may have no doubt heard of me. Although,' he added, 'you have heard no good of me.' 'Yes,' I candidly acknowledged, 'I have often heard of Wild Bill, and his reputation is not at all creditable to him. 'But,' I hastened to add, 'perhaps he is not so black as painted.' 'Well, as to that,' he replied, 'I suppose I am called a red-blooded murderer, which I deny. That I have killed men, I admit, but never unless in self-defense or in the performance of an official duty. I never, in my life, took any mean advantage of an enemy. Yet, understand, I never allow a man to get the drop on me. But I may yet die with my boots on,' he said, his face softening a little....After making a few queries relative to the Black Hills, which were politely answered, Wild Bill, with a gracious bow that would have done credit to a Chesterfield, passed on down the street out of sight...".

Whatever his nickname's origin, James Butler Hickok himself originated in Homer (now Troy Grove), Illinois, a small town about 100 miles southwest of Chicago, on May 27, 1837. "Jim," as the family called him, was the fourth of four sons born to William Alonzo and Polly Butler Hickok. Two daughters would follow. William Hickok had opened the town's first store prior to James' birth, but lost it in a serious financial panic that hit the country in 1837. To feed his family, William was forced into farming.

William Hickok was deeply religious, and also deeply opposed to slavery. The Hickok farm became a station on the Underground Railroad, which helped escaped slaves reach free states or Canada. But when the elder Hickok died in 1852, the family sold the farm and moved back into town. The Hickok boys found various jobs to support their mother and sisters. Jim worked briefly for a canal company, but left after a disagreement with the boss. The boss had mistreated some horses, and Hickok had mistreated the boss, by throwing him in the canal.

In 1856, Jim and his older brother Lorenzo ventured west, to the violence-torn territory of Kansas. There Jim became associated with a "Free State" militia group, was elected for a term as constable of the tiny village of Monticello, and did some farming. But none of it suited him, and he found himself too restless to settle. So in 1858, he took a job with the mammoth Russell, Majors and Waddell transportation company, driving freight wagons and stagecoaches as far west as Santa Fe, New Mexico.

He "was taciturn, even at that age," recalled Truman Blanchett, whose father ran a Colorado stage station at which Hickok stopped each week. "He talked little of himself or others...anyone who wanted to make the acquaintance of Hickok would mind their business and not get too inquisitive (and eventually) would find him a perfect gentleman in every way. In those days, he was not known as 'Wild Bill.'"

It was during this time that Hickok also met a boy who would come to emulate him, and help make both of them iconic symbols—or stereotypes—of the Wild West hero. In his autobiography, Will Cody insisted that he first met Hickok when Will was a 12-year-old employee of a Russell/Majors/Waddell wagon train. According to Cody, Hickok intervened when a bullying teamster threatened to beat the youngster. "'...If you ever again lay a hand on that boy—little Billy there—I'll give you such a pounding that you won't get over it in a month of Sundays,'" Cody quoted Hickok. He added "from that time forward, Wild Bill was my protector and friend and the friendship thus continued until his death."

Whether this happened is problematic, since it's doubtful both Bills were on the same wagon train at the same time. But it is a fact that Hickok knew the Cody family as early as 1857, and even spent the winter of 1859-60 at the Cody home/hotel near Leavenworth, Kansas. It's also a fact that Will Cody was heavily influenced by Hickok, who was 10 years his senior. "Buffalo Bill" would not only adopt "Wild Bill's" hair style and dress, but also appropriate some of Hickok's real-life experiences as the basis for scenes in Cody's stage performances and Wild West shows. "Of all the figures who formed William Cody's ambition to fulfill (or seem to fulfill) popular frontier fantasies," wrote Louis S. Warren, Cody's most thoughtful biographer, "none was greater than Hickok."

Not all of Hickok's "experiences" adapted for the stage were necessarily factual. One such story purportedly occurred in late 1860, when he was driving a freight wagon along a Rocky Mountain trail and encountered a cinnamon bear (a subspecies of black bear) and her two cubs. Hickok is said to have dismounted the wagon and waved his arms, expecting the bear to flee. She didn't. He then shot her—twice—which served only to make the bear angry. She charged, and before he could kill the bear with his Bowie knife, she had badly torn his left shoulder, crushed his left arm and left deep lacerations in his chest and left cheek. A teamster trailing behind Hickok found him and got him to a doctor just in time.

Several of Hickok's biographers doubt the story. But he was somehow sufficiently injured at the beginning of 1861 that the company took him off the road as a driver and assigned him in March to a freight and stage station at Rock Creek, in southeastern Nebraska. Before he left in July, Hickok would shoot three men, killing one of them, and be "credited" with killing 10 men single-handed in a battle that would assume mythical status in 19th century America's imagination.

What really happened is buried in umpteen layers of interpretation, speculation and fabrication. Stripped to probables and plausibles: Hickok was working as a station handyman for Horace Wellman, who ran the station for the Russell, Majors and Waddell company. The firm had purchased the station from Dave McCanles, a local landowner with a reputation as an enormously strong and loutish bully. When the company was slow to pay the mortgage, McCanles visited the station on July 12, 1861, with two other men and his 12-year-old son.

Heated words were exchanged, including a few between McCanles and Hickok. At some point McCanles made a movement with the shotgun he was carrying, whereupon Hickok shot him through the heart with a pistol. When the two men with McCanles rushed to the scene, Hickok shot them both, though not fatally. They were finished off by the station manager's wife and two other hired hands.

Hickok and the two other station workers were arrested and a preliminary hearing was held, at which they pleaded self-defense. A judge listened to the testimony of various witnesses—but for some strange reason not McCanles' son, who had seen the whole thing and swore his father was unarmed—and the defendants were acquitted. The "McCanles Massacre" would become the foundation for the legend of Wild Bill Hickok, but first America had to fight the Civil War.

Hickok's precise role in the war is a bit murky. Joseph G. Rosa, Wild Bill's most tireless and respected, if somewhat hagiographic, biographer, made exhaustive searches of Union Army records. Boiled down, Hickok served for almost the entire conflict, beginning in late July, 1861. He was definitely a scout, wagon master and military policeman; possibly a sniper during at least one battle, and probably a Union spy who operated for lengthy periods behind enemy lines. The war ended in April, 1865, and Hickok was officially mustered out on June 10 in Springfield, Missouri. Eleven days later, he took part in a gunfight that became the model for thousands of gunfights that would occur in fiction, and almost none—besides Hickok's—in fact.

Dave Tutt had Bill Hickok's pocket watch, and Bill Hickok wanted it back. Even without the dispute over the watch, there was bad blood between the two. Tutt had fought for the Confederacy, Hickok for the Union. There may also have been friction regarding Tutt taking up with Hickok's ex-girlfriend, or Hickok trifling with Tutt's sister. Or both, or neither, it isn't clear. What is clear is that about 6 p.m. on July 21, 1865, the *Missouri Weekly Patriot* reported, "David Tutt, of Yellville, Ark., was shot in the public square...by James B. Hickok, better known in Southwest Missouri as 'Wild Bill.' The difficulty occurred from a game of cards."

More specifically, Tutt claimed Hickok owed him $35, and grabbed a watch off the table as collateral. Wild Bill let it go at the time, out of deference to the owner of the hotel where the card game was taking place. But he warned Tutt not to wear the watch in public. Tutt, who was regarded as a tough egg and who was usually accompanied by a cadre of pals to back him up, ignored the warning. He appeared on the town square the following evening, sporting the time piece. Hickok spotted him and advised him not to cross the square with the watch. Tutt pulled a pistol and fired at Wild Bill. He missed; Hickok didn't. From a distance generally accepted at about 75 yards, Hickok put a bullet through Tutt's heart. In the next instant, he whirled on Tutt's associates and asked if any of them wanted to try their luck. None did.

For 21st century viewers of countless movie and television "high-noon-in-the-street," "draw, pardner," gunfights, the Hickok-Tutt shootout might seem pretty ho-hum. But in reality, it was as rare as a truthful infomercial. Most 19th century gunfights involved one or more drunks shooting at each other from a few feet away. Often, one of the men wasn't even armed, or had no idea someone was about to shoot at him. The fatal wound frequently came in the back. The Hickok-Tutt duel, face to face in the town's main square, in front of witnesses from all social strata, became Hollywood's archetypal setting for the ultimate confrontation between frontier good and evil.

By the way, Hickok was charged with manslaughter. All the witnesses testified that Tutt had shot first. But the judge instructed the jury that under Missouri law, Wild Bill could not claim self-defense if he was clearly willing to fight the deceased and did not try to avoid it. After brief deliberation, jurors acquitted him anyway. Wild Bill's cool nerve and uncanny accuracy, coupled with his striking appearance and catchy nickname, made him an irresistible subject for a Boston journalist who visited Springfield about a month after the trial. The journalist, in turn, made Wild Bill Hickok an American legend.

George Ward Nichols was a newspaper writer-turned-Army officer, still on active duty when he arrived in Springfield in September 1865.

While there, Nichols gathered material for what would become a cover story in *Harper's New Monthly Magazine*, entitled simply "Wild Bill." The title was the only simple element of the story. It took up 12 pages and included nine illustrations. Among these was a splendid line drawing on the magazine cover of a dashing Hickok, butt-first holstered pistol perched on his hip; a picture of Bill's horse "Black Nell," kneeling on a billiard table where Hickok had supposedly ordered her with a simple whistle, and re-creation of the 1861 fight at Rock Creek Station with Dave McCanles. This last picture depicted Hickok fighting three men simultaneously while three others lay dead or dying at his feet. Apparently, the artist couldn't find enough room for all 10 of the men Wild Bill reportedly killed in the fight.

"...You would not believe that you were looking into the eyes that have pointed the way to death for hundreds of men," Nichols breathlessly recounted about his meeting with Hickok. "Yes, Wild Bill with his own hands has killed hundreds of men. Of this I have no doubt."

Nichols' incompetence as a journalist matched his imagination—he managed throughout the piece to misspell his subject's name as "Hitchcock." But *Harper's* was no sensationalistic tabloid or cheesy barber shop magazine. It was a widely circulated national periodical, with a "respectable" readership of middle- and upper-class citizens. When the story was printed in February, 1867, Wild Bill became a national, and somewhat credible, celebrity.

Newspapers all over the country printed excerpts of the *Harper's* piece. The *New York Tribune* said, probably with tongue only partially in cheek, that the story referenced a man with the prowess of "the legends of Samson and Hercules combined...the deeds of Wild Bill are equaled only by the accomplishments of his miraculous horse, and the whole narrative affords a rich illustration of the romance of border life." By July, 1867, the publisher of Dewitt's Ten Cent Romances had churned out *Wild Bill, Indian Slayer*, followed in December by *Wild Bill's First Trail*. The real Wild Bill, meanwhile, was busy trying to add some veracity to the fiction writers' improbabilities.

In the six years following his gunfight with Dave Tutt, Wild Bill Hickok served as a U.S. deputy marshal; fought Indians as a cavalry scout, and was top lawman in two tough Kansas towns. He also killed at least five people, four of them on purpose. As a U.S. deputy marshal in central Kansas, Hickok's duties were mostly routine: tracking down Army deserters; chasing thieves who filched horses and mules from military posts, transporting prisoners from one jurisdiction to another.

His adventures as a scout for the 5th and 7th cavalries were considerably more exciting. In the winter of 1867-68, Hickok was part of an advance party of troops trapped for weeks by a blizzard. Starving and frostbitten, they were rescued by troops guided by none other than Hickok's pal, Buffalo Bill Cody. A year later, Hickok was alone, delivering messages to a fort, when he got into a running battle with several Cheyenne warriors. One of them got close enough to stick a lance into Hickok's leg. He was found the next day, afoot and limping to the fort using the lance as a crutch.

But it was as a Kansas lawman that Wild Bill attained mythic status. Hickok was a cautious lawman. He was well aware there was a target on his back for Texas cowboys who chafed at his occasional crackdowns on their fun, as well as the saloon keepers, pimps and gamblers who profited from the cowboys, and would-be shootists trying to make names for themselves as the man who killed Wild Bill. He walked down the middle of streets, avoiding dark alleys and sidewalks where he could be ambushed. His bedroom floor was covered with newspapers, to better detect footsteps in the night. He even poured his whisky with his left hand, to keep his right hand ready.

As sheriff of Ellis County for about five months in 1869, Hickok killed two men in separate incidents. The first involved Bill Mulvey, a revolver-wielding drunk in a Hays City saloon, who was reportedly threatening people, including Hickok. The second involved Sam Strawhun, another drunk in a Hays saloon, who reportedly threatened to bash Hickok in the face with a beer glass. "...Too much credit cannot be given to Wild Bill for his endeavors to rid the town of such desperate characters," a witness to the latter event told the newspapers.

Ellis County voters, however, were not overly grateful. In November, 1869, they elected one of Hickok's deputies as their new sheriff. Politics being politics, Wild Bill was known to have Republican leanings, and Ellis County was firmly Democrat. Hickok was not a sore loser, because he stuck around into the summer of 1870—or until his next gunfight.

On July 17, 1870, private citizen Bill Hickok was chatting with the bartender in a Hays saloon when Jeremiah Lonergan and John Kile, two members of the 7th Cavalry stationed at nearby Fort Hays, began giving him a hard time. The most accepted version of what occurred is that Lonergan grabbed Hickok from behind, pinning his arms back while wrestling him to the floor. Kile then pulled a pistol, put it to Hickok's ear, and pulled the trigger.

But the gun misfired. Wrenching one of his arms free, Hickok pulled one of his own pistols and shot Kile twice, once in the wrist and once in the side. He also put a bullet through one of Lonergan's knees. Getting to his feet, Wild Bill surveyed the barroom, which was full of other soldiers, and decided to skedaddle. He crashed through a window in the rear of the saloon, went to his hotel room, grabbed a rifle and a box of cartridges, and headed for the Hays cemetery. There he figured to make his last stand against the fallen soldiers' angry pals. (Kile died; Lonergan recovered long enough to get killed in another bar fight a few months later.) But no one found Wild Bill—or probably even looked hard for him—and he left town on a train the next morning.

In the spring of 1871, Hickok was offered the marshal's job in Abilene, which had become the first of the major Kansas cowtowns. While still careful to watch for ambush, however, Hickok was apparently in no danger of working too hard at the job. Critics complained he spent an inordinate amount of his time playing poker at the Alamo Saloon, Abilene's swankiest establishment. Town ordinances regarding carrying guns, gambling and prostitution were only sporadically enforced. But when he did act, people sometimes died.

Once again, he was a lawman for about half a year, and once again, he killed two men. One was Phil Coe, a saloon owner with whom Hickok had a personal feud as well as a legal one. Coe got off two shots at Hickok from eight feet away, and missed both times. Wild Bill got off two shots at Coe, and missed neither. But he also fired twice at someone who ran up during the gunfight. The someone turned out to be Mike Williams, a friend of Wild Bill's, who had hastened to assist Hickok in the gunfight with the bar owner. Hickok whirled and shot his friend before he realized who it was. He was Wild Bill's last victim.

In December, the Abilene city council decided it no longer needed Hickok's services, and fired him. The legendary man-killer needed a job, and eventually chose one that did not suit him at all.

"Bucking the Tiger"

If there was a single profession that captured the essence of 1876 America, it was gambling. The men and women who made their living from games of chance more often than not had the conscience of a congressman, the rapacity of a railroad tycoon and the inventiveness of an Edison. "They are to the rest (of humanity) what the man-eating shark is to the dog shark," the *Chicago Tribune* said of professional gamblers. They "are tireless in pursuit of their victim; merciless in their treatment of the unfortunate ones who fall into their clutches, infernally cunning in their wicked practices...cold, selfish, cruel."

They were also rather lazy. A member of the profession readily confessed that most of his colleagues were "probably raised without being accustomed to manual labor, (and) many of them cannot screw their courage up to the idea of performing hard work at so much a day." This may have been particularly true in the Wild West, where gambling was one of the least physically taxing, and potentially most lucrative, occupations available.

Storied figures who are celebrated in history as gunfighters and lawmen—Bat Masterson, Wyatt Earp, Wild Bill Hickok, Doc Holliday, Ben Thompson, Luke Short—spent far more time gambling than they ever did shooting it out in the streets at high noon, or tracking down desperadoes after a bank job. In fact, all of the aforementioned at one time or other owned part or all of gambling joints in Kansas, Colorado, Texas, Arizona, California and even Alaska.

But while movies and television shows have most often portrayed the denizens of the cowtowns and mining camps as seated around poker tables when they depict frontier gambling, the real king of the casino was a game that probably originated in France in the early 18th century. It was called faro, an Americanization of the French word "pharaon," which translated to "pharaoh" and arose from the depictions of ancient Egyptian potentates on the backs of a popular brand of French playing cards. A popular motif on the backs of American playing cards was a Bengal tiger, so "bucking the tiger" or "twisting the tiger's tail" became a common expression to describe faro playing, and pictures of tigers outside a building signaled there was a game inside.

It was very simple in concept. "The beauty of the game," a pro gambler explained, "is that you don't have to learn it—anybody can play it." Painted images of all 13 cards in a suit—it didn't matter which, although spades were the most popular—were displayed on a table. Players put their cash or "checks" (the preferred 19th century term for chips) on one of the images. The dealer then discarded the top card in a deck, and dealt two cards. The first card was a "loser," the second a "winner."

For example, if a player had bet on the king and any king (remember, suits didn't matter) was dealt first, he lost. If a king was dealt second, he won. If a king wasn't dealt at all, the player could remove his bet, let it stand, add to it or move it to another card. If two kings were dealt, the dealer took half the bet. A player could also choose to bet with the dealer, and bet on multiple cards. When there were only three cards left to be dealt, players could bet on which order they would appear. Here is where the house had an edge, since there were six different ways the three cards could appear, and the house usually only paid 3-to-1 or 4-to-1 on the bet.

As the game evolved, betting variations were added. But the basics remained the same, and faro offered a variety of advantages over other games. Unlike poker, it could be played by many bettors at once. It moved quickly, which allowed more betting. There was the thrill of winning on the turn of a single card. And if dealt honestly, the odds only slightly favored the house. It was therefore seldom dealt honestly.

After sleight-of-hand operators made dealing by hand highly unpopular with bettors, boxes were used to dispense the cards. But these were often rigged as well. “It is a notable fact that most all of these devices... are constructed on simple principles,” a reporter marveled. “In fact, like Edison’s phonograph, they are so simple that the wonder is they escape detection.” The swindling occurred on both sides of the table. One popular method for players was to attach an almost-invisible horsehair to a check or coin, then slide it off the table if the right card didn’t turn up. Cheating was so widespread that editions of *Hoyle’s Rules for Card Playing* in the early 1880s carried warnings that there were probably no honest faro games to be found in America.

Naturally all this chicanery was a dangerous proposition in a setting where many of the occupants carried firearms. To avoid having direct responsibility, many saloons and gambling halls rented space to independent faro operators, who paid the house a percentage of their take, and decided for themselves how much cheating they wanted to risk. This proved to be a sound arrangement for the owner of a Cheyenne, Wyoming joint in 1874, when a fellow wearing tinted spectacles and his hat pulled tight to his head grew irate at a duplicitous faro dealer who was running an independent game.

The player bashed the dealer over the head with his walking stick, stuffed fistfuls of money and checks into his pockets, toppled the table, drew two revolvers from his waist and invited anyone with objections to step forward. No one objected, seeing as it was Wild Bill Hickok sporting the glasses, with his tell-tale long brown hair tucked under his hat. The next day, the story goes, Bill had cooled off. To make amends, he returned to the saloon and split his "winnings" with the casino owner and the town marshal.

By the turn of the 20th century, faro had fallen out of favor, mostly because the game's operators couldn't reliably win without cheating, and Americans eventually got tired of being cheated. It's reckoned the last casino-run faro game closed down in Las Vegas in 1985.

It was a matter of money. Wild Bill needed some. Buffalo Bill had some—or at least a way to get it, by performing "Frontier" melodramas before Eastern audiences.

Will Cody and his stage partner, Texas Jack Omohundro, were in their second season "treading the boards" in 1873. They had parted company with writer/impresario Ned Buntline, and wanted a big audience magnet to replace him. Thanks to the *Harper's* article and his subsequent adventures, Wild Bill Hickok fit the bill nicely. But, as Cody noted in an 1888 memoir, Hickok needed coaxing. "Bill did not think well of our enterprise," Cody wrote, "on account of our unfamiliarity with the stage, but a large salary forced him to forgo his diffidence before the public."

Since leaving Abilene, Hickok had kicked around at various enterprises, mostly gambling. It was a profession where his skills were at best mediocre. In late August, 1872, he did appear as master of ceremonies for a "Grand Buffalo Hunt" at a fairground near Niagara Falls. This "spectacle," conceived by Sidney Barnett, a Buffalo (New York) museum owner, consisted of some Mexican vaqueros lassoing three lethargic bison, who were then released so about 50 Sac and Fox Indians could shoot at them with blunt tipped arrows. The "hunt" was a financial flop and Wild Bill returned to Missouri with a bad taste in his mouth for show biz and not much in his wallet.

It's unknown how large a salary Cody promised him, but Hickok did show up at a Brunswick, New Jersey theater on Sept. 8, 1873, to perform some shooting tricks, while Texas Jack showed off his skills with a rope and Buffalo Bill did a little of a lot of things. Then the combination began a tour of *The Scouts of the Plains*, which featured as villains two characters named "Dave Tutt," and "Jake McKandlass," names identical or very similar to real-life men whom Hickok had fought and killed.

Unlike Cody and Omohundro, Hickok could never overcome his stage fright, or distaste for play-acting. Wild Bill "possessed a good strong voice," Cody wrote, "yet when he went upon the stage before an audience, it was almost impossible for him to utter a word." Of course, it could have had something to do with having to say lines like "Fear not, fair maid! You are safe with Wild Bill, who is ever ready to risk his life and die, if need be, in defense of weak and defenseless womanhood!"

Because of his inability, or unwillingness, to deliver his lines with any enthusiasm, Hickok's speaking part was minimized. Bored, he sometimes amused himself by shooting his blanks near the legs of the "extras" playing Indians as they lay "dead" on the stage, thus making them yelp with painful powder burns. On one occasion, the scene called for the scouts to sit around a campfire, swapping tales while passing what was supposed to be a jug of whisky. Hickok took a swig—and promptly spit it out. "Cold tea don't count," he growled. "Either I get real whisky or I ain't telling no story." The audience howled with laughter. Cody choked down his ire, sent for some real liquor, and the show went on.

"The public uproar over him (Hickok) could not take seriously," recalled John Burke, Cody's longtime publicist. "It annoyed him. It made him tired. He couldn't endure it. The business seemed to him preposterous...with his good looks, striking figure and excellent speaking voice, he would have made a fine actor; but the fact is hated the business with a deep abomination."

Hickok stuck it out through March, 1874. Then, during a performance in Will Cody's "hometown" of Rochester, New York, Wild Bill walked out. When Cody came off stage, a stagehand told him "that long-haired gentleman who passed out of here a few minutes ago requested me to tell you that you could go to thunder with your old show."

Actually, the parting of the ways was mutual. Cody had had enough of Wild Bill's antics. He and Texas Jack graciously gave Hickok a $1,000 bonus (about $24,000 in 2022), as well as a handsome pistol. For his part, Hickok bowed out without criticizing his fellow scouts, or the theatrical life. The day after leaving the show, he told a Rochester reporter he had been called back to the West to scout for the Army.

In truth Wild Bill wasn't sure what to do. He is reported to have taken another show biz job with a New York City company performing *Daniel Boone*, but quit after one show. On his way back to Missouri, he happened to be passing through Scranton, Pennsylvania, when he was surprised to see his name still on the company's playbill. Enraged, he entered the theater and watched the imposter Hickok for a few minutes. Then he reportedly went on stage; beat the snot out of the imposter; was arrested; paid a $5 fine in the morning, and headed west.

James Butler Hickok met his future wife when the circus came to Abilene. In fact, the future Mrs. Hickok owned the circus. Agnes Lake was a woman of great accomplishments. "She enjoys the reputation of an excellent business woman," a Kansas newspaper noted, "and is a lady in every respect." She was also an innovator: the first American woman to own and operate a circus; the first to incorporate a dramatic play into a circus performance; the first woman to perform as a lion tamer. On top of all that, "she was accounted to be the best slack wire performer the sawdust ring ever saw, and she was also an unusually skilled rider."

Agnes grew up in Cincinnati. At the age of 16, a circus came to town. When it left, so did Agnes. She married a young and ambitious clown, William Lake Thatcher, who adopted the more show biz-friendly name Bill Lake. Eventually Lake came to own his own circus, and Agnes developed an impressive set of circus skills. The pair had a daughter (who would grow up to be one of the world's best equestriennes and perform with Buffalo

Bill's Wild West show), and got along nicely until 1869.

That's when a sullen thug in a small southwestern Missouri town shot and killed Bill Lake for refusing him free admission. Agnes took over the circus, and by the summer of 1871, the Lake Hippo-Olympiad and Mammoth Circus was "said to be the most complete circus in existence," featuring everything from "Madame Lake" performing the horseback drama *Mazeppa*, to the once-a-show ascension of a 90-foot-diameter hot-air balloon.

In late July, the circus hit Abilene, and love supposedly hit Agnes. "Madame Lake became infatuated with Bill," recalled Charlie Gross, a close friend of Hickok's. "...Bill was a handsome man, as you know, and she fell for him hard, all the way clear to the basement (and) tried to get him to marry her and run the circus." Hickok was attracted to Lake, despite the fact she was more than a decade older than he was. But Wild Bill Hickok had no interest in living in the East, or running a circus. "It's me for the West," he told Gross. "I would be lost back in the States." So he had Gross tell Madame Lake he was already married to a woman in Illinois. In actuality, Gross said, "he always had a mistress," but none of them meant much to him.

A seed, however, had been planted. Lake and Hickok corresponded for several years, and when they next saw each other in 1874, when Wild Bill was touring with Will Cody's theatrical troupe in Rochester, New York, things got serious. "I loved James for three years before I married him," Agnes wrote Hickok's mother in April, 1876, "but I would not marry before my daughter did. I wanted to see her settled in the world first."

With her daughter married and settled by March, 1876, Agnes and Bill were wed in Cheyenne, Wyoming. "'Wild Bill,' of Western fame, has conquered numerous Indians, outlaws, bears and buffaloes, but a charming widow has stolen the magic wand," the *Cheyenne Daily Leader* noted. "... He is a meek and gentle as a lamb."

He was also without visible means of support. Since leaving the Buffalo Bill combination, Hickok had spent most of his time in western Missouri or

Cheyenne, and derived what income he had from gambling. An arrest warrant for vagrancy was issued against him in Cheyenne in 1875, but none of the local law enforcement officers were in a hurry to serve it, and he was never arrested. Agnes Lake, meanwhile, had sold her circus and then gone bankrupt investing in other enterprises just before the economic Panic of 1873. By 1876, she had bounced back and was making a comfortable living appearing with other circuses. But Hickok made it clear he would not live off his wife's earnings. After honeymooning for two weeks in Cincinnati, he headed west again. The plan was for him to raise a stake in the Black Hills Gold Rush, and then send for her.

There was another problem—Wild Bill may have been losing his eyesight. There were contemporary reports that Hickok's eyes had been damaged by "the colored fire used during his theatrical tour" with Cody. When the journalist Leander P. Richardson met Wild Bill in Deadwood in July, 1876, he noted Hickok's eyes "were just beginning to regain their power after almost being blinded altogether by a terrible illness (and) were rather dull and expressionless in repose." Modern theories of Hickok's precise vision malady have ranged from the effects of venereal disease to glaucoma to trachoma to severe conjunctivitis—"pink eye." Whatever it was, and however serious, it augured ill for a man whose daily potential for being in a gunfight was as high as Wild Bill's.

Whether it was his eye problems, a paucity of funds, depression or just laziness, Hickok didn't exactly set any speed records getting to the Black Hills. After leaving his new bride in Cincinnati sometime in late March or early April, he went to Cheyenne and then to St. Louis after making a brief stop at the family home in Illinois.

In St. Louis, he set up a "headquarters" at a former train depot. And in early May—about the time the Centennial Exposition was starting in Philadelphia, Eli Lilly was opening his pharmaceutical business in Indianapolis, and Alexander Graham Bell was demonstrating his telephone in Boston, Wild Bill Hickok was advertising for 340 men to join him on an expedition to the Black Hills, which he would lead, presumably for a nice fee per prospective miner. "He can tell you all about the gold region, its prospects, etc." a newspaper ad promised, even though Hickok had never been to the area. "We want good men, who are willing to work and go to stay. The expedition is fast filling up."

Only it wasn't. The effort fizzled, and whatever there was a of Hickok-led expedition merged with a better organized group. Hickok himself went back to Cheyenne in early June. There he hooked up with Charlie Utter, who with his brother Steve was organizing a pony express-style mail delivery service to the Black Hills. On or about June 27, they left as part of a wagon train headed for Deadwood.

The trip took about two weeks, and Hickok's appearance in town was duly noticed. "Deadwood had only one narrow street, filled with stumps, boulders, lumber and logs," early resident E.L. "Doc" Peirce remembered, "with hundreds of men surging from saloon to saloon...whenever a gunman came to the gulch, the word was passed along as quickly as it would be in a ladies' sewing society."

One of those who might have noticed Hickok's arrival was a cross-eyed, Kentucky-born 25-year-old who occasionally used the alias "Bill Sutherland," but whose real name was John McCall. As the result of a pistol-whipping, his nose had been disfigured enough to earn him the nickname "Broken-Nosed Jack." Little is known about McCall other than that he probably drifted west about 1869, and may have been a buffalo hunter. In Deadwood, he was most likely a day laborer.Doc Peirce claimed to have known McCall fairly well, having briefly camped with him in the gulch. McCall was fine when sober, Peirce said, "but he was a demon when drinking."

It wasn't long before a rumor began to spread that Wild Bill was there to become Deadwood's first marshal, and crack down on things as he had supposedly done in Hays and Abilene. That was a highly unpopular prospect among the town's power structure, which consisted mainly of those who profited from the saloons, brothels and gambling joints.

But Hickok evinced no interest in any kind of job. He and Utter set up camp across Whitewood Creek from the main settlement. For much of the three weeks or so after their arrival, Utter was busy establishing his mail service. Wild Bill was not busy at all. According to the journalist Richardson, Hickok's daily routine seems to have been crawling out of his wagon in the morning, running "like a sprinter down the gulch to the nearest saloon," and strolling back with a drink or two for breakfast. Sometime around noon, he would visit a favorite saloon for some poker, then return about dusk to watch Utter cook dinner.

On the evening of August 1, Hickok was playing in a game in Nutall & Mann's No. 10, when Jack McCall took a stool (there were no chairs.) For once, Wild Bill had a run of luck. McCall didn't, and when he went broke, Hickok good-naturedly offered him enough money to get some supper, but McCall refused it.

The next afternoon, Hickok returned to the saloon. A three-handed game was in progress, and the only seat open had its back to the bar and the saloon's back door. That was an uncomfortable position for Wild Bill, who much preferred sitting with his back against a wall where he could watch the room. But the other players, all friends and acquaintances of his, refused to move and kidded him for being so nervous.

Sometime during the game, McCall slipped into the room, which in the afternoon had at most a dozen occupants. Quietly moving down the bar, he stopped behind Hickok, pulled a pistol from his belt and shot Wild Bill once through the base of the head. The bullet exited Hickok's right cheek and lodged in the wrist of another player.

"Damn you, take that!" McCall shouted as he fired. Even with the shot and shout, however, it took a few seconds before anyone in the room knew what had happened. Then they headed quickly for the front door. McCall snapped off shots at two of the closest witnesses, but both cartridges were duds. It appeared, in fact, that the only working bullet in Jack McCall's gun was the one he put through Bill Hickok's head. Even in death, Wild Bill never had much luck at the poker table.

McCall ran out the back door and tried to steal a horse. The owner, however, had loosened the cinch on the saddle to comfort the animal, and when McCall tried to mount, the saddle fell off. He then sought refuge in a nearby butcher shop, until a crowd and several rifles convinced him to surrender.

Meanwhile, Wild Bill was dead on the saloon floor. Doc Peirce, a barber who supposedly had some medical training, crouched over Hickok's body. He later wrote that Bill "had bled out quickly, and when he was laid out, he looked like a wax figure...Wild Bill was the prettiest corpse I have ever seen."

Writing 50 years after the event, Peirce also claimed Hickok was still holding his final hand: the aces of spades and clubs, and the eights of the same suits. He didn't identify the fifth card, but the queen of hearts or diamonds are the most popular speculations. However accurate Peirce's recollection and/or imagination was, black aces and eights have become globally known in poker as "the dead man's hand."

McCall was tried the next day in a theater by a hastily convened "miner's court," wherein various Deadwoodians were selected as judge, prosecuting and defense "lawyers" and jurors. "Never did a more forbidding countenance face court than that of Jack McCall," a reporter wrote. "His head, which is covered by a thick crop of chestnut hair, is very narrow as to the parts occupied by the intellectual part of the brain, while the animal development is exceedingly large."

McCall's defense boiled down to bogusly claiming Hickok had killed his non-existent brother in Kansas, and he had simply avenged the loss. That was good enough for the jury (one of whom, Frank Towie was shot and killed a few weeks after the trial while robbing a stagecoach.) McCall was acquitted. Whether some or all of the jurors were bribed, or just stupid, is still a subject of debate among Wild Bill aficionados. McCall, hung around for a few days, then left Deadwood. As it turned out (see Chapter 12), however, he wasn't done with the justice system when it came to killing a Wild West legend.

As the de facto undertaker, Peirce laid out Hickok's body for burial in the clothes he had on when he was shot: "He had no other clothes to put on." He was buried with his Yaeger rifle, but not his pistols. Before closing the coffin lid, Peirce snipped a 14-inch lock of Hickok's hair from the back of his head. Half of the lock when to Charlie Utter, the other half to the reporter Richardson. "It is as glossy as spun glass and soft as down," Richardson wrote in 1894. "Near the roots there is just a touch of roughness, where the life blood of a brave, great-hearted American man gushed out as the assassin's bullet burst through his brain." In 1907, just before Wild Bill's widow died, Richardson gave her the lock of her late husband's hair.

Charlie Utter oversaw Hickok's funeral, which was well-attended. A simple wooden marker was erected that correctly called Wild Bill "a brave man" and "the victim of an assassin," and incorrectly gave his age as 48. He was 39.

Chapter 7 Notes

Leander Pease Richardson Leander P. Richardson, "A Trip to the Black Hills." *Scribner's Monthly*, Vol. XIII, No. 6 (April 1877), p. 755.

Deadwood had been T.D. Griffith (ed.), *Deadwood: The Best Writings on the Most Notorious Town in the West*, p. 13.

"The streets present," *St. Louis Globe-Democrat*, Aug. 22, 1876, p. 1; *The New North West* (Deer Lodge, Mt.), August 25, 1876, p. 3.

Richardson had been Richardson, op. cit., p. 748.

Better, yet, he *Butte (Mt.) Weekly Miner*, June 29, 1878, p. 1.

Besides being a James D. McLaird, "I Know...Because I Was There." *South Dakota History*, Vol. 34, Nos. 3 and 4 (Fall/Winter 2001), pp. 241-243.

"Of course I" Richardson, op. cit., p. 755.

Just how he Frank J. Wilstach, *Wild Bill Hickok, Prince of the Pistoleers*, p. 273; Leander P. Richardson, "Last Days of a Plainsman," *True West Magazine*, Vol. 13, No. 2 (November-December 1965), p. 22.

It's just as well Richardson, "Last Days," pp. 22-23.

But Hickok's musings Joseph G. Rosa, *They Called Him Wild Bill*, p. 290; Wilstach, op. cit., p. 282.

More plausible J.W. Buel, *Life and Marvelous Adventures of Wild Bill, the Scout* (reprint), p. 7. See Joseph G. Rosa, *Wild Bill Hickok, the Man and His Myth*, pp. 20-25, for a detailed and somewhat pedantic discussion of Hickok's nickname.

Whatever its origin *The (Burlington, Ia.) Daily Hawkeye*, Jan. 29, 1886, p. 6; George A. Custer, *My Life on the Plains*, p. 40.

But acting aversion aside Louis S. Warren *Buffalo Bill's America*, pp. 65-66; George Ward Nichols, "Wild Bill," *Harper's New Monthly Magazine*, Vol. 34, No. 201 (February 1867), p. 286.

"He was about" George A. Custer, *My Life on the Plains*, p. 40.

"Whether on foot" Ibid.; Elizabeth Custer, *Following the Guidon*, pp. 153-54.

While not nearly Wilstach, op. cit., pp. xii—xiv; Richardson, "A Trip to the Black Hills," op. cit., p. 755.

Being quick was Rosa, op. cit., p. 347.

That advice assumed Ibid., p. 344.

As exaggerated as Wilstach, op. cit., p. 112.

"My name is Hickok" Ibid., pp. 240-242.

"He was taciturn" Rosa, op. cit., p. 29.

It was during Cody, op. cit., pp. 64-66.

Whether this happened, Louis S. Warren, *Buffalo Bill's America*, p. 61.

What really happened For more than you probably want to know about the McCanles incident, see Joseph G. Rosa's "*They Called Him Wild Bill,*" pp. 34-52.

Dave Tutt had (Springfield) *Missouri Weekly Patriot*, July 27, 1865, p. 3.

"...You would not" Nichols, op. cit., p. 274.

Newspapers all over *New York Tribune*, Jan. 24, 1867, p. 6.

As sheriff of *Leavenworth (Ks.) Daily Commercial*, Oct. 3, 1869, p. 4.

If there was *Chicago Tribune*, Nov. 6, 1866, p. 2.

They were also *Boston Weekly Globe*, Oct. 3, 1882, p. 6.

It was very *Chicago Tribune*, April 2, 1889, p. 5.

Will Cody and, Sandra A. Sagala, *Buffalo Bill on Stage*, p. 47.

Unlike Cody and Ibid., p. 49.

"The public uproar" Wilstach, op. cit., p. 225.

Hickok stuck it Cody, *Life of the Honorable William F. Cody*, p. 333.

In truth, Wild *Rochester (NY) Democrat & Chronicle*, March 26, 1874, p. 4.

James Butler Hickok *Topeka (Ks.) Daily Commonwealth*, July 30, 1871, p. 4;*Kansas City (Mo.) Times*, Aug. 23, 1907, p. 2.

That's when a *Corrine (Utah) Daily Reporter*, July 19, 1871, p. 3.

In late July Rosa, *They Called Him Wild Bill*, p. 237.

A seed, however, Ibid.

With her daughter, *Cheyenne Daily Leader*, March 7, 1876, p. 3.

There was another *The (Topeka, Ks.) Weekly Commonwealth*, July 23, 1874; Richardson, "Last Days of a Plainsman," p. 23.

In St. Louis, *St. Louis Globe-Democrat*, May 6, 1876, p. 8.

The trip took about Wilstach, op. cit., p. 267.

One of those Ibid., p. 296.

But Hickok evinced no "*A Trip to the Black Hills,*" p. 757.

Meanwhile, Wild Bill Wilstach, op. cit., pp. 284-85.

Writing 50 years Ibid.

McCall was tried *Kansas City Times*, Aug. 19, 1876, p. 2.

As the de facto *Deadwood Pioneer-Times*, Aug. 22, 1925, p. 1; Richardson, "*Last Days of a Plainsman,*" p. 24.

CHAPTER 8

"Get your guns, boys, they're robbing the bank!"

The last ride of the James-Younger Gang

SEPTEMBER

Two days after Wild Bill Hickok bled out on a Deadwood saloon floor, Hobbs Kerry spilled his guts in a Sedalia, Missouri, jail cell. Yes, he told the police on August 4, he had taken part in the masterfully executed train robbery near Otterville, Missouri, the month before. Yes, he knew the names of the other seven men involved, and yes, he would squeal on them in hopes of getting a lenient sentence.

The other robbers, he said, were Charlie Pitts and Bill Chadwell, from Kansas; Clell Miller, from Clay County, Missouri, and two sets of brothers, also from Missouri: Cole and Bob Younger, and Frank and Jesse James. "These names correspond with those already telegraphed" to pursuing posses all over southwest Missouri and southeast Kansas, the *Chicago Tribune* reported on August 7. "There seems to be no doubt now that the whole party will be arrested within two or three days, and this gang of robbers and desperadoes completely broken up and brought to justice."

The *Tribune* was wrong. None of the train robbers were caught, except the only amateur in the gang, who happened to be Kerry. At 23, Hobbs Kerry was a "very wiry and quick-motioned" little guy with "a large, sharp nose," and big dreams. He disliked working in the lead and zinc mines around the Southwest Missouri town of Granby. He wanted a career in the exciting world of armed robbery. Not only that, he wanted to break in with the best in the business: the James-Younger Gang.

For a solid decade, the gang had terrorized and titillated the entire country. The James Boys and Younger Brothers seemingly robbed whatever and wherever they wanted, and killed whomever they chose to kill. And if a robbery or killing was committed that they didn't do, they got the blame—or credit—for it anyway. They were simultaneously hated, feared, admired and respected.

"In all the history of medieval knight errantry and modern brigandage, there is nothing that equals the wild romance of the past few years' career of...Frank and Jesse James and the Younger Boys," a Missouri newspaper gushed after the gang had simultaneously robbed two stage coaches in 1874. "Their fame has become national, nay, world-wide...they have captured and pillaged whole railroad trains in Iowa, Missouri and Arkansas. They have dashed into towns and cleaned out banking houses in broad daylight...detectives who have attempted to ferret them out have been slain. Sheriffs' posses have been routed."

That was the kind of organization to which Hobbs Kerry aspired, and sometime in late June, through some go-between work by gang associate Charlie Pitts and Bruce Younger, an uncle of the Younger brothers, he got his chance to meet with the gang, and outline his plan to hold up a Granby mining company.

Only the brothers didn't like the idea. It smelled too much like a potential trap—which it might have turned into, since Kerry had shot off his amateur's mouth. Police in St. Louis had already learned of his mine-robbing idea, and had sent undercover cops to the Granby area to nose around. Instead, the assorted Jameses and Youngers decided to hit the Missouri-Pacific's No. 4 Express at a remote spot called Rocky Cut, about 100 miles east of Kansas City. But for some reason, the usually careful gang deviated from a longstanding practice of not trusting outsiders, and allowed Kerry to take part.

On the sultry, brightly moonlit night of July 7, the outlaws grabbed a railroad bridge watchman where the tracks crossed the Lamine River. After blocking the track with a pile of rail ties, they forced the watchman to flag down the train. When it stopped, they fired pistols into the air and whooped it up, with the intent of intimidating any would-be heroes among the passengers and crew. It worked, except for a 22-year-old "newsboy" who sold periodicals and snacks on the train, and had a lot more courage than sense. Louis Bales was toting a tiny-caliber pocket pistol, and fired it at one of the robbers. His target only laughed at the effort, and fired back a warning shot that convinced Bales to refrain from any more heroics.

In the baggage car, three gang members used a key taken from the car's attendant to open one of two express company safes, and a coal pick to smash a hole in the other safe, for which there was no key on board. As they worked, they took a brief break to gorge themselves on the candy, cakes, pies and fruit the newsboy Bales had been carrying for sale to passengers. Once the safes' contents—about $17,000 ($408,000 in 2022), $10,000 of which was in cash—were emptied into grain sacks, the gang advised the conductor to clear the tracks to protect following trains, then departed. None of the passengers were hurt or robbed, and the whole process took about an hour. "The band did their work with such coolness and precision," a St. Louis paper noted, "as to leave little doubt that some of their number at least had experience at the business."

After the robbery, Kerry returned to Granby, where he was already viewed as a suspicious character. He promptly began losing his $1,200 share of the loot playing faro and poker. "I don't know what I spent," he admitted later. "I drank a good deal." When he was arrested in a saloon, he had $20 left, and three revolvers. After being confronted with an incriminating letter he had written to a friend, which had been intercepted by the police, he agreed to squeal. (He ultimately did four years in prison for his part in the robbery, and then disappeared.)

One thing Kerry and some of the train witnesses agreed on was that as the gang rode away, the leader, described as having light sandy hair and fierce blue eyes that blinked repeatedly, shouted "Tell Alan Pinkerton and all his detectives to look for us in Hell!"

Jesse Woodson James—who had sandy hair, piercing blue eyes, and blinked a lot because of a granulated eyelid condition—had ample reason to hate Alan Pinkerton and "all his detectives." About 18 months before the train robbery, members of Pinkerton's Chicago-based National Detective Agency had crept up on the James family farm in Clay County, Missouri, about three miles from the town of Kearney. One of them threw a metal ball through a window. The device was meant to start a fire, driving the occupants out of the house. Dr. Reuben Samuel, the boys' stepfather, pushed the ball into the fireplace, where it exploded. Eight-year-old Archie Samuel, Frank and Jesse's half-brother, was killed. Their mother's right arm was so badly hurt it had to be amputated below the elbow. Neither Frank nor Jesse was in the house at the time. "The 'Grand Move,'" local lawman George Patton sarcastically wrote, "has made hundreds of friends for the James boys, where they had but few."

Patton was right. The killing of their half-brother and maiming of their mother resulted in a wave of sympathy for Frank and Jesse, which translated to deep and widespread hostility toward those trying to catch them. "It is generally believed...that (the James and Younger brothers) find a refuge from the penalty of their desperate exploits among (friendly) officers of the law and the communities in which they reside," a Kansas City paper commented. "...The cleverness with which they elude detection and arrest under all circumstances, the celerity of their movements, and the audacity and success of their operations, has created an impression that as capture was impossible, pursuit was useless."

There were faintly amusing and transparently ridiculous protests of innocence after the Otterville train robbery from the James family. A week or so after Kerry's finger-pointing confession, Zerelda Samuel, the James boys' mother, told a reporter that Kerry was lying because:A) She was pretty sure Frank and Jesse were in Philadelphia at the Centennial Exposition; B) Her boys "had been at swords' points with the Youngers for years and would have nothing to do with them," and C) If they had robbed that train, they most certainly would have shared the loot with their poor old mother.

She then showed the reporter the stump of her arm she had lost in the Pinkerton attack the year before. "With all the crimes charged upon the

James boys," she said, "they have never been accused of such inhuman and cowardly attacks on women and children. I'd rather they'd rob every bank in Kansas City than commit so dastardly a deed."

While their mom was protesting the James boys' innocence, the gang was already well on its way to its next robbery. This one would be a bank job, way up north, in Minnesota. It was apparently Jesse's idea, and there was some logic behind it. For one thing, Kerry's confession specifically naming the gang's members had made things hotter than usual around Missouri. For another, no one would expect the James-Younger bunch to strike so far north. Plus, Minnesota banks were reportedly ripe with Yankee cash, and Minnesota towns were unused to bold daylight bank robberies. And finally, there was a lawyer in St. Paul whom Jesse wanted to kill.

Samuel Hardwicke, a Clay County native, had spied on the James boys for the Pinkerton agency, and even been in on the 1875 raid of the James farm. After it was clear the brothers had escaped the attack—and another local who had helped the Pinkertons was found in his front yard with three bullets through his head—Hardwicke prudently moved his family to St. Paul. But he imprudently didn't cover his tracks, and the James boys knew exactly where he was.

Two of the Younger brothers were not enthusiastic about making the trip. Jim Younger had been summoned from California to replace the squealer Hobbs Kerry. Jim and Cole thought raiding into alien territory was too heavily laden with uncertainties. But Bob Younger was tight with Jesse, and when he insisted that he was going, his brothers gave in. Sometime in mid-August, Jesse and Frank James, Cole, Jim and Bob Younger, Clell Miller, Charlie Pitts and Bill Chadwell boarded a train, probably in St. Joseph, Missouri. Their eventual destination was figuratively, if not literally, to become something of a Civil War battlefield, 11 years after the war ended.

America's Civil War formally started on the morning of April 12, 1861, when Confederate forces fired upon the federal Fort Sumter at Charleston, South Carolina. But the citizenry of Missouri and Kansas had been holding blood-drenched dress rehearsals for years before then.

The root of the discord was slavery. Missouri was a slave state. It would benefit politically, economically and culturally if its neighboring territory to the west, Kansas, became a slave state when it entered the Union. Congress had left it up to Kansas residents to choose. But many of the thousands of settlers that flocked to Kansas beginning in 1854 were "free soilers," who either opposed slavery on moral grounds or simply did not want to compete with slave-based farms and plantations.

The result was a rift that began with sharply worded rhetoric and hotly contested elections, and deteriorated into human behavior at its most barbarous. It was generally referred to by its participants as "guerilla warfare," but it often degraded into unvarnished terrorism. Each side's "noble cause" masked acts of greed, revenge, fanaticism and brutality. If there was any saving grace in a cesspool of graceless acts, it was that rapes were relatively rare, and the murder of children was generally avoided.

By 1861, the border war had been subsumed by the national conflict, but it had by no means subsided. Some of the gangs and vigilante mobs took on a more military persona, while others morphed into criminal packs that preyed on the most profitable or least resistant targets, no matter which side they were on. There were shades of loyalties among non-combatants as well. Some pro-slavery Missourians nonetheless opposed secession from the Union. Some anti-slavery Kansans didn't mind if "the peculiar institution" continued outside Kansas' borders.

Both sides had few heroes, but plenty of villains. Among the leaders of the pro-Union Kansas "jayhawkers" and "Red Legs" were men like Charles "Doc" Jennison. Jennison was an undersized New York physician and ardent abolitionist who wore a tall fur hat and had a fondness for personally slicing the ears off prisoners. He led a mounted unit he described as "a self-sustaining regiment." Union Gen. Henry Halleck, on whose side

Jennison's men were ostensibly fighting, called them "no better than a band of robbers...(who) steal, plunder, and burn whatever they can lay their hands on."

Missouri's Confederacy-allied "bushwhackers" and "Border Ruffians" had William T. Anderson, a Kentucky-born horse thief who had lived in Kansas and Missouri. His long dark hair and beard, coupled with a rakish cap, made him appear more pirate than soldier, and his psychopathic personality earned him the nickname "Bloody Bill." He personally killed 14 unarmed men in a raid on Lawrence, Kansas, which saw the massacre of more than 150 men and boys. He also ordered the execution and post-mortem mutilations of Union soldiers who had surrendered after a battle near Centralia, Missouri. And Anderson had the distinction of being one of the few guerilla leaders who both countenanced and participated in rape.

Anderson's rationale for his murderous exertions was that he was seeking vengeance for crimes committed against his family. Those included the death of one sister and the crippling of another in August, 1863, when a makeshift Kansas City prison they were being held in, essentially as political prisoners, collapsed. "I'm here for revenge, and I have got it," he exclaimed during the killing spree in Lawrence a week after the prison collapse.

Of the eight men who headed to Minnesota in 1876 as the James-Younger gang, seven could tell stories of family tragedy similar to Anderson's. (The lone exception was Bill Chadwell.) At the age of 18 when the war began, Alexander Franklin "Frank" James was the oldest of the outlaw octet. His brother Jesse was going on 14. The boys' father, Robert James, was a well-educated minister who had left the family in 1850 for the gold fields of California, either to preach to the miners, search for gold, or just escape the domineering company of his wife. It wasn't clear, and didn't matter much, since he died soon after arriving.

Robert James' widow, Zerelda, was a fiercely independent and generally formidable woman. She ran the family's 200-acre farm in the wooded hill country of Clay County, Missouri, about 30 miles north of Kansas

City. The James clan grew tobacco and hemp. They were slave owners, and when the war began, Frank joined the Confederate army. But by the end of 1861, he had contracted measles, was captured by federal troops while recuperating in a hospital, and paroled home. Ignoring a promise to not take up arms again, he soon joined a guerilla group led by William Quantrill, a former school teacher who was only slightly less nuts than Bloody Bill Anderson.

Shortly after he joined Quantrill's Raiders, Union-allied militia visited the James farm, looking for Frank. They beat 16-year-old Jesse to a pulp, and tortured his step-father, Dr. Reuben Samuel, by hanging him briefly, letting him down, and then stringing him up again. He survived, but never fully recovered from the ordeal. The experience prompted Jesse to join Frank in June, 1864. At some point either just before or just after joining the guerillas, Jesse managed to shoot off the tip of a finger while loading a revolver, thus reportedly earning the nickname "Dingus."Two months later, he was shot through a lung by an old German farmer while stealing a saddle. Eight months after that, he was shot through the same lung by federal troops, apparently while trying to surrender. The second wound left him near death for nearly a year.

In between rather unglamorous shooting mishaps, however, Jesse and Frank earned well-deserved reputations as merciless killers, riding with Quantrill and then with Bill Anderson. They gunned down unarmed soldiers and civilians alike, justifying it as both righteous vengeance and the same treatment they would have received if the tables had been turned.

"Both sides did a lot of raiding and killing," Frank acknowledged in a 1903 interview. "...Those days, it was the way to fight. We did burn the houses of Yanks. We shot spies. So does everybody. If we hadn't, we wouldn't have lasted a week."

The Younger brothers were part of a large and prosperous family from Jackson County, Missouri, which encompassed Kansas City. The family patriarch, Henry Washington Younger, was a highly successful farmer, horse breeder, merchant and mail contractor. In his spare time, he sired

14 children. Henry Younger was a slave owner, but opposed secession. The distinction didn't matter to jayhawkers, who periodically stole Younger's horses.

After Henry's seventh child, Thomas Coleman, better known as Cole, punched a militia officer and subsequently fled to join Quantrill's Raiders, Henry was murdered by three militia members. Three months later, his widow was forced by the militia to burn down the family home. The following year, three of the Younger sisters and two cousins were arrested as "spies." They were in the same Kansas City prison as Bloody Bill Anderson's siblings when it collapsed, and one of the cousins was killed.

Cole, who began a lifelong friendship with Frank James as part of Quantrill's regiment, took part in the infamous raid on Lawrence, Kansas. In his autobiography, Cole admitted it "was a day of butchery," but made the questionable assertion he only killed combatants. In 1864, 16-year-old Jim Younger joined Quantrill. He was captured in early 1865, narrowly escaped execution and was imprisoned until the war's end. Bob Younger, who was only eight when the war began, did not fight, but did witness the outrages and tragedy that befell the family.

Of the other three men who rode to Minnesota with the James and Younger boys, Clell Miller was 14 when he joined Bill Anderson's guerillas. In Miller's first fight, Anderson was killed. (His head was cut off by his slayers and displayed on a telegraph pole.) Miller was badly wounded, and dodged being hanged only because the Union troops' leader was a friend of Miller's father. Charlie Pitts, whose real name was Samuel Wells, had grown up a friend and neighbor to the Youngers. His house was burned by jayhawkers, and his father killed by Union troops while he was watching a battle, as a civilian noncombatant, near the family farm. Pitts, at 15, joined the bushwhackers. The eighth member of the Minnesota-bound gang, Bill Chadwell, was originally from Illinois and only eight when the war began. He thus didn't participate in the pre-war hostilities or the war itself.

When the war ended, Pitts, Miller and the James and Younger brothers returned to a most unwelcome homecoming. A new Missouri state constitution had been adopted by the victors. It required potential voters to swear what was dubbed "The Iron Oath," in which they were obliged to aver they had never taken up arms against the federal government, nor aided those who had. Those who wanted to hold elective or government office, or be clergymen, lawyers or corporate officers had to take similar oaths. In essence, many native Missourians became second-class citizens, without basic legal rights and economic opportunities. In addition, pro-Union residents held all positions of authority and could enforce laws and dispense justice as they saw fit.

"It is safe to assume that nine-tenths of the outlawry in the West since the close of the rebellion was the outgrowth of that civil revolt," the *St. Louis Post-Dispatch* opined a decade after the war ended. "Too many men have become inured to bloodshed. It has been said that while the murderer will shudder at the contemplation of his first deed, the second has less revolting aspects, and so each subsequent taking of life is a matter of less solemn consequences to the perpetrators."

Frank James was less wordy and more colorful in his assessment. "We were outlaws the moment the South lost," he said. "Why, we had as much chance of settling down...as a tallow dog chasing an asbestos cat through Hell."

The difference between Frank and Jesse James, a friend and confidant of the brothers suggested, is that if they decided to kill you, you might be able to talk Jesse out of it, but stood no chance with Frank. "Jesse laughs at everything, Frank at nothing at all," wrote John Newman Edwards, a former Confederate officer and Missouri newspaperman who championed the "cause" of the outlaws. "Jesse is light-hearted, reckless, devil-may-care; Frank sober, sedate, a dangerous man always in ambush in the midst of society."

Being "light-hearted," however, didn't make Jesse any less reptilian than his brother when it came to killing people. In a letter to a newspaper, in which he apologized for accidentally shooting a little girl during a robbery, Jesse contended the gang never shot anyone on purpose, except in self-defense. His definition of "self-defense," was somewhat broad: "A man who is fool enough to refuse to open a safe or a vault when he is covered with a pistol ought to die...if he gives the alarm, or refuses to unlock, he gets killed."

At maybe 5'10 (at a time when the average American male was about 5'8"), Jesse was a bit heavier than his older brother, with sandy hair, a pug nose and generally pleasant features. Almost every description of him included a comment about his remarkable glacier-blue eyes, which seemed to be constantly in motion. He was considered fearless and generous by the other gang members, especially compared to the somewhat penny-pinching Frank. He also had a sly sense of humor. He liked to engage strangers in conversation while traveling incognito with the gang, then change the topic to "those notorious James and Younger boys," much to the discomfort of the other outlaws trying to keep a low profile. He was a great horseman, a lousy shot, and a fairly eloquent letter writer for a man with limited formal education.

Four years older than Jesse, Frank was thinner, taller and darker complected than his brother. Cole Younger, who liked Frank and disliked Jesse, said the older James was "always quiet and gentlemanly, while Jesse was likely to be quarrelsome." A robbery victim described Frank as appearing "like a man well educated, and very polite, and not inclined to talk much." When he did talk, Frank would sometimes startle people by quoting passages from the Bible or Shakespeare. He was also a prodigious tobacco chewer, which may be another reason he didn't talk much.

The Younger brothers were as disparate as the James boys. Cole was 6' tall, easily weighed more than 200 lbs.—and looked much bigger, with a thick chest and broad shoulders. Almost completely bald, he was described as having a "large Roman nose," "mild blue eyes," long sideburns and a dropping sandy mustache. Like Frank James, Cole was a Bible quoter. Unlike Frank, he was amiable and a good story-teller. "He looks anything but a villain," a reporter noted, "but every feature and expression indicates caution, shrewdness and a high order of intellect."

Jim Younger was a bit shorter and considerably lighter than Cole. He was also subject to wild mood swings. Jim, Cole said, "was either in the garret or way down in the cellar...he was either chipper as a canary bird or else he was very melancholy." At 6'2", Bob Younger was nonetheless the "baby brother." Muscular and handsome, with deep blue eyes and a neatly trimmed mustache, Bob was not as outgoing as Cole nor as bipolar as Jim. He had decided to quit the outlaw industry for farm life after the Minnesota raid.

Of the other three Minnesota-bound bandits, Clell Miller had the most experience. Stocky, with curly auburn hair, Miller was the smallest and chattiest of the gang. He had ridden with the James and Younger brothers on at least four other robberies, and had actually been arrested and tried after an Iowa bank job. He was acquitted, however, after providing numerous bogus alibis—and even got $120 from the court for his expenses.

Charlie Pitts and Bill Chadwell were close pals who got to know each other in Kansas, where they had robbed a bank together. Pitts was strongly built, with thick black hair and a full beard. He was considered an expert with horses. Chadwell was a towering 6'4, with a beardless baby face and a skill few would have deduced from his appearance: Cole Younger considered Chadwell one of the best poker players he ever saw.

At 23 in 1876, Chadwell and Bob Younger were the youngest of the eight. Frank James was the oldest, at 33, followed by Cole Younger at 32. All of them knew the outlaw trade, particularly Frank, Jesse and Cole. In the decade prior to the ride to Minnesota, various James-Younger gang members either participated in, or were blamed for, scores of bank, train and stagecoach robberies, as well as dozens of murders of former jayhawkers, Union soldiers, Pinkerton detectives and assorted squealers, snitchers and people who just looked at them wrong.

Some notable examples:

- On the afternoon of Feb. 13, 1866, a dozen men wearing blue army overcoats rode into Liberty, Missouri, not far from the James farm. Two of the men entered the Clay County Savings Association, owned mainly by pro-Union investors. Brandishing pistols, the two forced a pair of bank employees to fork over about $58,000 in cash and bearer bonds (about $950,000 in 2022), while the rest of the bandits in the street fired off pistols to cow the townsfolk. During the getaway, a 19-year-old college student was killed. Despite two large posses in pursuit, none of the bandits were caught. Among them were believed to be Cole Younger and Frank James. Jesse may have participated, although he was still recovering from his Civil War wounds.

- Shortly after lunch on Dec. 7, 1869, the James brothers rode into Gallatin, Missouri, about 70 miles north of Kansas City. Gallatin was the home of Samuel P. Cox, a former Union militia officer credited with killing guerilla leader Bloody Bill Anderson during the war. The James boys entered the Daviess County Savings Association, where, at point-blank range, Jesse put bullets through the chest and head of a man he had convinced himself was Cox. He also wounded the only other person in the bank before he and Frank fled, with about $700 ($14,000.) During their escape, Jesse's horse threw him, and the outlaw was dragged along the street for about 50 yards until freeing himself. Leaping up behind Frank, the brothers got away. Rather than having avenged the death of his former bushwhacker leader, however, Jesse had succeeded only in killing the principal owner of the bank, who had nothing to do with Anderson's death.

- On June 3, 1871, Cole, the James boys and Clell Miller robbed the bank in Corydon, Iowa, about 70 miles south of Des Moines. The bandits got $6,000 (about $132,000 in 2022), but no one noticed at the time, since most of the town was drinking free beer while listening to a speech by the then-famed orator Henry Clay Dean. Apparently vexed by the lack of attention, the gang interrupted the speech long enough for Frank James to inform the citizenry they had just been robbed, and wave some of the loot at them. The crowd ignored him as a heckler, and the gang rode off with their feelings ruffled, but unmolested by pursuers.

- Just about sundown on Sept. 26, 1872, the James brothers and Cole Younger approached a ticket booth at the fairgrounds in Kansas City, Missouri, where thousands of people were attending what was the equivalent of a state fair. Cole Younger seized the cash box from the cashier, who refused to let go. As an inducement, Jesse took a shot at him, but hit a little girl in the leg instead. He later apologized for his poor shooting, and offered to pay the girl's medical bills. The trio escaped on horseback with $978 ($21,500 in 2021). If they had arrived about a half-hour earlier, before the fair treasurer had collected the day's receipts, they would have scored about $12,000 ($263,800 in 2021).

- On the evening of July 21, 1873, the gang attempted its first train robbery, when it derailed an engine on the Chicago, Rock Island and Pacific line near Adair, Iowa, about midway between Des Moines and Omaha. The derailment broke the neck of the engineer, who was the robbery's only casualty. The gang, all but one of whom wore masks resembling those of the Ku Klux Klan, got $2,300 ($51,000 in 2021). The sole gang member without a mask was Jesse James. The outlaws knew in advance the train was carrying several tons of gold and silver bullion—only they may have thought "bullion" was some sort of coin. When they demanded it be handed over, and the conductor pointed out the stacks of heavy metal bars, they realized they had no way to carry it on horseback, and left it. The job only took about 10 minutes, no passengers were robbed, and Jesse expressed regret at the engineer's death before they rode off.

Between jobs, Jesse wrote letters to the newspapers, particularly the sympathetic *Kansas City Times,* operated and edited by his admirer, John Newman Edwards. In his missives, Jesse contradictorily portrayed the gang as modern-day Robin Hoods while simultaneously protesting their innocence of the crimes.

"Some editors call us thieves," he wrote. "We are not thieves—we are bold robbers. It hurts me very much to be called a thief...we are bold robbers and I am proud of the name." He went on to compare himself to "bold robbers" of the past, such as Alexander the Great and Julius Caesar, while contending the real thieves in the country were President Grant and the Republican Party. "They rob the rich and the poor. We rob the rich and give to the poor." But he failed to produce any evidence the gang had ever shared its spoils with anyone, rich or poor.

In a letter published in August, 1876, Jesse noted that "detectives have been trying for years to get positive proof against me for some criminal offense, so they could get a large reward offered for me dead or alive, and the same for Frank James and the Younger Boys, but they have been foiled at every turn." He added that he and the gang wanted no pardon, because they had done nothing to be pardoned for, but suggested lawmakers "pass a law having all those bogus warrants that are out for us destroyed, and let us go home and live in peace."

By the time the letter was printed, however, the James-Younger gang was not headed home, but headed north.

Stick 'Em Up

In a corner of the main building at Philadelphia's Centennial Exposition, a Connecticut company was attempting to make life harder for bank robbers. The Yale Lock Manufacturing firm's exhibit was tucked into a replica of a post office, complete with hundreds of lock boxes and drawers, each requiring a different key to be opened. But of much more consternation to would-be bandits was a display of Yale's newly patented "time" or "chronometer" locks, which were specifically designed for bank vaults, "and absolutely forbid the opening of the (vault) door before a certain hour."

For the relatively reasonable price of $450 ($10,800 in 2022), a bank could equip its vault with a device that would slide into place 12 sturdy steel bolts that could be not be opened until one of the device's two clocks reached a set time. (The other clock was a backup.) The time lock effectively eliminated a common bank-robbing tactic known as "bulldozing," wherein outlaws would kidnap a banker at home and force him to open the safe in the middle of the night, when outside interference was minimized. Bankers, a Kansas newspaper boasted, "need no longer feel afraid of being called upon at unreasonable times to open the vaults and safes for the benefit of rambling rangers like the James Brothers and Youngers."

The adoption of time locks was just one of the daunting obstacles faced by bank robbers in 1876. Most banks were located in the middle of towns, which made daylight robberies problematical. In addition, there were not a lot of banks to rob. A U.S. Treasury Dept. study estimated there were 2,762 federal- and state-chartered banks in the country in 1876, serving a population of roughly 45 million, or one bank for every 16,300 Americans. By way of comparison, the ratio in 2019 was one bank/branch for every 4,000 Americans, and that doesn't even include ATMs. In many small towns, particularly in the West, there was no formal bank, and financial transactions were either person-to-person, or conducted through a general store or other retail business.

The increasing ubiquity of telegraph service made it harder for bank robbers on horseback to quickly escape somewhere news of their crime hadn't reached. And as the novelty of post-Civil War bank jobs wore off, townspeople became more inclined to get involved when their bank was being robbed. "Men were no longer smitten with sudden surprise at the sound of horrid oaths and yells in their quiet streets," an early Jesse

James biographer noted. "They could no longer be terrorized by a reckless random firing of dragoon revolvers...people began to prepare for it."

Townspeople had a compelling reason to get involved when their bank was being robbed: It was their money. Prior to the adoption of federally guaranteed deposit insurance in the 1930s, customers were likely to be out of luck if the bank with which they did business was robbed. When the bank in Liberty, Missouri, was robbed in 1866, for example, the investors who had provided the bank's operating capital recovered 60 cents for every dollar they lost. Average depositors fared worse, at 30 cents on the dollar. That there was any compensation at all was due only to the fact that the bank's board of directors liquidated much of their personal assets to make good on at least a portion of the losses. The result was the bank went out of business.

If banks proved too tough a nut to crack, outlaws could always turn to stagecoaches. These were plentiful, not too heavily guarded and relatively easy to waylay. Despite the oft-repeated literary and cinematic stereotype of masked and mounted bandits riding down a coach after a desperate chase, most robberies actually occurred in steep uphill or narrow, twisting sections of a road, where the coaches had to slow down. There, dismounted gunmen in the road would flag down the coach. According to Arizona state historian Marshall Trimble, of the 129 stage robberies in Arizona between 1875 and 1903, only three were robbed by men on horseback chasing down a stage.

Stagecoach robbing provided not only the potential goodies in a strongbox, but whatever valuables the passengers carried. But the real money in the Wild West robbery business was to be made on rails. Not only did trains carry more passengers than stagecoaches, they often carried heavily laden safes. As the railroad system expanded in the western part of America, so did train robberies. It's estimated that at one point in the 1880s, trains were being robbed at the rate of one every four days.

An indignant Kansas City newspaper called train-robbing "a light, safe and profitable business...half a dozen resolute men, who understand the business and take pleasure in it, can stop a train at any time in some secluded spot and 'clean out' the express boxes in half an hour."

In the West, this "light, safe and profitable business" was launched on Nov. 4, 1870, when a gang led by Andrew Jackson Davis robbed a train just outside Reno, Nevada. Davis, a big, gregarious fellow better known as "Smiling Jack," used a number of tricks that became staples in real-life train robberies as well as in Hollywood versions. His gang of six relied on an informant to let them know the Central Pacific's Overland Express No. 1 was carrying $40,000-plus ($795,000 in 2022) in gold from San Francisco to Salt Lake City. They built a barrier on the track; boarded the train when it slowed to a crawl near the small town of Verdi, Nevada, and uncoupled the engine and express car from the rest of the train to reduce the possibility of outside interference during the robbery.

In fact, Davis' gang did everything right—except get away with it. The least experienced member of the gang was soon caught, confessed and ratted out everyone else. Davis himself did three years in prison, was paroled for good behavior—and eventually shot-gunned to death during a stagecoach robbery in California.

And while the Davis gang's train robbery was the first in the West, it was not unique for very long. About 20 hours and 320 miles after being robbed near the California-Nevada border, the Overland Express No. 1 stopped at a refueling spot about 50 miles from the Nevada-Utah border—where it was robbed again.

It would be something of a stretch to suggest Frank James put a bullet through Joe Heywood's brain because of grasshoppers. There were doubtless other cause-and-effect factors involved. Nonetheless, there may have been at least something of a link between the vicious and senseless murder of the 39-year-old husband and father, and a biblical-proportioned plague of insects that by 1876 had been ravaging western Minnesota for three years. "The damages done by the locusts during the past few years to the crops of Missouri, Iowa, Kansas, Nebraska and Minnesota may safely be estimated at one hundred million dollars ($2.4 billion in 2022)," a

Minneapolis newspaper reported in August.

Fortunately for the fertile farming area around the town of Northfield, Minnesota, the six-legged multitudes stayed away. Located about 40 miles south of Minneapolis-St. Paul, Northfield was just 21 years old in 1876. Settled first by New Englanders, who were followed by waves of Scandinavian immigrants, the town straddled the scenic Cannon River. The river provided a reliable source of hydropower, which in turn sparked the development of prosperous flour and lumber mills.

By 1876, Northfield had four churches, a lending library, a weekly newspaper, and schools to serve a population of about 2,000. The town was connected to the rest of the world by the Milwaukee & St. Paul Railroad, and Northfieldians prided themselves on staying up to date. Their bank even had recently installed one of the newly patented Yale time-locks on its vault.

Joseph Lee Heywood was the bookkeeper at the First National Bank of Northfield. He was also a pillar of the community: In addition to his duties at the town's only bank, Heywood was treasurer for both the municipal government and Carleton College, the seven-year-old institution of higher learning nestled on the north end of town.

Heywood moved to Northfield in 1867. Born in New Hampshire to a family whose members included Revolutionary War veterans, Heywood served in the Union Army for almost three years during the Civil War. He was involved in several key battles and suffered prolonged and life-threatening illnesses before being mustered out as a corporal in 1865. He married two years after settling in Northfield, had a daughter, and after his first wife died, re-married. Slender and darkly bearded, Heywood was quiet and almost painfully shy, but still well-liked and respected in the community.

He was also sandwiched on the town's socio-economic scale between two Northfield residents who, like him, would inadvertently play prominent roles in the most dramatic event in local history. One was Nicholas Gustafson, a 30-year-old Swedish immigrant who arrived in America in early July, 1876. Gustafson had come with his 11-year-old nephew to live with his brother on a farm just outside Northfield. He had no money, spoke no English, and was indeed a stranger in a strange land.

The other was Adelbert Ames. Like Gustafson, Ames was a newcomer to Northfield, but with a very different background. A 41-year-old native of Maine, Ames by 1876 had been a Medal of Honor-winning brigadier general in the Union Army, and both a post-war governor and U.S. senator from Mississippi. He was also the son-in-law of Benjamin Butler, a Massachusetts politician who during the Civil War had been the incompetent and dictatorial military governor of New Orleans, and was widely hated in the South.

Unlike his father-in-law, Adelbert Ames was considered both honest and capable. But he was literally driven from office in Mississippi because of his efforts to win economic and political rights for African-Americans, and after the federal government failed to intervene when widespread terrorism was instigated by the Ku Klux Klan and other groups. Disillusioned, Ames came to Northfield in mid-1876 to join the family business run by his father and brother. The Ames Flour Mill was among the region's most prominent concerns. Its products had just won honors at the Centennial Exposition, and the company not only owned 25 percent of the Northfield bank, Ames' father and brother were bank directors.

Now, whether it was the Ames connection to the Northfield bank; the grasshopper plague in western Minnesota; both, or something else entirely that resulted in Joe Heywood's murder is a matter of historical conjecture and dispute. One school of thought is that the James-Younger gang targeted the Northfield bank even before it left Missouri, because Jesse, made intensely bitter by the war, wanted to strike a blow against Ames and Butler. Another is that gang members cased banks in several other towns before settling on Northfield. According to this theory, the town of St. Peter was deemed too small, and the town of Madelia didn't have a bank. Mankato had three banks. But the pedestrian traffic in front of the banks was thought to be too heavy; the town's money would be split among the three institutions, making the potential payoffs iffy, and/or a former Missourian recognized Jesse on the street while the gang was looking things over, and the gang feared the town's banks would be on guard.

After the Northfield robbery, Bob Younger insisted they had simply come to Minnesota for a good time, but while there learned that Ames had money in the Northfield bank. Since Jesse had an ax to grind against Ames, Bob said, and because the trip had proved expensive, they decided to rob the bank. "The yarn," a Minneapolis paper noted skeptically, "contradicts others that have been told of their reasons for selecting the Northfield bank, and their movements before and after the attempt do not bear out their assertions that it was a pleasure trip."

An uncle of the Youngers in Missouri offered the explanation that the boys "were going to the British Dominion (Canada), where they hoped to get something to do, and settle down in peace. On the way there, the James Boys got to gambling and lost all their money...(and) swore they wouldn't travel without money and so resolved on the bank robbery."

Cole Younger told several versions. In one account, Cole wrote the gang "had been informed that ex-Gov. Ames of Mississippi and Gen. Benjamin Butler of Massachusetts had deposited $75,000 in the national bank of that place, and it was that information that caused us to select the Bank of Northfield." Cole denied they had been scared off in Mankato because someone had recognized Jesse. But he admitted "that we talked about the banks of that part of the state (western Minnesota)...but we came to the conclusion that they had enough to do to care for the farmers who had already suffered too much from grasshoppers to be troubled by us, therefore we went to Northfield...".

They took their time getting there. At least five of the gang checked into Minneapolis' Nicollet Hotel on August 23 and 24. According to Cole's autobiography, they spent the time "seeing the sights, playing poker and looking around for information, after which we spent a similar period in St. Paul." Although Jesse apparently did encounter a woman he knew while visiting a brothel, he either couldn't find Samuel Hardwicke, the traitorous Missouri lawyer he had planned to kill, or gave up the idea.

The gang hardly kept low profiles. Two of them gambled—and lost heavily—in the hotel's casino, and caused a stir by doffing their long linen "duster" coats and revealing big revolvers hanging from cartridge belts around their shoulders. Others amused themselves by dropping coins from a second-floor hotel balcony to an organ grinder on the first floor. They wore their pants tucked into their boots, constantly sported jingling spurs, failed to remove their hats while indoors, talked with distinctive Missouri accents, walked with swaggers and generally stood out like naked men at a church picnic.

After leaving the Twin Cities, the outlaws split up to case various potential targets and buy getaway necessities. They purchased the finest horses they could find, for as much as $150 ($3,600 in 2021), as well as good saddles. They also bought extra ammunition for their new-model Smith & Wesson No. 3 or Colt single-action Army revolvers, of which each robber carried from two to four.

Posing as cattle dealers, two of the gang—probably Clell Miller and Jesse—visited Northfield a few days before the robbery "and made inquiries concerning the price of land." Then about mid-morning on September 7, all eight rode into town. For about four hours, they hung around, in groups of two or three. They got change at the bank, nosed around the stores and ate lunch at the restaurants. One of them offered to bet a restaurant owner $100 that Minnesota would go Democrat in the upcoming presidential election. Then about 2 p.m., three of the bandits entered the bank. According to Cole, he later learned the trio had shared a quart of whisky after lunch. If it was meant to steady their nerves, however, it didn't do much for their judgement.

The robbery took less than 10 minutes. It did not go smoothly. "The first thing we knew, the three men were upon or over the counter, with revolvers pointed at our heads," recalled Frank Wilcox, the bank's assistant bookkeeper, "one of them exclaiming 'throw up your hands, for we intend to rob the bank, and if you halloo, we will blow your God-damned brains out,' and we could not do otherwise than comply."

Along with Wilcox, whose 28th birthday was scheduled for the next day, the bank was staffed that afternoon by 27-year-old Alonzo Bunker, the teller, and Joseph Heywood, the bookkeeper. Heywood was filling in as cashier and de-facto bank manager, since the regular teller and manager were attending the Centennial Exposition in Philadelphia. The bandit trio consisted of Bob Younger, Charlie Pitts and Frank James.

Heywood was ordered to open the safe, which contained about $15,000 ($360,000 in 2022), and actually wasn't locked anyway during normal business hours. He refused, however, claiming the time-lock could not be opened. When Frank entered the vault to check, Heywood shut the vault door on him. Pitts pulled Heywood away and freed Frank. Enraged, Frank pulled a Bowie knife and cut Heywood's throat slightly. He threatened to cut deeper if the safe weren't opened promptly. Instead, Heywood struggled with the robbers, shouting "Murder! Murder!" That earned him a blow on the skull from Frank's pistol butt.

While Heywood lay on the floor, dazed and bleeding, Frank fired a shot near his head, meant to intimidate him into cooperating. The distraction was enough to spur the teller Bunker to make a break for the bank's open back door. Pitts fired at him twice, hitting him in the shoulder, but Bunker escaped anyway. After a few more minutes of cursing and looking for cash not locked in the safe (they missed $2,000 in an unlocked drawer under the counter), the frustrated bandits left with a total of $26.70 in loose change—but not before Frank turned once again to Heywood. At point-blank range, he shot Heywood in the head. "The wound was a fearful one," a newspaper noted, "and must have produced instant death...literally blowing his brains out."

The five bandits outside the bank, meanwhile, were faring just as badly as their compatriots. Even before the shooting began inside the bank, hardware store owner J.S. Allen had smelled a rat. Allen tried to follow the three bandits into the bank, only to be halted by a gun-wielding Clell Miller. Miller, with Cole Younger, had been posted outside the building as lookouts while Jesse, Bill Chadwell and Jim Younger were mounted and waiting nearby as a rescue party should it be needed. "You son of a bitch,"

Miller snarled at the storekeeper, "don't you holler!" Allen ignored the advice. Breaking free from Miller's hold on his collar, Allen raced around the corner, shouting "grab your guns, boys, they're robbing the bank!"

The boys grabbed their guns, or at least whatever they could find. Several who couldn't find guns found rocks instead, and began hurling them at Cole and Miller, as well as the robbers leaving the bank. The three mounted bandits who had been waiting in reserve galloped in at the sound of shots from inside the bank. firing their revolvers in the air in an effort to cower the townspeople.

Only Northfield didn't cower. Farmer Elias Stacy snatched a shotgun loaded with birdshot from J.S. Allen's hardware store and fired at Clell Miller, hitting him in the face and knocking him off his horse. Anselm Manning, who owned another hardware store, pulled a rifle from his store window and killed Bob Younger's horse, which was being used as cover by the bandits.

Henry Wheeler, a 22-year-old University of Michigan medical student home on vacation, raced from where he had been loafing outside his father's pharmacy to a nearby hotel lobby. There, he grabbed a Civil War-era carbine, climbed to the third floor and put a bullet into Miller, killing him. Manning, the hardware store owner who had shot Bob Younger's horse, shot Cole Younger in the hip, reloaded, and killed Bill Chadwell. Medical student Wheeler shot Bob in the elbow, wounding him badly.

Despite his own wound, Cole managed to get his brother up behind him as the remnants of the gang galloped out of town. Jim Younger had taken a hit in the shoulder, and Frank James in the leg. Only Charlie Pitts and Jesse apparently escaped unharmed.

Not all of the casualties were gang members. Nicolaus Gustafson, the Swedish immigrant who had been in America all of two months, and in Northfield all of two weeks, did not understand the bandits' warnings to get off the street. He was shot in the head, either by Cole or by an errant ricochet from the hail of gunfire. Either way, he died four days later.

The body of Joseph Heywood, the martyred hero who had refused to hand over the town's money, was taken home. "...The courage he displayed was more than is found in the average man," the *Minneapolis Tribune* noted the next day. "...One who can stand unflinchingly in the face of loaded pistols and brandished knives and protect the trust in his hands is made of the stuff of which heroes are made ...". Heywood's grieving wife concurred: "I would not have had him do otherwise," she said.

While Northfield mourned its fallen hero, the bloodied and bedraggled bandits tried to find their way home. "We were in a strange country," Cole wrote. "On the prairie, our maps were all right, but when we got into the big woods and among the lakes, we were practically lost." At one point they kidnapped a farmer and forced him to guide them. When his usefulness proved doubtful, the James brothers wanted to kill him, according to Cole, but the rest of the gang voted to let him go. They extracted from him a vow not to talk. Upon his release, he made a beeline for the nearest posse.

There were plenty of posses from which to choose. Emboldened by hefty dead-or-alive rewards offered by the state and the Northfield bank, hundreds of men were hunting the gang. Most of the hunters were inept amateurs, or law enforcement officers whose jealousies of each other hampered efforts to organize the pursuit. Still, the sheer numbers meant there was no safe place to hide.

The gang's horses wore out, and after a few days, the outlaws were afoot, wearing boots meant for riding, not walking. They ate what they could find—green corn, watermelons, wild plums and almost no meat or hot food. The Youngers' wounds, especially Bob's, meant they could only travel short distances before being forced to stop and rest. Even the weather conspired against them: It rained almost incessantly.

A week after the robbery, still resting and hiding more than moving, Jesse and Frank decided to take off on their own, after failing to convince

Cole and Jim Younger to abandon—or even "mercy kill"—Bob. Charlie Pitts chose to stay with the Youngers, perhaps proving there *is* honor among at least some thieves. The James boys managed to steal a series of horses, boldly stopping from time to time at farmhouses for food. They briefly kidnapped a doctor and forced him to give them his pants and coat to replace their bullet-riddled attire before releasing him. And they kept moving, for several hundred miles, across Minnesota and finally home to Missouri. They had nothing to show for their raid north, but they had escaped.

The rest of the gang was not as lucky. On Sept. 21, two weeks after the robbery and only 80 miles from Northfield, the 17-year-old son of a farmer spotted the desperadoes near the town of Madelia and alerted the local authorities. A posse of about 40 quickly formed and cornered the outlaws in brush and woods along a riverbank. The Youngers and Pitts decided to fight it out. When Cole told the as-yet uninjured Pitts he might consider surrendering, Charlie replied "I'll not go...I can die as well as you can."

As it turned out, he could die better, or at least faster. When seven members of the posse finally summoned the courage to charge the bandits, Pitts was killed almost immediately. All three of the Youngers were also shot: Jim four times, including in the jaw and back; Bob in the right lung, and Cole a staggering eight times, one bullet lodging behind his right eye. In addition to their gunshot wounds, they were so weather-beaten and water-logged that when Cole's boots were removed, all of his toenails fell off. But miraculously, none of them died.

The prisoners were taken to Madelia. As they slowly recovered, the jailed Youngers became tourist attractions—and even objects of some sympathy and respect for their daring and endurance—and for resolutely denying the two bandits who escaped were Jesse and Frank James. Instead, the Youngers insisted, the two were fellows named Howard and Woods.

"The attempt to rob a bank in the heart of a town of two thousand population, in open day, was a deed requiring much physical courage," the *Minneapolis Tribune* scolded the outlaws' admirers, "but after all, it was a dastardly crime...better we say that the men who committed the crime should have escaped altogether than that being apprehended, society should surrender to them morbid sympathy for their suffering, or a mistaken admiration for their courage...Their hands are red with the blood of the innocent and unoffending; and women and men should look on them with loathing, and rather rejoice in their suffering as the merited reward of their crimes...".

Once they had healed enough to travel, the Youngers were moved to the town of Faribault, which was about 13 miles from Northfield and the government seat of Rice County. Their trial, for the murders of Joseph Heywood and Nicolaus Gustafson, the wounding of Alonzo Bunker, and the bank robbery itself, was set for November.

Also set for November was America's presidential election. It would prove to be a much bigger crime than the raid on Northfield.

Chapter 8 Notes

The other robbers *Chicago Tribune*, Aug. 7, 1876, p. 5.

The *Tribune* was *St. Louis Republican*, Aug. 4, 1876, p. 5.

"In all the" *Lexington (Mo.) Weekly Caucasian*, Sept. 5, 1874, p. 1.

On the sultry, Mark Lee Gardner, *Shot All to Hell*, p. 11.

In the baggage *St. Louis Republican*, Aug. 4, 1876, p. 5.

After the robbery *Kansas City (Mo.) Times*, Aug. 15, 1876, p. 2.

Jesse Woodson James T.J. Stiles, *Jesse James, Last Rebel of the Civil War*, p. 285.

Patton was right *Kansas City (Mo.) Daily Journal of Commerce*, Aug. 13, 1876, p. 1.

Although virtually no one Ibid.

She then showed Ibid.

Both sides had Thomas Goodrich, *Black Flag: Guerilla Warfare on the Frontier, 1861-1865*, p. 10; p. 26.

Missouri's "bushwhackers" and Ibid., pp. 135-145.

Anderson's rationale for Stiles, op. cit., p. 111.

"Both sides did" *Pittsburgh Press*, March 21, 1915, p. 58.

Cole, who began, Cole Younger, *The Story of Cole Younger, by Himself*, p. 40.

Of the other three Some authors believe Bill Chadwell was an alias for Minnesota-born horse thief Bill Stiles; that Stiles was the one who talked Jesse James into the Minnesota foray, or that Chadwell and Stiles were two different men and Stiles was an undetected ninth man on the raid. But in his 2013 book, *Shot All to Hell*, author Mark Lee Gardner makes a convincing case that Chadwell and Stiles were different individuals, and that Stiles had nothing to do with the robbery. Based on the available evidence, I concur with Gardner.

"It is safe" *St. Louis Post-Dispatch*, July 13, 1876, p. 2.

Frank James was *Pittsburgh Press*, March 21, 1915, p. 58.

The difference between John Newman Edwards, "A Terrible Quintette," p. 6.

Being light-hearted *Kansas City Times*, Oct. 15, 1872, p. 4.

Four years older, *Winona (Mn.) Daily Republican*, Oct. 13, 1883, p. 1; Stiles, op. cit., p. 234.

The Younger brothers *St. Louis Globe-Democrat*, Sept. 27, 1876, p. 1.

Some notable examples For detailed accounts of these and other robberies during the decade leading to the Northfield raid, see both T.J. Stiles' *Jesse James, Last Rebel of the Civil War*, and Ted Yeatman's *Frank and Jesse James: The Story Behind the Legend*. Both are excellent, and for the most part complement, rather than contradict, each other.

"Some editors call us" *Kansas City Times*, Oct. 15, 1872, p. 4.

"In a letter published Kansas *City Times*, Aug. 18, 1876, p. 4; Aug. 23, 1876, p. 2.

In a corner *St. Johnsbury (Vt.) Caledonian*, Aug. 11, 1876, p. 2

For the relatively *Lawrence (Ks.) Daily Journal*, Oct. 19, 1876, p. 3.

The increasing ubiquity Frank Triplett, *Jesse James*, p. 169.

If banks proved, Marshall Trimble, "How Common Were Stagecoach Robberies in the Old West?" *True West Magazine* Blog, Oct. 23, 2010.

An indignant Kansas *Kansas City Times*, Aug. 18, 1876, p. 2

In the West, See Eric Cachinero, "Highwaymen: Nevada outlaws conducted the first train robbery in the West," *Nevada Magazine*, Vol. 78, No. 2 (March/April 2018), pp. 72-78.

It would be *Minneapolis Tribune*, Aug. 19, 1876, p. 2.

Located about 40 Much of the information on the town of Northfield was gathered from the Northfield Historical Society's website and at the bank museum in Northfield itself.

Joe Heywood moved See Gerald D. Otis, *Joseph Lee Heywood, His Life and Tragic Death*. Self-published, 2013.

One school of For the various theories and arguments of why the gang selected Northfield, see Mark Lee Gardner's *Shot All to Hell*; T.J. Stiles' *Jesse James, Last Rebel of the Civil War*, and Ted Yeatman's *Frank and Jesse James*. All present thoughtful arguments for their version; none are overwhelmingly convincing.

After the Northfield *Minneapolis Tribune*, Sept. 25, 1876, p. 1.

An uncle in *St. Louis Republican*, Oct. 22, 1876, p. 7.

Cole Younger told *St. Paul Globe*, July 4, 1897, p. 1.

They took their Younger, op. cit., p. 62.

Posing as cattle *St. Louis Globe-Democrat*, Sept. 11, 1876, p. 1.

The robbery took *Chicago Tribune*, Sept. 11, 1876, p. 5.

Along with Wilcox While most writers and historians agree Bob Younger and Pitts were two of the three robbers who entered the bank, there is some question as to whether the third was Frank or Jesse James. Based on witness descriptions and other evidence, I think it was almost certainly Frank.

While Heywood lay *St. Louis Globe-Democrat*, Sept. 11, 1876, p. 1.

The body of *Minneapolis Tribune*, Sept. 8, 1876, p. 2; Gardner, op. cit., p. 99.

While Northfield mourned, Younger, op. cit., p. 67.

The rest of the gang Ibid., p. 69.

"The attempt to" *Minneapolis Tribune*, Sept. 25, 1876, p. 1.

CHAPTER 9

"Seven can't beat eight"

Stealing a president—and the presidency

INTERLUDE

On the evening of Nov. 7, 1876, while the Younger Brothers were in a Minnesota jail awaiting trial and the rest of America waited to learn the outcome of a bitterly contested presidential election, seven shoeless men huddled in the cold, dark silence of a tomb, in a cemetery just outside Springfield, Illinois. They were waiting for grave robbers. More precisely, they were waiting for kidnappers, who planned to steal a body and hold it for ransom. The corpse in question was Abraham Lincoln's.

Since his assassination more than 11 years before, the martyred president had reposed in a lead-lined cedar coffin, which was inside a marble sarcophagus, which was inside a large and handsome tomb in the Oak Ridge Cemetery, about two miles outside central Springfield. The tomb, which Lincoln shared with two sons who had preceded him in death, was secured with a simple padlock. There were no guards or caretakers on the grounds. So unthinkable was the idea that anyone would desecrate Lincoln's resting place that the sarcophagus had been sealed with plaster of Paris rather than cement.

But James "Big Jim" Kennally had thought the unthinkable. Kennally was essentially a Midwest gangster. He ran a livery stable in St. Louis and owned part of a bar in Chicago. His main business, however, was as a wholesaler of counterfeit currency. He sold bogus bills to "boodle carriers," who then passed them off a few at a time at banks and retail establishments. Kennally, however, had a problem. Benjamin Boyd, the master counterfeiter who produced Kennally's merchandise, had been caught and was doing a 10-year prison stretch. So Kennally came up with a plan as simple in concept as it was audacious in scale.

He would steal Lincoln's remains, secreting them in the sands of a seldom-visited stretch of Lake Michigan's coastline. He would then demand the immediate pardon of Boyd, plus a $200,000 ransom ($4.8 million in 2022) from the federal government, in exchange for revealing the remains' whereabouts. Election Day was the perfect time to pull the caper, as everyone in Springfield would be attending rallies and awaiting poll results rather than hanging around a graveyard.

To carry out his scheme, Kennally enlisted three men. One was Terrence Mullen, a Chicago saloon keeper. Another was Jack Hughes, an accomplished counterfeit money passer. The third was Lewis Swegles, who had a solid reputation in the Chicago underworld as a horse thief and all-around crook. In reality, however, Swegles was a "roper," slang for a paid police informant. As the plot unfolded, Swegles spilled every detail to Patrick D. Tyrell, who headed the Chicago branch of the U.S. Secret Service. In 1876, the chief duty of the service was not to guard the president (a task not formalized until 1894) but to deal with America's severe counterfeiting problem. So serious was the issue that at the time the Secret Service was formed in 1865, it was estimated that the half the currency in circulation was phony.

Since grave-robbing wasn't a crime that fell under the service's official purview, Tyrell put together an ad hoc group that included two private detectives from the Pinkerton Agency, as well as a few other acquaintances of Tyrell. His idea was to catch the ghouls in the act. Because the tomb resoundingly echoed the slightest sound, Tyrell's group removed their shoes and waited for two hours in total silence and pitch blackness for the grave robbers.

When the bad guys finally showed up, however, the grisly drama took on comic-opera overtones. The robbers broke the tool they had brought to destroy the tomb lock. They had to resort to a hacksaw, which took more than a half-hour to accomplish the task. Then they discovered they couldn't lift the 500-pound casket out of the sarcophagus. Tired of waiting,

Tyrell's detectives decided to close in. In doing so one of the Pinkerton detectives accidentally fired his pistol, causing the robbers to flee. In the ensuing chase, the good guys ended up shooting at each other, and the robbers escaped.

But not for long. Not suspecting he was already known as one of the grave robbers and was under surveillance, Mullen returned to his Chicago bar. When Hughes showed up at the saloon on Nov. 17, both men were arrested. Since there was no specific Illinois law against body snatching, the pair were charged with attempting to steal Lincoln's coffin, valued at $75 ($1,800 in 2021). They were convicted and did a year in jail. Kennally, the plot's mastermind, was not charged. Fearful of another attempt, the memorial's overseers secretly buried Lincoln's body in the tomb's basement, in a shallow unmarked grave. In 1901 it was relocated again, this time in a 10-foot-deep vault that was filled with tons of concrete.

The caper was so incredible, many Americans didn't believe it. Some thought it was a tasteless and feeble election-year stunt by the Democrats or the Republicans. Others deemed it a scheme to enable one of the Secret Service agents who had been involved in foiling the plot to regain his former job as Chicago's chief of police. Still others thought it was an effort by unrepentant former Confederates to avenge themselves on Lincoln. "The crime was too horrible for belief," noted the *Chicago Tribune*, which published a lengthy and detailed account the day after Mullen and Hughes were arrested. "Nothing of the kind had ever before occurred in the country; and it is not to be wondered at that nine-tenths of those who read the dispatch giving the particulars were loath to believe the statements made."

But as startling as the idea of stealing Lincoln's body was, it wasn't even the year's most outrageous event surrounding American presidents. That event involved stealing the presidency itself.

As America's 16th chief executive's eternal rest was being disturbed by grave robbers in Illinois, the 19th president-to-be was going to bed in New York City. At least that's who Samuel J. Tilden thought he was. After all, Tilden, the governor of New York and Democratic presidential candidate, had garnered a quarter of a million more popular votes more than Rutherford B. Hayes, his Republican rival in the heated campaign that had concluded that day.More important, by the time Tilden drifted off to sleep in his handsome Victorian mansion, off New York City's tony Gramercy Park, it was projected his share of the nation's electoral votes would top 200—and in 1876, it took only 185 to win the White House.

At 62, Tilden's drooping left eyelid and ghostly pallor were testimonials to a lifetime of ill health. He was short and thin, clean-shaven in a time of full, manly beards, and had a prominent nose—all of which may have contributed to him being a lifelong bachelor. But that status might also have stemmed from a seeming indifference to human intimacy of any kind. He was undeniably intelligent and industrious. The son of a prosperous upstate New York store owner, Tilden compensated for his sickly childhood by devouring every book he could get his hands on, developed an appetite for politics and fought off a seemingly unbroken string of illnesses long enough to finish law school.

He had a knack for business. If not handsome, by 1876 he was handsomely wealthy, with an estimated worth of at least $5 million ($120 million in 2022.) Most of his wealth was earned as a corporate lawyer, often for the era's great robber barons. He had a particular talent for "healing" financially ailing railroads through adroit mergers and divestments, and timely acquisitions. His coldly calculating methods earned him a nickname: "The Great Forecloser."

Tilden was also extraordinarily adept at politics, a somewhat surprising gift in light of hiscold-fish personality. His climb up the political ladder included stops as corporate counsel for New York City, state legislator, and chairman of the Democratic Party in New York. He was a vocal opponent of fighting a war to preserve the Union, and campaigned against Abraham

Lincoln in both 1860 and 1864, which were not as unpopular stances in New York as they were in most of the rest of the North. In 1874, Tilden was elected governor of New York in a landslide, due mainly to his key role in toppling America's biggest crook.

In the Gilded Age, that was saying something. But if there was a poster boy for the era's rampant political corruption, it was William Magear "Boss" Tweed. Sporting an outlandish wardrobe to cover his mountainous girth, Tweed rose from a lowly volunteer firefighter and city alderman to congressman and state senator—and ruler of an extensive network of elected officials, government workers and private contractors. The "Tweed Ring" systematically looted tens of millions from New York City's treasury, mostly through kickbacks on public works projects and acquisitions. When an electrician submitted a $60,000 bid to install fire alarms, for example, Tweed countered "if we get you a contract for $450,000, will you give us $225,000?"

In 1872, the *New York Times* exposed the ring—after beating back an attempt by Tweed to buy the paper and stop the story from being printed. Genuinely outraged at Tweed's excesses, Tilden jumped to the front of a crusade to topple "The Boss." Utilizing his analytical acumen, he pored over Tweed's bank records and compiled a damning affidavit that confirmed the *Times'* charges. New Yorkers, Tilden declared in a stirring speech in October, 1872, "have been the subject of a conspiracy, the most audacious and most wicked ever known...I come before you to advocate a union of all honest men against a combination of plunderers." Tweed would eventually die in jail, after a spectacular-if-temporary escape to Cuba and then Spain. "I guess Tilden and (prosecutor Charles S.) Fairchild have killed me at last," Tweed said from his cell. "I hope they will be satisfied now."

As governor, Tilden built on his reputation as a reformer, fighting a well-publicized battle against a gang of state legislators who were milking funds from New York's canal system. Given the myriad incidents that had mired Congress and the Grant Administration in a swamp of scandal, "Tilden and Reform" seemed to be a timely campaign slogan. On June 28, three days after Custer's demise at the Little Bighorn (a fact still unknown to virtually all of America for another week), Democratic national convention delegates in St. Louis unanimously nominated Tilden on the second ballot.

"The government no longer exists for the people," Tilden told a crowd in Albany after winning the nomination, "the people exist only for the government...now, I ask, what is the remedy for these public evils, for the private distress, for this disorder in business which carries suffering into every household?...it is comprised in one word 'Reform.'"

While reform gave him a solid issue on which to run, Tilden had other assets as well. He had a genius for organizing and analyzing demographic data, and he recognized, well before most politicians of his time, the value of marketing. His presidential campaign featured a "Newspaper Popularity Bureau," whose team of writers churned out hundreds of flattering articles and distributed them to newspapers across the country. A "Literary Bureau" produced advertising that ranged from the print equivalent of infomercials to over-the-top handbills that would have made P.T. Barnum envious. The political calculus was that if Tilden could win his home state and most or all of the former Confederate states, where the Republican Party of Lincoln was widely loathed, Democrats had a better-than-even chance of winning the White House in 1876, for the first time in 20 years.

By the end of Election Day, a stunning 81.6 percent of America's eligible voters had exercised their franchise, still the highest rate in U.S. history for a presidential election. Tilden spent the late afternoon at the Everett House, a posh hotel not far from his home, and the headquarters of the Democratic National Committee. Later, he walked home through the bracing November evening with a coterie of friends and followers. His mansion was equipped with a ticker tape machine that allowed the group to monitor the returns. Since not everyone was an admirer of his reform efforts, and politics in 1876 could be a brutal business, Tilden's mansion was also equipped with steel doors and a secret escape passage to a side street.

A bit more than 500 miles west of the Manhattan mansion of "Centennial Sam," as Tilden had recently been dubbed, his GOP presidential rival was entertaining a small group of increasingly despondent friends. The house Ohio Gov. Rutherford B. Hayes was renting on the outskirts of Columbus—there was no Ohio governor's mansion at the time and the state's chief executives were on their own when it came to housing in the capital—was nice enough. The two-story building was almost surrounded by a cluster of tall trees, and had a handsome columned porch running the length of the front.

Inside, Lucy Hayes, the candidate's wife of 24 years, was serving refreshments—no liquor, as both she and the governor were teetotalers—while the group monitored the gloomy election returns: New Jersey for Tilden; New York for Tilden, even Hayes' home state of Ohio seemingly in doubt. Eventually, Lucy fled to her bedroom with a migraine, leaving Rutherford, known as "Ruddy" or "Rud" to his family and friends, to carry on hosting duties. He did so, Hayes noted in the diary he had kept faithfully since he was 12, "without difficulty or much effort. I became the most composed and cheerful of the party."

"Composed and cheerful" was a common condition for the 54-year-old Hayes. People found him easy to like, with a modest demeanor, a self-deprecating sense of humor, and a knack for listening as well as talking. He was physically impressive as well, handsomely bedecked with a full mustache and beard, and a full head of light brown hair just beginning to gray. He had deep-set blue eyes, broad shoulders and a deep voice. The portrait of 19th century manliness was rounded out by his favorite exercise, boxing, and also by being the father of four sons and a daughter.

He had not been born rich or privileged, but he was lucky. His father, a whiskey distiller, died a month before Hayes was born, leaving him with a sister (two other siblings died in childhood) and an overprotective but unsupportive mother. But he also had an uncle, who had made a fortune in the mercantile and banking business in the town of Fremont, Ohio, about midway between Toledo and Cleveland. The uncle made Rud Hayes his heir, and left him with a tidy fortune that by 1876 was reckoned at around $500,000 ($12 million in 2022.) But it did not leave him with a swelled head.

"He was a very modest boy," the Democratic editor of a Fremont newspaper recalled not long after Hayes won the GOP nomination, "and while I suppose he had a good enough opinion of himself, he never was an upstart...I don't believe in Hayes politically, and shan't vote for him, but he's a square man, and if elected will make an honest president."

After graduating from Harvard Law School (the first lawyer-president to actually go to a law school), Hayes set out his attorney's shingle first in his hometown of Fremont, then in Cincinnati. There he gained a sterling reputation as a criminal defense lawyer, in several cases defending fugitive slaves. He was elected the city's attorney, but joined the Union Army when the war broke out. Wounded several times, once severely, Hayes was commended by Gen. Grant for "conspicuous gallantry" and by war's end had risen to the rank of brigadier general.

In 1864, without his knowledge, he was nominated by friends for a seat in Congress. He agreed to run, but refused to ask for a leave so he could campaign. "An officer fit for duty who at this crisis would abandon his post to electioneer for a seat in Congress ought to be scalped," he lectured a friend who had suggested the idea of a furlough. "You may feel perfectly sure I shall do no such thing."

He won anyway, and served most of two terms before quitting to run for governor of Ohio. Hayes narrowly won in an election that otherwise went solidly for Democrats, and was re-elected two years later. In 1873, he left office, but was talked into running for, and won, a third term in 1875. He was personally popular in a politically up-for-grabs state, but little known outside Ohio as 1876 began. So Hayes was considered at best a possible GOP vice presidential choice when the Republican nominating convention began in June in Cincinnati.

On the first ballot, he got just 65 votes, which was good for fifth place. But supporters of the four men in front of him—Rep. James Blaine of Maine, Sen. Oliver Morton of Indiana, former Treasury Secretary Benjamin

Bristow and Sen. Roscoe Conkling of New York—could not or would not coalesce behind any of the front-runners. On the seventh ballot, Hayes was deemed an acceptable alternative by 384 delegates, five more than needed for the nomination.

It was hardly the resounding show of support Democrats accorded Tilden, and Hayes was realistic about his chances to win the presidency. "...I find myself strangely calm and indifferent about it," Hayes wrote two days before the election, adding on Election Day, "I still think Democratic chances the best." Late on Election Night, Hayes climbed into bed. "Talked with Lucy, consoling her," he noted a few days later. "We soon fell into a refreshing sleep, and the affair seemed over."

While Hayes and Tilden slumbered, a 57-year-old one-legged fellow with a luxuriant mustache, receding hairline, beady eyes and well-earned nickname—"Devil Dan"—was stumping around the Republican Party's national headquarters. This was located in the Fifth Avenue Hotel, a splendid six-story marble building just off New York City's Madison Square.

On the scale of humanity, Daniel B. Sickles was somewhere between "colorful character" and "murderous scoundrel." The scion of a wealthy New York family, Sickles was an up-and-coming star in the Democratic Party, until 1859. That was when he shot and killed an unarmed man on a New York sidewalk. The man had been fooling around with Sickles' wife. Tried for murder, Sickles employed the then almost unheard-of strategy of pleading temporary insanity, even though the murder was so clearly planned that Sickles had waited in ambush and was carrying not one, but three, pistols. In any event, it worked, and he was acquitted. He then reconciled with his wife, while continuing to engage in numerous affairs himself.

However, the incident did dash his hopes of winning high political office. Undaunted, Sickles obtained an officer's commission in the Union Army when the war broke out, eventually rising to the rank of brigadier general. At the Battle of Gettysburg, he grew bored with his unit's assignment away from the main action, and rashly moved his unit without permission. The move almost proved disastrous for the Union Army as it

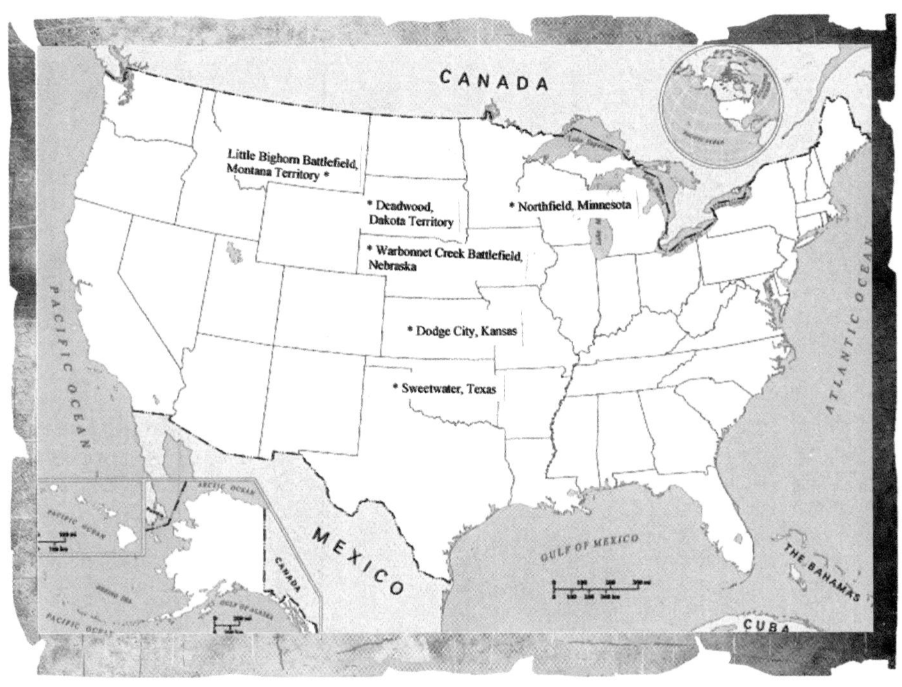

Where the West was Wild in 1876.

Bat Masterson in his mid-20s. He has already been a buffalo hunter, Indian fighter, deputy marshal, county sheriff — and gunfighter. — *Courtesy Kansas State Historical Society*

A 1910 newspaper ad of the by-then-portly New York City journalist Bat Masterson, plugging for an automatic pistol.

An irreverent lizard suns himself on the tombstone of 'Sweetwater Shootout' victim Mollie Brennan. — *Ceil Dolan Wiegand*

Actor Gene Barry as TV's version of Bat, on the cover of a 1950s comic book.

Dodge City entrepreneur Charlie Rath sits atop a mound of 40,000 buffalo hides waiting for shipment back east in 1874. — *Courtesy Kansas State Historical Society*

The interior of Dodge City's Long Branch Saloon, circa late 1870s. There was no real Matt Dillon, but there was a real Bat and Wyatt to keep order.

Wyatt Earp, seated, and Bat Masterson, probably taken in 1876, while both were deputy marshals in Dodge City.

Wyatt Earp, about the age of 21. At the time, he was a police constable in Missouri.

Wyatt Earp sometime in the 1880s, after Tombstone and the OK Corral gunfight.

An elderly Wyatt Earp gazes in 1926 across the Colorado River from California into Arizona, where his status as a Wild West legend was forever established.
— *Courtesy Arizona Historical Society*

Actor Hugh O'Brian as the iconic 1950s TV version of Wyatt Earp.

Modern Dodge City's larger-than-life bronze statue of Wyatt.
— Ceil Dolan Wiegand.

Lt. Col. George Armstrong Custer in 1875, a year before the Little Bighorn battle.
— *Library of Congress*

Elizabeth Custer as a young Civil War bride.
— *Library of Congress*

CUSTER'S LAST FIGHT.

'Custer's Last Fight,' as depicted in Frederick Whittaker's slavish biography published just months after the battle.

Where Custer fell at the Little Bighorn. His is the only marker with a name.
— Ceil Dolan Wiegand

Cheyenne warrior Lame White Man's marker at the Little Bighorn monument. It took 123 years for him to get it.
— Ceil Dolan Wiegand

Part of the Little Bighorn's memorial to the battle's winners, installed in 2003.
— Ceil Dolan Wiegand

Will Cody in his late teens.
— Courtesy Buffalo Bill Center of the West

From left, Wild Bill Hickok, Texas Jack Omohundro and Buffalo Bill Cody, circa 1872-73, while touring as 'actors.'
— Courtesy Buffalo Bill Center of the West

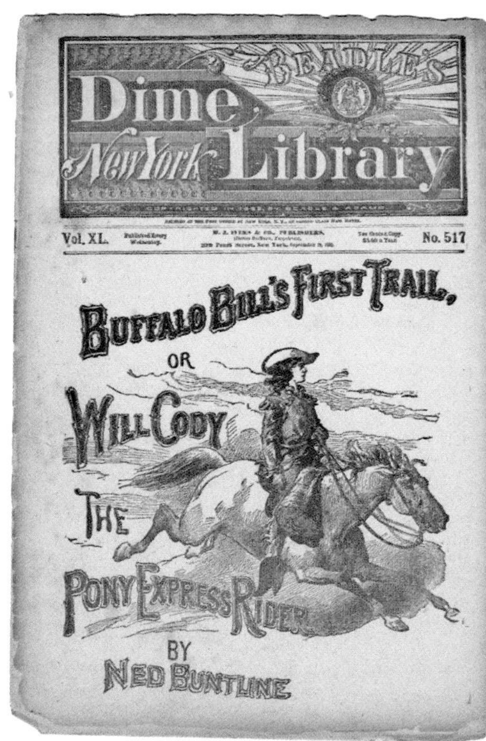

The cover of an 1888 Buffalo Bill Dime Novel, by Ned Buntline. It was Buntline who convinced Cody to try stage acting.

Artist Robert Lindneux's highly exaggerated 1928 painting of Buffalo Bill taking the 'First Scalp for Custer' at Warbonnet Creek.
— *Courtesy of Buffalo Bill Center of the West.*

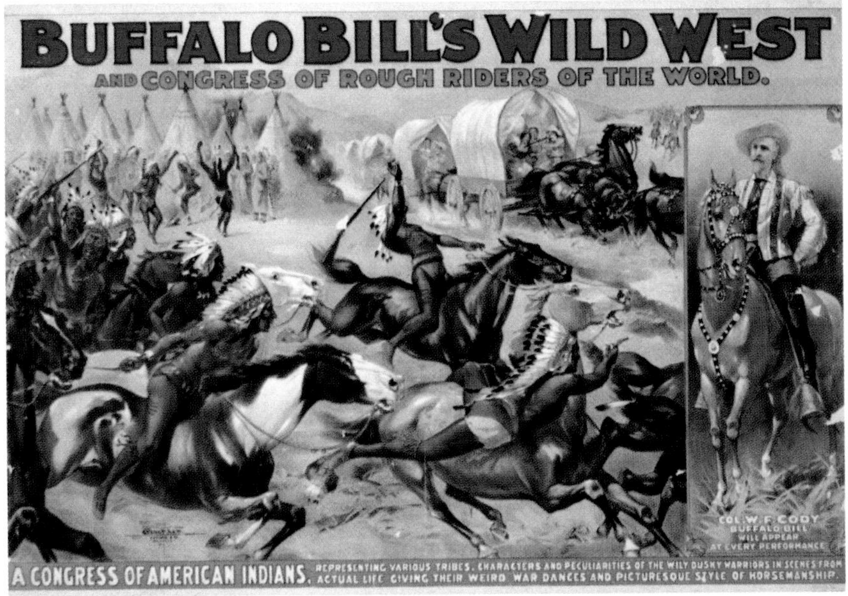

An 1898 advertising poster for Cody's Wild West Show. — *Library of Congress.*

Buffalo Bill Cody in stage attire circa 1877. He wore this outfit or something very similar in the fight at Warbonnet Creek. — *Courtesy Buffalo Bill Center of the West*

Sitting Bull and Buffalo Bill in a publicity pose that appeared on everything from postcards to rifle ads. — *Courtesy Buffalo Bill Center of the West*

Col. William F. Cody in 1907, at the age of 61.
— *Library of Congress*

The Warbonnet Creek Battlefield Memorial in Northwest Nebraska. That's it - the whole memorial.
— *Ceil Dolan Wiegand.*

WILD BILL.

SEVERAL months after the ending of the civil war I visited the city of Springfield in Southwest Missouri. Springfield is not a burgh of extensive dimensions, yet it is the largest in that part of the State, and all roads lead to it—which is one reason why it was the *point d'ap-*

Vol. XXXIV.—No. 201.—T

The 1867 magazine story that launched the myth of Wild Bill Hickok.

Wild Bill Hickok, circa early 1870s. —*Courtesy of Kansas State Historical Society*

Actor Guy Madison as the 1950s' Wild Bill, promoting breakfast cereal.

One of the few known photos of Agnes Lake Hickok, American circus innovator and widow of Wild Bill. — *Courtesy Kansas State Historical Society.*

An 1895 portrait of Martha Jane Canary, AKA 'Calamity Jane.' Caption repeats Jane's claim to have been a U.S. Cavalry scout. —*Library of Congress*

Downtown Deadwood in 1876. —*Library of Congress*

Downtown Deadwood in 2021. — *Ceil Dolan Wiegand*

Steve Utter, left, and Wild Bill's partner, Charlie Utter, at Hickok's original grave site.

Wild Bill's grave in 2021.
— *Ceil Dolan Wiegand*

Jesse James in 1875, a year before the Northfield bank raid.
— Courtesy State Historical Society of Missouri

A young Cole Younger, probably taken about 1862.

Frank James at the end of the Civil War in 1865.
— Courtesy State Historical Society of Missouri

The Northfield First National Bank in 1874. The bank entrance is by the wagon to the left in the photo.
—Courtesy Northfield Historical Society

The Northfield bank museum in 2021.
— Ceil Dolan Wiegand

A dime novel depiction of the Northfield Bank Robbery.
— *Courtesy of Gould Library Special Collections, Carleton College*

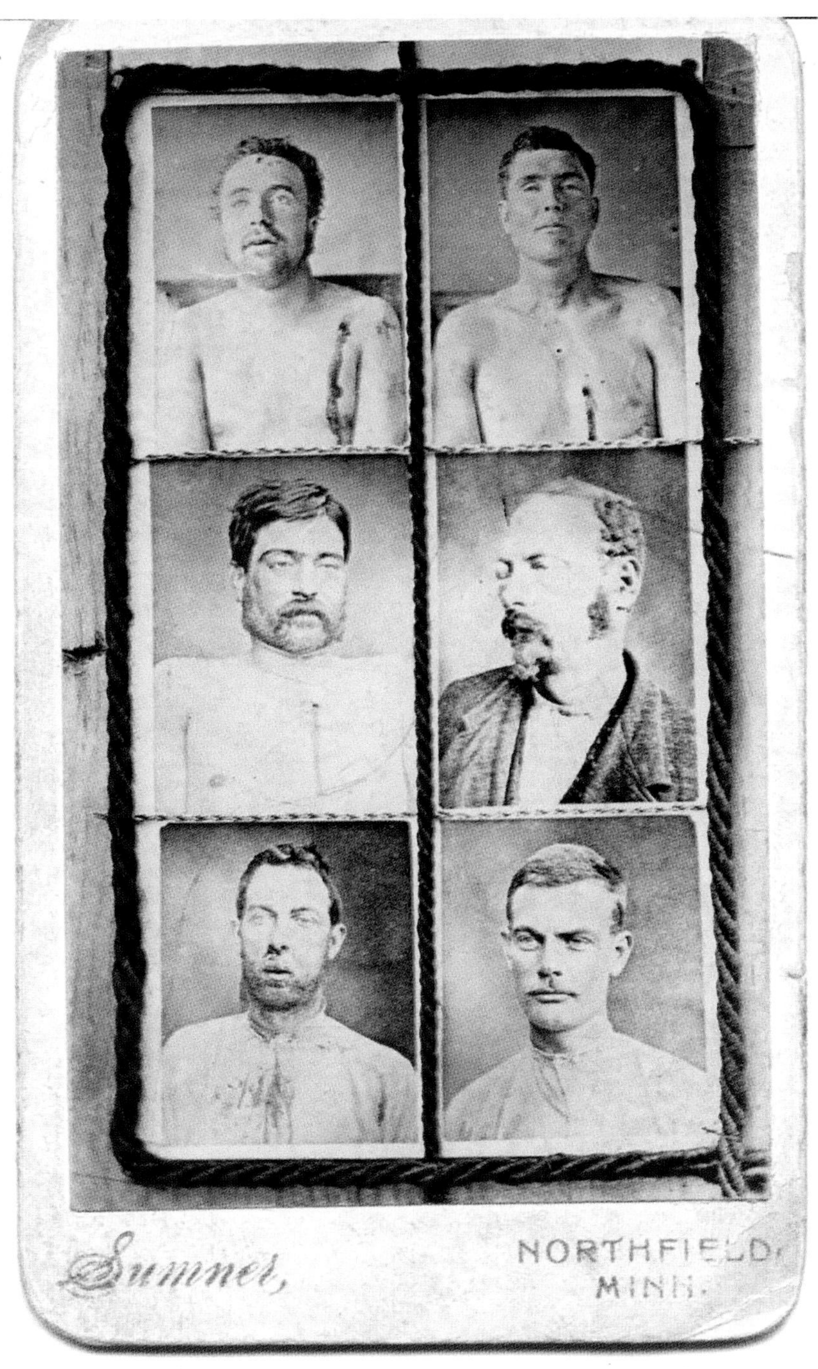

The Northfield bandits. The first three are the slain robbers; the last three are the wounded and captured Younger Brothers. Only the James Boys escaped.
— Courtesy Northfield Historical Society

The murder of Jesse James, as depicted in Frank Triplett's hastily concocted 1882 biography.
—Courtesy State Historical Society of Missouri

The body of Jesse James, following his 1882 murder at the hands of a gang member.
—Courtesy State Historical Society of Missouri

Frank James in 1898.
—Library of Congress

Cole Younger in 1915,
a year before his death.
—Library of Congress

No telling who a Wild West legend might have to tangle with...

WEEKLY. [MAY 13, 1876.

P. T. BARNUM'S NEW AND GREATEST SHOW ON EARTH!

My great Traveling Centennial Academy of Object Teaching cost a million and a half of dollars, employs 1100 persons, 600 horses and ponies, and will be transported East to Maine and West to Missouri on 100 solid steel railroad cars. It by far surpasses all my former efforts; consists of sixty cages of rare wild animals and amphibia, including Barnum's $25,000 *Behemoth*, the only HIPPOPOTAMUS in America; vast Centennial Museum of living Mechanical Automata and other curiosities; a CENTENNIAL PORTRAIT GALLERY; BEST CIRCUS IN THE WORLD. A JUBILEE of Patriotic Song and Splendor; superb Historical Tableaux; National Anthems by several hundred trained voices, accompanied by music and roar of cannon; *the whole audience to rise and join in singing the national hymn,* "*America.*" I carry my own park of Cannon and a large Church Bell, fire a national salute of 13 guns each morning, accompanied by the public bells, and give the most extensive and gorgeous STREET PAGEANT ever witnessed, glittering with patriotic features, and attended by three bands of music. Each night a grand display of Patriotic Fireworks, showing WASHINGTON, American Flags, &c., in national colors of fine red, white, and blue, fine Balloons, &c. You will never see the like again. Admission to all, 50 cents. Children under nine, Half Price. P. T. BARNUM.

An 1876 ad for master showman P.T. Barnum's centennial year circus, featuring America's only living hippo, Behemoth.

Evangelist Dwight Moody preaches to a packed New York City auditorium in Spring 1876. At the time, he was one of the most famous Americans in the world.

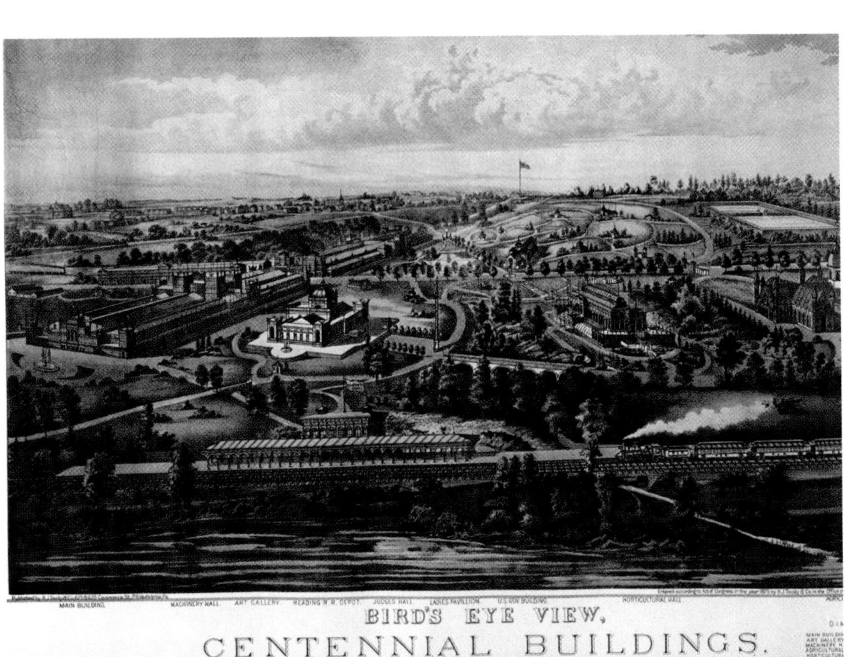

A poster depicting the 1876 Centennial Exposition grounds in Philadelphia, America's first World's Fair. —*Library of Congress*

President Grant and Brazilian Emperor Dom Pedro start the mighty Corliss Engine at the Centennial Expo.

FRANK LESLIE'S ILLUSTRATED NEWSPAPER

No. 1,077—Vol. XLII.] NEW YORK, MAY 20, 1876. [Price, 10 Cents.

PHILADELPHIA PA.—OPENING OF THE CENTENNIAL EXPOSITION, MAY 10th—MACHINERY HALL.—THE GREAT CORLISS ENGINE—PRESIDENT GRANT STARTING THE MACHINERY.—From Sketches by our Special Artists.—See Page 179.

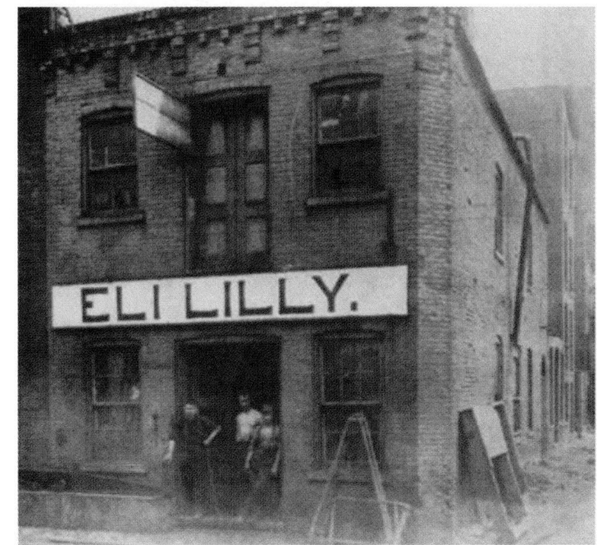

Eli Lilly, center, poses with his entire staff in door of his new drug company in Indianapolis in 1876. Lilly's young son is to his right.

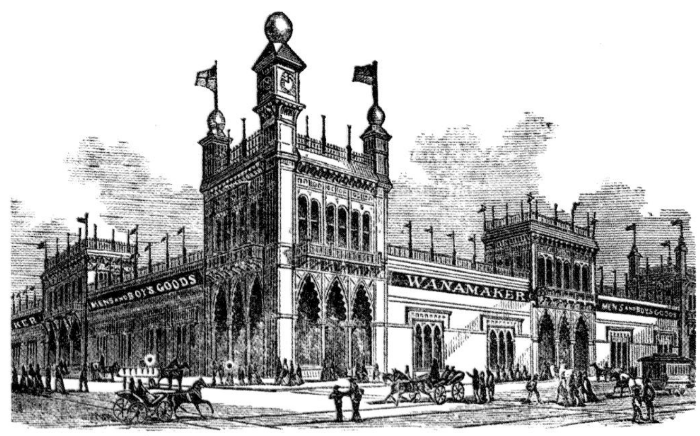

Wanamaker's Department Store in 1876. Opened at the same time as the Centennial Expo, the Philadelphia store revolutionized retail merchandising in America.

An 1899 magazine depiction of a faro game, by far the most popular form of gambling in the 19th century Wild West.

A female delegation explains to a congressional committee why the 14th and 15th Amendments should cover women. They are preaching to the deaf—and dumb.

A bronze Doc Holliday sits outside Dodge City's Boot Hill Museum, waiting for tourists to make a wrong move. — *Ceil Dolan Wiegand*

A life-sized statue of actor James Arness as Dodge's fictional U.S. Marshal Matt Dillon at the Dodge City Visitor's Center — *Ceil Dolan Wiegand*

Wild West-style champion shooter Frank Spence, a great -grandson of one of the Cowboys who battled the Earp Brothers and Doc Holliday.
— Courtesy of Frank Spence

Frank Spence as his Cowboy Shooting alias 'Frank Stilwell' would have appeared in Tombstone Az. in 1881. *— Courtesy of Frank Spence*

exposed its flank, and it took a heroic stand by another brigade to save the day. Sickles, meanwhile, was busy having a leg so badly wounded by a cannon ball, the limb had to be amputated. For losing his leg, but not losing the battle, Sickles was inexplicably awarded the Medal of Honor. He donated his severed limb to an army medical museum, where it was preserved and where he visited it from time to time.

After the war, Sickles switched his political allegiance to the Republican Party, and was named U.S. minister to Spain by President Grant. He promptly caused another scandal by having an affair with Isabella II, who had recently been deposed as the Spanish queen. By 1876, he had no real job, but occasionally volunteered his questionable talents to the GOP. He functioned mainly as a jack-of-all-trades, while keeping his eyes open for a possible post-election government appointment.

On Election Night, Sickles went to the theater and had a late supper with friends. Unable to sleep, and morose at the prospect of a Democratic victory and the accompanying dashed hopes of a cushy job under Hayes, he wandered over to the almost-deserted Republican headquarters about midnight. There he began perusing the telegraphed returns on the desk of the party's chairman, Zachariah Chandler.

"...After a careful scrutiny (I) reached the conclusion that the contest was really very close and doubtful, but by no means hopeless," he recalled in a 1902 memoir. "According to my figures, based on fair probabilities, Hayes was elected by at least one (vote) in the Electoral College. This estimate assumed that Hayes would receive the votes of South Carolina, Louisiana, Florida and Oregon."

It was a big assumption. Sickles realized it would take some very fancy footwork to make the "official" vote tallies work in Hayes' favor, no matter what the actual vote tallies were. The first step was to concede nothing. "With your state sure for Hayes, he is elected," Sickles wired Republican officials in the affected states. "HOLD YOUR STATE." To add weight to the admonitions, he signed the telegrams with the name of GOP national chairman Chandler. Then, about dawn, "Devil Dan" went home to bed.

Despite its nostalgic revelry and justifiable pride in all its technological advancements, America was in many ways a troubled country in its centennial year. There was the protracted economic recession. High unemployment rates were exacerbated by massive immigration, which flooded the labor market at precisely the wrong time. Coupled with the deepening schism between the very rich and most of the rest of America, labor unrest grew throughout 1876, and boiled over in massive and bloody strikes the following year.

There was deep partisan political division, widespread—and bipartisan—political corruption, and geographic sectional discord. Westward expansion had resulted in wars with Native Americans, which in turn accelerated their cultural and physical destruction. And topping the list of problems in 1876 was finding a way to expiate America from its "Original Sin:" slavery.

It had been 11 years since the North won the Civil War and preserved the Union. The war effort had been replaced by the monumental task of "reconstructing" the shattered South, while carving out a just and equal place in America for the country's 3.9 million former slaves. The effort largely failed, due to a host of elements that included the desire for revenge on the part of many Northerners; the refusal on the part of many Southerners to accept that a social, economic and political system based on slavery was gone, and an absence of fair, firm and compassionate leaders at all levels of government.

True, the 13th, 14th and 15th amendments to the Constitution had been ratified, abolishing slavery, extending equal legal protections and rights—at least ostensibly—to former slaves, and guaranteeing—again, ostensibly—the right to vote to adult to Blacks, assuming they were male. But as the "Rebels' Revenge" overtones of the Northfield bank robbery by the James-Younger gang suggested, the aftershocks of America's bloodiest conflict seemed to taint every aspect of life and society's institutions.

Despite all the constitutional additions, for example, the progress of "Freedmen" (a term meant to include freed women and children as well) had been halting, at best. There were exceptions: On November 7, the very same day Hayes and Tilden were pondering their presidential chances and Lincoln's eternal rest was being disturbed, 24-year-old Edward A. Bouchet was being awarded a doctoral degree in physics from Yale University. That made Bouchet, the son of a former slave, the first Black to earn a PhD from an American university. And the federal Freedman's Bureau, created in 1865 to help freed slaves transition to their new status, provided food, education and other support. By 1868, the bureau had helped as many as 200,000 former slaves learn to read, and about 10,000 black families were settled on land that had been confiscated during the war by Union troops.

But far more common was the Freedman who traded slavery for sharecropping. Former slaves farmed land owned by someone else—often their former owners—with the hope of sharing in the profits. But there seldom were profits, at least not for the sharecropper. To make ends meet while waiting for the harvest, they had to borrow, and often ended up owing more than their share of the proceeds. The result was perpetual debt for the sharecropper, and a pretty good deal for the landowner, who no longer had to directly feed and clothe his "freed" workers as he had been obligated to do for his slaves. "What's the use of being free," a sharecropper bitterly wrote to *New York Tribune* editor Whitelaw Reid, "if you don't even own enough land to be buried in?"

Of course African Americans had no monopoly on poverty. But they were unique in being the specific targets of sets of laws known as the "Black Codes." These were dictates approved by Southern state legislatures that were designed, in the words of a South Carolina politician, to ensure Blacks were "kept as near to the condition of slavery as possible and as far from the condition of the white man as practicable."

The codes varied from state to state. In Mississippi, Blacks could not own land outside a city or town limits, thus preventing them from farming their own land. In South Carolina, Blacks who were arbitrarily deemed unfit parents could have their children taken away and placed as unpaid "apprentices" with white families. In Louisiana, cursing in front of an employer's family was prohibited. In most Southern states, carrying a gun, quitting a job, traveling without permission or acting insolent toward whites were all forbidden for Blacks.

And if the Black Codes weren't enough to remind Freedmen how illusory freedom could be, there was also the very real threat of being whipped, beaten or murdered by the various terrorist groups that sprang up across the region after the war. The Ku Klux Klan, Knights of the White Camelia and other loosely organized gangs adopted tactics that ran the gamut from cross burning to church burning to people burning. During just one 90-day stretch in 1868 in Georgia, a federal agency recorded 142 attacks by terrorist groups that included 31 murders, 41 shootings, 55 beatings, five stabbings and eight whippings of at least 300 lashes.

"When the war ended, I had four brothers and two sons, and my wife had two brothers," Henry Woolfolk, a former Alabama slave, told a Chicago reporter in October, 1876. "Today, me and the old woman are all that are left. Eight strong, able-bodied farm hands have gone over Jordan, and white man's bullets were what sent them on that long journey...it is a terrible price to pay for freedom, and if we are defeated (in the election) this year, we will either go back to slavery or leave the country."

Woolfolk's reference to "we" meant the Republican Party. From the end of the war until 1874, the GOP had dominated all three branches of the federal government, and the party of Lincoln had become the party of the Freedmen. A Republican-controlled Congress had temporarily divided the south into five military divisions, forcing Southern states to ratify the 14th and 15th Amendments as a condition of re-entry into the Union. Thousands of federal troops were dispatched in an effort to enforce congressional edicts and afford Freedmen some protection in exercising their new rights, including that of voting. The result was Republican legislatures and governors in many Southern states, and a hefty percentage of Black state and local elected officials.

But the presence of "Yankee Bluecoats" 11 years after the war had ended rankled even those Southerners who had accepted defeat. It absolutely infuriated those who didn't. That hatred, in turn, contributed to the rise of the KKK and similar groups. And as the groups' efforts in intimidating would-be black voters increased, fewer Blacks risked it—with good reason.

In a single Louisiana parish in 1874, it was estimated 60 black would-be voters were murdered before an election. In one heavily black Mississippi parish with 12,000 residents, only seven registered Republicans showed up at an 1875 election.In contrast, 90 percent of the state's eligible white voters turned out, almost all of them Democrats, and Mississippi fell back into Democratic hands. By 1876, only three state governments in the once solidly Republican South were still under GOP control: Louisiana, Florida and South Carolina.

Tensions over the looming election periodically boiled over into bloody confrontations in the South that were seized on and sensationalized by pro-Republican elements of the Northern press. A July 4 incident in which four Blacks were murdered in South Carolina became known as "The Hamburg Massacre." A larger fight in September that resulted in 17 deaths in the same state was labeled "The Three Days War." "The Blacks fired in self-defense only," the *New York Times* claimed after the September incident. "It closely resembled...the dozen or so other outrages that the White Democrats of the South have committed for political purposes."

Black political leaders warned President Grant that "unless you do something, "our folks will not dare go to the polls." Grant did something. Hundreds more federal troops were dispatched to the South to protect political rallies and oversee polling places on Election Day. As a result, Nov. 7 came and went almost without incident—at least as far as violent incidents were concerned.

While adult male Blacks in 1876 had the constitutional, albeit potentially hazardous, right to vote, a massive segment of the American populace was still banned at the polls. Of the approximately 24.5 million females in the country, about half were 21 years old or older. Among that population, approximately 0.00175 percent—those adult women who happened to live in the territories of Wyoming and Utah—were eligible to vote.

"Liberty today is but the heritage of one-half the people, and the Centennial will be but the celebration of the independence of one-half the nation," wrote Matilda Joslyn Gage, a leading advocate for the cause of giving women the vote. "The men alone of this country live in a Republic, the women enter the second hundred years of national life as slaves."

On May 10, Gage presided over the opening of a meeting in New York City of the National Woman Suffrage Association. That was the very same day the Centennial Expo was opening in Philadelphia; Wyatt Earp was being run out of Wichita; Eli Lilly was starting his pharmaceutical company in Indianapolis; George Custer was on a train headed west to begin his final campaign against the Plains tribes; Alexander Graham Bell was demonstrating his telephonic device to a group of scientists in Boston, and Cole Younger and the James Boys were, at least according to published reports, robbing a stagecoach near Kingsbury, Texas. It was a busy day in America.

At the Masonic Temple on New York's 6th Avenue, a veritable who's who of American suffragists had gathered to, in the words of one speaker, "foment a rebellion." There were the movement's best-known champions: Elizabeth Cady Stanton and Lucretia Mott, who had helped organize the first women's rights convention in 1848; Susan B. Anthony, who had been fined in 1872 for having dared to vote in the presidential election, refused to pay and cowed the local officials into dropping the matter; Belva Lockwood, the first female attorney to argue a case before the U.S. Supreme Court; Amelia Jenks Bloomer, a pioneering journalist whose advocacy of women's right to wear pantaloons earned the attire the name "bloomers."

And then there were the Smith sisters, Julia and Abby, of Glastonbury, Connecticut. Wealthy and somewhat eccentric octogenarians, the siblings had attracted national attention for refusing to pay local property taxes because they weren't allowed to vote, even after several of their pet cows were confiscated. Like many in the group, the Smiths first became politically active fighting for the cause of abolition. So vital had the role of women been that when Lincoln met Harriet Beecher Stowe, the author of the hugely popular anti-slavery novel *Uncle Tom's Cabin*, he is said to have remarked "so, you're the little woman that wrote the book that made this great war."

Having helped to end slavery, the suffragists were furious at the indifference, and often outright opposition, to their cause by most of the male abolitionists they had aided. One angry suffragist confronted the Black orator Frederick Douglass after he had spoken at the Republican nominating convention in June. "How can you, so lately made a citizen, speak of the continued disabilities of your race and not say one word for the women of this land?" A greatly mollified Douglass apologized by saying "I would have spoken for you if I had thought of it."

At the New York women's convention in May, the press reported, Gage "contended that women were as equally inventive as men, and as capable of filling any position where brains, intelligence and more than ordinary ability were required." The group issued a list of demands that ranged from women's right to have an equal say in how the federal government spent the public's money to the right "to demand an allowance of money from her husband without being obliged to account for it." This last declaration, the *New York Times* noted, was "a sentiment which was greeted with applause."

But the single biggest demand was the right to vote. Women, Susan B. Anthony thundered, should "declare themselves free and independent, no longer bound to obey laws in whose making they have no voice." A few days later, Anthony and several others quietly opened a "Centennial headquarters" in Philadelphia and began laying plans to make their voices more widely heard during the country's 100th birthday celebration

It was an uphill task. It was argued women voters would cast ballots exactly as their husbands dictated; or would vote as they pleased, creating widespread marital discord. They would be too easily swept up by sentiment and emotion, or they would be coarsened by politics and rendered less feminine. What they could not possibly do, Mark Twain wryly observed, was a more effective job of electing incompetent and corrupt officials than American men routinely did.

Voting wasn't the only right prohibited to American women in 1876. Under a longstanding legal doctrine known as *coverture*, married women were generally restricted or banned outright from owning real property in their own name, controlling income they earned, seeking an education without their husband's permission, or denying him sexual relations. In some jurisdictions, they were considered not liable for committing some crimes, since it was assumed they were simply obeying their spouses. If they were charged with a crime, they were denied the right to be tried by a jury of their peers, since women were not allowed to serve on juries.

Western women were marginally better off than their eastern counterparts when it came to equal rights. States and territories in the West often had more liberal divorce laws, allowed women to own and operate their own businesses, and even paid female schoolteachers the same paltry salaries as male teachers. Women were accorded fairer treatment not so much because western men were less chauvinistic, but as a practical matter: With fewer people of any gender to assume roles in public life, it made sense to extend opportunities for anyone willing to take them.

In December, 1869, the Wyoming territorial government extended the right to vote to women. Utah Territory extended the ballot to women soon after Wyoming. But the West's progressivism did not extend elsewhere.In 1875, the U.S. Supreme Court unanimously ruled that the 14th Amendment did not extend the right to vote to adult females. "For nearly 90 years, the people have acted upon the idea that the Constitution, when it conferred citizenship, did not necessarily confer the right of suffrage," wrote Chief Justice Morrison Waite. "Our province is to decide what the law is, not to declare what it should be...If the law is wrong, it ought to be changed, but the power for that is not with us."

Stymied by the courts and most state and territorial legislatures, suffragists decided to take their case to a larger stage in 1876. Representatives from the National Woman Suffrage Association were sent to both of the national presidential nominating conventions, where all of the delegates at each were men. At the Republican convention in Cincinnati, Sara J. Spencer, whom the press dismissed as "a woman of uncertain age, sharp features, acidulous (and) without distinction in any respect," was given 10 minutes to make her case. It fell largely on deaf ears, although the GOP did include in its platform the bland statement that the suffragists' "claims are entitled to respectful consideration," presumably sometime well after 1876.

Possibly rattled by the reception Spencer received from the Republicans, the suffragists took a different tack when the Democrats met in St. Louis. There the chosen speaker was a strikingly attractive 32-year-old local woman, Phoebe Wilson Couzins. Not only was Couzins comely, she was accomplished: among the first women to graduate law school and begin a legal practice, and eventually the first female deputy U.S. marshal.

Speaking with what the press described as "much self-possession," Couzins coyly pointed out that 1876 was a leap year, and tradition demanded males accept proposals from "fair women." Accordingly, she proposed a platform plank that pledged Democrats "to secure the right of suffrage to the women of the United States on equal terms with men." Although "she was greeted with loud cheers and listened to with attention," the delegates ignored her proposal. In fact, the only mention of women at all in the Democrats' platform was a vague promise to aid the widows of servicemen.

Strike three came at the Centennial Expo in Philadelphia. The suffragists' association had requested to be a formal part of the exposition's 4th of July festivities. The group hoped to read, or at least present, its recently drafted "Declaration and Protest of the Women of the United States." But the Centennial Commission's chairman, Gen. Joseph Hawley, refused. "If your request were granted," he explained frankly, "it would be the event of the day—the topic of discussion to the exclusion of all others...we cannot grant it."

Undaunted, five of the suffragists—Susan Anthony, Matilda Gage, Sara Spencer, Phoebe Couzins and Connecticut novelist Lillie Blake—conspired to crash the nation's party. Armed with press passes that gave them access near the stage in Independence Square, where more than 100,000 people had gathered to wish America a happy 100th birthday, the quintet waited until a dignitary finished reading the Declaration of Independence.

Then they strode on to the stage and after a few words from Anthony, they handed their document to a startled Thomas Ferry, the U.S. Senate majority leader who was standing in for President Grant, and who, according to Gage "looked paler than he will when he is in his coffin." As they departed, they handed out copies of their declaration, and marched to a nearby bandstand, where Anthony read the entire 2,300-word manifesto.

"It is with sorrow we come to strike the one discordant note, on this hundredth anniversary of our country's birth," Anthony said. "we cannot forget, even in this glad hour, that while all men of every race, and clime, and condition, have been invested with the full rights of citizenship, under our hospitable flag, all women still suffer the degradation of disfranchisement. Our history, the past hundred years, has been a series of assumptions and usurpations of power over woman, in direct opposition to the principles of just government...".

The suffragists' bold effort was generally ignored, overshadowed by centennial celebratory events around the country—and also the rapidly spreading news of the defeat of Custer and the 7th Cavalry at the Battle of the Little Bighorn just 10 days before. But Centennial officials did patronizingly throw women a bone on Election Day, three days before the expo closed. November 7, officials decided, would be "Women's Day" at the fair. After all, the menfolk would be busy with voting.

A favorite pose of 19th century presidential candidates was that of the Reluctant Warrior. They seldom, if ever, took receipt of their parties' nomination when it was accorded them at the conventions. Instead, they pretended for a week or two to ponder shouldering the burden before finally issuing a letter of acceptance that dripped with appropriate amounts of gratitude, humility and pledges to try hard to live up to the responsibility.

Hayes responded on July 8 to the GOP's "official communication," two weeks after winning the nomination. In his brief acceptance letter, he promised to reform the civil service system (which angered President Grant, who saw it as a dig at Grant's ineffectiveness in that arena); pledged not to seek a second presidential term if he won a first one, and confirmed his support of a constitutional amendment to prevent religious groups from interfering with public schools. He also pledged to protect the constitutional rights of all residents of Southern states, mainly by relying on "honest and capable local government" to ensure such protections. This last pledge was read by many as a tacit promise to end the use of federal troops to enforce civil rights protections for African Americans in the South.

Tilden responded to the Democratic nomination on July 31, more than a month after it was offered. Unlike Hayes' short, bland and generally vague acceptance letter, Tilden's was long and tediously detailed. He promised not only government reform, but also cuts in government spending and taxes; protection of civil rights for all, and changes in the nation's monetary system. The promises were so meticulously laid out, a reader complained, it was "like a chapter from some German work in metaphysics."

In addition to being publicly coy about accepting nominations, 19th century presidential aspirants very rarely campaigned in person. For the most part, Tilden remained in New York and Hayes in Ohio throughout the summer and fall, although both did make obligatory trips to the Centennial

Expo in Philadelphia. This ivory tower approach left the tasks of rallying voters and slinging mud to surrogates. While Tilden relied heavily on his "Newspaper Popularity Bureau" and "Literary Bureau" to flood the nation with printed propaganda, the Hayes camp leaned on a small army of orators, with directions to play up the candidate's military service.

Both sides employed the modern campaign tactics of lying and spreading unfounded and vicious rumors about the opposition. Hayes, it was said, was anti-Catholic and anti-immigrant; Tilden a lackey of the railroad industry. Hayes may have once shot his own mother during a fit of lunacy; Tilden was probably gay. Imaginative metaphors were sometimes employed by the often rabidly partisan press. The *Chicago Tribune*, for example, referred to Tilden in a Page One story as "a small, lazy, odorous, ungainly, trickling stream, winding along among the weeds ...".

Both candidates faced more significant, if not necessarily more substantive, charges. In August, the *New York Times* reported that Tilden had "contrived in very questionable ways to pay just as little as possible" in federal income taxes, which had first been imposed in 1862 to help pay for the North's war effort. "Can Mr. Tilden produce," the *Times* rhetorically asked, "any reason why...he should not be branded as a swindler and a perjurer?"

Mr. Tilden could not, at least not for some weeks. After frantically digging through piles of years-old financial documents, the Tilden camp put together plausible evidence that showed the candidate had complied with all the tax laws at the time and paid what he had owed. Although damaging, the impact of the charges could have been much worse—except Tilden's GOP opponent discovered he hadn't bothered to file *any* tax returns himself for 1868 and 1869. Hayes kept quiet about it—and just as quietly advised his supporters not to push too hard on the charges against Tilden.

Hayes had to deal with accusations of theft during his Civil War service. The incident involved $400 Hayes had allegedly been given by a soldier who was to be executed for desertion. Hayes, it was charged, failed to pass the money along to the soldier's family. Based only on differing memories and he-said/he-said statements, the charge failed to create a lasting stir in the press or among voters.

Dubious personal attacks aside, both parties had larger, authentic and effective themes on which to base their campaigns. For the Democrats, it was the rampant corruption in which Washington had wallowed for more than a decade—a period in which Republicans had almost completely controlled both Congress and the White House. Although Hayes was not widely considered to be personally corrupt, Democrats contended, "he was a loyal lieutenant in the Republican camp, an enthusiastic adherent of Grant and of the latter's corrupt vassals...and now we are to trust the mere paper promises of such a man who turns whithersoever the wind blows?"

More important to most Americans was the fact the country had been settled for three years at the bottom of an economic abyss. "In the low places, at the cabin door, in the ruts of industry, upon the fields of labor, the voice of want is heard rolling and rumbling from the mouths of three millions of people out of bread, out of work, in want," roared a typical Democratic speaker at a rally in Kansas City. "...These hard times must be laid at the door of the party who controls the government."

Hayes was well aware of the dangers of having the nation's economic woes laid on the GOP doorstep. In a letter to former presidential rival-turned-key ally James G. Blaine, Hayes noted "our strong ground is the dread of a solid South, rebel rule, etc. etc. I hope you will make these topics prominent in your speeches. It leads people away from 'hard times,' which is our deadliest foe."

Hayes' references to "solid South" and "rebel rule" alluded to the chief weapon in the Republican arsenal: "waving the bloody shirt." The term sprang from an apocryphal incident in which a GOP congressman on the House floor in 1868 had supposedly brandished the whip-shredded garment of a federal official who had been brutally beaten by a mob of unrepentant Southerners. The moral of the tale was that the South had failed to learn from its defeat in a war it started—and the South was full of Democrats. At every opportunity, GOP speakers contended that while not all Democrats had been Rebels, all Rebels had been Democrats.

"Every state that seceded from the Union was a Democrat," bellowed Robert Ingersoll, an Illinois lawyer and the Republican Party's most eloquent orator, at a mass rally in Chicago. "Every Union soldier that carries a scar upon his body today carries with him a souvenir of the Democratic Party...the man that shot Abraham Lincoln was a Democrat...every man that was sorry to see the institution of slavery abolished was a Democrat."

In addition to the "bloody shirt," the Republicans also had more campaign money. In large part this was due to a party requirement that federal officeholders who made more than $1,000 a year ($24,000 in 2021 currency) pony up 2 percent of their salaries to the GOP. Failure to do so could result in demotion, transfer to a dead-end post, the loss of any chance for promotion, or even outright dismissal.

But having a deeper-pocketed campaign than his opponent and fanning the embers of a war that had been over for 11 years did not fill Ruddy Hayes with confidence. "I am looking anxiously forward to the end of the contest," he confided to his journal, 45 days before Election Day. "...I am prepared for any event...I shall find reasons enough for satisfaction with the result, if I am defeated." He jotted down his fears that because the country was so divided, a narrow outcome either way might result in bloody conflict. And he also expressed dissatisfaction with the fact that several states—Ohio, Indiana and the new state of Colorado—had already voted in order to consolidate the presidential vote with local elections to save money.

In the case of Colorado, Democrats in Congress could have prevented it from becoming a state until after the election. But they were confident the state would go for Tilden. They were wrong, and Colorado's three electoral votes were secured in October by Hayes. No one in the Tilden camp was overly alarmed. Three measly votes out of 369 weren't likely to matter much.

America woke up confused the day after the election, and with good reason. In Chicago, readers of the *Tribune* learned from the headlines that the election was "LOST...The Country Given Over to Greed and Plunder... Tilden and the Solid South to Rule the Nation." *Cincinnati Enquirer* subscribers were greeted with "Victory! Tilden Elected by Immense Majorities...A Waterloo for the Republicans." And in New York City, the *Herald* declared the results were "Something that No Fellow Can Understand...Impossible to Name Our Next President."

The *New York Times* found itself in rare agreement with the rival *Herald*. Under a "Results Still Uncertain" headline, the paper noted that "at the hour of sending *The Times* to press this morning, the result of the Presidential election held yesterday is still in doubt." The *Times'* breakdown of the electoral vote count, based mainly on speculative hope, gave Tilden 184—one short of the bare majority needed to win. Hayes had 166, according to the *Times*, with 19 votes still in play from South Carolina (7), Louisiana (8) and Florida (5). One of three electoral votes in Oregon was also in dispute, but the *Times* summarily—and presciently—gave it to Hayes.

Two days later, the *Times* decided Hayes had won after all. "The National Victory," its Page One headline proclaimed, "The Republican Majorities Everywhere Increasing." The *New York Sun* demurred. "Samuel J. Tilden Fairly Elected...The Democrats Jubilant." In the days that followed, the uncertainty grew. Republican hopes flickered a bit brighter. Democrats bit their nails shorter. Both sides hurriedly sent trainloads of "observers" to "oversee" the vote tallies and election certifications, which had been stalled by the frantic telegrams from "Devil Dan" Sickles and other GOP officials.

At the White House, President Grant told reporters that since "'everything now depends upon a fair count,'" he was sending "men of irreproachable character and respectability" to the three Southern states. He also sent federal troops to the states' capitals. "Should there be any grounds of suspicion or fraudulent counting on either side, it should be reported and denounced at once," Grant telegraphed William T. Sherman, the army's commanding general. "...Either party can afford to be disappointed in the result, but the Country cannot afford to have the result tainted by the suspicion of illegal or false returns."

Actually, there was little suspicion of chicanery. Almost everyone was absolutely certain it had occurred. Both parties had brazenly constructed mountain-sized piles of fraud both before and after the election. In Florida, for example, Democrats had distributed ballots bearing the Republican emblem—a portrait of Lincoln—in hopes of tricking illiterate and semi-literate voters into casting their votes for the Democratic slate that was listed on the ballots. Merchants offered outright bribes of items, such as a pair of shoes, in return for voting Democrat. They also threatened to impose a "traitor's tax" on goods if shoppers, particularly African-Americans, were suspected of voting for Republicans. For their part, Republicans produced what were called "little jokers" that could be slipped into ballot boxes by partisan clerks and counted for the GOP.

After the election, the Republican majority on the canvassing board charged with certifying the results in Louisiana faced a dilemma in which the Democratic elector with the least number of votes still had 6,000 more than any Republican elector. The board solved the problem by throwing out 2,000 "questionable" ballots for the Republican—and 13,000 for the Democrat. This "solution" was arrived at only after several GOP board members offered to deliver the state to Tilden in return for $200,000 ($4.8 million in 2022.) Tilden declined the offer.

"Conscience offers no restraint," Republican observer Lew Wallace wrote to his wife. "Nothing is so common as the resort to perjury...If we win, our methods are subject to impeachment for possible fraud. If the enemy win, it is the same thing, exactly—doubt, suspicion, irritation go with the consequence, whatever it might be." It should be noted that Wallace, an Indiana native and former Union Army general, didn't let his conscience bother him in public. He endorsed the GOP-dominated canvassing boards' decisions, and was eventually rewarded by being named territorial governor of New Mexico. There he completed his biblical novel,

Ben-Hur. He also earned a place in Wild West history by double-crossing Billy the Kid, offering the Kid a pardon in return for surrendering, then reneging on the offer after the Kid turned himself in.

As weeks went by, the situation grew uglier. Someone fired a shot through a window of the Hayes residence in Ohio while the family was dining. Some congressmen started carrying guns in the Capitol. When a colleague began haranguing Rep. Lucius Q.C. Lamar of Mississippi on the House floor, Lamar drew a derringer, pointed it at his verbal assailant, and snarled to startled onlookers "take him away, or I'll present him to a cemetery!" Northern Democrats who were Union Army veterans began to re-form into units and drill, as rumors spread of a march on Washington to ensure Tilden's apparent victory. In response, Grant ordered troops to guard key sites in and around the capital.

By mid-December, the three contested states had all sent competing sets of electors to Congress. And Congress, with Republicans in control of the Senate and Democrats in control of the House, punted the issue. On Jan. 26, 1877—80 days after the election and only 37 before the March 4 date then in place for presidential inaugurations—a 15-member Electoral Commission was created to examine the claims of each party on the disputed electoral votes. It seemed a Solomonic solution: The Senate would appoint three Republicans and two Democrats; the House three Democrats and two Republicans. Two Supreme Court justices from each party would also be named. The 15th member would be Justice David Davis, a political independent who had been appointed to the court by his friend and former Illinois legal associate, Abe Lincoln.

But this was Gilded Age politics, where the end not only justified the means, it reveled in the means' slime. The Illinois legislature, dominated by Democrats and hoping to curry Davis' favorable support of Tilden, promptly elected Davis to a vacant U.S. Senate seat from the state. Davis, perhaps proving his independence, promptly accepted the Senate seat, but refused to stay on the Electoral Commission, and resigned. The Democrats had double-crossed themselves. Davis was replaced by the next most senior justice, Joseph P. Bradley, a Republican appointee of Grant's. That gave the GOP the majority.

On Feb. 7, the commission began handing down its decisions. All of them were strictly along party lines, and as a cheerful GOP ditty noted: *"Hold the fort for Hayes is coming / Keep the banners straight; / The Boys on guard are loudly drumming; / Seven can't beat eight."* Democratic newspapers countered with references to Hayes as "Rutherfraud," and "His Fraudulency."

The protracted political drama had one more act, however. House Democrats could filibuster, a parliamentary tactic that might delay the election confirmation process until after March 4, at which point there was a chance the Electoral Commission's decision might be disregarded in favor of some new scheme. But Southern Democrats thought there might be some political profit to be made, even in a Hayes victory. Negotiations with the Hayes camp, which had actually begun privately some weeks before, culminated in a deal on February 26, the day before the commission awarded Hayes South Carolina's seven electoral votes, pushing him to the magical plateau of 185.

In return for Southern Democrats declining to support a filibuster, Hayes agreed to appoint one of their own—as it turned out, a former Confederate officer—as postmaster general. This was considered the plumb of all cabinet posts: The postmaster general controlled hundreds of federal jobs, which he could dole out to friends, family and supporters, presumably all of them Democrats. In addition, Hayes gave vague –and eventually unkept—promises to support construction of a transcontinental railroad that would link the South with the West Coast, a potentially huge economic boost for the region.

Finally, and most important, he agreed to withdraw almost all federal troops from Southern states, and end federal intervention in states' internal affairs. By the end of his term, Southern states would begin enacting "Jim Crow" laws that memorialized racial segregation, and ranged from the substantively evil—banning Blacks from white schools, restaurants and drinking fountains—to the stupidly trivial—requiring Blacks to be sworn in on different bibles from whites when testifying in courts. The laws ensured white political, economic and social supremacy over African Americans in the South for decades to come.

At 4:10 a.m. on March 2, the Senate took its final vote to confirm the election results. Tilden, who had been mostly silent during the long and painful process except to occasionally urge against violence, threw in the towel. "I can retire to private life with the consciousness that I shall receive from posterity the credit for having been elected to the highest position...without the cares." He then sailed to Europe for a year-long vacation, and into historical semi-obscurity.

Hayes became the only president to be sworn in twice for the same term, first at the White House in a private ceremony late on March 3, just in case there was any last-minute trouble, and again a day later at a public event. A highlight—perhaps *the* highlight—of his single term was the establishment of the annual Children's Easter Egg Hunt on the White House lawn.

But while generally regarded as a quintessentially mediocre president, Hayes did become a hero in Paraguay. In 1878, he agreed to settle a bloody, decades-long border dispute between that South American country and Argentina. He found in favor of Paraguay, thereby almost doubling the size of the country. November 12 is still celebrated there as a provincial holiday in honor of Hayes. Both a city and the Paraguayan equivalent of a state are named after him, and he appears on a Paraguayan postage stamp.He is accorded no such honors in this country. And no one, so far as is known, has tried to kidnap the body of Rutherford B. Hayes and hold it for ransom.

Chapter 9 Notes

On the evening of For an entertaining and well-written account of the plot to steal Abe Lincoln's corpse, see Thomas J. Craughwell's 2007 book, *Stealing Lincoln's Body* (Belknap Press.)

"The crime was" *Chicago Tribune*, Nov. 18, 1876, p. 1.

As America's 16th For all of the gory details of the 1876 presidential race, I highly recommend *Fraud of the Century*, (Simon & Schuster, 2003), by Roy Morris Jr. It's jammed with detail, drama and sparkling writing.

But if there was Morris, op. cit., p. 100.

In 1872, the Ibid., p. 104.

"The government no longer" *Brooklyn Daily Eagle*, June 30, 1876, p. 2.

Inside, Hayes' wife Rutherford B. Hayes, *Diary and Letters of Rutherford B. Hayes*, Vol. III, p. 374.

"He was a very" *New York Daily Herald*, July 5, 1876, p. 6.

In 1864, without Hayes, op. cit., Vol. II, p. 497.

It was hardly Hayes, op. cit., Vol. III, pp. 374-376.

"...After a careful" Jerome L. Sternstein, "The Sickles Memorandum: Another Look at the Hayes-Tilden Election Night Controversy," *The Journal of Southern History*, Vol. 32, No. 3, p. 354.

It was a big Ibid., p. 356.

But far more Hugh Brogan, *The Penguin History of the United States of America*, p. 356.

Of course African Hodding Carter, *The Angry Scar: The Story of Reconstruction*, p. 136.

If the Black Codes Morris, op. cit., p. 33.

"When the war" *Chicago Weekly Tribune*, Oct. 4, 1876, p. 6.

Tensions over the *New York Times*, Oct. 31, 1876, p. 2.

Black political leaders Chernow, op. cit., p. 842

"Liberty today is" *Chicago Weekly Post and Mail*, May 11, 1876, p. 1.

Having helped to Dee Brown, *The Year of the Century*, p. 148.

At the New York *Burlington (Vt.) Free Press*, May 16, 1876, p. 3; *New York Times*, May 11, 1876, p. 5.

But the single Brown, op. cit., p. 145.

In 1875, the *New York Daily Herald*, Oct. 5, 1875, p. 4.

Stymied by the *New York Daily Herald*, June 15, 1876, p. 4.

Speaking with what *Port Huron (Mich.) Times Herald*, June 28, 1876, p. 1; Brown, op. cit., p. 151.

Strike three came Brown, op. cit., p. 152.

Then they strode *The (Philadelphia) Times*, July 6, 1876, p. 2.

"It is with sorrow" *Declaration and Protest of the Women of the United States by the National Woman Suffrage Association, July 4th, 1876,* Library of Congress online microfilm collection.

Tilden responded to *New York Daily Herald*, Aug. 5, 1876, p. 4.

Both sides employed *Chicago Tribune*, Aug. 3, 1876, p.1.

Both candidates faced *New York Times*, Aug. 22, 1876, p. 4.

Dubious personal attacks *Greenville (Oh.) Democrat*, Oct. 4, 1876, p. 1.

More important to *Kansas City (Mo.) Times*, Oct. 13, 1876, p. 4.

Hayes was well, Morris, op. cit., p. 120.

"Every state that" *Janesville (Wisc.) Daily Gazette*, Oct. 24, 1876, p. 1.

But having a Hayes, op. cit., Vol. III, p. 363.

America woke up *Chicago Tribune*, Nov. 8, 1876, p. 1; *Cincinnati Enquirer*, Nov. 8, 1876, p. 1; *New York Daily Herald*, Nov. 8, 1876, p. 3.

The New York *New York Times*, Nov. 8, 1876, p. 1.

Two days later *New York Times*, Nov. 10, 1876, p. 1; *New York Sun*, Nov.

10, 1876, p. 1.

At the White House *New York Daily Herald*, Nov. 12, 1876, p. 5; Chernow, op. cit., p. 844.

"Conscience offers no" Morris, op. cit., p. 196.

As weeks went Ibid., p. 236.

On Feb. 7 *Waukegan (Ill.) Weekly Gazette*, March 17, 1877, p. 2.

At 4:10 a.m. Andrew Glass, "Presidential election results left in doubt, Nov. 7, 1876," *Politico.com*, Nov. 6, 2016.

PART II

CHAPTER 10

"The last of the greatest"

The two lives of Bat Masterson

He had slaughtered buffalo, fought Indians and faced down mobs of drunken cowboys. He had been branded a troublemaker in Denver, arrested as a con man in New York City and received as a welcome guest at the White House. It had been a long ride since that frozen January night in 1876 when he lay bleeding heavily on the floor of a Texas Panhandle dancehall, having just killed a man.

Now he was a month from his 68th birthday. He was diabetic, asthmatic, overweight and fighting the aftereffects of a bad cold that had plagued him for two weeks. But he had a column to write. So on a fair, cool October morning in 1921, he trudged the few blocks from his Manhattan apartment to the former horsecar railroad barn at West 50th Street and Eighth Avenue that housed the *Morning Telegraph*.

Over 18 years, he had scribbled out several million words for the *Telegraph*, mostly about boxing and horseracing, but periodically veering to presidential politics, grisly murders or whatever other topic on which he felt like expounding. He often mangled syntax, but he seldom minced words. On this particular morning, his subject was the hefty paydays being collected by prizefighters of only modest abilities for lackluster performances.

"Just think of an honest, hard-working farmer laboring from daylight to dark for forty years of his life, and lucky if he finishes with as much as one of these birds gets in an hour," he wrote. "Yet there are those who argue that everything breaks even in this old dump of a world of ours. I suppose these ginks who argue that would hold that because the rich man gets ice in the summer and the poor man gets it in the winter things are breaking even for both. Maybe so, but I'll swear I can't see it that way."

While he was writing, a few colleagues popped their heads in his office to see how he was feeling. He assured them he was okay. But he wasn't. A few minutes before noon, an assistant found him slumped over his rolltop desk, clutching his copy. What arrows, fists and lead slugs couldn't do, a massive heart attack could. William Barclay Masterson was dead.

Assuming he didn't too much mind being dead, Bat Masterson would almost certainly have enjoyed both the kind words and the nonsense in his obituaries Most of them were composed of admiration, nostalgia and horse manure, in about equal parts. The *St. Louis Post-Dispatch* called him "quite the deadliest man in America for standup gunfighting. Had he cared to commemorate his homicidal achievements in the orthodox way, it is estimated that his pistol handle would have been decorated with from 22 to 28 notches."

The *Washington Herald* credited him with killing a man during a poker game, helping to carry the body outside, then resuming the game. In Kansas, where he had conducted most of his law-enforcement career, the *Coffeyville Morning News* reported Bat had in the space of a few hours hunted down and killed four cowboys who had shot down his brother Ed. The *New York Times* had Bat holding off 300 Indians for three weeks, with only eight companions, at the "Battle of 'Dobe (sic) Walls." Not to be outdone, the *Louisville Courier-Journal* made it "nearly a thousand" Indians and only six companions.

While he died just once, Bat Masterson had lived two lives. The first, as plainsman, lawman, gunfighter and gambler, was thoroughly-if-inaccurately covered in his death notices. The second, as businessman, prizefighting authority, journalist (but still a gambler), was perfunctorily mentioned. Even his good pal, the celebrated columnist Damon Runyon, waited until the 18th paragraph of his nationally syndicated 23-paragraph ode to Masterson to mention that Bat had lived the last two decades of his life amid New York City skyscrapers rather than Kansas sagebrush.

Masterson may have had mixed feelings about the imbalance. On the one hand, as the Coffeyville paper noted, "Bat was one of the last survivors of the Old West, but he never capitalized on his past, never became a circus plainsman." He thus might have been irked at the obits' emphasis on the shoot- 'em-up phase of his life. On the other hand, as Runyon pointed out, "he had a great sense of humor and a marvelous fund of reminiscence, and was one of the most entertaining companions we have ever known." So he might have gotten a giggle from the factual liberties the obituaries took.

The accuracy of Runyon's observation about Bat's sense of humor and fondness for spinning tales was demonstrated by a meeting Masterson had with a young reporter in a hotel lobby in 1910. The reporter wanted to talk about gunfights. The former gunfighter wanted to talk about almost anything else. "If there's anything that makes me tired," Bat said, "it's these young fellows who insist on writing a lot of trash about events that happened twenty years before they began yelling for their living. If they'd tell the truth, it wouldn't be so bad, but they have to dress it up and tell the public that a peaceable man like me has twenty-seven notches on his gun. Now don't you say anything about those notches and I'll let you have a few unvarnished facts." Masterson then proceeded to give him an entire newspaper page full of highly varnished facts—and tossed in a few dubious anecdotes at no extra charge.

A few years later, when an old acquaintance and ardent collector of Wild West memorabilia pleaded with Masterson to sell him one of his guns, Bat finally agreed. According to his friend Wyatt Earp, Masterson went to a pawn shop and bought an old Colt 45. To sweeten the appeal of the "souvenir," he then carved 22 notches in the gun's handle. When the collector asked if the notches represented men Masterson had killed, "I didn't tell him yes and I didn't tell him no," Bat reportedly told Earp. "I simply said I hadn't counted either Mexicans or Indians, and he went away tickled to death."

Actually, by his own reckoning in testimony at various trials, as well as historical evidence—and if you exclude his participation in battles with Native Americans—Bat Masterson shot at other men just six times in his gunfighting career. The first was the 1876 Sweetwater Shootout described in Chapter 1, in which he killed Melvin King and was himself severely wounded. The last was in 1897, when he accidentally shot and slightly wounded a precinct clerk at a Denver polling place during a voting eligibility ruckus. No charges were filed in either case.

Sandwiched in between were four incidents in and around Dodge City. The tally of casualties in the four events came to one or possibly two men killed by Masterson; one man definitely wounded by Bat and another possibly wounded by him, and a horse killed by Bat and his brother Ed while they were shooting at the Texas cowboy on its back. The cowboy was unhurt. This count does not include an occurrence in a Denver barroom in which Masterson was pistol-whipping an adversary when a fleeing patron dropped a gun and inadvertently shot Bat in the leg. The injury proved to be only a flesh wound.

So, where did all that 22-27-28 notches malarkey originate? Apparently in the bar of the Tabor House hotel in Gunnison Colorado in the wee hours of an August, 1881, morning. It seems William Young, the *New York Sun*'s managing editor, was having a drink or two with several U.S. Army officers. These included William Suddath Cockrell, an army surgeon who was the son of a prominent U.S. senator from Missouri. Young asked if there was the least truth in any of the myriad lurid tales of man-killers and shootists he had heard while visiting the mining boomtowns of the West. Cockrell solemnly conceded that most of the stories were either highly embellished or outright lies. But he then pointed to what he said was an exception: a pleasant-looking, average-sized young man standing in the doorway of the hotel's billiard room.

"'There is a man,' Dr. Cockrell said, "'who has killed twenty-six men, and he is only twenty-seven years of age. He is W.B. Masterson of Dodge City, Kan. He killed his men in the interest of law and order.'" Among his victims, the good doctor continued—almost certainly with as straight a face as he could maintain—were seven men Masterson had killed within a few minutes of each other. The "squad of ruffians" had just killed Masterson's brother, and he dispatched them with two pistols held with his hands crossed in an X pattern so he could cover the field.

In another case, Cockrell continued, Masterson tracked down a father-son duo of Mexican killers who had $500 prices on their heads. Literally. Having shot them both, Masterson decapitated them and carried their heads back to town in a sack as proof of his deed. "'A two-days' ride under a hot sun swelled and disfigured the heads so that they were unrecognizable,'" Cockrell told the furiously scribbling journalist. Masterson was thus cheated of the rewards.

Whether he believed it or not, Young dutifully heeded the time-tested newspaperman's doctrine to never let the facts get in the way of a good story. His account made it into the *Sun* in the fall of 1881, and was reprinted in big and small newspapers across the country. Masterson may or may not have been amused, particularly since he wasn't even the man Cockrell pointed to in the billiard room doorway. But when the doctor eventually apologized in person to Bat for the practical joke that went national, Masterson didn't shoot him. The *Sun's* gullible yarn was subsequently supplemented in an interview of Bat by a Kansas City Missouri reporter. Masterson, the reporter claimed, told him he had been tried and acquitted four times for murder, and that as far as the Mexican bandits were concerned, "the story is straight, except that I did not cut off their heads." Bat Masterson the Wild West legend and Bat Masterson the reality were now popularly accepted as one and the same.

What was a fact was that Masterson had a genuine knack for getting people out of deep trouble without firing a shot. Five examples spring to mind, all but one of which occurred without him shooting at anyone.

In 1878, the famed vaudevillian Eddie Foy was in a makeshift dressing room at Dodge City's Comique theatre, Foy recalled in his memoir, when the notorious gunman Ben Thompson, "about two-thirds drunk, blundered in." Thompson announced he was going to shoot out an oil lamp on a table beside Foy, and demanded the entertainer move out of the way. "I was seized with a sudden foolish obstinacy," the diminutive comic wrote. He refused to move. An enraged Thompson pointed his gun directly at Foy's head. "For a long moment, we confronted each other thus—and then Bat Masterson burst into the scene, threw the muzzle of Thompson's gun upward, and partly by coaxing, partly by shoving, got him out...I was limp for the rest of the evening."

In 1880, it was Ben Thompson's turn to ask Bat a favor. Ben's brother, "Texas Billy" Thompson, was a hot-headed killer who may have saved Bat from vengeful soldiers in the wake of the Sweetwater Shootout (see Chapter 1.) Now Billy was in trouble in Ogallala, Nebraska. It seems that in a shootout with a popular local saloon owner, Billy had mangled the barkeep's hand, and in turn was the recipient of a serious shotgun wound. Word was that when he recovered, there was a lynch rope waiting for him. Ben Thompson was a wanted man in the region and couldn't attempt a rescue of his brother himself. So he asked Masterson. Bat thereupon went to Ogallala; persuaded a bartender friend to drug the drink of the guard outside Billy's hotel door, and spirited the wounded Thompson onto a train bound for North Platte, about 55 miles away.

In North Platte, Bat ran into Will Cody, and asked for his help. The adventure-loving Buffalo Bill leapt at the chance. Cody hid the pair for a day or two, then loaned Masterson the use of his wife's fancy new carriage, which Bat drove the 230 miles to Dodge. The *Dodge City Times* laconically noted that Bat "arrived from a visit to Ogallala this week...he came by wagon and was accompanied by Texas Billy Thompson. The latter has recovered from his wounds." Buffalo Bill, by the way, had to buy his wife a new carriage.

The next of Masterson's quintet of notable rescues was the only one that involved gunfire—or a relative. The spring of 1881 found Bat in Tombstone, Arizona. There he was dealing faro in the Oriental Saloon and generally watching the backs of his pals, the Earp Brothers. The Earps were wading deeper and deeper into a feud with a group of locals that would eventually develop into the most famous shootout in Wild West history. But Masterson would miss it, because of a telegram he received in April that his brother Jim was in trouble in Dodge City.

James Masterson had been a deputy marshal and marshal of Dodge. The least likeable of the Masterson Brothers, Jim, along with a fellow named A.J. Peacock, owned the town's Lady Gay Saloon. Peacock, had hired his brother-in-law, Al Updegraff, as a bartender. Updegraff was an alcoholic who habitually dipped his hands into the saloon's cash till, and Jim Masterson wanted to fire him. Peacock demurred. Tempers escalated. Threats were made. Guns were drawn, although no one was shot—until Bat stepped off the train in Dodge.

What became known locally as the "Battle of the Plaza" began when Bat spotted Peacock and Updegraff as he alighted. He shouted at them, they ducked for cover, and the shooting started. Other citizens joined in on both sides, and someone shot Updegraff through the right lung. When the firing ceased, Bat was arrested. Since it was unclear just who shot Updegraff, Masterson was charged only with "felonious discharge (of) a pistol" within town limits, and fined $10. Peacock hurriedly agreed to buy James Masterson out, and the brothers left Dodge that evening. Updegraff recovered from his wound, only to die of smallpox two years later.

But the incident left a bad taste in the mouths of many Dodge citizens toward the Mastersons. "The firing on the street by Bat Masterson...is severely condemned by our people," the *Dodge City Times* editorialized, "and the good opinion many citizens had of Bat has been changed to one of contempt...there is good reason to believe (he) will never darken Dodge City anymore." But he would.

Although Masterson apparently did not get on all that well with his brother Jim, he certainly liked him a good deal more than the fellow he rescued in Colorado from almost-certain death the following year. "Doc Holliday had a mean disposition and an ungovernable temper, and under the influence of liquor was a most dangerous man," Masterson wrote in a

1907 magazine profile of John Henry Holliday, a professional gambler and unquestionably the West's most dangerous dentist. "He was hot-headed and impetuous, and very much given to drinking and quarreling, and among men who did not fear him, was very much disliked."

But Holliday was a close friend of Wyatt Earp, who was a close friend of Bat's. So when Wyatt asked Masterson to help Holliday out of a precarious situation, Bat assented. The situation sprang from a series of bloody incidents that took place in Arizona in late 1881 and early 1882, and of which the patient reader will be apprised in the next chapter. Suffice to say here that Holliday was wanted for murder in Arizona. He was arrested in Denver, and Arizona authorities had requested he be turned over for trial. But Holliday and nearly everyone else, including Colorado Gov. Frederick W. Pitkin, knew that if Holliday were to be extradited, the odds were good he would be murdered or lynched. "If I am taken back to Arizona," Holliday told a reporter, "that is the last of Holliday."

Masterson had recently been appointed city marshal in Trinidad, Colorado. As such, he had some connections—and a plan to keep Doc in the state. From Denver, he wired Henry Jamieson, a pal who happened to be the city marshal of Pueblo, Colorado. Together, the two marshals presented state authorities with a warrant for the arrest of Doc Holliday, on a charge of fleecing a sucker of $150 in a con game in Pueblo. The charge was completely fabricated, but it gave Gov. Pitkin the excuse he needed to deny Arizona's extradition request, since the Pueblo warrant took precedence. Holliday was taken back to Pueblo, released on $300 bail, and the case was promptly forgotten. Holliday would never return to Arizona.

The last of the Masterson rescues recounted here involved the aptly named Luke Short. At 5'6" and maybe 135 pounds, Short, in Bat's words, "was a small package, but one of great dynamic force." He was a federal fugitive for selling whisky to Indians, a gambler and a saloon owner, and "quick as a flash" with a revolver. Short killed two men in gunfights: one in Tombstone, one in Fort Worth, Texas, and both of them with Bat Masterson as a witness.

In the spring of 1883, Short was co-owner of Dodge City's handsome Long Branch Saloon. His partner, Bill Harris, had run for the mayoralty of Dodge, but lost to Larry Deger, the obese ex-city marshal for whom Wyatt Earp and Jim and Bat Masterson had been deputies in 1876. Deger was the front man for a cadre of other saloon owners who coveted the brisk business done by the Long Branch. Shortly after Deger's election, the town council passed a sheaf of "reform" ordinances that cracked down on gambling, prostitution, loitering and even musical performances in saloons.

But the ordinances were only selectively enforced, against the Long Branch and a couple of other joints. After a flurry of disputes and a shooting scrape between Short and a deputy in which no one was hurt, Short and several others were escorted to an eastbound train by a large and heavily armed group of city officials, and instructed not to return.

Short didn't, at least not until he sent some telegrams from the safety of Kansas City. Several were to various state officials, demanding justice. One was to Bat Masterson. Bat, in turn, wired Wyatt Earp about Short's situation, and Earp gathered a group of noted gunmen that included Texas Jack Vermillion, Charlie Bassett, Dan Tipton and Shotgun Collins. The group drifted into Dodge while Bat and Short waited in Kansas City.

Hysteria gripped Short's Dodge adversaries. They pleaded with the governor to send in the state militia to avert what would surely be a bloodbath. Newspapers around the country got wind of the state of affairs, and stories of the looming "Dodge City War" entertained Americans whose perception of the Wild West dovetailed nicely with the situation. Only nothing happened. Intimidated by the gaggle of gunfighters, and with their plea for state help refused by the governor, city officials gave in to a series of demands from Short and Masterson.

"I arrived here (Dodge) yesterday and was met at the train by a delegation of friends," Bat wrote with sarcastic glee in a letter printed in the *Topeka State Journal*. "...I think the inflammatory reports published about Dodge City and its inhabitants have been greatly exaggerated, and if at any time they did 'don the war paint,' it was completely washed away before I arrived here. I never met a more gracious lot of people in my life."

Masterson was accompanied by Short, who resumed control of the Long Branch and was unmolested by town officials until November, when he voluntarily sold his interest in the saloon and left Dodge. Before they left Dodge, Masterson, Earp, Short and five others somewhat smugly posed for an iconic Wild West photograph that became known as the "Dodge City Peace Commission."

"Our city trouble is about over," the *Ford County Globe* philosophized, "and things in general will be conducted as of old. All parties that were run out have returned and no further effort will be made to drive them away... so here the battle ends and we trust that we may have no more internal insurrections in Dodge City."

Notwithstanding Masterson's comments about Dodge City being full of "gracious" people, the truth was Bat had a long rollercoaster relationship with the town. In 1883, he declared "I have long since bequeathed my interest in Dodge City and Ford County to the few vampires and murdering band of stranglers who have controlled its political and moral machinery in the last few years." By 1885, he was accepting a gold watch chain and gold-capped cane after being voted "the most popular man in Dodge" at a July 4th celebration.

The rollercoaster began in 1877, during which Bat was named county undersheriff, bought an interest in the Lone Star Dancehall, and was arrested in June for coming to the rescue of a drunk being abused by city Marshal Larry Deger. While the drunk temporarily escaped, Masterson was arrested—but it took Deger, a deputy and a bunch of bystanders to do it. Bat, the *Dodge City Times* reported, "seemed possessed of extraordinary strength, and every inch of the way was closely contested, but the city dungeon was reached at last, and in he went." It cost him $25 ($631 in 2022) to get out the next day.

In October, the 23-year-old Masterson announced he was running for the Ford County sheriff's job—against his old nemesis Deger. He would make no campaign pledges, he said, "as pledges are usually considered, before elections, as mere clap-trap...I am no politician." In the same edition as his announcement, editors of the *Times* declared "Bat is well-known as a young man of nerve and coolness in cases of danger...and knows just how to gather in the sinners. He is qualified to fill the office and if elected will never shrink from danger." The *Times* hedged its bets by referring to Deger in the same column as a "substantial honest and upright man" worthy of voters' "fair consideration." It turned out to be a close race, with Bat winning 266-263.

As sheriff, Masterson got generally high marks. He captured most of a gang of would-be train robbers led by "Dirty Dave" Rudabaugh; ran down, wounded and arrested the Texas cowboy who murdered the Dodge City mayor's mistress, and routinely tracked and caught horse thieves, a crime more serious in 1870s Kansas than it would appear to be now. "Sheriff W.B. Masterson and deputy William Duffy are indefatigable in their efforts to ferret out and arrest people," the *Dodge City Times* noted approvingly. "Scarcely a day passes without reward for their vigilance and promptness."

Not only was Bat "indefatigable" as sheriff; he was uninjured. Tragically, the same could not be said for his slightly older brother Ed. As a deputy city marshal in November 1877, Ed attempted to gently break up a dancehall dispute between two men. One of them, Bob Shaw, shot Ed in the right breast, temporarily paralyzing his gun hand. As he fell, Ed managed to transfer his gun to his left hand and pump two shots into his assailant. Both men recovered. Shaw wasn't charged with a crime, on the head-scratching grounds that he had never shot anyone before, and "Shaw's family are highly respectable people, and he has concluded to quit the Far West and go back to live under his parents' roof" in Georgia. Ed was awarded $18 ($450 in 2022) by the town council to cover his medical bills.

Five months later, Ed's affability got him killed. He had become Dodge's marshal, succeeding Bat's old rival Larry Deger. In the Lady Gay

Saloon one night in April, 1878, Ed spotted Jack Wagner, a drunken Texas cowboy, carrying a pistol in violation of city ordinances. He relieved the cowboy of the weapon and handed it to Wagner's trail boss, Alf Walker, with instructions for Walker to give the gun to the bartender. A short time later, Ed saw the cowboy on the street, with his gun. A scuffle began between the two, and then a shot was fired. A bullet from Wagner's revolver slammed a hole through Ed's abdomen "large enough for the introduction of the whole pistol," according to a newspaper account. His coat smoldering from the shot, Ed staggered across the street and collapsed. He died 40 minutes later.

Hearing the shot, Bat raced to the scene and emptied his revolver at the two Texans, seriously wounding Walker and killing Wagner. Walker was eventually taken back to Texas, and may have died from his wounds there. After waiting with Ed until he died, Bat then rounded up four cowboys that had been with Wagner and Walker, coolly refraining from shooting them too. They were released after it became clear they had nothing to do with Ed's death.

Dodge went into mourning for its well-liked marshal. The *Times* noted "his geniality of temperament, kindness of heart and richness of personal bravery." The *Globe,* its columns lined in black ink, wrote that "everyone in the city knew Ed Masterson and liked him. They liked him as a boy, they liked him as a man, and they liked him as an officer."

Bat went home with the sad news to his parents' farm near Sedgewick, Kansas, about 150 miles east of Dodge. He was back on the job within a week. But sympathy for Masterson's loss of a brother extended only so far among Ford County voters when Bat came up for re-election in November, 1879. His opponent, a bartender named George Hinkle, was backed by a "reform" group. The reformers were basically big landowners who wanted to see more farmers and a larger permanent population for Dodge, or merchants who did not profit directly from the cowboys and thus didn't care if Dodge was a hospitable host to them, and also a few people who actually opposed drinking, gambling and prostitution.

Hinkle's backers accused Masterson of being too lax when it came to jail escapes, too loose with county funds and too tight with "the Gang." This was a group led by Mayor James "Dog" Kelly, a slight, sloppily dressed former Confederate soldier. Kelly's nickname derived from his inordinate fondness for hunting dogs, several of which had been given him by George Custer. The Kelly-led gang was an alliance of the old buffalo-hunting fraternity, gamblers, saloon and dancehall operators and merchants who profited directly from a Dodge City that was amenable to indulging the vices of the cattle drovers.

The reformers won, and Hinkle rather decisively whipped Masterson. Bat did not take defeat well. In a letter to the *Dodge City Times*, he responded to a post-election charge by the editor of the *Spearville News* that Masterson had threatened his political opponents with violence. "I will say it is as false and flagrant a lie as was ever uttered," Bat wrote, "but I did say this: That I would lick him (the editor), the s-- of a b----, if he made any more dirty talk about me, and the words s—of a b---- I strictly confine to the Spearville editor, for I don't know any other in Ford County."

For the last two decades of the 19th century, Bat Masterson did pretty much whatever caught his attention at the time, which more often than not was a little of this, a little of that. He hung his trademark derby hat in Kansas City, Tombstone, Dodge City, Fort Worth and several cities and towns in Colorado. Census records and city directories listed him as everything from a "laborer" to a "sporting man." The latter designation was far closer to the truth—and the truth was he was everything from a law dog to a, well, sporting man.

"I can't say that I have been prosperous, although I have not suffered much from adversity," Bat wrote in 1898 to a friend from his Army scouting days. "I came into the world without anything and have held my own up to date...In the gambling business (I) have experienced the vicissitudes (of) the business. Some days—plenty, and more days—nothing."

His law-enforcement experience—and greatly inflated gunfighter reputation—convinced the town council of Trinidad, Colorado to appoint him city marshal in 1882, possibly to the displeasure of his brother Jim, who was already on the police force and coveted the top job himself. As marshal, Bat kept the peace in Trinidad, despite being batted over the head, improbably enough, with a cane while arresting a drunk. There was only one fatal shooting during his one-year tenure, and that occurred in a fight between two cops. But in late 1883, the Trinidad marshal's job was made an elective office. Masterson ran, lost, and moved on.

He combined his next experience in politics with his first foray into journalism. Still smarting from his loss of the Ford County sheriff's job, Masterson returned to Dodge City in late 1884 to get revenge on his political enemies. He did it by publishing a four-page newspaper he called *Vox Populi* a few days before a local election. Except for four small ads, the edition consisted entirely of imaginative and bile-dripping invective toward candidates he disliked. They were "scum and filth," "crawling reptiles" and "thieves and liars." He parodied them as a menagerie that included "a peculiar kind of winged thing, allied in habits to the magpie and crow," "a cross between a chimpanzee and baboon," and "a sort of badger, prowling by night and having a chemical fang that could soften iron." How much impact it had is uncertain, but what was certain was that all of Masterson's political foes lost. The *Vox Populi* promptly went out of business after the single edition. "While its existence was comparatively of short duration," Bat crowed in another paper, "the wonders it performed was simply miraculous."

With his political career permanently over and his journalism career indefinitely suspended, Masterson returned to more familiar environs. In late March, 1889, Colorado papers carried the news that "W.B. Masterson... has just been named manager of the Palace Theater at Denver. Good order will prevail there, and no mistake."

The Palace Variety Theater and Gambling Parlor was in dire need of good order. Opened in 1865, the handsome brick building housed a large vaudeville stage fronted by seating for 750, a 60-foot-long bar and two dozen gambling tables that could accommodate 250 players at a time. It also had a reputation, in the words of one editorialist, as "a disgrace to the state and the rendezvous of prostitutes, gamblers, bunko men and pick-pockets." Two murders in 1888 didn't help the joint's image either, and city officials were compelled to close it down for a while. After it reopened with Bat as its manager, and eventually its owner, the Palace's murder rate dropped to zero.

Masterson also strove to improve the Palace's entertainment. In an ad placed in vaudeville trade journals, he advised acts hoping to work there to "state the quality and quantity of their wardrobes and amount of salary they will work for, not what they want." He added that "variety ladies with more than three husbands need not write to this house for a date."

Masterson, however, did not object at all to "variety ladies" with only one husband. In fact, even before taking over the Palace he had made news by beating up a fellow who for some reason objected to his wife sitting on Bat's lap in a Denver theater box. Masterson, the newspapers said, was "a handsome man who pleases the ladies." At the Palace, one of the pleased ladies would become his wife.

In later years, a reporter would interview Emma Matilda Walter Masterson and describe her as "a woman of retiring disposition." She liked reading and housekeeping, the reporter reported, and was definitely "not the type of new woman" who would ever have done anything more exciting than marrying a famous gunfighter. The reporter had clearly not done his homework.

In fact, Emma Masterson had a pretty exciting life before she ever met Bat Masterson. Born in Philadelphia in 1857, she left home in her early teens seeking a show business career. What she found was Ed "the Gopher Boy" Moulton, a professional foot racer. Foot racing was a popular Gilded Age sport. It was easy to stage, easy to bet on, and easy to fix the outcome.

Moulton was very fast, so much so that he sometimes couldn't find a challenger. When he couldn't, Emma would don racy racing tights, be given a 25-yard head start in a 125-yard race, and run against her husband. She even would win once in a while. The couple also sold photographs of Emma in her racing attire, which were often more popular than the races. To further supplement their income, Emma became exceedingly dexterous at swinging "Indian clubs," the bowling-pin-like exercise equipment. Indian club swinging was a popular fad at the time, and Emma was good enough to become a featured variety show act as "The Queen of Clubs." In 1888 and 1889, she performed at the Palace in Denver, and met Bat.

Although they didn't marry (if they ever legally did) until 1893, Emma and Bat became a couple shortly after meeting, and would remain so until his death. (As a consolation prize, Ed Moulton went on to become a nationally known track coach who trained several Olympic medalists and had a long career as the head track coach for Stanford University.)

The 39-year-old man Emma may or may not have married in 1893 was at the time, according to a Kansas City journalist, about 5'9" in height and 165 pounds in weight, with closely cropped dark hair, a neatly trimmed mustache and a complexion "inclined to be florid, evidently from dissipation." Bat was sporting a black derby hat and was attired in "a Spring suit of clothes, light in color and beautifully made. He is not flashy in any respect...is extremely polite in manner, talks well and easily and uses good English...this is the man who is said to have killed as many men as any others of the border characters."

In the West, that was sometimes a handy reputation to have. After selling the Palace Theater, Masterson moved to the new Colorado mining boomtown of Creede to manage the Denver Exchange, a large saloon and gambling hall. About 250 miles southwest of Denver, Creede was "a typical Western town without a government." Much of the population of about 5,000 crammed into "hotels" consisting of "sleeping rooms" that contained from 20 to 60 cots. Many of the hastily erected structures hugged a stream that not only provided the town's drinking water but was also "the repository for all the offal and filth that accumulates in a large city."

It was the kind of burg that attracted tough hombres, and Bat was "generally recognized as the nerviest man of all the fighters here," a St. Louis reporter wrote. "He has a record for cool bravery unsurpassed by any man in the West...Masterson walks around the (saloon) sixteen hours of the twenty-four and knows exactly what is going on...all the toughs and thugs fear him as they do not any other dozen men in camp. Let an incipient riot start and all that is necessary to quell it is the whisper 'there comes Masterson.'"

However seriously Masterson took his job and his reputation, he invariably had time for practical jokes. One night an itinerant preacher named Parson Tom Uzzell came into the saloon and asked Bat if he could deliver a sermon. Bat reluctantly agreed to pause activity at the gaming tables, and when Uzzell was done, Masterson suggested he pass the hat. The preacher did so, and gratefully departed with several hundred dollars. But when several of the gamblers subsequently expressed their regrets of not giving more, Bat had an idea. A couple of light-fingered associates were dispatched to Uzzell's tent, where they stealthily snatched his pants while he slept. Early the next morning, Uzzell indignantly stomped into the saloon in his long-johns, howling his pants had been stolen. After the laughter died down, Masterson handed the preacher his trousers, with twice as much money in the pockets as had been there the night before.

But if there was one thing Bat Masterson loved more than practical jokes, boomtowns—and maybe as much as Emma—it was boxing. In September 1892, Masterson got wind of an upcoming heavyweight championship fight in New Orleans. He promptly packed his bags, said goodbye to Creede and headed east.

Unarmed mano-a-mano combat for money or other prizes had been around in America since before George Washington was a pup, but it was most often a ruleless, brutal fight that involved more eye-gouging, nose-biting and testicle-pummeling than left hooks or right jabs. After the Civil War, however, efforts were made to standardize boxing matches by adopting the "Marquess of Queensbury Rules." These were regulations developed in Britain and so named because a Scottish nobleman who was a boxing enthusiast heartily endorsed and promoted them. The rules included standard ring dimensions, three-minute rounds with one minute between each round, a prescribed number of rounds in a fight, a ten-second count for a fighter to resume the match, and greater discretion for referees. Wrestling, biting and hitting below the belt were disallowed.

Even with the new rules, most U.S. states continued to ban prizefighting through the 1880s. Such bans were often circumvented by promoting bouts as merely "exhibitions" of the sport and not serious for-money fights, even though everyone and his brother knew that big purses and serious betting surrounded them.

Although never a prizefighter himself, Bat Masterson passionately embraced the sport. As early as 1882, he had promoted a fight in Dodge City. At one time or other, he managed fighters and acted as a timekeeper or referee, or provided security—a much-needed service at events where large sums of money were at stake. "Gunmen were an important part of the pugilistic picture," noted the esteemed boxing historian Nat Fleischer, "when fair play was being maintained by a judicious display of force on both sides."

In the last 40 years of his life, Bat attended virtually every major bout in the country as a gambler, official or journalist. These included serving as security chief for an 1892 match on an island in the Rio Grande between Mexico and Texas. It was held there because neither jurisdiction would allow it on their soil. After weeks of controversy and herculean efforts to erect a site on the sandy spit, the fight itself last 125 seconds.

Even Emma Masterson got enthused about the sport. In 1891, Emma accompanied Bat to a boxing match in New Orleans, despite the fact that women were prohibited from attending prizefights. The day after the fight, the press reported that "a handsome short-haired woman" who identified herself as "a variety actress from Denver, had her sex penetrated by a police lieutenant just as she was taking a seat in a box" near ringside. Dressed as a man, Emma was arrested for violating a city ordinance against cross-dressing. She was released the next day, and later complained her disguise failed when a single lock of her hair fell from beneath the cap she was wearing. That was some sharp-eyed cop.

By 1893, Bat was dubbed "the King of Western sporting men" by the *National Police Gazette*, a publication that was a Gilded Age combination of *Playboy, Sports Illustrated* and the *National Enquirer*, and was the bible of the boxing world. Masterson, the *Gazette* proclaimed, "is a general sport (who) backs pugilists, can play any game on the green with a full deck and handles a Bowie (knife) or revolver with the determination of a Napoleon."

The Gazette's fulsome praise, however, omitted the sad fact that Masterson almost invariably let his personal feelings toward fighters or their managers cloud his judgement when it came to picking winners. As a result, he seldom profited from the often-heavy wagers he laid on matches. Eventually, he figured there was a surer way to make a living in the fight game.

In 1899, he entered a partnership with Otto Floto, a fat fight fan from California. Floto had recently been named sports editor of the *Denver Post,* reportedly for no other reason than that the paper's owner liked saying his name. Colorado had recently legalized boxing, and Floto and Masterson opened the Colorado Athletic Association, with the aim of training fighters, staging and promoting matches and generally monopolizing the sport within the state. Only Floto quickly lined up enough financial backing to force Masterson out and take entire control.

An outraged Masterson countered by opening a rival company, the Olympic Athletic Club. He also secured a column in a rival newspaper to the *Post.* For the next year or so, Floto and Masterson sparred continually in print and in person. At one point they even came to blows in the street. The local papers gleefully reported the absurdly hilarious sight of two overweight middle-aged men "kicking each other in the groin." The fight concluded with Masterson chasing—or trying to chase—Floto down the street. "I used to think I was a pretty good runner," Bat wheezed afterward, "but that fellow started to pull away from me on the jump...there are some fellows you can deal with and talk them into being decent, and there are others just like a stubborn mule that you have to beat to death to teach them...".

Later, there were rumors Floto had hired a gunman to dispose of Masterson. If so, he never showed up. In 1900, Masterson decided the future of boxing in Denver wasn't worth fighting over. A story circulated that the final straw was broken when a woman at a polling place challenged his eligibility to vote by beating him over the head with her umbrella. Another was that after Bat engaged in a drunken shooting spree, he was told to leave town—or else—by an old friend who was a deputy U.S. marshal. In any event, the Mastersons headed east again in 1902, this time to stay.

Bat Masterson loved New York City, and that mystified Billy Dixon. "It always seemed strange to me that he finally should prefer life in a big city after having lived in the West," Dixon said about his old buffalo-hunting pal and compadre at the Battle of Adobe Walls. "I have been told that he said that he had no wish to live over those old days, that they no longer appealed to him, but I never believed it. Such psychology is contrary to human nature."

But it was true. Nearly four decades—and 50 pounds—had been added since the days of the buffalo. As far as Bat was concerned, cutting into a sizzling steak at a table in Shanley's Grill on 43rd and Broadway beat the hell out of spooning into a cold can of beans at a bison dung-fueled fire in the Texas Panhandle. "I don't care if I ever see those dreary old prairies again," he said, even as he regaled newspaper proteges and other assorted Manhattan denizens with tales of the Wild West.

Masterson had his first taste of life in Gotham in 1895, and it quite agreed with him. It seems George Gould, the son of the fabulously wealthy robber baron Jay Gould, had been receiving death threats from a jilted suitor of his sister, and needed a bodyguard. The New York City police commissioner, who had met and befriended Bat in North Dakota a decade earlier, recommended Masterson for the job. Bat accepted, and for eight months enjoyed living in luxury: long days at the racetrack, betting Gould's money; idyllic weekends on elegant yachts, sumptuous living quarters. When the gig ended with the arrest of the stalker, Masterson was decidedly grateful to the police commissioner who had recommended him for it. The commissioner was a chap named Theodore Roosevelt.

Those surprised by Masterson's embrace of the East might have been more surprised by the fact that his original intention was to go even further east than New York. With a Chicago gambling pal, Charles "Parson" Davies, Bat's plan was to sail to England and promote boxing matches there in conjunction with the national celebrations surrounding the coronation of the new king, Edward VI. But the day before he was to sail, he was arrested while getting his shoes shined. Masterson was charged with bilking a Mormon clergyman in a rigged faro game, and illegally carrying a large revolver. The faro game charges were bogus, and dropped. The concealed weapons charge was true, and Bat was fined $10. Worse, he missed his boat.

But if you will pardon the following string of cliches, missing the boat turned out to be a blessing in disguise, because Bat had friends in high places. One was the former New York City police commissioner. As vice president of the United States, Theodore Roosevelt had ascended to the presidency with the assassination of William McKinley in September 1901, and was elected in his own right in 1904. Soon thereafter, he arranged the appointment of W.B. Masterson as deputy U.S. marshal in New York City. The salary was $2,000 per year ($62,300 in 2022), which was more than twice what all but four of the 24 other deputies in the office were making.

"I want you to be not only a vigilant, courteous and efficient officer,"

Roosevelt wrote Bat, "...but I also want you to carry yourself so that no one can find in any action of yours cause for scandal or complaint." The president also asked Masterson to refrain from gambling. During his 52 months in the job, Bat faithfully showed up at the marshal's office on payday, and very rarely, if ever, at any other time. He also blithely ignored Roosevelt's admonition about gambling.

But he did limit the scandals to perhaps only one incident. In 1906, Bat had an altercation with two men in a New York hotel. After being struck in the face by one of them, Masterson knocked his attacker down, then thrust his hand in his pocket, pointed it at the other fellow and invited him to leave. The fellow did so. When a reporter asked to see Bat's pocketed weapon, he smilingly obliged by producing a pack of cigarettes.

More important to Bat than his friend in the White House was his friendship with two brothers whom he had also met out west, and who greatly admired his real and imagined exploits. Alfred Henry Lewis had traveled west in the 1880s, working as a cowhand and ferreting out material for a series of stories that by the start of the 20th century would make him America's highest-paid magazine writer, and eventually author of 18 books.

One of Lewis' books, a "biographical novel" called *The Sunset Trail*, starred Bat Masterson and added new luster to Bat's status as a Wild West legend. As editor of a glossy magazine called *Human Life*, Lewis also persuaded Masterson to pen a series of profiles of the famous and infamous gunfighters Bat had known, such as Wyatt Earp and Doc Holliday. When Bat declined to include an autobiographical sketch, Lewis wrote one for him. Some of it was true. Most of it was like this: "To a courage that is proud, he adds a genius for justice and carries honesty to the pitch of romanticism...add the claws of a grizzly bear, and you will have a picture of Mr. Masterson."

The other Lewis brother, William Eugene, was editor of *The Morning Telegraph*, a tabloid heavy on sports news, scandal, gossip and show business. The *Telegraph* specialized in covering horseracing, and eventually

Hollywood, and habitually featured Page One drawings or photos of curvaceous showgirls. A standing New York joke was that a "whore's breakfast" consisted of a pack of cigarettes and *The Morning Telegraph*.

For a perverse little tabloid (the *Telegraph* delighted in bragging that it cost a dime, twice what its competitors charged), its staff included a fair number of people who would achieve widespread celebrity. There was Louella Parsons, who would head west to become the queen of the Hollywood gossip columnists. Young reporter Heywood Hale Broun would become one of the country's most respected journalists and the first president of the American Newspaper Guild. Another young reporter, Stuart Lake, became so enthralled with Bat Masterson's stories about Wyatt Earp he would seek Earp out and write a biography of him that more than anything else would elevate Earp above all his gunslinging contemporaries. A staff caricaturist named John Barrymore gave up newspaper artwork for the theatrical arts, and became one of the brightest stars of the stage and screen. And then there was Masterson,

In 1903, Gene Lewis offered Bat a job as a columnist. For the next 18 years, Masterson would churn out pieces that at first focused on boxing and horseracing but evolved into an array of subjects so broad the column came to be called "Masterson's Views on Timely Topics." His journalistic musings ranged from choleric rants to witty aphorisms. In the former category was his description of boxers who dodged military service in World War I as "a craven-hearted, low-down set of measly microbes." Among his pithy observations was that "when a man is at the racetrack, he roars longer and louder about the twenty-five cents he loses through a hole in the bottom of his pocket than he does the $25 he loses through the hole in the top of his pocket."

Damon Runyon, one of Masterson's cocktail table acolytes, recalled "Bat had no literary style, but he had plenty of moxie." Runyon would rise to fame as both a columnist and short story writer. He would base one of his most memorable characters, the gambler Sky Masterson (played by Marlon Brando in the musical adaptation *Guys and Dolls*), on Bat. And in Bat's case moxie trumped style. His fearlessness in pointing out corruption in the boxing industry led to nationwide stature as a prizefighting analyst, and he often was asked to write "guest" columns for papers across the country.

One such fearless column led to an interesting revisiting of his Wild West reputation. In 1911, Masterson accused boxing manager Frank Ufer of fixing a fight. Ufer responded in a *New York Globe* article that Bat had made his reputation "by shooting drunken Mexicans and Indians in the back." Bat sued the *Globe* for libel, seeking $25,000 in damages. Among the attorneys the *Globe* hired to defend it was 41-year-old Benjamin H. Cardozo, who would go on to have a distinguished legal career capped by becoming a U.S. Supreme Court justice.

But he was no match for Masterson. In making his case, Bat testified that he had never shot a Mexican in the back or the front; had fought Indians but didn't know for sure if he had killed any, and certainly hadn't killed 27 or 28 men in gunfights, as was often related. When pressed, he estimated he had killed three, one in self-defense and the other two in the line of duty as a peace officer.

"I don't think about being proud of it," he replied when Cardozo asked if it was true he basked in his reputation. "I do not feel that I ought to be ashamed of it either; I feel perfectly justified. The mere fact I was charged with killing a man, standing by itself, I have never considered an attack upon my reputation." The jury decided Bat had been at least somewhat wronged by Ufer's base accusation, and awarded Masterson $3,500, plus court costs. On appeal, the award was reduced to $1,000. But the moral victory remained Bat's.

In early October 1921, Masterson's 19th century past again met the 20th century in the form of a visit Bat received from actor William S. Hart. A trained stage actor, Hart had become a leading screenwriter, director and producer in the film industry, and one of Hollywood's biggest stars of Western movies. He was enthralled to meet the real thing in Masterson. For his part, Bat, who liked Western movies, was probably a little star-struck too. The two men talked for several hours and posed for pictures at the newspaper. At the urging of Louella Parsons, Hart also agreed to write a column for the *Telegraph* about his reverence for those whom he portrayed on the screen.

"Now, I am just an actor—a mere player—seeking to reproduce the lives of those great gunmen who molded a new country for us to live in and enjoy peace and prosperity," Hart gushed. "And we have today in America two of these men in the flesh...one is Wyatt Earp, the other William B. (Bat) Masterson...they are the last of the greatest band of gun-fighters... let us not forget these living Americans who, when they pass on, will be remembered by hundreds of generations."

Less than three weeks after Hart's visit, Bat Masterson passed on. Whether "hundreds of generations" will remember him, however, is somewhat problematical. "At one time Masterson was said to have been the best-known man between the Mississippi and the Pacific Coast," the *New York Times* wrote at the time of Masterson's death, "and his exploits as a gunfighter have become part of the tradition of the Middle West of many years ago. He was the last of the old-time gunfighters."

But he wasn't. Wyatt Earp would outlive his old pal by a bit more than seven years, and would continue to cast his shadow over Masterson's memory in print, film and television for the following century. While dozens of books have been written about Earp, only two Masterson biographers of any substance have appeared to date. The first, in 1957, was a veritable word machine named Richard O'Connor. To say O'Connor was prolific is to say the Pacific Ocean is wet. In a 59-year life, he produced more than 50 books, from biographies to historical fiction. His *Bat Masterson* is somewhere in between. O'Connor candidly admitted that he had to crank out two books a year "or I couldn't make a living," and thus had little time for research. As a sympathetic reviewer put it, O'Connor "learned early that most readers prefer a smooth-running, entertaining book to one jammed with footnotes."

At least O'Connor's timing was good. Television was awash with Westerns in the late 1950s: In the 1958-59 season, seven of the 10 top-rated shows featured gun-toting people on horseback, and half of the top 30. NBC's *Bat Masterson*, based on O'Connor's book and starring second-tier movie actor Gene Barry in the title role, debuted in October, 1958. O'Connor served as a show consultant and the series helped make the biography O'Connor's most successful book.

Barry portrayed Bat as a foppish dude, resplendent in tailored dark suit, spangly vest and revolver rakishly carried on his left hip, with the butt facing his navel so he could affect a fancy cross-draw. For a TV shoot-'em-up, however, Barry's Masterson rarely drew his gun. Instead, he relied on suave manners, sharp wits and a gold-capped cane that he annoyingly twirled like a high school band leader. Despite the lack of violence and a theme song that rhymed "trigger" with "figger," the show lasted 3 seasons and 108 episodes. It also spurred a 10-issue comic book series and the sales of hundreds of thousands of plastic canes and black derby hats.

The Masterson character also appeared in 34 episodes of the much more successful ABC show *The Life and Legend of Wyatt Earp*. Played by actor Mason Alan Dinehart, Masterson was portrayed as an eager apprentice to the god-like Earp, to the absurd point of Wyatt teaching Bat how to use a pistol. Masterson also fared much worse than Earp in the movies. Bat was the featured character in perhaps a dozen films, all of them forgettable and some of them—1954's *Masterson of Kansas* comes to mind—downright painful to watch.

Fortunately for Masterson's legacy, there was Robert K. DeArment. Like Masterson, DeArment led two lives. The first was as a World War II combat infantry veteran who through 45 years worked his way up from the factory floor to the executive offices at the Champion Spark Plug company in Toledo, Ohio. But somewhere along the way, DeArment was bitten by the Wild West bug. Before he died in 2021, at the age of 95, he wrote more than 20 books and dozens of articles on the subject, and became the field's go-to expert on Bat Masterson in particular. He wrote not one, but two Masterson biographies. The first, published in 1979, focused on Bat's pre-New York days. The second, released in 2013, concentrated on Masterson's later life.

Both of DeArment's biographies were painstakingly researched and well-written, "full of anecdotes and local color," as one reviewer put it. Moreover, DeArment had the literary integrity to correct mistakes and update information from one book to the next. "In the history of the American West," a reviewer noted, "such candor is as charming as it is rare."

But even DeArment apparently had his misgivings about the staying power of Bat Masterson's legacy. In his second biography of Masterson, he recounted a story about his wife conversing with a big-league base ball coach on a long flight. When she mentioned her husband was the definitive biographer of Bat Masterson, the coach replied "Who did he play for?"

Chapter 10 Notes

"Just think of" Masterson's last column appeared in the *Telegraph* Oct. 27, 1921, the day of his funeral.

Assuming he didn't *St. Louis Post-Dispatch*, Oct. 25, 1921, p, 1;

The *Washington Herald* *Washington Herald*, Oct. 26, 1921, p. 8; *Coffeyville (Ks.) Morning News*, Oct. 26, 1921, p. 1; New York Times, Oct. 26, 1921, p. 14; *Louisville (Ky.) Courier-Journal*, Oct. 26, 1921, p. 6.

While he died, *San Francisco Examiner*, Nov. 2, 1921, p. 16.

The accuracy of *Salt Lake Tribune*, July 17, 1910, p. 40.

A few years later Stuart Lake, *Wyatt Earp, Frontier Marshal*, p. 40.

"There is a man" *Dodge City Globe*, Nov. 22, 1881, p. 3.

Whether he believed Robert K. DeArment, *Bat Masterson, the Man and the Legend*, p. 5.

In 1878, the Eddie Foy, *Clowning Through Life*, pp. 109-110.

In 1880, it *Dodge City Times*, July 17, 1880, p. 5.

But the incident *Dodge City Times*, April 21, 1881, p. 8.

Although Bat apparently W.B. Masterson, *Famous Gunfighters of the Western Frontier*, pp. 35-36.

But Holliday was *Denver Republican*, May 22, 1882, p. 1.

The last of the Masterson, op. cit., p. 8.

"I arrived here" *Topeka State Journal*, June 9, 1883, p. 4.

"Our city trouble" *Ford County Globe*, June 12, 1883, p. 2.

Notwithstanding Masterson's *Ford County Globe*, Feb. 10, 1883, p. 3; *Dodge City Globe*, July 7, 1885, p. 5.

In 1877 alone *Dodge City Times*, June 9, 1877, p. 4.

In October, Masterson *Dodge City Times*, Oct. 13, 1877, p. 4.

As sheriff, Masterson *Dodge City Times*, Aug. 17, 1878, p. 2.

Not only was *Dodge City Times*, Nov. 17, 1877, p. 4.

Five months later, *Ford County Globe*, April 16, 1878, p. 2.

Hearing the shot The shooting of the two cowboys who killed Ed Masterson has been endlessly debated by historians. In the immediate wake of the incident, local newspapers reported that Ed had shot his two assailants. But it's possible either the papers were trying to puff up Ed's legacy, or protect Bat from revenge by the cowboys' friends. In an 1885 trial that had nothing to do with the shooting, several witnesses and Bat himself testified under oath that he was the one who shot his brother's killers. The testimony, coupled with other accounts and the fact Ed was almost certainly in no condition to get off five shots, convinces me it was Bat.

Dodge went into *Dodge City Times*, April 13, 1878, p. 4; *Ford County Globe*, April 16, 1878, p. 2.

The reformers won *Dodge City Times*, Nov. 12, 1879, p. 8.

"I can't say," Robert K. DeArment, *Gunfighter in Gotham*, p. 43.

He combined his Dodge City *Vox Populi*, Nov. 1, 1884; *Globe Live Stock Journal* (Dodge City), Nov. 11, 1884.

With his political *Lamar (Co.) Register*, March 30, 1889, p. 2.

The Palace Variety *Fort Collins (Co.) Express*, March 4, 1882, p. 2.

Masterson also strived DeArment, op. cit., p. 40.

Masterson, however, Ibid., p. 34.

The 39-year-old *Kansas City Times*, April 27, 1893, p. 4.

In the West *Chicago Tribune*, March 5, 1892, p. 12.

It was the *St. Louis Globe-Democrat*, March 5, 1892, p. 6.

Although never a DeArment, op. cit., p. 14.

In 1891, Emma *Fort Wayne (Ind.) Sentinel*, Jan. 15, 1891, p. 1

By 1893, Bat DeArment, op. cit., p. 22.

An outraged Masterson, Ibid., p. 47.

Bat Masterson loved Olive K. Dixon, *Life of Billy Dixon*, p. 178.

But it was true Richard O'Connor, *Bat Masterson*, p. 252.

"I want you" Jack DeMattos, *Masterson and Roosevelt*, pp. 22-23.

One of Lewis' *Omaha Daily Bee*, Dec. 8, 1907, p. 5.

In 1903, Gene DeArment, op. cit., p. 204.

Damon Runyon, one *San Francisco Examiner*, Nov. 2, 1921, p. 16.

One such fearless William H. Manz, "Benjamin Cardozo Meets Gunslinger Bat Masterson," *New York State Bar Assn. Journal*, July/August 2004, pp. 9-17.

"Now I am just" *New York Morning Telegraph*, Oct. 4, 1921.

Less than three *New York Times*, Oct. 26, 1921, p. 14.

But he wasn't. *Miami Herald*, Oct. 8, 1958, p. 17; *El Paso Times*, March 11, 1975, p. 123.

Both of DeArment's *San Francisco Examiner*, Feb. 3, 1980, p. 283; *Lincoln (Neb.) Star*, Feb. 10, 1980, p. 79.

But even DeArment DeArment, op. cit., p. 8.

"The bloke from Arizona"

Wyatt goes Hollywood

One day in the spring of 1914, the swashbuckling actor/director Raoul Walsh was relaxing between takes at the Mutual Film Company's new Hollywood studio, when a security guard approached him. There were two men at the gate, the guard said, who wanted to talk to Walsh about his latest escapade.

Thie escapade in question consisted of Walsh having spent three months in Mexico, riding with the army of the celebrated revolutionary/bandit Pancho Villa and filming Villa and his soldiers during actual battles. At times, the cameras had been so close that one was blown up by an artillery shell and the tripod of another destroyed by machine gun fire. The 27-year-old Walsh, who also acted in the film, portraying a younger version of the general, was putting the finishing touches to *The Life of General Villa*, and was in an expansive mood. So he agreed to talk to the two visitors. "That," Walsh wrote in a 1974 memoir, "was how I met Jack London and Wyatt Earp."

Meeting the first American writer to earn a million dollars from his profession *and* a real-life gunfighter at the same time impressed Walsh more than a little. London, he wrote, "was getting on in years, but his seamed face was still as rugged as his stories...the legendary Earp was tall and a little stooped, but I could still see him as the marshal of Tombstone." The writer and ex-lawman had met in Alaska, Walsh learned. They became friends despite a 26-year age difference. London, in fact, had been born in 1876, three days after Earp had almost shot himself by dropping his pistol while lounging in a Wichita saloon. London was thinking of writing a book about Villa, and wanted to learn more about the man from Walsh.

The 66-year-old Earp, who by this time was a resident of Los Angeles, had apparently come along because he had little else to do.

Raoul Walsh was not a man to be easily impressed. His own 60-year career would see him play roles from John Wilkes Booth in D.W. Griffith's epic (though execrably racist) *Birth of a Nation* to femme fatale Gloria Swanson's lover in the racy 1928 version of *Sadie Thompson*. He would direct the trail-blazing *Thief of Bagdad*, starring Douglas Fairbanks, and *The Big Trail*, which featured John Wayne in his first starring role. He would also direct Errol Flynn as George Custer in *They Died with Their Boots On*, Humphrey Bogart in *High Sierra* and Jimmy Cagney in *White Heat*. And he would do most of it sporting a rakish eyepatch, the result of losing his right eye when a jackrabbit jumped through the car windshield while Walsh was driving through an Arizona desert.

Still, he was definitely impressed by his visitors. Walsh invited them to be his guests that night at Levy's Café, famous for its oyster cocktails, thick steaks and star-studded clientele that made it Los Angeles' "first major movie industry hangout." Over dinner, Walsh "tried to draw both men out about their doings. Neither wanted to talk about himself, although I did manage to get a few good details from Earp about the Clanton family and the famous shootout at the O.K. Corral."

At one point, Walsh interrupted their meal by calling over a short, dapper fellow from a nearby table, who was entertaining the diners by pretending he was a waiter, complete with towel over forearm and order pad in hand. Walsh introduced his dinner companions to Charlie Chaplin, a former British vaudevillian who was on his way to becoming the wealthiest and most famous film star in the world.

"When I introduced my guests," Walsh recalled, "he viewed Earp with evident awe. 'You're the bloke from Arizona, aren't you? Tamed the baddies, huh?' He looked at London and nodded. 'I know you too. You almost made me go to Alaska and dig for gold.'" Chaplin then sat down and shared stories of his youth in England. "I had a fine time listening to them," Walsh wrote, "and later wished I had some way of recording their conversation."

That Walsh got Wyatt Earp to talk at all about the most defining event in Earp's life was something of a coup. It was not his favorite subject. "There are more corpses in *Hamlet* than there was at the O.K. Corral, and with less reason," he complained late in life to an interviewer, "...That fight didn't last but thirty seconds, and it seems like in my going on 80 years, we could find some other happenings to discuss."

As much as he disliked discussing the subject, it was an inescapable fact that the events of Oct. 26, 1881, would do more to establish the American icon that Wyatt Earp became than the rest of his life's experiences combined. In fact, it could be reasonably argued that absent a bloody 30-second slice of a cold and blustery Wednesday afternoon in Tombstone, Arizona, relatively few people in 2022 would have ever heard of Wyatt Earp.

It was true Earp had developed a solid, though limited, regional reputation as a lawman in Dodge City. When he returned to the town in mid-1877 after his time in Deadwood as a firewood entrepreneur, the *Dodge City Times* expressed its "hope he will accept a position in the (police) force once more. He had a quiet way of taking the most desperate character into custody...it wasn't (good) policy to draw a gun on Wyatt unless you got the drop and meant to burn powder without any preliminary talk." A year later, the *Ford County Globe* noted "Wyatt Earp is doing his duty as assistant marshal in a very creditable manner—adding new laurels to his splendid record every day."

But while Earp's time in Dodge laid the foundation for his legendary status, he was involved in only two shootings of note there. The first was in July 1878, when a group of Texas cowboys hurrahed the town at 3 a.m. on their way back to camp. When some of the cowboys' shots perforated a dance hall, Wyatt and fellow policeman Jim Masterson ran into the street and fired at the mounted cowboys. One of them, George Hoy, was felled with a shoulder wound, from which he died a month later. The incident gave Wyatt his first widespread publicity when the *National Police Gazette* reported the story and praised Earp as "a good fellow and brave officer." The accolade was slightly marred by the fact the *Gazette* spelled his last name "Erpe."

The second incident occurred three months later. James "Spike" Kenedy, the son of a wealthy Texas rancher, was jealous of Dodge Mayor James "Dog" Kelly. The mayor had won the affections of the beautiful and popular saloon entertainer Fannie Keenan, aka Dora Hand. The lovesick Kenedy rode past Kelly's house one night and pumped a bullet or two through a wall. But Kelly—and his wife—weren't home, and Fannie was. A shot killed her. Kenedy fled. A determined posse, led by Bat Masterson and including Wyatt and veteran lawmen Bill Tilghman and Charlie Bassett, chased Kenedy through rain and snow for two days before overtaking him. Wyatt shot Kenedy's horse; Bat shot Kenedy. The horse died. Kenedy did not, and was eventually acquitted, quite possibly through the influence of his father's fat wallet on the judicial process.

When the cattle drives ended in the fall and the need for law enforcement in Dodge waned, Wyatt would head south to make a living dealing faro in Texas or doing freelance detective work for the railroads. On one such excursion in early 1878, he met a pale, thin and pugnacious gambler from Georgia named John Henry Holliday. The 27-year-old Holliday was in some ways a tragic figure. Educated as a dentist at the University of Pennsylvania, Holliday had drifted west after a death-sentence diagnosis of tuberculosis and an unrequited love affair with a cousin.

In the West, he all but gave up dentistry: Patients were understandably nervous at having someone who frequently coughed, occasionally spit up blood and had a nasty disposition in the first place put his hands in their mouths. Although Holliday advertised his dental services in a Dodge City paper and even offered a money-back guarantee of satisfaction, he mostly played poker for a living.

Bat Masterson considered "Doc" Holliday a jerk. "Holliday had few real friends anywhere in the West," Masterson wrote in his magazine profile of

Holliday. "He was selfish and had a perverse nature—traits not calculated to make a man more popular in the early days of the frontier." But Wyatt Earp liked him. While vague on details, Earp often claimed that Holliday had once saved his life by backing him in a Dodge saloon confrontation with a dozen or so Texas cowboys. "With all of Doc's shortcomings and his undeniably poor disposition," Wyatt insisted, "I found him a loyal friend and good company."

By 1879, Wyatt realized his life was on a treadmill. He had been doing the same job for nearly five years, counting his time in Wichita, for basically the same salary, and he had put his 31st birthday astern. Besides, Earp recalled years later, "Dodge City was beginning to lose much of the snap which had given it a charm to men of restless breed, and I decided to move to Tombstone, which was just building up a reputation."

In September, Earp left Dodge, accompanied by his brother James, James' wife, and Celia "Mattie" Blaylock, a former prostitute who had become Wyatt's common law wife. They stopped in Las Vegas, New Mexico, to pick up Doc Holliday, who was running a saloon there. Holliday had recently shot and killed a former U.S. Army scout who had been shooting up the saloon, and Doc was ready to move on. Big Nose Kate Elder, Holliday's paramour, came along too. The party then dropped by Prescott, Arizona, to gather Virgil Earp, who was a town constable. Holliday and Elder lingered behind before rejoining the Earps in Tombstone in the fall of 1880.Two more Earp bothers, Morgan and Warren, also eventually meandered into town.

The arrival of the Earp brothers did not go unnoticed. "The Earp Brothers—tall, gaunt, intrepid—caused considerable comment when they first arrived, particularly because of Wyatt's reputation in Dodge City, Kansas," wrote John Clum, editor of the *Tombstone Epitaph* and the town's mayor. "All the cattle rustlers in Kansas, Colorado, New Mexico and western Texas knew—and feared—Wyatt Earp."

But the Earps were much less interested in pursuing rustlers than they were in pursuing money, and they quickly began looking for ways to find it in large quantities. They had limited success. Virgil returned to law enforcement. James ran a no-frills bar. Morgan did this and that, but mostly avoided long-term employment. Wyatt ran faro games and occasionally rode shotgun on Wells Fargo stagecoaches. He also plotted to become Cochise County sheriff, a lucrative post because the sheriff kept a percentage of the taxes he collected.Collectively, the brothers bought and sold mining claims, but there was little profit in it.

Wyatt did find time between money-making schemes to strike up an acquaintance with Josephine Sarah Marcus, the beautiful 20-year-old consort of Sheriff Johnny Behan. Most people called her Josie. Wyatt would come to call her Sadie. She was from a San Francisco family and had left home at an early age to become an actress. Appearing in Tombstone in a Gilbert & Sullivan operetta, she caught Behan's eye, and ended up as his housemate. At some point she also caught Wyatt Earp's eye. By the end of 1882, Wyatt and Sadie would be an inseparable couple for the rest of Wyatt's life. Earp would abandon Mattie Blaylock, the woman with whom he had come to Tombstone. She would die alone of an opiate-and-alcohol overdose in a desolate Arizona mining town hotel in 1888.

But first the Earps would become part of a many-level struggle in Tombstone that involved partisan politics, urban-rural rivalries, old Civil War grudges, semi-organized crime, greed, lust and good old fashioned personal hatreds. The most infamous result of the struggle was also the most iconic—and possibly the most overblown—shootout in Wild West history.

Dozens of books, some of them excellent, have recounted in minute detail the causes and consequences of the Gunfight at the O.K. Corral. The assessments have ranged from the assertion that it was basically an extension of the Civil War to the observation it was basically a bungled arrest for a misdemeanor offense, and "solved nothing, proved nothing, meant nothing." For our purposes, we'll stick to the basics—although even some of those are still hotly debated between those who admire or despise Wyatt Earp.

Tombstone was, and still is, about 70 miles southeast of Tucson and just 30 miles from the border with Mexico. By 1881, thanks to an 1877 silver strike, the town had swollen to perhaps as many as 10,000 inhabitants. Like Wild West mining towns before and after it, Tombstone had delusions of grandeur that vanished when the mines played out, which in its case was relatively quickly. "The really profitable mines that are being worked throughout Arizona can be counted on the fingers of one hand," a *New York Tribune* correspondent reported less than two weeks before the gunfight, "and there will still be a finger or two to spare."

Among those who didn't make a living directly from the mines and lived in the area outside town was a large and very loosely affiliated assemblage known, disparagingly, as "Cowboys." Among this group, many were engaged in some aspect of the cattle rustling industry; some were stagecoach robbers, and a few were killers. The Cowboys' ranks included Ike and Billy Clanton, Frank and Tom McLaury, and Billy Claiborne. Billy Clanton and the McLaury brothers would be active and unfortunate participants in the gunfight. Neither Ike nor Claiborne were armed when the shooting started. Claiborne fled before the first shots and Ike just after.

The Cowboys' opponents in the Oct. 26 shootout were led by Virgil Earp, not Wyatt. A deputy U.S. marshal and veteran lawman, Virgil had been appointed Tombstone's chief of police by the town council about five months before the fight. The job was vacant because Virgil's predecessor had skipped town with $1,000 (about $26,000 in 2022) of the Tombstone treasury, never to be heard from again. Virgil was considered by most to be a worthy successor. Experienced and even-tempered, he was also impartial in carrying out his duties: During his tenure he had arrested both his brother Wyatt for causing a saloon ruckus, and John Clum, the town mayor, for recklessly driving a carriage. On the day of the fight, Virgil turned down offers of help from a vigilante group of the town's businessmen and leading citizens. Instead, he was backed by his brothers Wyatt and Morgan as special policemen, and the quarrelsome Doc Holliday.

There were preliminary bouts before the main event, all of which contributed to the seeming inevitability of the shootout. The night before, Holliday and Ike Clanton, both drunk, engaged in a loud argument in an establishment that was the 1880s equivalent of a fast-food joint, and Ike threatened to gun down Holliday and the Earp Brothers. Later, Ike, Virgil, Tom McLaury and the county sheriff, Johnny Behan, played poker until dawn. When the game ended, Ike continued his litany of threats against Doc and the Earps.

Around noon on the day of the fight, Virgil spotted Ike on the street carrying a revolver and Winchester rifle, walked up behind him and whacked him over the head with his pistol. Ike was arrested and subsequently fined $25 for illegally carrying firearms within the town limits. Later, Wyatt and Tom McLaury had an argument that ended when Wyatt "buffaloed" McLaury, leaving him semi-conscious in the street. By 3 p.m., there were probably enough hard feelings to ignite a war, let alone a gunfight. Virgil felt pushed into a corner. The Cowboys were still in town, still carrying guns in open defiance of the town ordinance, and doing so in open view of the "upright" citizenry the marshal was supposed to protect. He decided to arrest them. Accompanied by his brothers and Holliday, Virgil strode down Fourth Street, and took a left when they got to Freemont Street.

The two sides faced off in a narrow lot, between a residence and a photographic gallery, a few doors down from the rear entrance to the O.K. Corral. (Because "Gunfight at the O.K. Corral" was much more euphonious than "Gunfight Next to Fly's Photographic Studio," writers and Hollywood producers moved the location in their depictions of the event, and the name stuck.) At some point Virgil told the Cowboys they were under arrest and to throw up their hands. Then someone got trigger-happy.

While it has never been conclusively established exactly who started it, historians generally agree that about 30 shots were fired in about half a minute, with some of the combatants no more than 10 feet apart. If so, the fight said volumes about the poor marksmanship of the combatants and/or the inaccuracy of their weapons since a total of only nine bullet or buckshot wounds were suffered. When it was over, Tom and Frank McLaury and Billy Clanton were dead. Morgan Earp was somehow shot through one shoulder with the bullet exiting the other shoulder, and Virgil through a calf. Doc Holliday was slightly wounded in the hip. Only Wyatt Earp emerged unscathed, save for a bullet hole in his coat.

The battle was little noted outside Arizona and California, at least not immediately. Two days after the fight, *The New York Times, Brooklyn Union, Chicago Inter-Ocean* and *Philadelphia Times* all used the same one-paragraph wire service story. The piece managed to misspell the names of the Clantons and McLaurys, listed Wyatt as the only Earp wounded and most laughable of all referred to Doc Holliday as "City Judge Halliday." The *St. Louis Globe-Democrat* sneeringly referred to the Cowboys as "good Sunday-School boys" and noted approvingly that "these Earps seem to have the right grit for the place." And the *Alameda (Ca.,) Daily Argus* opined that "the administration of law (in Arizona) is a little different from that of California. Somehow the right man gets killed down there."

But some Tombstonians weren't so sure. There was widespread sentiment that the Earps and Doc had killed the wrong Clanton and that perhaps they had goaded the well-liked McLaurys into the fight. "Opinion is pretty fairly divided as to the justification of the killing," wrote Clara Spalding Brown, the wife of a Tombstone mining engineer and a correspondent for the *San Diego Union*. "You may meet one man who will support the Earps, and declare that no other course was possible to save their own lives, and the next man is just as likely to assert that there was no occasion whatever for bloodshed and that this will be a 'warm place' for the Earps hereafter."

In the wake of the fight, both Wyatt and Doc were briefly jailed. Ike Clanton swore out a murder complaint against Holliday and all three Earp Brothers. Under territorial law, the quartet was not immediately put on trial. Instead, a hearing before Justice of the Peace Wells Spicer was convened to see if a trial was warranted. The hearing began on Halloween, five days after the fight, and took a month to conclude. In the end, Spicer sharply criticized Virgil for deputizing his brothers and Doc, all of whom had personal grudges against the Cowboys. But he ruled "that the defendants were fully justified in committing these homicides—that (it) was a necessary act, done in the discharge of an official duty." There was no subsequent trial.

While the legal battle was done, however, the killing had just begun. To shorthand the fallout from the gunfight:

- Three nights after Christmas, Virgil was patrolling the town when he was ambushed by shotgun-wielding assailants. He survived, but lost more than five inches of bone from his left arm and was crippled for life.
- On the cold and rainy night of March 18, 1882, Morgan and Wyatt were at a popular Tombstone billiards parlor when rifle shots smashed through a glass door. One shot hit the wall just above Wyatt's head. Another ripped its way through Morgan's back. He died 40 minutes later.
- Two days after Morgan's murder, Wyatt and a contingent of friends accompanied Virgil and his wife to Tucson, where they were to take a train to the Earp family home in Colton, California. At the depot, Wyatt spotted Ike Clanton and a Cowboy named Frank Stilwell. Convinced they were there to finish off Virgil, Wyatt chased Stilwell down. "As I rushed upon him, he got out his hands and clutched my shotgun," Wyatt told a reporter 11 years later. "I let go both barrels and he tumbled over dead and mangled at my feet."

Thus began what became known as "The Vendetta Ride." Wyatt had recently been appointed a deputy U.S. marshal, with the authority to arrest the men who he believed had killed Morgan and maimed Virgil. But he was also now a wanted man for killing Stilwell. Armed with arrest warrants, a posse led by Sheriff Behan and composed mostly of Cowboys hunted for Earp and the men with him.

Undaunted by being pursued, and accompanied by Doc, Wyatt's younger brother Warren, former Cowboy Sherm McMaster and shootists Texas Jack Vermillion and Turkey Creek Jack Johnson, Wyatt began his hunt. He was not interested in bringing in suspects alive—a fact not lost on many Arizonans. "Their path is strewn with blood," the Tucson-based *Arizona Star* wrote about the Earp posse. "Wherever they halt in a settlement...human life ceases to be sacred. Their late escapades in Tombstone are only their records repeated in other frontier towns."

Wyatt's group found and killed two more men suspected of being in on his brothers' ambushes. One was Florentino Cruz, aka "Indian Charlie," whom the group cut down at a wood cutting camp owned by Pete Spence, another suspect in the killing of Morgan. The other was Curly Bill Brocious, a notorious Cowboy leader. Brocious' demise came during a running fight between Earp's group and eight or nine Cowboys. "I fired both barrels of my (shotgun) into him," Wyatt recalled in 1896, "blowing him all to pieces." In doing so, Earp's remarkable luck in gunfights continued. His saddle horn was shot off, he was hit in the heel of one boot and one or two slugs perforated his coat. Through it all, he was unhurt.

By mid-April, however, the Vendetta riders were physically spent and mentally exhausted. They rode into New Mexico, then dispersed. Wyatt and Doc quarreled in Albuquerque, and went separately to Colorado. The precise subject of the spat is unknown, but it might have been sparked by an anti-Semitic remark by Holliday about Wyatt's soon-to-be wife, Sadie Marcus, who was Jewish. Doc and Wyatt eventually patched things up, although they saw little of each other after Tombstone and the Vendetta Ride. Holliday would spend the last six years of his life in various Colorado towns, gambling, drinking and slowly but steadily dying of tuberculosis.

In contrast, Wyatt Earp would wander the West for nearly half a century after the last significant events in his career as a lawman and gunfighter were over. He would never escape the events of his two years in Arizona. The stories would twist and turn in their retelling. By 1888, the versions included accounts that had Ike Clanton courting a wholly fictional

Earp sister named Jessie; Curly Bill Brocious fighting alongside the Earps as their cousin, and a full-scale battle waged between 50 or so Cowboys and the Earp clan at a fortress-like castle in the desert.

And even as he was chased by Tombstone, Wyatt would himself chase rainbows, from goldfields to gambling halls and from one century to the next, seeking affirmation of his self-image as a man who was unafraid to do his version of the right thing, and vindication of the things he had already done. He would find neither during his lifetime—and immortality after his death.

Wyatt spent much of his first post-Tombstone year in the silver boomtown of Gunnison, Colorado. He ran a faro game and generally tried to keep a low profile in an effort to avoid extradition to Arizona, where he was wanted for murder. But the silver boom in Gunnison was all but over by the end of 1883, and Wyatt moved on to the Idaho gold camp of Eagle City, where he and brother James ran a saloon called the "White Elephant" and a dance hall located in a large tent, and were later accused of claim-jumping and otherwise terrorizing the settlement.

In 1885, Wyatt decided to find another way to make a living other than mining miners. He and Sadie settled in the bustling California border town of San Diego. Nestled in the extreme southwest corner of the country, San Diego's main economic attraction was neither gold nor silver, but—surprise!—real estate. A railroad line connecting the town to the rest of the country was completed in 1885, and over the next five years the population would explode by 500 percent, to about 16,000. The resulting land boom saw as much as $200,000 ($5.5 million in 2022) in property sales in a single day.

Wyatt bought at least eight lots around town, all but one of them vacant. But his real interest was in San Diego's "Stingaree District," so named because it was said you could be stung there as easily as you could by the bottom-dwelling denizens of the adjacent bay. The district, according to a *San Diego Union* survey, housed most of the city's 50 licensed saloons (and dozens of unlicensed ones); 35 brothels; 120 "lewd women" who presumably were independent sex contractors, and three opium dens. Most or all of the vice establishments listed by the *Union* were periodically outlawed by the city council, but only in a technical sense. The saloon lobby controlled many local politicians, and the police were unofficially instructed not to enter gambling joints unless it was to address a non-gambling issue.

With a partner, Wyatt opened a gambling house on the second floor of a building owned by a city councilman who operated a saloon on the first floor. It didn't hurt that Wyatt became friends with the chief of police, and was already friends with the mayor, a former Tombstone lawyer who had been part of the defense team in the post-O.K. Corral legal proceedings. When friendship wasn't sufficient Earp reportedly resorted to other forms of insurance against outside interference in his main gambling joint, or two the others in which he had an interest. When a cop inadvertently walked into one, Wyatt supposedly told him "if you come after my game, you will get into your coffin."

It was in San Diego that Earp became enamored with both horse racing and prizefighting. To indulge his passion for the former, he assembled a stable of both thoroughbreds and harness racing horses and traveled throughout California and as far east as Kansas City, Missouri, to race them. His personal reputation as a tough guy who could keep order in the ring led to him refereeing about three dozen fights in San Diego and across the border in Baja California. Both pastimes involved wagering, and as a professional gambler, Wyatt much preferred "sure things" to "square deals." It was thus inevitable that he would be accused of fixing races and throwing fights. But given his reputation, such accusations were only discreetly and quietly uttered, and were left unverified.

Just eight years after the Gunfight Sort of Near the O.K. Corral, the San Diego city directory listed Wyatt Earp's occupation as "capitalist." But his shady image, deserved or not, stretched across the country. In a January 1889 story that recounted the Tombstone street fight, the *New York Sun* sardonically noted Earp was "a common everyday sort of sport who will obey the law if he must," and "is more particular about his reputation now than he was (in Tombstone.) He recently appeared in print in San Diego for the purpose of denying an allegation that he had contributed a sum of money to a corruption fund for use in local political affairs."

By 1891, the real estate bubble throughout California had burst. All the properties Wyatt had bought were sold, lost to foreclosure for unpaid taxes, or reverted to the previous owner. His equine assets were likewise liquidated. Coupled with his natural restlessness and a local crackdown on the vice industry, the land bust compelled Wyatt and Sadie to seek greener pastures. They headed north, to Sadie's hometown of San Francisco.

Sweets made life sweet for the couple's six years in San Francisco—and boxing made it bitter. The sweets were provided, literally and figuratively, by Sadie's brother-in-law. Emil Henry Lehnhardt owned a confectionery shop in nearby Oakland that sold "the most acceptably flavored ice-cream and the most toothsome candies in Alameda County." He sold so much of it there was apparently enough wealth for the whole family. (When Lehnhardt decided for some reason in 1912 to go down to the store's basement and shoot himself in the head, he left his widow, Sadie's sister, an estate worth $257,000, or about $7 million in 2022 currency.)

The Earps also benefitted from the largesse of Wyatt's pal, Elias "Lucky" Baldwin. An extremely rich and savvy businessman whose nickname derived from his consistently good investment choices, Baldwin shared Wyatt's love of horse racing, and Sadie loved that Baldwin would lend her money to cover her frequent gambling debts. In her highly fanciful memoir, Sadie wrote that she and Wyatt were officially married in 1892 aboard Baldwin's yacht. No official record of the nuptials, however, has been found.

With friends like Baldwin and *San Francisco Examiner* publisher William Randolph Hearst, Wyatt developed a taste for the good life: long days at the racetrack, custom suits, jewelry for Sadie, and even a trip to the 1893 world's fair in Chicago. But while he worked as a horse trainer for a woman in nearby Santa Rosa, his main income still derived from gambling, an occupation that decidedly has its ups and downs. In need of additional funds, Wyatt agreed in 1896 to become a bodyguard for Andrew Lawrence, the *Examiner's* editor. Lawrence was much despised for his habit of blackmailing people who wanted to keep their names *out* of the paper. Earp also agreed, presumably for a fee, to submit to long interviews with an Examiner reporter. The interviews were turned into a three-part series that appeared in August under Wyatt's name.

"You will never know the frontier until you have read Wyatt Earp," an *Examiner* promo breathlessly exclaimed. "Why, there is nothing in fiction to compare with the cold record of the man's experience. His mind is simply saturated with the vivid colors that bedaub the life of the plains and the mining camp. And he has the gift to bestow those colors upon the canvas so that people who live in cities and never heard the cracking of the six-shooter may know the life for what it really was."

In reality, the ghostwriter "bedaubed" the stories with a heaping helping of hooey, either from his own oversaturated imagination or Wyatt's highly selective memory. The lengthy pieces, which ran on three consecutive Sundays, were replete with exaggerated or invented anecdotes about Doc Holliday, Bat Masterson and Wyatt and his brothers. "It may be that the trail of blood will seem to lie too thickly over the pages that I write," the first story began. "If I had it in me to invent a tale, I would fain lighten the crimson stain...but half a lifetime on the frontier attunes a man's hand to the six-shooter rather than the pen, and it is lucky that I am asked only for facts, for more than facts I could not give." And so on.

What the articles gave Earp was an even higher profile in the Bay Area than he already had. The notoriety may also have led to him being selected to referee a boxing match on December 2 to decide the heavyweight championship of the world. Or it may have been just because he was willing to be bribed.

The fight, for a winner's purse of $10,000 ($315,000 in 2022), was between "Ruby Bob" Fitzsimmons and "Sailor" Tom Sharkey. Fitzsimmons, a red-headed former blacksmith from New Zealand, was the reigning champ. At 165 pounds, Fitzsimmons was light for a heavyweight, but tall, quick and a hard-hitter. His opponent, the Ireland-born Sharkey, was a U.S. Navy veteran. Sharkey was 12 pounds heavier, three inches shorter and eight years younger than Fitzsimmons. He was also more of a brawler than a boxer, and Fitzsimmons was a 3-to-1 favorite to retain his title—if the fight took place.

Prizefighting was technically illegal in San Francisco, and absent a governing body, it was up to the fighters' managers and match promoters to agree on a referee. On the morning of the fight, after weeks of haggling, they decided on Wyatt Earp. "Well," Wyatt reportedly said after some hesitation, "I consider it an honor and consent to serve...It would be a little bit of tone to act as referee when the two best men in the world were to come together." He would regret his decision.

The trouble began before the fight did, which was shortly before 11 p.m. at the cavernous Mechanics' Pavilion. As Wyatt entered the ring, San Francisco Police Captain Charles Wittman noticed a bulge beneath Earp's coat. It was a very long-barreled Colt's revolver, of which the captain relieved the referee. Earp later claimed to have been toting the gun because he had a large amount of cash on him from a foray to the racetrack, and had forgotten he was still toting it. He was subsequently fined $50 for carrying a concealed weapon. That turned out to be the least of his troubles.

As the now-gunless Wyatt climbed between the ropes, Fitzsimmons' manager and brother-in-law, Martin Julian, shouted to the estimated crowd of 10,000 that he objected to Earp as referee. Conceding he had originally consented to the choice, Julian said he had since come to believe rumors that Wyatt had been promised $2,500 ($79,000 in 2022) to disqualify Fitzsimmons at some point and award the purse and title to Sharkey. "We are satisfied with any other man in the house, but we don't want this man," he said, pointing to Earp. An embarrassed Wyatt offered to withdraw.

But an impatient Fitzsimmons overruled his manager: "I have given into everything in this matter, and I will give into this. Let's get at it."

So they did. Fitzsimmons dominated the fight up to and including the eighth round. With Sharkey struggling to stay on his feet—he had already been knocked down twice—the champ delivered his famous "solar plexus blow." Sharkey went down, seemingly writhing in pain. But Wyatt—almost alone among the 10,000 pairs of eyes watching—saw the blow illegally landing south of the solar plexus. He stopped the fight and awarded the decision to Sharkey before quickly leaving the ring.

The decision triggered a national uproar. Professional boxing, particularly at the heavyweight level, was with horseracing the most popular spectator sport in America. The *San Francisco Call* denounced Earp as "the ex-faro-dealing sharp" whose "false reputation as a bad man from Arizona would not have saved his hide had the crowd been able to get hands on him." Across the continent, the *New York Daily Herald* ran a cartoon of Wyatt wearing an oversized sombrero and clenching a knife between his teeth as he pointed a gun at Fitzsimmons and handed a $10,000 money-bag to Sharkey.

Earp adamantly denied taking a bribe, and insisted he had called the fight as he saw it. His defenders asserted that had Earp wanted to throw the fight, he would not have waited until the eighth round to see a low blow, and risk Sharkey being knocked out before then. Earp pointed out that Bat Masterson, "the best friend I have on Earth...had every dollar he could raise on Fitzsimmons." Masterson, who was in Denver at the time of the fight, not only backed Wyatt's claim, but soundly thrashed another gambler who dared to criticize Earp to Bat's face.

Fitzsimmons went to court to prevent Sharkey from cashing the winner's check. During the hearing, Wyatt was further embarrassed when he acknowledged he was broke. "The announcement of his absolute poverty seemed to affect him greatly," The *San Francisco Chronicle* reported, with a fair degree of sarcasm: "He laid his head in a melancholy manner on the four-carat diamond that adorned his little finger." The paper also ran a cartoon of a dejected Wyatt on the witness stand, "confessing that his lively career has not brought him a fortune."

Worse, several of Earp's numerous creditors showed up at the hearing to present him with various legal documents demanding payment. "The troubles of the Tombstone Terror are increasing," the *Chronicle* chortled, "and his recently acquired notoriety as a prize-fight referee seems to be drawing down on his head several legal thunderbolts from all parts of the country."

In the end, the judge ruled that since the fight was illegal in the first place, the court had no jurisdiction. Sharkey kept the check. He and Fitzsimmons fought again four years later in New York, and this time "Ruby Bob" knocked out "The Sailor" in the second round.

Earp's reputation, meanwhile, was in tatters. The term "Wyatt Earped" became widely used as a synonym for "cheated:" A Philadelphia boxer claimed to have been "Wyatt Earped" in a bout; horseracing officials in St. Louis "Wyatt Earped" a winning horse by disqualifying it; an Ohio politician was said to "be only too glad to be Wyatt Earped into the (U.S.) Senate."

Humiliated, Wyatt and Sadie left California in 1897. They spent some time in Arizona—avoiding Tombstone—before being lured by yet another siren song from the mining camps of a new gold rush, this time in Alaska. "Wyatt Earp, whose career as a fighting man in the palmy and riotous days of Tombstone, Arizona, left Yuma, where he has been for several months past, for Dawson City," the *San Francisco Call* sneered. "...It is supposed by the famous gambler-fighter and friends who are backing him that there will be millions to be made if the cards are properly handled."

Earp handled the cards he was dealt during his time in Alaska the way he had always done it. There were some flush times, when the money seemed easy. There were a few dustups—bar fights and relatively minor legal confrontations. And there were the omnipresent fanciful and farcical tales of his activities.

From 1897 to 1901, he managed various saloons and gambling halls, eventually becoming a partner in the Dexter, which was a combination saloon, hotel, clubroom and probably brothel in Nome. Summers, he and Sadie stayed north. When winter came, they moved south again, to Seattle or the San Francisco Bay area. "Wyatt Earp, the noted sport and frontiersman...is making money perhaps faster than he ever made it before," the *San Francisco Examiner* reported in November, 1899, "and he has told his friends that if business runs with him next summer as it did after his arrival in the camp...he will be able to retire with all the money he desires."

But the "noted sport" wasn't one to let financial success get in the way of his penchant for finding trouble. In May, 1900, he was knocked out in a saloon while visiting San Francisco, by a horseracing acquaintance with whom he had a disagreement over the riding abilities of a particular jockey. Later that year in Nome, Earp was arrested for allegedly interfering with police who were breaking up a street brawl. Wyatt claimed he was only trying to help the cops, and the charges were dismissed.

Even when he didn't do anything incriminating or embarrassing, newspapers periodically came up with something for him. In July, 1900, the *New York Tribune* ran a Page One piece headlined "The Arizona Bad Man Not Quick Enough With His Gun." The story claimed Wyatt had been shot through the right arm and seriously wounded by a customer whom Wyatt had been bullying in Earp's Alaska saloon. The story was wholly fabricated. Even more bizarre was a widely published yarn about how a five-foot-tall Royal Canadian Mounted Policeman had cowed Earp into meekly handing over his gun after Wyatt had drunkenly shot up a saloon in the Yukon Territory's Dawson City. Trouble was, Earp was never in Dawson City.

By 1901, the winds of wanderlust had caught Earp up again. With what relatives later said was a hefty sum of money in his pockets, Wyatt and Sadie left Alaska to spend a few years in western Nevada mining towns, such as Tonopah and Goldfield. But for the last three decades of his life, the "Terror of Tombstone" mostly led a life of restless poverty. Winters were spent in a humble shack near Wyatt's incongruously named and parsimoniously producing "Happy Days" gold and copper mines, in the Mohave Desert near the California/Arizona border. During summers, Wyatt and Sadie mooched off friends in Los Angeles or Sadie's candy heiress sister in Oakland, or rented modest bungalows in L.A.

In his 60s, there is evidence Earp occasionally moonlighted as an off-the-books agent for the Los Angeles Police Department. This meant doing jobs considered too dicey for regular cops, such as slipping into Mexico to drag back wanted suspects without the benefit of an extradition warrant. He also worked at driving wagons or acting as security in a mining dispute near Death Valley. Sadie, meanwhile, spent every dollar she could find to feed her compulsive gambling habit.

And Wyatt continued to show up in the newspapers from time to time, very seldom in a flattering way. In 1911, his arrest for trying to fleece a sucker in a bogus faro game was widely reported. (He escaped jail on a technicality—the police had busted up the scam before any money had changed hands, so no crime had actually been committed.) In 1922, the *Los Angeles Times* ran an atrociously inaccurate tale in which the Earp brothers were depicted as stagecoach robbers, Doc Holliday killed a man in Los Angeles and Wyatt himself was killed in Colton, California. The *Saturday Evening Post* and *Scribner's* magazines ran similar stories.

"Notoriety has been the bane of my life," a bitter and frustrated Wyatt wrote an acquaintance. "I detest it, and I never have put forth any effort to check the tales that have been published in recent years of the exploits in which my brothers and I are supposed to have been the principal participants. Not one of them is correct. My friends have urged that I make this known on printed sheet. Perhaps I shall; it will correct many mythic tales." So Wyatt Earp spent the last years of his life trying to set the record straight. He failed, which for the sake of his legend was probably the best thing that could have happened.

Wyatt Earp liked Western movies, even if he wasn't always impressed by people pretending to do things he had actually done. In his dotage, he enjoyed hanging around studios and film backlots, and the presence of the tall, erect somber old man with the big drooping mustache either dazzled or puzzled employees. Western movie legend John Wayne contended he had chats with Earp that influenced Wayne's signature onscreen way of walking and talking. Fabled director John Ford claimed Earp drew a diagram for him of the Tombstone gunfight. Both claims have at least an even chance of being baloney.

But Wyatt really was pals with Tom Mix and William S. Hart, two of the biggest Western film stars of the 1920s. Mix had some legitimate skills in the saddle. His father had been a stable master, and Mix grew up to be an expert horseman, a skilled working cowboy and wild west show performer. Hart was a theater-trained actor, screenwriter and director who idolized real-life Wild West legends such as Earp and Bat Masterson. His films were gritty and realistic, usually culminating with a moral lesson. He and Earp became fast friends, so much so that Wyatt, anxious to polish his legacy, pitched Hart on helping him out.

"Many wrong impressions of the early days of Tombstone and myself have been created," Earp wrote Hart in 1923. "I am not going to live to the age of Methuselah, and any wrong impression I want to make right before I go away. The screen could do all this, I know, with you as the master mind. Not that I want to obligate you because of our friendship, but because I know I can come to you with this ...".

Hart's career, however, was already on the wane—he would make his last picture in 1925—and he had little pull left with studio moguls. The best be could do was include a character named "Wyatt Earp," along with one named "Bat Masterson," in a 1923 film in which Hart himself played the title character— *Wild Bill Hickok.*

His dreams of absolution by film thwarted, Earp turned to the printed word. After rejecting the literary efforts of the wife of an old friend, Wyatt began recounting his life story to John H. Flood Jr. in 1925. Flood, a mining engineer who was all of 3 years old when the Tombstone shootout took place, revered Earp and served as Wyatt's unpaid personal assistant in the last years of Earp's life.

According to the most accepted version of events, Flood dutifully sat at the kitchen table of the Earps' tiny L.A. bungalow each Sunday, taking down Wyatt's recollections. Many of the stories would then be sanitized or censored by Sadie, who would occasionally substitute outright fabrications designed to put a shinier polish on Wyatt's armor. She also insisted on more dime novel-quality "pep." Coupled with Flood's uncanny inability to write a coherent sentence, the resulting 348-page manuscript was absolute dreck. How bad was it? The venerable Western author, artist and magazine publisher Bob Boze Bell claims to have counted 104 "CRACKs!", three "INGs" and one "BANG!" in just the chapter on the shootout. Not surprisingly, the effort was unanimously rejected by publishers, despite an impassioned plea by William S. Hart that it be published "in the interest for the furtherance of true American history."

Earp then turned to a real writer. Walter Noble Burns was a 60-year-old Kentucky-born journalist who had spent a year on a whaling ship, joined the army during the Spanish-American War, accompanied General "Black Jack" Pershing on his fruitless attempt to catch the Mexican bandit Pancho Villa, and emerged as Chicago's leading crime reporter during the early years of the city's Al Capone-bootleggers-and-gangsters era.

Burns had also written a best-selling book, *The Saga of Billy the Kid*. Looking for another legendary Western figure to profile, he approached Earp in August 1926. But Wyatt turned him down, since at the time he was still working with Flood. When the Flood effort floundered, Earp reconsidered Burn's offer. Burns, however, had already completed a new book: *Tombstone: An Iliad of the Southwest*. Diligently if not always accurately researched, the book was about two-thirds the history of the town and about one-third the history of Earp. Wyatt was flatteringly portrayed as "the Lion of Tombstone." "Whatever else he may have been," Burns wrote, "he was brave. Not even his enemies have sought to deny his splendid courage."

But Wyatt was outraged. First, he felt double-crossed because he had shared stories with Burns under the assumption the writer was researching a biography of Doc Holliday. Second, and far more important, he and Sadie didn't stand to make a dime from Burns' book. To their credit, Burns and his publisher offered the Earps $1,000 (about $15,000 in 2022), plus 25 percent of any sale of movie rights. Wyatt wanted half of everything. He got nothing.

That is, he got nothing until Christmas Day, 1927, when he got a letter that would begin the molding of Earp's popular cultural image for decades to come. The letter was from Stuart N. Lake, a San Diego journalist, publicist and frustrated screenwriter. Lake was a 38-year-old New York native whose resume included working as a professional wrestling promoter; a press aide to Theodore Roosevelt after TR had left the presidency; a World War I veteran who suffered an injury to his left leg that left it 4 inches short than the right one, and a New York City reporter who learned about Wyatt Earp from no less an authority than Bat Masterson. Now Lake wanted to write Wyatt's memoirs.

Besides being an able writer, Lake had two attributes—imagination and patience—that would prove invaluable in dealing with Earp. After some correspondence, the two finally met in mid-1928. Wyatt liked Lake. He just didn't like talking to him. "As a matter of cold fact, Wyatt never 'dictated' a word to me," Lake wrote to a friend years later. "I spent hours and days and weeks with him—and I wish you could see my notes! They consist entirely of the barest facts...I was pumping, pumping, pumping, for names and incidents and sidelights; all of which Wyatt could supply but none of which he handed out in any sort of narrative form...he was delightfully laconic, or exasperatingly so."

As Earp and Lake labored, Billy Breakenridge, a former deputy to

Sheriff Johnny Behan, Wyatt's Tombstone adversary, published a ghost-written autobiography called *Helldorado.* The book portrayed Earp as more career opportunist than frontier hero. Wyatt was both angry and hurt, since he had provided material to Breakenridge for the book.

Meanwhile, the resourceful Lake compensated for his subject's reluctance to talk by putting words in Wyatt's mouth. He did it by stitching together the reminiscences of those who had known Earp and whom Lake interviewed, as well as what documentary material he could find. The result was a book that while enjoyable to read, was undependable as a source of historical fact.

No matter. When *Wyatt Earp: Frontier Marshal* was released in mid-1931, at a list price of $3.50 ($61 in 2022), readers snapped it up. The book quickly sold 7,000 copies, no mean feat in an America facing the deepest part of the worst economic depression in its history. Mostly broke, and bewildered as to just why they were broke, Americans were increasingly intrigued by larger-than-life characters who seemed to live outside the system, whether it was heroes like aviator Charles Lindbergh and base ball icon Babe Ruth, or outlaws like John Dillinger and Bonnie and Clyde. Earp fit the bill, even if it was somewhere in between the good guys and the bad guys

The reviews of Lake's effort were generally good. The *Los Angeles Times* called it "a thrilling Western narrative of absorbing interest to all who have a spark of interest in tales of frontier life." The *New York Times* said it was "vivid and detailed," and compared 1881 Tombstone to 1931 New York City and Chicago. "What both those cities need," the reviewer observed, "seems to be a few Wyatt Earps." Of course not all the reviews were positive. The Tucson-based *Arizona Star* charged that Lake had "whitewashed his hero at the expense of his (Earp's) associates...Mr. Lake has written his story only as Earp has told it, without historical justification."

Wyatt, however, did not live to bask in the book's success or fume at the criticism. On January 13, 1929, two months short of his 81st birthday, he lost his years-long fight with kidney problems. Among his pall bearers were his movie star pals Tom Mix and William S. Hart, as well as old Arizona chums like former Tombstone mayor John Clum. Sadie eventually had his remains cremated and interred in a Jewish cemetery in Colma, California, near San Francisco.

Earp's obituary appeared in hundreds of newspapers across the country, although the tone and content varied widely. The *Chicago Tribune* took a respectful approach: "Wyatt Earp, slim, erect, forceful, the last of the celebrated gunmen whose guns blazed on the side of law and order, died peacefully in his Hollywood home in the arms of his wife...". The *New York Daily News* breezily headlined its obit "Wyatt Earp, Frontier Hero, Dies, Boots Off." Some papers ran the death notice on the entertainment page, alongside the local movie listings. Others had it on the sports page and devoted as much space to Earp's role as referee of the Sharkey-Fitzsimmons fight as to the Tombstone shootout.

In 1932, Lake sold the movie rights to his book to Fox Studios for $6,750 ($130,500 in 2022) and split it with Sadie. She wanted more. "I'll put it this way," an exasperated Lake wrote his editor. "I think Mrs. Earp is very completely unwell, mentally...I feel sorry for her, very sorry. She is, however, the most suspicious person whom I have ever encountered."

In 1934, Fox released *Frontier Marshal*, starring a largely now-forgotten actor named George O'Brien as "Michael Wyatt." Wyatt Earp's name wasn't mentioned, mainly because Sadie had threatened to sue Fox for $50,000 if it was. Few people saw the film, and even fewer reviewed it. In 1939, 20th Century Fox tried again with another *Frontier Marshal*, this one starring Randolph Scott. Scott's character was called "Wyatt Earp," but only after Fox agreed to drop Earp's name from the movie's title and pay Sadie $5,000. Doc Holliday, played by Cesar Romero, was changed to "Halliday" to avoid threatened legal action by the deceased dentist's family. Lake's story was changed from being somewhat true to ridiculous mish-mash.

Sadie Earp died in 1944 at the age of 84, to almost no one's regret. In 1946, director John Ford had no compunctions about using the names "Earp" "Clanton" and "Holliday" in *My Darling Clementine.* Loosely—very loosely—based on the events leading up to the iconic fight on the streets of Tombstone and starring Henry Fonda as Wyatt, Ford's film has been hailed as one of the greatest Westerns ever made—a clear case of well-told legend besting well-known facts.

The Ford film helped unleash a barrage of more than 40 Hollywood movies in years to come that featured Wyatt Earp as a leading or ancillary character. Notable among them were *Gunfight at the O.K. Corral* (1957); *Hour of the Gun* (1967); *Tombstone* (1993) and *Wyatt Earp* (1994). Wyatt himself was played by such Hollywood luminaries as Burt Lancaster, James Garner, Kurt Russell and Kevin Costner.

In almost all of his screen depictions, Wyatt Earp was portrayed as either a sympathetic or heroic figure, or both. Nowhere was this truer than on a television series that premiered in 1955 and ran for six seasons and 229 episodes. *The Life and Legend of Wyatt Earp* was hailed by critics as an "adult Western" that emphasized character development over fist-fights and trick roping. Audiences loved it too, and the show consistently had Top 25 ratings during its run.

The star was Hugh O'Brian, a tall, square-jawed and darkly handsome actor who had the dual distinctions of having been the youngest drill instructor in the history of the United States Marine Corps, and the last character to be killed by John Wayne on screen (in 1976's *The Shootist.*) O'Brian's characterization of Earp was heavily influenced by the fact Stuart Lake served for two seasons as a consultant to the show. "I'm convinced that Earp was a thoroughly honest man, righteous, utterly fearless," O'Brian said in 1956. "He was essentially an easy-moving, relaxed type of guy—but he could tense up like a coiled spring, and he had fabulous reflexes."

Or at least that's how O'Brian played him, and how millions of Americans came to view Wyatt Earp. In 1979, for example, a security guard in Gettysburg, Pennsylvania, who had watched the movies and TV show paid the "frontier marshal" the ultimate compliment: He changed his legal name to Wyatt Earp. "He was one great guy," said the former Don Trappler. "He's my No. 1 hero." Earp's name has also been bestowed on suburban subdivision streets, deli sandwiches and a 7,800-feet-high mountain in Antarctica.

But maybe it should be left to Walter Noble Burns, the author whose words Wyatt didn't mind but whose ethics he despised—to sum up the man. "There was no flinching in what he did, and no alibis or apologies afterward," Burns wrote in his 1927 book on Earp and Tombstone. "He was unaffectedly genuine. Right or wrong, he believed with absolute faith in the righteousness of the justice he administered at the muzzle of a gun."

Chapter 11 Notes

This consisted of Raoul Walsh, *Each Man in His Time*, p. 102.

Still, he was *Los Angeles Times*, April 28, 2004; Walsh, op. cit., p. 103.

"When I introduced" Walsh, op. cit., pp. 103-04.

That Walsh got *Corpus Christi (Tx) Caller Times*, May 22, 1960, p. 96.

It was true *Dodge City Times*, July 7, 1877; *Ford County Globe*, June 18, 1878.

But while Earp *National Police Gazette*, Aug. 10, 1878.

Bat Masterson considered W.B. Masterson, *Famous Gunfighters of the Western Frontier*, pp. 35-36.

After four years Casey Tefertiller, *Wyatt Earp, the Life Behind the Legend*, p. 32.

The arrival of Allen Barra, *Inventing Wyatt Earp*, p. 388.

Dozens of books Two well-researched and highly engaging books on the subject are *The Last Gunfight*, by Jeff Guinn (Simon & Schuster, 2011) and John Boessenecker's *Ride the Devil's Herd* (Hanover Square Press, 2020). I think the best biography of Wyatt Earp himself is Casey Tefertiller's *Wyatt Earp: The Life Behind the Legend*. The quote here summarizing the fight as much ado about very little comes from a piece novelist Larry McMurtry wrote for the *New York Review of Books*, in the March 24, 2005 edition.

Tombstone was about *New York Tribune*, Oct. 15, 1881, p. 2.

The battle was *New York Times*, Oct. 28, 1881, p. 2; *Brooklyn Union*, Oct. 28, 1881, p. 1; *Chicago Inter-Ocean*, Oct. 28, 1881, p. 5; *Philadelphia Times*, Oct. 28,1881, p. 1; *St. Louis Globe-Democrat*, Dec. 16, 1881, p. 7; *Alameda Daily Argus*, Oct. 28, 1881, p. 3.

But some Tombstonians Jeff Guinn, *The Last Gunfight*, p. 235.

In the wake of Tefertiller, op. cit., pp. 252-253

Two days after *Denver Republican*, May 14, 1893, p. 2.

Undaunted by being *Arizona Star*, March 22, 1882, p. 2.

Wyatt's posse found *San Francisco Examiner*, Aug. 2, 1896, p. 27.

But by 1885 Andrew C. Isenberg, *Wyatt Earp: A Vigilante Life*, p. 183.

In contrast he One hilarious account of the Tombstone shootout was spun by a

Charles H. Hopkins, who claimed to be a newspaper editor in Tombstone at the time. Hopkins was in Tombstone, but as a teamster who had been arrested for drunkenness by one of the Earps. His Ike Clanton-woos-Jessie Earp yarn appeared in papers across the country, including the *Buffalo (NY) Times*, Feb. 29, 1888, p. 3

Wyatt bought at *San Diego Union*, April 3, 1887, p. 1.

With a partner *San Diego Union*, May 10, 1888.

Just eight years *New York Sun*, Jan. 6, 1889, p. 10.

Sweets made life *Oakland Tribune*, July 3, 1902, p. 3; *Oakland Tribune*, Sept. 23, 1912, p. 1.

"You will never" *San Francisco Examiner*, Aug. 7, 1896, p. 6.

In reality, the *San Francisco Examiner*, Aug. 2, 1876, p. 27.

Prizefighting was technically *San Francisco Call*, Dec. 7, 1896, p. 1; Dec. 16, 1896, p. 1.

As the now-gunless *San Francisco Call*, Dec. 7, 1896, p. 1.

The decision triggered *San Francisco Call*, Dec. 3, 1896, p. 1; *New York Daily Herald*, Dec. 10, 1896, p. 1.

Earp adamantly denied *San Francisco Chronicle*, Dec. 3, 1896, p. 11.

Fitzsimmons went to *San Francisco Chronicle*, Dec. 9, 1896, p. 9

Worse, several of Ibid.

Earp's reputation was *Buffalo (N.Y.) Courier*, Dec. 12, 1896, p. 11; *New Orleans Times-Democrat*, Dec. 27, 1896, p. 3; *Kansas City (Mo.) Times*, Nov. 5, 1897, p. 4.

Humiliated, Wyatt and *San Francisco Call*, Aug. 6, 1897, p. 1.

From 1897 to *San Francisco Examiner*, Nov. 13, 1899, p. 4.

Even when he *New York Tribune*, July 15, 1900, p. 1; *Buffalo (NY) Sunday Morning News*, Oct. 4, 1903, p. 22.

"Notoriety has been" John Richard Stephens, *Wyatt Earp Speaks!*, p. 228.

"Many wrong impressions" Tefertiller, op. cit., p. 320.

According to the Bob Boze Bell, "Wyatt Earp in Hollywood," *True West Magazine*, October 2015. P. 28; Isenberg, op. cit., p. 203.

Burns had also Walter Noble Burns, *Tombstone: An Iliad of the Southwest*, p. 252.

Besides being an Tefertiller, op. cit., p. 326.

The reviews were *Los Angeles Times*, Nov. 8, 1931, p. 44; *New York Times*, Jan. 10, 1932, p. 74; (Tucson) *Arizona Star*, Nov. 1, 1931, p. 16.

In 1932, Lake Tefertiller, op. cit., p. 331.

The star was Marshal Earp: How an Actor Brought a Legend Back to Life," *TV Guide*, Jan. 21-27, 1956, p. 8.

Or at least *Gettysburg (Pa.) Times*, Oct. 8, 1979, p. 2.

But maybe it Burns, op. cit., p. 252.

CHAPTER 12

"The women who weep"

Two widows and a Calamity

George Custer's funeral was held 471 days after he died. Many thought it was worth the wait. "Thousands of people lined the banks on either side of the roadway as the procession approached, and stood in silence until it passed," *Harper's Weekly* reported about the Oct. 10, 1877, ceremony, which took place at the U.S. Military Academy at West Point, New York.

The formalities took six hours, including the procession, chapel service and burial, but not including the 30-mile boat ride down the Hudson River from Poughkeepsie, where Custer had been in cold storage for a few months.What was left of the "Boy General" had been shipped from the Little Bighorn battlefield in Montana during the summer. But because classes were out at West Point, it was decided there wouldn't be enough cadets around to do it up properly until the fall. After the service, a "battalion of three hundred cadets fired three volleys over the grave...and the body of the brave Custer was left to rest where his comrades had laid him."

Maybe. There is speculation by some historians and forensic anthropologists that the human remains lying in the West Point grave are actually those of an unidentified enlisted man, and that Custer's bones are still somewhere at the battlefield.

The uncertainty arises from the callous and haphazard way the federal government handled things after the battle. Almost all of the 7th Cavalry's dead were hastily covered with a few inches of soil where they fell, and just as quickly uncovered by prairie scavengers and the elements. George Custer and his brother Tom, however, were accorded more protection. Their bodies were put together in an 18-inch-deep hole, covered with blankets, a tarp and a leather stretcher weighed down with rocks. A map was made showing where each body was located.

But it was nearly 11 months before the War Department grudgingly gave in to pressure from the fallen soldiers' families and allocated $1,000 ($24,000 in 2022) for a nobler handling of the remains. On June 25, 1877—precisely a year to the day after Custer's demise—a detail from the 7th showed up at the battlefield. The idea was to move the officers to military cemeteries or private burial places, and bury the enlisted men in a common grave on-site. At the request of George Custer's wife, Elizabeth, his body was to be buried at West Point, from whence he had graduated just 16 years before.

Trouble was, the grave marked as George and Tom Custer's on the map didn't contain the two bodies, or the tarp, or the blankets, or the stretcher. Instead, there was a skeleton wearing a rotting corporal's uniform. So, the burial detail moved to another grave, found a skull, ribcage and leg bone, and decided that was George.

"It may be some consolation for you to know that I personally superintended the transfer of the remains from the box in which they came from the battlefield to the casket which conveys them to West Point," Major Joseph G. Tilford wrote to Mrs. Custer. Tilford also thoughtfully enclosed in the envelope what he said was a lock of Custer's hair. But however much consolation it provided, and whether it was even from George's head, a lock of hair wasn't going to pay the bills for Libbie Custer. To do that, she would need her husband's legendary status to live long and prosper.

Elizabeth Bacon Custer was a soldier's wife. She knew how to endure dreary postings, long separations from her husband, petty gossip from other officers' wives, infuriating politics that impeded promotion, mediocre income and paltry pensions. But she was also *George Custer's* wife. She nurtured his astounding narcissism, put up with his infidelities (while maybe having one or two of her own), and reveled in the fact that of all the women who swooned at the cavalier general, she was the one married to him. All that took pragmatism—and grit.

Elizabeth Clift Bacon was born in Monroe, Michigan, in 1842. Her father was by turns a schoolteacher, lawyer, state legislator, judge, bank president and railroad director. He made lots of money doing one or more of those things: For her ninth birthday, "Libbie," as she was called by nearly everyone, received a piano that in today's currency would cost $9,800. She was essentially an only child, as two siblings died in infancy and a third before the age of eight. Her mother died when she was 12, and Libbie was left to live at the school she was attending until her father remarried.

She was valedictorian of her class, and by age 20 was considered by all to be bright, personable and more than a little attractive. "Libbie has a splendid disposition and lovely temperament," a cousin wrote. "I never saw her superior in qualities that go to make up a noble woman." Neither had another Monroe resident, who at the time was a rising star in the Union Army.

Libbie Bacon met George Custer at a party on Thanksgiving night in 1862. She thought he was incredibly handsome and insufferably full of himself. He was deeply smitten. She got over her initial aversion to his arrogance, and they were married in February 1864. For the next 12-plus years, Libbie followed George to stations in Texas, Kentucky, Kansas and North Dakota; waited while he campaigned against Native Americans in the West and politicked and partied in the East, and listened in shock to the terse message delivered to her on July 6, 1876, at Fort Lincoln: "None wounded, none missing, all dead."

After learning of George's death, Libbie accompanied an officer and the Fort Lincoln post's surgeon to visit the wives of other dead officers and tell them the news. "From that time on, the life went out of the hearts of the 'women who weep,'" she wrote in the first of three memoirs, "and God asked them to walk on alone and in the shadows." When the grim news had been delivered, she helped out with the wounded in the post hospital.

And then she almost fell apart. “Mrs. Custer is not strong, and I would not be surprised if she did not improve,” Gen. Nelson Miles wrote his wife after visiting Libbie at Fort Lincoln. “She seemed so depressed and in such disrepair.” Another observer wrote she had “so little strength left that she could scarcely reach the top of the stairway.” But the U.S. Army made no provisions for the widows of dead officers, and Libbie and the other bereft women were compelled to leave the fort two weeks after learning of their husbands’ deaths. Libbie went home to Monroe.

At home, Libbie gradually recovered enough to go through the papers Custer had left behind and assess her situation. There was the $2,500 mortgage on the house ($60,000 in 2022), unpaid promissory notes—and a love letter to George from an acquaintance of Libbie’s. On the plus side, there was money from a *New York Daily Herald* widow’s fund, a cash gift from Grand Duke Alexi of Russia, a small check from the U.S. Treasury for Custer’s testimony before a congressional committee, a life insurance policy, and the promise of a $600 ($14,400 in 2022) annual pension from Congress. When she added it all up, she figured it would be a good idea to make some money.

She decided to earn it herself, turning down offers to hold fundraising benefits on her behalf. “Mrs. Custer appears to have been the right kind of wife for such a man (as Custer),” the *Cincinnati Enquirer* noted approvingly. “...She has insisted upon paying all of her husband’s debts in full.” But if Libbie was “the right kind of wife” for Custer, Custer was the right kind of late husband to have for Libbie as well. For most of her remaining 56 years, the Widow Custer made a handsome living writing and lecturing about her life as an army wife.

She published three critically praised and brisk-selling memoirs: *Boots and Saddles* (1885); *Following the Guidon* (1890), and *Tenting on the Plains* (1893). Each dealt with a different period of the Custers’ marriage. Each was lucid, well-organized and almost devoid of maudlin sentimentality, while still managing to portray George Custer as a swell guy with only minor flaws. They were also surprisingly informative. As a typical reviewer of *Boots and Saddles* wrote, a reader "will feel that he has incurred a debt of gratitude to the sweet-voiced, clear-souled loyal woman, who with wifely devotion has given him the priceless glimpse of a soldier's home life...the little book is full of vivid and realistic anecdotes which show the keen spirit of fun which possessed the young wife and her hero through the days of happiness and hardship."

Libbie supplemented her handsome income from the books with a lucrative lecture schedule. At the lectern, she stuck to the formula that made the books successful. She avoided seeking audiences' sympathies, and emphasized just how wonderful it had been to be Mrs. George Custer. "The tragedy of Gen. Custer's last battle was fresh in everybody's mind," a charmed reporter wrote after one of her talks, "but there was not a hint of it in the sweet cheerfulness of the narrative which held the audience spell-bound. A slight tremor of the voice told how difficult certain passages were to read, but there was no other reference to the sad ending of the delightful domestic drama which she presented."

It would be unfair, however, to leave the impression that Libbie Custer's literary and rhetorical exertions were motivated only by the expectation of financial gain. She had adored George Custer. Despite his post-mortem popularity with the general public, he had also been harshly criticized as a swaggering boob who got what he deserved at the Little Bighorn, while the men he led there did not. Libbie was determined to protect his memory.

A shining—or glaring—example of her efforts was the statue of Custer she lobbied federal officials to erect on his West Point gravesite. Constructed of bronze from 20 obsolete cannon and funded with $10,000 in private and public contributions, the statue depicted Custer standing on a pedestal, wielding a saber in one hand and a revolver in the other. Libbie hated it. She objected to not having been consulted in its design and claimed it was demeaning to a cavalryman to be posed without a horse beneath him. The statue was removed. "I literally cried it off its pedestal," she triumphantly said. It was replaced, with her consent, with a stone obelisk that looks a bit like the Washington Monument and is still a popular tourist stop at the academy.She also pushed successfully for Custer memorials to be placed in her hometown of Monroe, Michigan, and Custer's birthplace in New Rumley, Ohio.

Custer's widow had help in her quest to perpetuate the public's veneration of her "martyred" husband. In late 1886, Buffalo Bill Cody added "Custer's Last Rally" to his Wild West show. The performance, which formed the show's final act, had Custer heroically fighting Indians hand-to-hand until at last he is the final soldier to succumb. Cody initially played the role himself, donning a long yellow wig and wildly waving a saber, despite the fact that Custer had neither long hair nor a saber at the Little Bighorn. Libbie, who attended rehearsals of the drama as well as the show itself, wrote Cody to congratulate him for "teaching the youth the history of our country, where the noble officers, soldiers and scouts sacrificed so much for the sake of our native land." The show, which played all over America and large parts of Europe, was an immense boost to Custer's image.

Another, more unlikely, image booster came in the form of an 1896 lithograph called "Custer's Last Fight." Distributed by the Anheuser-Busch Brewing Company to thousands of bars and saloons around the country as an advertising poster, the lithograph was based on an 1888 painting by Cassilly Adams, an Ohio-born artist of almost no lasting repute. It depicted a long-haired Custer (who, by the by, was a teetotaler,) in a buckskin jacket, brandishing a saber above his head while encircled by a horde of Indians, several of whom in the foreground are mercilessly butchering fallen soldiers.

As an 1897 newspaper description put it, "the scene graphically pictures the dreadful massacre of the Little Big Horn, the story of which is so familiar to every school boy and girl of America, where General Custer and his handful of brave men were surrounded and shot down like dogs by a host of bloodthirsty redskins but a quarter century ago." Over succeeding decades, the lithograph became the primary mind's-eye image of the battle for millions of Americans.

But more immediately beneficial to Libbie's cause was a biography of Custer published less than six months after his death. The author, Frederick Whittaker, was a London-born Union Army veteran who after the war bestowed upon himself the rank of captain and became a prolific, if not particularly talented, writer. He churned out more than 80 dime novels, along with numerous magazine articles, and eventually became the assistant editor of *Army and Navy Journal*, a periodical that had no official connection with the U.S. military but was nonetheless influential in Washington.

Whittaker had met George Custer once, in the offices of *The Galaxy* magazine for which Custer had written a series of articles that later became the bulk of his best-selling memoir, *My Life on the Plains*. The "captain" (who was really a second lieutenant) was besotted with admiration for "the general" (who was really a lieutenant colonel.) Within weeks of Custer's death in late June, Whittaker wrote a mawkish article for *The Galaxy*, and an even more sentimental poem for *Army and Navy Journal*. *The Galaxy's* editors were impressed enough to commission Whittaker to produce a rush-job biography of Custer.

In early December, *A Complete Life of General George A. Custer* went on sale at a hefty $4.25 a copy ($102 in 2022). Buyers were lucky it wasn't sold by the pound. Whittaker's book was 650 pages long, a size *The Nation* magazine's reviewer accurately described as "repellently large and heavy."

Whittaker laid it on thick from the very first line: "This book aims to give the world the life of a very great man, one of the few really great men that America has produced." It ended—finally—with the assertion that "we have followed him through his life...without finding one deed to bring shame to soldier or man." In between, Whittaker excoriated Custer's subordinates at the Little Bighorn, Major Marcus Reno and Captain Frederick Benteen. Reno, according to Whittaker, had behaved cowardly and Benteen had disobeyed orders. That, he concluded, was why the Custer column was wiped out. He also criticized President Grant for not being nicer to Custer, and called for a military court of inquiry. "The nation demands such a court," Whittaker wrote, "to vindicate the name of a dead hero from the pitiless malignancy that first slew him and then pursued him beyond the grave."

Critics were generally kind. While acknowledging the book "would have gained by compression," the *Chicago Tribune* praised it as "a fitting tribute to the memory of a noble man." Without a trace of discernable sarcasm, the *Fall River (Ma.) Daily Evening News* said "the tale reads agreeably as a story of romance and fiction." But sales were only moderate, owing largely to the book's high price, its great bulk and the fact the U.S. economy was pretty much in the toilet at the time of its release.

Whittaker's charges against Reno and Benteen, however, coupled with Libbie's unrelenting efforts to deify her late husband, began to stir up a controversy over a question the Army and War Department wished would just go away: Whose fault was the defeat at Little Bighorn? The flap exacerbated by Whittaker's book was noticed as far away as London, where *The Examiner* said the book "throws great doubt upon the actions of Reno and Benteen and suggests that to the want of promptness and obedience on their part is to be attributed the deaths of Custer and his companions."

Benteen and President Grant mostly ignored Whittaker. But Reno, who since the battle had been court-martialed and suspended from the army for a separate scandal involving the wife of another officer, felt increasingly pressured to clear his name. The final straw may have come in November 1877, when none other than Sitting Bull piled on. The great Lakota spiritual and political leader was interviewed in Canada, where he had taken his people after the Little Bighorn battle to escape the U.S. Army. He told *New York Daily Herald* correspondent James B. Stillson that "the Long Hair" (Custer) fought bravely, standing "like a sheaf of corn with all the ears fallen around him." But he sneered at Reno's refusal to move his men from their defensive positions on a butte a few miles away and come to Custer's aid. All of the warriors were fighting Custer, Sitting Bull said, and "there were none but squaws and papooses in front of them (Reno's men) that afternoon."

On June 23, 1878, Reno formally asked for a court of inquiry to convene so he could defend himself. The request was granted two days later—precisely on the second anniversary of Custer's death. The hearing was postponed until January 1879 because the 7th Cavalry was still in the field in the aftermath of the Sioux War, and many of its officers were unavailable to testify until winter set in.

When the proceedings finally began, they took 26 days, featured 23 witnesses and produced 1,300 pages of official records. Bafflingly, the records were kept under lock and key by the government until 1941, even though they consisted mainly of newspaper clippings and the hearings had been open to the press and public. In the end, Custer and his men were still dead, and the three-member court cleared Reno while, in the words of one of the judges, "damning him with faint praise." The court noted that "the conduct of the officers throughout (the battle) was excellent, and while subordinates in some instances did more for the safety of the command by brilliant displays of courage than Maj. Reno, there was nothing in his conduct which requires animadversion (censure) from this court."

To this day, Custer's admirers contend, with substantial evidence, that the inquiry was a sham. Its preordained goal, they argue, was to protect the image of the 7th and the integrity of the Army, particularly at a time when a cost-cutting Congress was looking for reasons to slash military spending. Whittaker, who had led the charge to vindicate his hero and paste the scapegoat's horns on someone else's head, was livid. "Had Reno fought like a soldier instead of fleeing like a coward, Custer would have defeated the Indians," he wrote to a Philadelphia newspaper. "Every officer in the Seventh knows this to-day." After the letter, Whittaker faded from public view. In 1889, he was found at the bottom of his home's stairway with a bullet in his head. It was never settled whether it was a result of murder, suicide or clumsiness.

By the end of 1879, Reno had been court-martialed again, this time for assaulting a subordinate. He was thrown out of the army in April 1880, and died in 1889. In one of history's perverse little twists, a military review board in 1967 reinstated Reno and gave him an honorable discharge. That cleared the way for him to be reinterred, with full honors, in the national military cemetery at the Little Bighorn battle site. And that makes Reno the 7th Cavalry's highest-ranking officer who took part in the fight to be buried on the scene—unless Custer's bones are there instead of at West Point.

Benteen remained in the Army until 1888, when he received a disability discharge. He went to his grave (in 1898) still openly critical of Custer's leadership and bitter about having been "so grievously assailed by penny-a-liners and novel writers hunting for an easy market for their wares." He also blamed Libbie Custer's labors "to keep the name of Gen. Custer fresh in the memories of the public, that in her lectures to that generous public she may receive a fitting audience."

As for Libbie, the "generous public" that Benteen so disdained continued to buy her books and attend her talks, and for the most part admire her late husband. Her efforts were boosted by Custer biographies in 1926 and 1928 that were scarcely less fawning than Whittaker's. She traveled extensively around the world, but never visited the Little Bighorn. When she finally died, four days short of her 91st birthday and 56 years after her husband's demise, she left most of her sizeable estate to Vassar College, with the stipulation that it be used to aid students who were the daughters of commissioned military officers.

But with her death in 1933, cracks began to appear in George Custer's public image. A year after Libbie died. Frederic F. Van de Water, a New York book critic and novelist, published *Glory-Hunter: A Life of General Custer*. Van de Water's take on Custer, and his book's opening lines, were polar opposites from those of Frederick Whittaker. "He followed Glory all his days," Van de Water began. "He was her lifelong devotee. She gave him favor withheld from most men, and denied herself when his need of her was sorest."

Van de Water stumbled across Custer as a subject only because he was researching the Sioux War for a novel that featured a Native American as the protagonist. His Custer was personally brave, but also selfish, insubordinate, cruel, reckless and foolish: "He loved fame with insatiable ardor. His pursuit of renown was medieval and adolescent...his fall was not star-ordained. It was in himself."

Van de Water's book-critic brethren liked his wait-a-minute approach to a legendary American. The *New York Times Book Review* noted "Mr. Van de Water has accumulated evidence until it can hardly be questioned. There is enough of it to damn the man as cruel and irresponsible. Yet the Custer portrayed is a thousand times more fascinating, has far more claim to sympathy, than the plaster saint of poor Mrs. Custer's loving narrations." The *Brooklyn Times-Union* said the book "pricks the bubble of fame created by newspapermen of Custer's day" that was perpetuated "by history text books, which have always been too prone to make heroes."

The influence of Van de Water's disassembling of George Custer's image stretched almost as far as Libbie Custer's assembly of it. In a 1988 introduction to a new edition of Van de Water's book, eminent Western historian Paul Andrew Hutton called it "without a doubt, the most influential book ever written on Custer." Most subsequent novels, Custer biographies and histories of the Indian wars consistently portrayed Custer under a harsh light.

In films, Custer's character varied, but not often favorably. In 1965's *The Great Sioux Massacre*, actor Philip Carey portrayed him as a decent enough fellow who runs afoul of the Grant Administration and is seduced by the promise of a bright future in politics if he can only score a big win against the Indians. It does not turn out well for Carey's Custer. In 1968's *Custer of the West,* Robert Shaw's Custer is a sardonic figure who is disgusted by the government's treatment of Native Americans but loves the traditions of the U.S. Cavalry too much to resist an opportunity to kill Indians in large numbers. Like Carey's, Shaw's Custer ends badly.

Heavily influenced by the Civil Rights Movement and growing opposition to America's involvement in Vietnam's civil war, 1970's *Little Big Man* has Richard Mulligan as a Custer who is a bat-poop-crazy racist, and whose death is more comic relief than tragedy. *Son of the Morning Star*, a 1991 two-part television series based on Evan Connell's nonfiction work of the same name, told the story from the perspective of Libbie Custer and a fictional Cheyenne woman. Among its Emmy nominations were those for best costuming and best hairstyling.

Of course there have been exceptions to the anti-Custer trend, on both the screen and in print. Directed by Raoul Walsh and starring Errol Flynn, 1940's *They Died With Their Boots On* was released on the eve of America's entry into World War II. As such it was a flag-waving film designed to stir patriotic feelings for America's past. Flynn's Custer had tremendous sympathy for Native Americans, and the real bad guys were duplicitous politicians and sleazy Indian agents. Even so, Flynn still dies at the end.

In 2015, *The Last Days of George Armstrong Custer*, by Western history writer Thom Hatch, was released. It was an unapologetic apologia that contended Custer's military career was "by any measurement one of the finest in American history," and that his reputation had "fallen prey to the academic and pop-culture bullies who cannot accept the premise...that great men have actually walked the earth."

Other recent Custer biographers, such as Robert M. Utley, James Donovan and Nathaniel Philbrick, have taken a more nuanced approach than Hatch. But despite the fact that George Custer remains one of the two or three most written-about Americans ever, it's likely Libbie Custer wouldn't care for the prevailing 21st century public perception of her husband.

"The only regret she expressed when dying was that Custer's detractors would now be free to tarnish his image," the Native American novelist James Welch wrote in 1994. "Sixty years later, it would seem her fear has been justified...Custer's Last Stand has become a cautionary tale, and the Custer myth, unhappily for Libbie's ghost, has turned to tarnished brass."

Unlike George Armstrong Custer, it's pretty certain James Butler Hickok is occupying the grave site to which he was assigned. The problem with Wild Bill has been trying to preserve what's on top of him.

Hickok was assassinated in Deadwood, South Dakota, on August 2, 1876, just 38 days after Custer was killed. He was planted the next day in what was then the town's cemetery, conveniently located part way up what would come to be called Mount Moriah, on the east side of and close to the town's main drag. Bill's pal, Colorado Charlie Utter, supervised the interment. Utter put up a board that described Hickok as "a brave man; the victim of an assassin." A bit later, the head board was replaced with one that read "Wild Bill—J.B. Hickok. Killed by the assassin Jack McCall in Deadwood Black Hills. August 2nd, 1876. Pard we will meet again in the Happy Hunting ground to part no more. Good Bye—Colorado Charlie. C.H. Utter."

But Charlie didn't have to wait until the "Happy Hunting ground" to meet Hickok again. By August, 1879, Deadwood had grown so fast that people were living on top of the dead. It was decided to move the cemetery further up the hill, and Charlie supervised Wild Bill's disinterring and relocation. What he found was a surprise: The corpse that weighed maybe 180 pounds in 1876 now weighed in the neighborhood of 300. Due possibly to minerals in water that seeped into the grave, "the body was thoroughly petrified," newspapers reported. "The features of the deceased were as natural as life, save that a whiteness o'erspread all (and) gave to the face and neck the appearance of chiseled marble."

It took four men to move Bill up the hill to a new grave, over which was placed the wooden headboard of the old one. But it didn't last long. Hickok's grave became an instant tourist attraction, and since most 19th century tourists lacked cellphones to take selfies, they made do with pocket knives and carved off bits of the headboard until not much was left.

In 1891, J.H. Riordan, a New Yorker who had never met Hickok but greatly admired him anyway, shelled out the money for a nine-foot-tall stone monument at the grave, topped with a bust of Wild Bill and decorated with two crossed pistols. Within a decade, the monument had been chipped to pieces by souvenir hunters who had traded in their pocket knives for hammers and chisels.

In 1903, the busted bust was replaced by a life-sized statue of Hickok, carved by local sculptor Alvin Smith. A reviewer from Abilene, Kansas, where Wild Bill had been city marshal for about six months in 1871, patronizingly noted that it was "a rude statue in red sandstone... intended to represent Wild Bill. It is a good deal of a caricature, but was well-intended...".

This time Deadwood's officials erected a wire fence around the memorial. By the 1940s, the fence was more holes than wire; tourists posed for photos standing on Bill's grave, and the statue's head, arms and other accoutrements were gone.

The covetous folks in Abilene had seen enough. In June, 1953, a group calling itself the Wild Bill Hickok Foundation asserted that since Bill had actually been a city official in Abilene and only a visitor in Deadwood, his final resting place should be moved. They eagerly pointed out the continued desecration of the Deadwood grave, and a bit more quietly acknowledged that Abilene could use a tourist attraction. Deadwood courteously declined the proposal. "We are capable of seeing to it that in the final analysis, the grave will be preserved for future generations with all the glory and historical aura to which it is entitled," said Deadwood Mayor R.L. Ewing.

Two months later, Deadwood officials removed the remains of the statue and replaced it with a replica of the original wooden headboard erected by Charlie Utter. Three years later, someone stole it. For the next half century or so, Wild Bill rested in an unkempt plot. But in the late 1980s, South Dakota voters approved casino gambling in Deadwood. Awash in newfound cash, city officials eventually launched an ambitious three-year, $4.6 million renovation of the Mt. Moriah cemetery. Part of the refurbishing was a handsome bronze bust of Wild Bill mounted on a pedestal, that resembled the 1891 marker. This time it was ensconced by a chest-high wrought iron fence. And as of this writing, it is still there.

But the Abilene foundation was not the first entity to try and snatch Wild Bill from the Black Hills. That distinction would fall to his widow.

Like Libbie Custer, Agnes Hickok was stunned to hear the news of her husband's sudden violent death. That, however, is where similarities of the two widows ended. For one thing, Wild Bill wasn't the first husband Agnes had lost to murder. While still in her teens, she had married William Lake Thatcher, a circus clown. Adapting the catchier name "Bill Lake," Agnes' spouse became a highly successful circus owner—until a night in 1869 when he was shot to death by a worthless punk in a dispute over an unpaid admission. Also unlike Libbie, Agnes had not lived in the shadows of either of her husbands, or basked in their reflected glory.

As Agnes Lake, she had not only been Bill Lake's business partner, but was the circus' brightest star as a wire walker and equestrienne. "I thrived on work," she told an interviewer in 1907. "First, I gave the outside wire walking spectacle, then rode in the grand entrée, was the chief feature of *Mazeppa* (a theatrical drama performed on horseback), and also did another riding turn. Frequently I appeared in the (post-circus) concert as well. All this twice a day ...". During her five-year relationship and five-month marriage to Hickok, Agnes had built a sizeable nest egg, lost it, and rebuilt it while Wild Bill, financially speaking, was just squeaking by.

Still, Bill's death stung hard. In November 1876, she wrote to Hickok's mother, explaining that she had been dealing not only with his loss, but with the harrowing pregnancy of her beloved daughter Emma, a product of her first marriage. "My daughter has had a hard time of it, and the Baby is so cross that there is no rest with her night or day...I am longing to pay you all a visit this Spring before going West to remain next to the scenes that my beloved Husband loved so well and try to end my days out West. I am going to the Black Hills and remain near his grave."

In the summer of 1877, Agnes did go west, but she neither remained very long near Bill's grave nor ended her days anywhere near it. In mid-August she took the train to Cheyenne, Wyoming. From there she traced the 275-mile trail north that Bill Hickok had taken with Charlie Utter the year before. The 50-year-old Agnes traveled with "Texas George" Carson, a "widely and favorably known" frontiersman, and Mr. and Mrs. "Buckskin Charley" Dalton, a ranching couple who had apparently known Hickok. It was a somewhat eventful trip. Agnes reported that when a sway brace broke on the wagon she was driving, she was thrown under the horses pulling it. "...I got off with plenty of bruises, from which I am very sore," she wrote, "but thanks to the Ruler of all things, no limbs broken."

Agnes' original intention had been to make arrangements to ship Hickok's body east. She changed her mind, however, after Deadwood locals assured her a suitable and protected monument would soon be erected to honor Bill's memory. We all know now how that turned out. How serious she was about moving Bill is questionable anyway, since she revealed she was returning to Cheyenne to pick up two horses being trained for the circus, and then joining her daughter for a tour that would go through New York City and end in Havana, Cuba.

She also may or may not have planned to marry her guide, George Carson. Records show the two took out a marriage license in Cheyenne, but there were no recorded nuptials, and no mention of Carson again past Cheyenne. In fact, Agnes spent most of the rest of her long life in the company of her daughter, Emma Robinson. Emma was a chip off the old horse hoof. Hailed as America's finest equestrienne, she performed with the Barnum & Bailey Circus and Buffalo Bill's Wild West show. "Mrs. Agnes Lake accompanies her daughter everywhere and is her constant companion," the *Cheyenne Daily Leader* reported. "She has herself 36 years of experience with the circuses, and what she don't know about them is not worth thinking about."

In later years, Agnes settled near Jersey City, New Jersey, where she lived quietly near her daughter and son-in-law. Their homes were near a spacious indoor riding facility where Emma could practice during the winter. Agnes lived so quietly, in fact, that she triggered a spate of stories in 1906 by reporters surprised she was still alive. On Aug. 31, 1907, she wasn't. Agnes died two days short of her 81st birthday, and a bit more than 31 years after Wild Bill.

Her death merited newspaper stories across the country. Some, like the *Kansas City Star's*, played up her connection with Hickok and sported headlines like "Wild Bill's Widow Dead." Others, like the *New York Times*, didn't mention Wild Bill until the last paragraph or two, and focused mainly on Agnes' milestone-setting circus career, such as the fact she was America's first female circus owner, the first to routinely move her show by train, and the inventor of the multi-ring performance. Still others, like the *Washington (D.C.) Evening Star*, didn't mention Wild Bill at all. (The Star's headline was a bit tacky: "Old Circus Queen Dead.")

Despite her celebrity at the time of her death, however, Agnes Lake Hickok's connection to the legendary Wild Bill was eventually obscured by his almost entirely fanciful connection to a foul-mouthed, alcoholic cross-dressing woman he barely knew. She is addressed in the pantheon of Wild West legends as Calamity Jane.

Martha Jane Canary said she was born in Missouri. That was true. Almost everything else Martha Jane Canary ever said about herself merits the utmost scrutiny. "Quite a few scholars have researched her life in the last couple of decades in an effort to sift out fact from fiction," said James D. McLaird, a South Dakota historian. "When they get done discarding the legends, there's not much left. All I can tell you is that she was probably an alcoholic prostitute who was kind of fun to have around. She was boisterous and friendly... but it's pretty easy to show that almost everything she said was a lie."

Among the sifted nuggets that appear to be true are that she was born in 1852; was the eldest of six children; was orphaned at the age of 15, and assumed responsibility for her siblings by working at whatever job she could find to sustain them. Then it gets murky. As a young adult, she claimed to have disguised herself as a man and fought Indians as a cavalry scout and freight wagon driver. But there is far more evidence she was a prostitute, dancehall performer and "camp follower," meaning she moved around military posts entertaining the troops in a horizontal manner.

Contemporary newspapers and her acquaintances somewhat unkindly suggested it was easier to believe Calamity Jane's alleged exploits disguised as a man than anything she did as a woman. "It is doubtful she ever had a skirt on in her life," sniffed the *Chicago Tribune*. "...She has always been associated with men and lived a man's life." A Deadwood associate described Jane as "about the roughest looking human being I ever saw," and another said she was "real tall and built like a busted bale of hay."

Jane claimed her nickname was given her by a wounded cavalry officer she saved from Indians by throwing him on her horse during a battle and galloping to safety. A friend, the well-known Black Hills madam Dora DuFran, said it stemmed from Jane always being sent for in Deadwood when there was a calamity, such as a disease outbreak. Perhaps closest to the truth was the theory the nickname derived from what occurred in a saloon after Jane was there for more than 20 minutes and began an unbearable howling.

In any event, her name became nationally known within her lifetime as the heroine of dozens of dime novels. In many of them, she was paired with a hero known as Deadwood Dick. Like the 21st century's Paris Hilton and the Kardashians, Jane Canary was a walking example of historian Daniel Boorstin's definition of a celebrity: "A person who is well-known for (her) well-knownness." In actuality, if Calamity Jane performed any real heroics in her life, it was probably confined to tending the sick during Deadwood's smallpox outbreak in the winter of 1876-77.

Whatever she was, she was decidedly *not* a wife, lover or even good friend with James Butler Hickok. She probably knew him slightly, and may even have traveled in the same wagon train that brought Hickok to Deadwood in 1876. But there is no evidence to back her claim—after Bill's death—that the two of them were secretly married in 1873. "I have gone up and down the eastern side of the Rocky Mountains and have talked with every man I could find who knew Wild Bill personally," Deadwood old-timer O.W. Coursey wrote in 1925, "and all of them, without a single exception, deny that Bill was ever in any way intimate with Jane, or cared anything about her; in fact, the evidence is overwhelming that he shunned her."

But despite all the evidence to the contrary, two events that occurred years after Hickok died added to the widespread belief that Bill and Jane were a thing. The first was on Aug. 4, 1903. That was the day Martha Jane Canary achieved the lasting celebrity she had always craved by being buried next to James Butler Hickok in Deadwood's Mt. Moriah Cemetery. The purported reason was that it had been poor Jane's last request. But the reality was that several of Deadwood's civic leaders decided over more than a few drinks to recognize Jane's service to the town during the 1876 smallpox epidemic—and prank Wild Bill in the process.

"Someone suggested it would be a good joke on Wild Bill if she would be buried alongside of him," it was revealed in a letter decades later. "... As the conversation proceeded, they were *sure* it would be a good joke on Bill if he knew that he would lay up with Jane for eternity." They say that on moonlit nights, when the wind gently nudges the cemetery's towering pines that look down over Deadwood, if you listen closely, you can hear Wild Bill *not* laughing.

The second indignity the deceased Hickok suffered came at the hands of Jean Hickok Burkhead McCormick in 1941. McCormick was a 67-year-old Montana woman who claimed she was the legitimate daughter of Calamity Jane and Wild Bill. The claim was accepted by the U.S. Department of Public Welfare as part of a process granting McCormick an old age assistance pension. The government's guileless acceptance led to a tidal wave of newspaper and radio stories about "Wild Bill's Lost Daughter!"

The complete lack of evidence to substantiate McCormick's claim led to it ultimately being deemed bogus by historians, but it did serve to once again link Jane and Bill in the public eye.

Calamity Jane lived for 27 years past Wild Bill Hickok, scraping out an existence as an innkeeper, a cook in a brothel run by her friend Dora DuFran, and a raconteur at various "dime museums" in the Midwest. These latter establishments were basically freak shows, featuring diversions such as "the living half horse, half human," "the one-armed whittler," and "Uzee, the aboriginal albino beauty." Jane was billed as "scout, trapper and Indian slayer." Her act consisted of telling lies and peddling a poorly written seven-page "autobiography" that she apparently had dictated to someone only slightly more literate than she was.

In 1901, a New York philanthropist, Josephine Brake, "rescued" Jane from life as a destitute drunk and brought her to live in Buffalo. Cynics at the time pointed out Brake was probably less motivated by charity than she was at the chance to exploit Jane's celebrity status in plugging a romance novel Brake had recently written. The cynics were correct. Jane's "adoption" coincided with the presence in Buffalo of the 1901 Pan American Exposition. The expo included performances by Frederick T. Cummins' Wild West Congress. Cummins hired Jane to perform with his show, but she quickly drank her way out of it. When Will Cody came to town with his show, Jane begged enough money from Cody for a train ticket west.

Two years later, she was dead, at the age of 51. She looked to be much older. Reviews of her passing were mixed. Close to home, the *Black Hills Union* rather nastily complained that mythologizing figures such as Jane Canary sent a terrible message to the nation's youth. "Ask the honest pioneer what Jane was famous for," the *Union* suggested, "and he will tell you she was noted for the amount of bad whiskey she could get away with and for being so low and debased that she was fit company only for dogs."

But the *New York Times* eulogized her as a "woman who became famous as an Indian fighter...wearing men's clothes she served with Gens.

Custer and Miles," and was "the most picturesque character in the West." The *Times* also reported that it was none other than Calamity Jane who tracked down Bill Hickok's killer, Jack McCall, while McCall was cowering in a Deadwood butcher's shop, and brought McCall to justice with the aid of a meat cleaver. None of that was true. Justice, however, did catch up with Broken-Nosed Jack.

He couldn't leave well enough alone. Sure, he had just killed the most famous gunfighter in the West by sneaking up behind him and putting a bullet in the back of the seated fellow's head. Sure, he had been acquitted in a hastily convened "miners' court" by a dozen drunk and/or bribed jurors, and somehow escaped being shot before he left town.

But despite sometimes being moody—and always dangerous—Wild Bill Hickok had friends. If Jack McCall had known what was good for him, he would have skedaddled out of the Great Plains after murdering Hickok in Deadwood. He would have moved to California, or back home to Kentucky. Or at the very least kept a low profile for a while. But no one ever accused Jack McCall of being the sharpest knife in the drawer. Besides, what's the point of killing a legend if you can't brag about it?

So McCall did. After leaving Deadwood, he went to Wyoming, where he boasted of his deed in saloons in Cheyenne, Horse Creek and Laramie. He admitted he made up the story he had told the miners' court about how he was only avenging the killing of his brother by Wild Bill in Kansas. In fact, McCall never had a brother. He said he really killed Hickok because the two had quarreled during a poker game the day before, and that after he slapped Wild Bill, Hickok merely smiled at him.

Among McCall's listeners one night in late August was Col. George May, an Illinois-trained attorney who had served as the prosecutor at the miners' court trial in Deadwood. He was outraged by the acquittal, and had trailed McCall to Wyoming.May alerted law enforcement elements about McCall's boasts, and the killer was arrested in Laramie by a deputy U.S. marshal.

It turned out McCall's belief that he couldn't be tried again for the murder had a geopolitical flaw. Deadwood was an illegal settlement. It was located on land the federal government had ceded to the Lakota Nation as reservation land and was therefore under federal supervision. The miners' court thus had no legal standing, and McCall had not been acquitted of anything. After his arrest, he was extradited to Yankton, South Dakota, about 400 miles southeast of Deadwood, and indicted for Hickok's murder.

After an escape attempt failed, McCall tried to at least partially exculpate himself by claiming he had been hired to kill Hickok by a John Varnes. McCall claimed Varnes was sore because Hickok had made him look small by interfering in a fight Varnes had with another man. McCall offered to turn states' evidence, but Varnes was never found, in part because not much effort was made to find him.

McCall's trial began on Dec. 1, the same day Deadwood was linked to the rest of the world by completion of a telegraph line into the town. The trial took five days and the jury took three hours to return a guilty verdict. McCall's defense attorneys called no witnesses in his behalf, but did try a variety of legal maneuvers to obtain a new trial. They failed, and McCall was sentenced to death. A subsequent clemency appeal to the White House on the grounds McCall was drunk at the time of the murder was denied. On March 1, 1877, three days before Rutherford B. Hayes was sworn in as the 19th U.S. president, Jack McCall was hanged. He was buried with the noose still around his neck.

"The best that can be said of him is that although he lived like a ruffian, he died like a man," the *New York Daily Herald* observed. "Trying to maintain his stolidity, he nonetheless spent his last moments with the crucifix clasped tightly in his hands...the world is better off by having lost him."

If McCall had hoped to grab a piece of immortality by killing a legend, it might be of some comfort to him to know that Yankton still features two plaques memorializing his time there—along with hosting the remains of

McCall himself. One of the plaques, on a downtown red brick building that was the former courthouse and now houses health and social services organizations, tells the story of McCall's trial. The second, much rustier, plaque is mounted on a pole in a grassy field next to a soccer complex and across the street from a Wal-Mart. It marks the spot where McCall was hanged.

In the nearby Sacred Heart Catholic Cemetery is McCall. The front of his modest stone marker bears his name, the year of his birth, and the date of his death. On the back is a biblical quotation: "Their sins and lawless acts I will remember no more." In McCall's case, it could not be more inaccurate.

Wild Bill's murder didn't make much of a national stir, perhaps because it occurred in such a far-flung outpost as Deadwood and came just weeks after George Custer's widely publicized death. But it was prime fodder for the dime novelists. Ned Buntline, who disliked Hickok, and whom Hickok despised, had the last laugh by cranking out *Wild Bill's Last Trail*. It depicts Hickok as a drunken bully who is afraid of ghosts, threatens to kill women and is himself killed by a righteously vengeful Jack McCall.

On the "non-fiction" side, the stream of biographies, which was still flowing through 2019 with Tom Clavin's *Wild Bill: The True Story of the American Frontier's First Gunfighter*, began in 1880 with a book by one of America's most popular and prolific Gilded Age authors. James W. Buel, a former schoolteacher and journalist, produced more than 50 titles during his career. The topics ranged from a 15-volume history of the United States to a history of the Bible that sold an astounding 1.35 million copies.

Like much of his other work, Buell's *The True Story of "Wild Bill" Hickok* was short on accuracy and long on enthusiasm. In between claiming Hickok was the kind of vigilante law America needed to tame the West and calling for a monument to be erected to Wild Bill, Buell included such imaginary incidents as the time Hickok simultaneously took on four men at a Nebraska stagecoach stop, killing three and wounding the other.

Buell's sole source for the story was a man "who at the time lived within a few miles of where the fight occurred and heard the details from several eyewitnesses."

Roughly a half-century later, a well-known theatrical press agent took a literary whack at Wild Bill. Frank Wilstach grew intrigued with the Hickok story while working as an advance man for various circuses and Wild West shows in the Midwest. The result was *Wild Bill Hickok, Prince of the Pistoleers*, which was released in 1926 and serialized in newspapers across the country. Wilstach said his aim was "to find out what was real and what imaginary in the tales about him (Hickok) that have been current for upwards of 60 years." Wilstach talked to some people who knew Hickok, and debunked several of the more outlandish parts of the legend. But he couldn't resist creating dramatic scenes, complete with dialogue, to dramatize factually dubious events. And like Buel, he claimed to have relied on notebooks and journals kept by Hickok that apparently very few people besides Buel and Wilstach ever saw.

It fell to a 32-year-old copywriter and teletype operator who had never been west of Ireland to put Bill Hickok's biography on the right track. As a boy growing up in the London suburb of Middlesex, Joseph G. Rosa became entranced with James Butler Hickok—or at least as he was portrayed by Gary Cooper in the 1936 film *The Plainsman*. "It was the enigma of a man who was both a romantic and tragic figure that appealed to me," Rosa said in a 2001 interview.

Thus entranced, Rosa spent years ferreting out documents and other information about Hickok from sources that included surviving members of the Hickok family. More amazing, he did it long-distance. Rosa estimated he sent and received more than 3,000 letters across the Atlantic during his research. The result was the publication in 1964 of *They Called Him Wild Bill: The Life and Adventures of Wild Bill Hickok*.

The book was immediately deemed the Bible of Bill. The *New York Times* called it "the most thorough and accurate biography of Wild Bill that has yet been published." The *Los Angeles Times* said that while "this book may not be the last word on Wild Bill Hickok...it will long be a standard." As it turned out, it wasn't even the last word on Hickok by Rosa. Before his death in 2015, the Englishman produced a dozen more books about various aspects of Wild Bill and on the mythos of gunfighters and the Wild West in general. "It is my hope," Rosa said, "that Hickok emerges as a man and not a legend."

Unfortunately for Rosa, the very medium that inspired his passion has pretty much stomped all over his hope. Hollywood's Hickok has ranged from the knight in shining buckskin, portrayed by Gary Cooper in *The Plainsman* (1936) to the crabby opium-smoking tough guy who has a phobia about people touching his hat, portrayed by Jeff Bridges in *Wild Bill* (1995). On television's HBO series *Deadwood*, Keith Carradine's Hickok appeared in only four of the series' 36 episodes, which is just as well unless you like your Wild Bill on the cartoonish side. *The Adventures of Wild Bill Hickok*, which ran for eight seasons and 113 episodes on ABC and CBS in the 1950s, was clearly a kids-oriented shoot-'em-up. The show's star was Guy Madison, a veteran of seemingly dozens of B-movie Westerns. But his Hickok was so antiseptically clean, he could have worked in a microchip factory when not running down desperadoes.

The closest to the real Wild Bill, at least in terms of moral ambivalence, may be actor Sam Shepard's Hickok in the 2013 made-for-television film *Purgatory*. Wild Bill is marshal in a town full of dead Wild West legends who have to behave—meaning no gunplay—for a prescribed number of years before they can move on to Heaven. Hickok risks eternal damnation to defend the town against a gang of vicious outlaws. Putting the real Wild Bill somewhere between angelic and hellish seems about right, as I suppose it does for most people.

So far, however, TV and the movies have yet to fulfill Joseph G. Rosa's hope of depicting a man instead of a legend. Or as Tom Selleck's character, Matthew Quigley, puts it to the evil Australian land baron before the climactic gunfight in 1990's *Quigley Down Under:* "This ain't Dodge City, and you ain't Bill Hickok." How true.

Chapter 12 Notes

George Custer's funeral *Harper's Weekly, Oct. 27, 1877, p. 841.*

The ceremony took Ibid.

"It may be" Thom Hatch, *The Last Days of George Armstrong Custer*, p. 201.

She was valedictorian Marguerite Merrington (ed.) *The Custer Story*, p. 43.

After learning, 10 Elizabeth B. Custer, *"Boots and Saddles,"* p. 269.

And then she James Donovan, *A Terrible Glory*, p. 342.

She decided to *Cincinnati Enquirer*, March 23, 1877, p. 2.

She published three *Detroit Free Press*, April 5, 1885, p. 24.

Libbie supplemented her *Buffalo (N.Y.) Courier*, March 15, 1892, p. 9.

A shining—Merrington, op. cit., p. 327.

Custer's widow had Louis S. Warren, *Buffalo Bill's America*, p. 274.

As an 1897 *Fort Wayne (Ind.) News*, May 21, 1897, p. 5.

In early December "Frederick Whittaker's Custer," *The Nation*, Vol. 24, No. 612 (March 22, 1877), p. 180.

Whittaker laid it Frederick Whittaker, *A Complete Life of General George A. Custer*, p. 1; p. 628, p. 608.

Critics were generally *Chicago Tribune*, Dec. 22, 1876, p. 9*; Fall River (Ma.) Daily Evening News*, Dec. 18, 1876, p. 2.

But Whittaker's charges *The Examiner* (London, England), April 14, 1877, p. 25.

Benteen and President *New York Daily Herald*, Nov. 16, 1877, pp. 3-4.

When the proceedings Donovan, op. cit., p. 378.

To this day, *Philadelphia Times*, March 30, 1879, p. 7.

Benteen remained in Howard Kazanjian and Chris Enss, *None Wounded, None Missing, All Dead*, p. 162.

But with her Frederic Van de Water, *Glory-Hunter: A Life of General Custer*, p. 17.

Van de Water Ibid., p. 370.

Van de Water's *Sioux City (Iowa) Journal*, Dec. 1, 1934, p. 5; *Brooklyn Times*

Union, Nov. 7, 1934, p. 6.

The influence of Van de Water, op. cit., p. 13.

In 2015 The Hatch, op. cit., p. 271.

"The only regret" James Welch and Paul Stekler. *Killing Custer: The Battle of the Little Bighorn and the Fate of the Plains Indians*, p. 287.

But Charley didn't (Reno) *Nevada State Journal*, Nov. 18, 1879, p. 1.

In 1903, the *Abilene Weekly Reflector*, Sept. 2, 1909, p. 1.

The covetous folks *Lead (SD) Daily Call*, June 19, 1953, p. 1.

As Agnes Lake, *Jersey City Morning Telegraph*, Aug. 23, 1907.

Still, Bill's death Joseph G. Rosa, *They Called Him Wild Bill*, p. 308.

In the summer Ibid.; *Black Hills Weekly Times*, Sept. 7, 1877, p. 1.

She also may *Cheyenne Daily Leader*, Aug. 3, 1880, p. 3.

Martha Jane Canary *Chicago Tribune*, March 6, 1994, p. 25.

Contemporary newspapers and *Chicago Tribune*, March 3, 1901, p, 2; Watson Parker, Deadwood, the Golden Years, p. 198.

In any event Daniel Boorstin, *The Image, or What Happened to the American Dream*, pp. 57-58.

Whatever she was *Daily Deadwood Pioneer Times*, Aug. 22, 1925, p. 1.

Someone suggested it Russell Thorp to Fred M. Mazzula, Aug. 31, 1960, Vincent Mercaldo Collection, 1850-1945, Buffalo Bill Center of the West Archives.

Two years later *Black Hills Union* (Rapid City, SD), Aug. 14, 1903, p. 4.

But the New *New York Times*, Aug, 2, 1903, p. 2.

The best that *New York Daily Herald*, March 2, 1877, p. 2.

Roughly a half-century *Fort Worth Record-Telegraph*, Dec. 24, 1926, p. 1.

It fell to "Joseph Rosa on Obsession, Possession and Wild Bill," *True West*, Vol. 48, No. 6 (August/September 2001), p. 59.

The book was immediately *New York Times*, May 31, 1964, p. 90; *Los Angeles Times*, April 12, 1964, p. 467; *Great Falls (MT) Tribune*, March 8, 1964, p. 48.

CHAPTER 13

"Is that you, Buck?"

Old outlaws and a "dirty little coward"

Sometime on the snowy morning of Feb. 16, 1903, a bald and portly 59-year-old man in the small farm village of Lee's Summit, Missouri, picked up the receiver from a telephone box and made a long-distance call. The fellow he was calling was a mustachioed and thin 60-year-old man in Kearney, Missouri, about 40 miles away.

"Is that you, Buck?" the caller asked. "Yes," replied the other man. "Is that you, Curiosity?" It was the first time in more than 26 years that Cole Younger had spoken to Frank James. Employing the wariness that had through decades of violent living kept them breathing long enough to get old, the two referred to each other by the code names they had used as Confederate guerillas during the Civil War. No sense taking chances when you can't see who you're talking to and might not recognize them anyway after a quarter of a century.

Once satisfied that each was the genuine article, the two shared some chuckles over old memories and agreed to meet that night in Independence, about halfway between Lee's Summit and Kearney. Cole had a bone to pick with Frank.

The last time the two had seen each other was in a rain-soaked patch of woods on the banks of the Blue Earth River, a bit southwest of Mankato, Minnesota. Less than a week before, on Sept. 7, 1876, Frank, Cole and six other men had robbed the bank in Northfield, Minnesota. Four men had been killed, including bank employee Joseph Heywood, who had refused to open the bank's vault and was shot in the head by an enraged Frank James. In addition to the murder of Heywood inside the bank, an unarmed farmer and two of the robbers were killed in a fierce gunfight in the streets outside between the gang and Northfield's citizenry. Cole, Frank and Cole's brothers Jim and Bob had all been wounded. They got away, temporarily, with $26.70 ($679 in 2022)

That came to about 42 cents ($11) for each of the cumulative 63 years the Younger Brothers spent in a Minnesota prison for the crimes. Through all their years behind bars, the Youngers steadfastly refused to rat out Frank and Jesse James as having been at Northfield. The Youngers' loyalty was all the more remarkable in light of the fact that the James Boys had left them in the woods because Bob Younger's wound was so bad it was slowing down the escape.

"Be true to your friends, if the heavens fall," was Cole's written response to questions about which of the robbers had killed Heywood. As a result, although he weathered some legal problems of his own in Missouri and Alabama, Frank James had escaped any legal ramifications for his part in the Northfield robbery. But Cole wasn't sore about that.

What vexed him was a rumor than Frank had accepted a lucrative offer to appear—as Cole Younger—in a play called *Younger Brothers, Bank Robbers*. "Frank James is not going on the stage in a play with my name on it," Cole told a reporter the day after meeting with Frank. "He told me to tell you that the report he was is a malicious lie...Frank swore to me that he had never intended to go on the stage. I will not permit any play to be used with my name on it or represent my deeds...my name is my trademark and no man or set of men shall use it on the stage or anywhere else."

Unless of course the men doing so were Frank James and Cole Younger themselves.

The Youngers had not been taken easily after the Northfield job. By the time they finally surrendered, after a two-week chase and an intense shootout with a pursuing posse, Jim had received four bullet wounds, including two in the back and one that carried away part of his lower jaw;

Bob was shot through a lung and already had a crippled right arm from the fight at Northfield, and Cole had been hit eight times, including behind the right eye.

They were treated with surprising humanity, considering their crimes. The Youngers reciprocated by courteously and patiently enduring a steady stream of sight-seers. The tourists first paraded past them while they were still in their makeshift hospital beds, and later while in their cells in the Faribault, Minnesota jail, where they were held awaiting trial. Some of the visitors brought little gifts such as tobacco and handkerchiefs, especially for Bob. At 23, he was the youngest of the Youngers. In conversations, the brothers cannily evoked sympathy by playing up their upbringing in Missouri by pious and honest parents. They also forthrightly took responsibility for their actions, even while implying they had been traumatized into a life of crime by the horrors their family suffered during the Civil War.

The Minnesota newspapers wrote of them as if they were some exotic species. Cole could actually quote the poet Lord Byron and was "calm and thoughtful," and Jim "has an expression of shrewdness." Bob was "young and handsome, courageous and frank," and "has a peculiarly winning and gentle voice." Their popularity, however, went only so far: As a special excursion train of visitors left Faribault to return to Minneapolis-St. Paul, a reporter polled the passengers as to the fate they favored for the Youngers. There were 71 votes to hang them, six not to hang them, three unsure—and one young woman who voted to "hang all except Bob."

As facetious as it was, the poll reflected a widespread sentiment. There was serious talk of lynching the Youngers, as well as serious fears the James brothers or other outlaw associates would try to spring them. Security was so tight and tense that a jumpy jail guard shot and killed a Faribault policeman who approached the jail early one morning and failed to give the necessary password.

The necktie party talk was fueled by a relatively new law in Minnesota. Under it, defendants who pleaded guilty to murder could not be executed.

The idea behind the law was to save the state the expense of protracted death penalty cases. What it saved was the Youngers. "Any innocent soul who supposes the robbers can be adequately punished labors under a grave mistake," the *St. Paul Pioneer Press* opined. "Their lives are as safe as that of the saintliest person in the state."

The newspaper was right. Faced with overwhelming evidence, as well as another state law that allowed for them to be convicted of the killings of the bank worker and the farmer even if they hadn't pulled the triggers themselves, the Youngers pleaded guilty to robbery, assault and murder. They were sentenced to life in prison. None of them spoke during the proceedings other than to enter their guilty pleas, nor showed too much anxiety over their fates. "I have seen a good deal of the world," Cole shrugged after the sentencing, "and might as well retire anyway."

The sentences mollified all but the most bloodthirsty. "It would have been gratifying to have seen the death penalty inflicted in punishment of their crimes," editorialized the *Chicago Tribune*, "but they have been overtaken by a doom scarcely less terrible and appalling to men of their years—a life imprisonment which no governor of Minnesota will ever dare shorten by as much as a day."

The Youngers' prison was on the outskirts of Stillwater, a town on the St. Croix River, about 25 miles east of Minneapolis-St. Paul. Finished in 1853, the prison was crowded, dark and damp. Each cell was amply supplied with cockroaches and bedbugs, and the food sometimes featured ingredients that could move around on their own. Even so, it was a fairly progressive lockup by Gilded Age standards. The facility included a library, classrooms, a yarn manufacturing plant and eventually America's first prison newspaper. Convicts who behaved could have their sentences reduced by up to 25 percent—unless their surname was Younger.

Cole was initially assigned his own rifle-toting guard who had orders to shoot to kill at the first sign of an escape attempt. But it was wasted taxpayers' money: Cole turned out to be a model prisoner. He graduated from a job making washtubs to running the library, then became the head nurse at the prison hospital. He graciously granted interviews to reporters, expressed repentance for his actions to visiting reform groups and delivered sermons during prison religious services. He even allowed the bumps on his head to be analyzed by a professor of phrenology—the 19th century fad of discerning character by charting the geography of the human skull. The phrenologist proclaimed Cole had the head of "a national leader," and contended that had Younger attended West Point, he would have doubtless become a top general.

Bob and Jim, however, did not fare as well. Bob, who took a bullet through a lung during the shootout before their surrender, developed tuberculosis and died in 1889, at the age of 36. He was denied a pardon, even when doctors pronounced he had only weeks to live. Jim, who had lost a sizeable chunk of his lower jaw to a bullet, could not eat solid food and had a speech impediment. A voracious reader, he assumed Cole's job as prison librarian. He adopted a canary he named Dickie, which he taught to do tricks. But moody before he even got to prison, he was now often sullen and depressed, and avoided visitors when he could. He also gradually embraced socialism, not a popular political perspective with prison or other government officials.

In 1882, Cole had a visitor who was uninterested in his head bumps but very interested in getting Jim, Bob and Cole out of prison. Warren Bronaugh was a former Confederate soldier and Missouri farmer who one day happened to see a picture of Cole in a newspaper. He recognized him as the man who in 1862 had saved his life by stopping Bronaugh from riding straight into a nest of Union soldiers. The farmer told Cole he would do whatever he could to get the Youngers sprung. For the next two decades, Bronaugh would spend most of his time and money writing hundreds of letters, incessantly lobbying politicians in Minnesota and Washington and haranguing editorial writers in his efforts to win paroles or pardons for the Youngers.

It was a formidable task. There were successes. Stephen Elkins, a U.S. senator from West Virginia, joined the effort. Elkins had been a pro-Union teacher of Jim and Cole, and Cole had saved him from being hanged by guerillas during the war. Ignatius Donnelly, a well-known Minnesota congressman, also became a supporter. But for every small victory, there were sizeable setbacks. In 1886, a story that had originally appeared in an 1875 book about the Youngers began circulating in newspapers. The story was that during the war, Cole had lined up 15 Union prisoners and then killed them while trying to see how many men an Enfield rifle bullet could pass through.

"...It is false from beginning to end," Cole protested in a letter to Minnesota Gov. William Marshall. "The whole thing was so absurd that I never supposed any sensible man would believe it. I had always supposed the story was gotten up by some reporter as a burlesque of the sensational newspapers."

Whether he believed it or not, Marshall, like other Minnesota governors before and after him, deemed pardons for the Youngers too hot a political potato to even consider. But in 1897, the task was handed off to a newly legislated three-man Board of Pardons. At the request of Stillwater Prison Warden Henry Wolfer, Cole composed his version of what happened at Northfield to present to the board. Some of it was true, and some needed an entire shaker of salt to consume. Cole contended the gang had agreed among themselves before the robbery to shoot only in self-defense, and blamed the killings on the questionable "fact" that the three robbers who entered the bank were drunk.

Circumstances aside, the key sticking point was the Youngers' refusal to say who killed bank employee Joseph Heywood and bystander Nicholas Gustafson. A case could be made that Gustafson's death was caused by a ricocheting bullet, although lots of witnesses' fingers pointed at Cole as the killer. But Gustafson was a newly arrived immigrant who spoke no English and was thus callously dismissed by many Minnesotans as far less important than the heroic Heywood, a pillar of the community. Heywood's murderer had to be brought to account.

"Good faith on their part demands that they disclose the name of the man who killed cashier Heywood, and that man be brought back to Minnesota and punished," Faribault Mayor A.D. Keyes testified. "If the murderer was Frank James, as we are led to believe, then he has never suffered anything for the crime. He has never even been imprisoned, and it is no more than right that he should suffer the penalty in some measure at least."

The pardons board unanimously, if somewhat reluctantly, agreed. It took four more years before Minnesotans' memories, and demands for Frank James' scalp, faded enough for the board to grant paroles to the Youngers. But on the stiflingly hot Sunday morning of July 14, 1901, Cole and Jim Younger left the prison in which they had spent 8,999 days. Give or take a day.

"Twenty-five years ago, the Youngers were outlaws," the *Minneapolis Star-Tribune* noted. "For 25 years they have been exemplary prisoners... now they go forth as men who have been mentally, morally and physically reconstructed under the penal system of the United States. What will be the result?"

It would be decidedly mixed. After two weeks of semi-adjusting to a strange new world full of marvelous and intimidating wonders—electric streetcars, automobiles, telephones, phonographs—Cole and Jim began their new lives as reconstructed members of the workforce. The two main conditions of their paroles were that they had to stay in Minnesota, and they could not exploit their celebrity status for profit. Neither could prospective employers, which considerably narrowed the job offers they could accept.

So state officials settled them in the slightly bizarre jobs of peddling tombstones for a St. Paul company. For $60 a month (about $1,900 in 2022), Cole and Jim drove one-horse carriages around the state, stopping at farmhouses and in towns, soliciting customers to invest in what Cole came to euphemistically refer to as "future memorials."

But while lots of people were eager to chat with the famous former outlaws, they were decidedly less eager to buy tombstones from them.

Worse, the long drives began to wear down Jim physically and mentally. After an injury, he switched to working in a cigar store. That resulted in a steady stream of ex-cons and bums coming by to beg or borrow money from a "successful" former inmate.

The worst problem for Jim Younger, however, was falling in love. During his last year in prison, Jim met Alix Muller, an attractive young reporter for the *St. Paul Pioneer Press*. After winning over her family, the two planned to marry on Jim's release. But they ran smack into an arcane state law concerning parolees. Under Minnesota law, a man on parole was legally dead. And since dead men could not marry, neither could parolees.

In late 1901, the Youngers applied for pardons, a condition that would remove Jim and Alix's obstacle. The application was denied. Jim fought deep depression for most of 1902. Then in mid-October, he told a friend "I am a mere nothing in the world's affairs...I'm a ghost, the ghost of Jim Younger." Two days later, he killed himself with a bullet to the brain.

The Minnesota Pardons Board decided Jim's death was enough punishment for Cole. On Feb. 4, 1903, he was granted a pardon, with two conditions attached. One was that he leave Minnesota and never come back. The second was that he never "exhibit himself or allow himself to be exhibited, as an actor or participant, in any public performance, museum, circus, theater, opera house or any other place of public amusement or assembly where a charge is made for admission."

Cole signed his agreement to the conditions, settled his affairs in St. Paul, and headed home to Missouri—and a career in show business.

After the debacle at Northfield and their departure from the Youngers, Frank and Jesse James ran home to Mother. More accurately, they rode—long and hard. Although their precise route isn't known, a best guess is they moved west through Minnesota into the Dakota Territory, then south into Iowa and maybe Nebraska. Various accounts have them traveling by river barge part of the way, or swinging through Kansas and into the Indian Territory (now Oklahoma) and sneaking into Missouri from the south.

Both brothers were wounded, Frank in the knee from the fight in Northfield, Jesse from a shotgun blast in the shoulder during a skirmish with one of the scores of posses chasing them. At one point they had to give up their horses and rigs at a guarded river crossing so they could slip past a picket line. Making saddles from grain bags filled with hay and rope stirrups, they stole two sturdy wagon horses and rode them for 150 miles before their mounts broke down. Then they stole two fine-looking steeds only to discover one was blind and the other half-blind. They rode for hours at a stretch, stopping only long enough at isolated farmhouses for a bite to eat, a few hours of fitful sleep, or to steal fresh horses.

Even their pursuers were impressed. "Their endurance on horseback for days and nights, wounded and almost starving and without sleep are without parallel in the history of crime," wrote a posse member who chased them for weeks. "Pursued by over one thousand men thirsting for their blood, they ran the gauntlets of Minnesota and Dakota for a distance of 490 miles...".

Sometime in early to mid-October 1876, Frank and Jesse made it back to the familiar environs of Clay County, Missouri. They stopped at the family farm to say hello to their mother. Then they periodically shifted from home to temporary refuges with friends and sympathizers, often sleeping in the woods near their benefactors' residences for fear of being trapped if someone snitched. Even on their home turf, they couldn't relax.

On the evening of November 22, the Younger brothers were spending their third night in Stillwater Prison. William M. "Boss" Tweed, the corrupt former political czar of New York City, was spending his last night aboard the U.S. Naval frigate *Franklin*, on his way back to prison in New York after having briefly escaped to Spain. P.T. Barnum was advertising a new illustrated book he had written for children on how to collect wild animals. Students at Princeton and Yale were excitedly awaiting the nation's first Thanksgiving Day football game, scheduled for the following week. And Americans were impatiently but peacefully still awaiting the result of the Hayes-Tilden presidential election that had concluded two weeks previous.

At the James Farm, Frank had stepped outside into the cold, rainy evening when he caught a glimpse of men moving in the trees around the house. He quickly fired into the air to alert Jesse inside, then took a few shots at the posse behind the trees. The brothers managed to get to their horses, mainly because some posse members refused to even fire at them, let alone close in. "Come on, you cowardly sons of bitches," Frank or Jesse shouted as they rode away. (To rub salt in the posse members' wounded pride, county officials later refused to pay them.)

Despite periodic reports of sightings (one of which had Jesse playing poker in Las Vegas, New Mexico, with Billy the Kid), various crimes attributed to them (a string of train robberies in Colorado) and even accounts of their deaths (the boys' mom claimed Frank had died in Texas of tuberculosis), for the next three years Frank and Jesse James disappeared.

More accurately, they hid in plain sight. Even more accurately, they hid in plain sight in Tennessee: Here's Frank, alias "B.J. Woodson," winning ribbons at regional fairs for his prize Poland China hogs. There's Jesse, aka "J.D. Howard," winning races with his prize horse Red Fox. Both men and their wives would have children born in the state. Both were friends with men who were in local law enforcement or government. Both frequented the faro games around Nashville, often together. And nobody knew who they really were. That is, Frank explained in an 1882 newspaper interview, "nobody but those who were members of my household or Jesse's."

Frank arrived in Nashville in mid-1877 after hiding out for a time with relatives in Kentucky. He rented a farm and, by his account at least, worked it like a real farmer," seldom failing to put in my full ten hours per day in the fields." He also hired out as a timber hauler for a local lumber company, "taking my meals in the woods with the darkies and never giving less than a full hand's work." He became a Methodist and gave up swearing. And, he said, he was happy. "Those years of quiet upright life were...the happiest I have spent since my boyhood, notwithstanding the hard labor attending them. My old life grew more detestable the further I got from it."

Jesse rented a farm as well near Waverly, Tennessee, about 75 miles west of Nashville, before relocating to the Nashville area. To neighbors, Frank "seemed to be a man of education and was really fond of reading newspapers." As for Jesse, "there was always something mysterious about the man and he was regarded with suspicion" when he first arrived. A doctor who treated Frank for what might have been malaria noted that "Mr. Howard (Jesse) was absent frequently for as much as three weeks at a time and didn't seem to do any work whatever."

In fact, Jesse was working—at putting together a new gang. He was bored with "normal" life, uncomfortable being out of the public spotlight and disdainful of the concept of actually earning a living. In the late summer of 1879, he frequently visited Southwest Missouri to recruit men who had been too young to fight in the war but grew up with the romanticized tales of the fabled James-Younger gang.

His recruits included two of his cousins, Wood and Clarence Hite; Ed Miller, brother of the Clell Miller who had been killed at Northfield; Bill Ryan, an Irish-born tough guy with an overfondness for strong drink; Dick Liddil, a convicted horse thief; "Windy Jim" Cummins, a likeable but jumpy fellow who made Jesse nervous, and Tucker Basham, who was so dim he made the rest of the gang look like Rhodes Scholars. The gang's aptitude for outlawry was amply summed up by the fact one of them once showed up for a train robbery with no guns.

On Oct. 8, 1879, Jesse and five of the new men rode into Glendale, Missouri, a smudge of a settlement about 15 miles east of Kansas City and on the Chicago and Alton Railroad line. The gang rounded up a dozen or so locals and herded them into the train depot, where Jesse stuck a pistol barrel into the mouth of the telegraph operator and convinced him to flag down the next train. The bandits believed it was carrying nearly $400,000 in gold and silver bullion (about $10.7 million today). But they had the wrong train, and made off with only about $6,000 ($160,000) instead.

Other than the express car attendant, who was smacked by a pistol for trying to sneak off with the safe's contents, no one was hurt. The train's passengers were left alone. Before he rode off, Jesse gave the telegraph operator a press release. "We are boys that are hard to handle, and we'll make it hot for the party that ever tries to take us," the message read. It was signed with six aliases—and "the James Brothers --" even though Frank had nothing to do with it.

Jesse wanted America to know he was back in business. But America wasn't the same country in the autumn of 1879 that it had been in the autumn of 1876, when the James Boys began their three-year hiatus. Then, they were often viewed in the South, as "Knights of the Lost Cause." Many people saw Jesse and Frank as striking back at the North's vengeance-driven Reconstruction policies and an influx of rapacious Yankee carpetbaggers. They were thus willing and sometimes eager to offer the outlaws food, shelter and protection from the authorities.

But the protracted and negotiated election of Rutherford B. Hayes as president in the months following the Northfield raid had ended Reconstruction. The federal government largely halted its efforts to protect the constitutional rights African Americans ostensibly won after the Civil War. Southern Democrats, most of whom had supported secession and the Confederacy, regained control of the region. "Jim Crow" laws that formally institutionalized a racially based caste system were just over the horizon. The South's "Lost Cause" wasn't so lost anymore. In 1869, a train robbery could be glossed over with a veneer of "striking a blow against Yankee oppression." In 1879, it was just robbery.

"It is a shame and disgrace that such things occur in our midst," a Missouri newspaper fumed the day after the Glendale job. "The only way to stop such hellish deeds is to give the perpetrators hell—shoot 'em down wherever they are found."

In 1880, Missourians elected a new governor. Thomas T. Crittenden was a hybrid Southern politician—a Democrat who was pro-Union. During the war, he had been a Union Army officer and the state's attorney general.

After the war, he served two terms in Congress. As governor, he vowed in his inaugural address to rid the state of its image as a robbers' roost by getting rid of the robbers. "Missouri cannot be the home and abiding place of lawlessness of any character," he said. "...When crime is committed, pursuit and punishment will be inflicted under the forms of law, without fear, favor or affection."

Jesse James was not impressed. He had followed the Glendale train robbery with a series of jobs in 1880 that included the audacious holdup of a tourist stagecoach visiting the Mammoth Cave in Kentucky. Two months after Crittenden's speech, he and two others made off with an Army engineers' payroll of $5,200 ($136,500 in 2022) near Muscle Shoals, Alabama. But he was increasingly concerned about the trustworthiness of his new gang. Tucker Basham had been caught after the Glendale job, and sung like a canary. Bill Ryan was arrested after the Alabama robbery, and his arrest came just outside Nashville, not far from the homes of Jesse and Frank.

Fearful Ryan would turn informant, Jesse decided to leave Tennessee. This time, Frank could not avoid getting involved. "Try as we might to break off from our Bohemian life," he said, clearly speaking with an editorial "we" and not for Jesse, "something would always occur to drive us back. It was with a sense of despair that I drove away from our little house."

Driven back to the "Bohemian life," or else just broke, Frank joined Jesse and three others to rob a train near Winston, Missouri, about 60 miles northeast of Kansas City, on July 15, 1881. It happened to be just one day after Lincoln County Sheriff Pat Garrett gunned down Billy the Kid at Fort Sumner, New Mexico. The Kid was the only Western outlaw who came close to matching Jesse's national notoriety. Now Jesse had the field to himself.

Sporting a full beard, dyed black, Jesse killed the train conductor during the robbery, and he or Frank killed a passenger. Just why is disputed. Gang members and some witnesses said the killings were accidents, the results of errant shots at the ceiling that were meant to intimidate. Others said that while the passenger's death may have been accidental, the conductor was shot deliberately. The conductor, it turned out, was part of the 1875 raid on the James farm that resulted in the death of Jesse and Frank's half-brother and maiming of their mother. Either way, two men were dead, all for a grand haul of $600 ($15,800 in 2022.)

The killings intensified Missouri's national image as a dangerous place, which naturally didn't help attract visitors or outside business investment. "This fresh outrage once more calls public attention to the lawlessness which goes unrebuked in Missouri," warned the *Chicago Tribune,* "and if something is not promptly done to check it, then travelers should give that state a wide berth."

The robbery also deepened anger within the state against law enforcement's seeming impotence. "The hunt for the Winston train robbers is rapidly degenerating into a farce," complained the *Kansas City Star*. "... Jesse James and his gang will continue to rob and kill until old age palsies their arms...They will only be captured when a big price (is) put upon their heads or when the entire country arouses as at Northfield and overwhelms them with an avalanche of wrath."

The chances of an avalanche of Missouri citizens' wrath appeared slim. While many Southwest Missouri residents had once protected Frank and Jesse out of friendship or empathy, they now did so out of fear. As one old timer who had sold horses to the gang put it, "He (Jesse) comes along with his gang and asks for food and lodging. So you suppose I refuse and have my house and barn burned and my stock and maybe my family killed? Not much. I simply say 'glad to see you Jesse, come in and make yourself to home. How are the children and the old lady?'"

But the idea of posting a big reward for Frank and Jesse had potential. It might not only encourage the average Missourian to get over his or her trepidation, but might also spur a gang member to turn traitor. Ten days after the Winston robbery, Gov. Crittenden met secretly in St. Louis with a dozen railroad and express company executives. At meeting's end, the railroad poohbahs agreed to fund $10,000 rewards for the capture of Frank and Jesse (about $262,000 in 2022), and $5,000 for each of the other participants in the Glendale and Winston robberies.

Announcement of the rewards irritated Jesse. He responded with another train robbery. On September 7, Frank, Jesse and four others piled rocks on a curve in the track at a spot called Blue Cut, not far from Independence, Missouri. This time, they robbed the passengers, and made a show of it. When the brakeman said he only had 50 cents, Jesse gave him a dollar. A woman fainted; Jesse helped revive her with a wet handkerchief and returned the two dollars she had given up. He gave the engineer two dollars and told him to "buy a drink in the morning and drink it for Jesse James." He even offered to help remove the rocks from the track. The offer was declined, the engineer politely explaining he would rather the gang just depart quickly.

Jesse made it clear the robbery was as much an act of defiance as a profit-making enterprise, although the gang still managed to collect about $3,000 in cash, watches and jewelry. "They can't stop us from robbing trains; it's our business," he told his captive audience. "We could do it just the same if the baggage car was full of soldiers...If we are going to be wicked, we might as well make a good job of it." As he departed, he bowed deeply and said "good bye, this is the last time you will see Jesse James." He was right.

By the beginning of 1882, Jesse James' "new" gang had disintegrated. After the Blue Cut robbery, brother Frank moved east, first back to Tennessee and then to North Carolina before settling, uneasily, in Lynchburg, Virginia. Tucker Basham and Bill Ryan had been arrested. Dick Liddil, assisted by a young fellow named Bob Ford, had killed Wood Hite, Jesse's cousin, in a fight over the affections of Ford's sister. Liddil eventually decided to cooperate with law enforcement officials rather than risk Jesse's wrath. Jesse himself killed Ed Miller when he decided Miller talked too much. Windy Jim Cummins vamoosed, lest he wind up like Ed Miller.

That left two brothers. The aforementioned Ed Miller had introduced Jesse James to Charley and Bob Ford in the summer of 1879. The Fords were part of a large Virginia family from that settled after the war in Richmond, Missouri, about 25 miles from the James farm. Jesse took an immediate liking to Charley, but not to Bob. "Jesse never trusted Bob," Frank James recalled. "He loved Charley, but always suspected Bob of treachery." For his part, the 20-year-old Bob had little respect for the 34-year-old legend. Jesse, Bob told a reporter, "had outlived his greatness as a bandit...as a leader, he was dead. There were but few men who would place themselves in his clutches. Even his brother Frank kept continuously hundreds of miles away...it was his (Jesse's) tyranny among his fellows that wrecked his empire."

Despite his increasing paranoia, Jesse continued to hide in plain sight after leaving Tennessee. He audaciously moved his wife and two children to Kansas City, even though he was well-known enough in the area to be recognized by many people. The Jameses then moved to St. Joseph, about 75 miles north. Charley Ford, who had become a semi-permanent guest, moved with the family. In March 1882, Charley accompanied Jesse to Nebraska to case banks in several small towns. On their return, however, Jesse changed his plans and decided to rob a bank in Platte City, Missouri, 25 miles north of Kansas City, on April 4. A big murder trial was under way there, Jesse told both Fords, and with the town distracted, the bank would be easy pickings for the trio.

But Bob Ford had plans of his own. He had met secretly in January with Gov. Crittenden and Clay County Sheriff Henry Timberlake, an ex-Confederate guerilla. Crittenden, Bob maintained later, promised him $10,000 ($262,000 in 2022) each for Jesse and Frank, dead or alive. Bob figured "dead" was a much safer route to take, and talked Charley into coming along for the ride. The brothers waited for their chance.

It came at the Jameses' St. Joseph residence on April 3, the day before the planned Platte City bank robbery. It was a warm morning, and Jesse doffed his coat and vest while talking with the Fords. Concerned that a neighbor might glimpse through a window and wonder why "Mr. Howard" was toting two .45 caliber revolvers around his waist, Jesse also removed his guns. He turned his back on the brothers and climbed onto a chair to dust some wall hangings. Then he heard the familiar "click" of a pistol hammer behind him.

"When he turned his back, I gave my brother the wink," Charley testified at a coroner's jury that afternoon. "My brother had a Smith & Wesson and could get (his gun) out sooner than I could. I had my finger on the trigger but my brother fired first and I saw that it was a death shot and did not fire." The shot, from less than four feet away, caught Jesse below the right ear and lodged in his brain. He lived long enough for his wife Zee and children to rush from the adjoining kitchen at the sound of the gunfire, but died in his wife's arms without saying anything. The Fords lamely protested a pistol "accidentally had gone off." "Yes," Zee replied, "I guess it went off on purpose."

The legal system moved swiftly in the case of Bob and Charley Ford. They were indicted for murder and candidly confessed they had planned to shoot an unarmed man in the back. "I knew he was quicker than me and I wouldn't try it while he had his arms on," Charley testified. "He was so watchful no man could get the drop on him." The jury dutifully returned guilty verdicts; the judge just as dutifully sentenced them to hang, and Gov. Crittenden pardoned them within hours of the sentencing.

"I have no excuses to make," the governor said, "no apologies to render to any living man for the part I played in this bloody drama." Crittenden pointed out there was a chance some innocent person might have been killed had the Platte City robbery occurred. "The life of one honest law-abiding man however humble is worth more to society, to a state, than a legion of Jesse Jameses."

Crittenden's end-justifies-the-means stance was generally supported, even if the means made a lot of people squeamish. "In the light of all moral reasoning the shooting was unjustifiable," the *St. Joseph Weekly Transcript* philosophized. "But the law is vindicated and the $10,000 reward offered by the state for the body of the brigand, dead or alive, will doubtless go to the man who had the courage to draw a revolver on the notorious outlaw even when his back was turned."

The Fords, however, apparently saw only a portion of the reward. There were believable stories that Clay County Sheriff Henry Timberlake and Kansas City Police Commissioner Enos Craig, who had been in on the plan, also got shares. The rest of the brothers' lives didn't go so well either. After appearing briefly with Bob in a show called *I Shot Jesse James*, Charley contracted tuberculosis and became a morphine addict. He killed himself slightly more than two years after he helped kill Jesse James.

Bob exhibited himself on stages and in dime museums for a while, and served briefly as a policeman in Las Vegas, New Mexico. But he hurriedly left town after being challenged to a duel by a former pal of Billy the Kid, and moved to Colorado. There he opened a dance hall in the mining boomtown of Creede and replaced it with a tent saloon when the dance hall burned down. One afternoon in 1892 a fellow named Ed O'Kelley shot-gunned Bob to death for no discernable reason. O'Kelley did 10 years for the murder, and got out in time to be shot to death himself by an Oklahoma City policeman. Justice had a funny way of moving full circle in the Wild West.

While the Fords were awaiting trial, Jesse James was being planted on the family farm. The funeral service was held in Kearney, about four miles from the farm. Hundreds of friends, acquaintances and perfect strangers lined up to see the outlaw lying in an open metal casket. Several reporters and detectives checked the corpse against known photographs of Jesse, just to make sure it was the right man being buried. The Baptist minister who gave the eulogy skipped over details of Jesse's life and character and focused instead on the idea that everyone dies, sometimes unexpectedly.

Jesse's mother Zerelda so long and loudly lamented her lost son that a reporter snidely suggested her performance, "had she been educated for the stage, would have placed her in the first rank of tragediennes." Jesse's remains were transported to the farm and buried there, it was said, so Zerelda could protect it from body snatchers. "Because my darling boy was too confiding, he was shot down like a dog," she wailed, "by a man he had fed and trusted, who did it for money, money, money!"

Later that day, Zerelda stopped lamenting long enough to make some money herself by selling sell a painting in the house to a reporter for $10 ($262 in 2022), after he bargained her down from $50. (Within 18 months, she would be charging tourists 25 cents ($6.61) to view the grave and listen to tales about her boys' adventures and travails. Another two bits secured visitors an actual pebble from the grave. When the pebbles ran low, there were plenty more in the nearby streambed.)

At one point during the day, Zerelda loudly proclaimed "thank God Frank is beyond their reach; he is dead." But Frank James wasn't dead. He was in Virginia, thinking hard about what to do with the rest of his life.

Frank was tired. "I am tired of this life of night-riding and day-hiding," he told a St. Louis reporter in September, 1882, "tired of seeing Judas in the face of every friend...tired of the saddle, the revolver and the cartridge belt...and I want to see if there is not some way out of it."

Left unsaid was his desire that "the way out" include not being shot by a government-approved assassin; not being sent back to Minnesota to face murder charges from the Northfield robbery, and in fact not being too inconvenienced at all. In a long interview, he played up his virtuous and hard-working life in Tennessee and declined to mention his roles in the Winston and Blue Cut train robberies. And with either remarkable hypocrisy or a wicked sense of humor, he added "I always held that there are few crimes in the world more hideous or dastardly than the killing of any man for money."

Even as he talked to the reporter, however, Frank's "way out" was being paved by an old friend. John Newman Edwards was perhaps the best-known journalist in Missouri. A former Confederate major with an enviable war record, he was also so ardent a Rebel that at war's end he exiled himself to Mexico for three years rather than formally surrender. He returned in 1867 and began work at newspapers all over the state, moving on when a better job was offered or his crippling battle with alcoholism got him fired.

Throughout his career, he had defended the Jameses and Youngers with over-the-top eloquence and flame-thrower rhetoric. In 1872, for example, he compared the gang to the knights of King Arthur's Round Table. To Edwards, their acts rose above those of common criminals. They performed "feats of stupendous nerve and fearlessness that makes one's hair rise to think of it...with them robbery is but the second thought; the wild drama of the adventure (is) first." When Jesse was killed, Edwards excoriated the entire state: "Tear the two bears from the flag of Missouri. Put thereon...a thief blowing out the brains of an unarmed victim, and a brazen harlot, naked to the waist and splashed to the brows in blood."

Edwards was also a skilled deal maker. In the wake of Jesse's death, he began negotiating with Gov. Crittenden on Frank's behalf. The biggest hurdle was extracting a promise that Frank would not be extradited to Minnesota. Edwards figured Frank's chances with any Missouri jury were pretty good. But Minnesota had revoked the law that banned executions for those who pleaded guilty to murder, which had saved the Youngers from the gallows. If Frank went back, he would most certainly be hanged.

After weeks of talks, a deal was struck. Crittenden's price was a dramatic formal surrender by Frank—to the governor himself. On October 5, seven months after Jesse's murder, Frank and Edwards walked into Crittenden's private Capitol office in Jefferson City. He was expected: Crittenden had invited friends and some prominent citizens to attend without telling them what they were attending. Frank announced himself, then yanked a pistol from its holster and handed it butt-first to the governor. "I make you a present of this revolver," he said, "and you are the first, except myself, who has laid hands on it since 1864." That was a lie, since the gun in question was an 1875-model Remington. But it was after all the gesture that mattered.

Frank was taken to jail in Independence to await trial. He spent his days entertaining friends, well-wishers and tourists, often with his wife and son on hand. One of his visitors was a man Frank didn't recognize, but who recognized him. Frank Wilcox had been the assistant bookkeeper at the Bank of Northfield on Sept. 7, 1876. He had watched the brain of his friend Joe Heywood get splattered on the floor by a slug from Frank James' gun. And he was willing to testify to it. For his part, Frank James claimed he was willing to go to Minnesota as long as he was given a fair trial. "I was never in Minnesota in my life and it is all nonsense to connect me with the Northfield robbery," he said.

As it turned out, Wilcox didn't get to testify and Frank didn't have to go north. Crittenden turned down a request for extradition from Minnesota's governor, on the grounds that Missouri had first dibs on trying Frank James. It did so in August, 1883, when Frank went on trial for the murder of Frank McMillan, the passenger who was killed during the Winston robbery. Under Missouri law, all of the train robbers—who included Frank—were equally culpable for the homicide no matter who had shot whom. The trial was somewhat fittingly held in an opera house to accommodate an overflow crowd. Despite witnesses that included robber-turned-rat Dick Liddil, Frank's seven lawyers and the presence of a heavily armed group of Frank's friends convinced the jury to acquit him.

He was then tried in a federal court in Alabama for the 1881 robbery of the army engineers' payroll at Muscle Shoals. He was quickly acquitted there too, which in this case was fair, because he wasn't there and didn't do it. All other charges pending against him elsewhere were eventually dismissed for lack of evidence or because witnesses had died.

Frank faced one last hurdle. Governor Crittenden left office in January 1885, and since there was no statute of limitations for the Northfield killings, it was possible Crittenden's successor might honor a Minnesota extradition request. But Edwards went to Jefferson City again to have a talk with the new governor, who happened to be a former major general in the Confederate Army. In March, Edwards wrote Frank with a message from Gov. John S. Marmaduke: "Go on a farm and go immediately to work... keep out of the newspapers. Keep away from fairs and fast horses and keep out of sight for a year." Edwards added "under no circumstances will Gov. Marmaduke ever surrender you to the Minnesota authorities." Frank James, robber and killer, was off the legal hook.

For the next 16 years, Frank made a modest living at various jobs in various states. He sold shoes, clerked in a dry goods store, tended horses and worked as a ticket taker at a St. Louis burlesque theater. He rejected numerous financially attractive offers to take advantage of his notoriety by appearing on stage or other public venues.

But that changed in 1901. Encouraged by several politician friends, Frank lobbied for the post of doorkeeper for the Missouri House of Representatives. "I wanted the office (sort of a sergeant-of-arms thing) to show the people I was desirous of holding a place of trust," he explained later. But the politicians who had egged him on to seek the job got cold feet about handing a government job to an ex-train robber. Rebuffed, Frank James was driven to a life of acting.

Sort of. He announced in November, 1901, he had accepted a small role in a touring drama called *Across the Desert*. The 58-year-old Frank explained he was doing it to provide for his family and his empty retirement nest. He added he had declined previous offers because he wanted nothing to do with any show "that idealizes law-breaking and makes a hero out of the lawbreaker...what I appear in will be clean and wholesome." He also made clear that "I do not expect to become an actor in the true sense of the word...my appearance will be more of a personal exhibition than a dramatic performance."

He was right on all counts. His part, which was shoe-horned into what was regarded as a well-written and smartly produced drama, consisted of two scenes and about six lines. Frank portrayed "a prosperous Westerner" who breaks up a quarrel between two other characters. Despite the paucity of his appearances during the play, Frank's name was prominently featured in the production's advance publicity, and he was interviewed in nearly every town on the tour.

The interviews boosted ticket sales, and the only small controversy arose in Canton, Ohio, when two churches and the local YMCA asked the mayor to shut down the show "to prevent the exhibition of this wholesale assassin in this city." The mayor declined, pointing out Frank "had as much right to appear before the public as the reformed gamblers and drunkards who sometimes hold forth in our best churches."

Frank frankly told reporters he liked everything about show business except the actual performing. "I cannot get accustomed to the stage," he said, "and really dread it more than I ever did a fight in the Civil War." Still, he generally got kind reviews, and one of his lines invariably drew big applause: "The man who refuses to forgive his fellow man burns the bridge over which he himself must pass."

Frank continued to perform seasonally in *Across the Desert* and two other plays into early 1903. Cole Younger, meanwhile, was seeking ways to circumvent his pardon's prohibition of making money off his name and past. He had written a self-serving and generously fictionalized autobiography and hoped to go on the lecture circuit to help promote it. But he realized that would be a direct violation of his pardon.

Instead, he worked out a deal with Val Hoffman, the son of a wealthy Chicago brewer, and U.S. Sen. Steve Elkins of West Virginia, whose life Cole had saved during the war. The arrangement called for Hoffman and Elkins (who was in on the deal as a silent partner) to put up $67,000 and buy out the Buckskin Bill Wild West Show from a shady ex-con named H.E. Allot. The refurbished show would be renamed The Great Cole Younger and Frank James Historical Wild West Show. Cole would manage it, for 25 percent of the net profits. Frank would be the arena manager for $300 a week ($9,100 in 2022.) Allot would remain on as assistant manager.

To make it seem as if he were actually trying to adhere to his pardon condition, Cole would not appear in the show. But he would be in the audience for each performance in case customers wanted to shake hands or chat. Frank would play a passenger in a stagecoach robbery act, and ride in the show's grand entrance parade. Minnesota officials fumed at the subterfuge, but took no action other than to write stern letters to Cole. Despite the limited performing roles of the two big names, the show's advertising promised a spectacle of cowboys, cowgirls, American Indians, Hungarian cavalry, Russian Cossacks and Roosevelt Rough Riders, as well as "the two famous men, Cole Younger and Frank James, who will review the rough riders in a gorgeous military tournament." Whatever that was.

Occupying 30 train cars, the tour began promisingly in May in Illinois and headed east. But it soon became a magnet for con artists, grifters and gamblers who attached themselves leech-like to the show, following it from town to town. Many of them, it turned out, were confederates of Allot, the assistant manager and former show owner. In most of the towns in which the production performed, there were vociferous and numerous complaints. "They have a regular gambling concern in the sideshow which swindled people out of from $1 to $20," the *Knoxville (Tn.) Sentinel* reported, "and this seems to be part of the show."

On top of that, the performances were at best mediocre. "The James-Younger aggregation of poor horses and painted men is a bum show, according to the testimony of a large majority of those who paid their money and wasted their time going to see it," a Tennessee paper noted. There was also grousing about Cole and Frank turning "a doubtfully honest penny by making profit of a notoriously dishonest past."

By September, the wheels had come off. In Osceola, Missouri, some of the tag-along thugs cornered Frank and threatened to kill him for attempting to drive them away. Fortunately, Cole was nearby, and both ex-desperadoes were toting .38 revolvers. The thugs backed off. Soon after, Cole sued the show's owners over unpaid debts and they retaliated by having him arrested for embezzlement. The legal spats were soon sorted out, but Frank and Cole had had enough.

"We have severed all connections with the James-Younger Wild West Show," they announced in a Chicago paper. "The management was duly notified to choose between the grafters and us. They refused to eliminate the grafters; hence we refuse to allow our names to be used with a thieving outfit." The show closed for good a few weeks later.

Cole and Frank parted ways in business, but remained close friends the rest of their lives. Cole ignored his pardon's restrictions and eked out a living appearing in various venues that included a traveling exhibit of guns and saddles and a "moving picture film" depicting a train robbery. He also periodically lectured on how being a criminal was wrong, and wrote another book, this one about his years in prison. Cole died on March 21, 1916, at the age of 72. Before he went, he reportedly summoned Jesse James' only son to tell him his father had not killed anyone at Northfield, and the Youngers bore no grudges for being left behind.

Frank went back to the stage for two more years, grew pears on a farm in Oklahoma, and moved back to the family farm in Kearney after his mother died in 1911. He raised the price for visitors from 25 cents to 50 cents, and banned photographs. He would occasionally visit the famed Excelsior Springs health resort nearby, sit in a rocking chair near the front entrance and, depending on his mood, chat with or growl at the hotel's guests. He died, also at the age of 72, on Feb. 18, 1915.

Frank's last interview appeared in the Sept, 26, 1914 issue of *Collier's Weekly*. Tucked among news reports about German army's conquest of Belgium and subsequent march toward Paris, and ads extolling the virtues of the new Maxwell automobile (on sale for $695, or $18,560 in 2022 dollars), Frank's comments were mostly pat generalities, hoary metaphors and made-up anecdotes. He did emphatically state his support of women's suffrage. When the reporter asked him why he didn't want to talk about the old days, he paused for a moment. "If I admitted these stories were true," he replied, "people would say 'there's the greatest scoundrel unhung,' and if I denied 'em, they'd say 'there's the greatest liar on earth.' So I just say nothing."

"Jesse James," the poet Carl Sandburg wrote in *The American Songbag*, his classic 1927 anthology of U.S. folk music, "is the only American bandit who is classical...whose exploits are so close to the mythical and apocryphal."

That's not to say other American criminals haven't been idealized or distorted in popular culture. In the 1930s, for example, cold-blooded killers such as John Dillinger and Bonnie and Clyde were widely admired by many Americans who were suffering through an economic catastrophe they didn't understand and didn't believe they had any role in causing. To many, the bank robbers and kidnappers were only thumbing their noses at the Big Shots who *had* caused the Great Depression. The public's fascination with bad guys and girls was encouraged by the media. Newspapers assigned catchy nicknames to crooks—"Baby Face," "Mad Dog" "Pretty Boy"—and Hollywood cranked out films that made a criminal's life look exciting and glamorous.

But as Sandburg correctly pointed out, no American criminal has come close (with the possible exception of Billy the Kid) to Jesse James when it comes to reaching mythical status. Heck, he didn't even need a nickname. The alliterative flow of his name alone was enough to become ubiquitous in American culture: An anti-trust lawyer complaining about the merger of two giant drug companies says the deal "is like giving Jesse James a bigger gun;" a company advertising coins for sale suggests "Jesse James may have once stolen the very silver dollar you can acquired;" Linda Ronstadt tunefully laments that her lover "really worked me over good, just like Jesse James."

The legend-building started early. In 1877, the Jameses' champion, John Newman Edwards, published *Noted Guerillas*, which included the James Boys and Younger Brothers. In 1880, *The Life and Adventures of Frank and Jesse James and the Younger Brothers*, by St. Louis newspaperman J.A. Dacus reportedly sold 21,000 copies. Not to be outdone, the prolific and imaginative James W. Buell put out two books in 1881, *The Border Bandits* and *The Border Outlaws.*

Following Jesse's murder, Frank Triplett, a mining engineer and mediocre author, scribbled out a Jesse James biography in just seven weeks. The book is notable for two reasons: Its formal title is 66 words long, and it was or wasn't authorized by Jesse's widow and mother. Triplett said it was. In ads soliciting sales agents to peddle the book, Triplett claimed it was "written by the wife and mother!...a true life by the only persons in possession of the facts—a faithful wife and mother!" Zee James and Zerelda James Samuel, however, disagreed. They sued Triplett and were awarded $942 ($25,900 in 2022).

Nearly all of the early biographies of the James-Younger gang heavily focused on Jesse, and were heavily sympathetic. Two themes ran through most of them. The first was the outlaws were victims of post-Civil War trauma and forced into criminality by lack of other options. The second was that they were some sort of Robin Hoods, striking righteous blows at evil railroads, banks and other tyrannical institutions. Never mind the hundreds of thousands of other war veterans didn't turn to crime after 1865, or that there is no evidence the James-Younger gang shared its loot with anyone.

The Robin Hood theme made its way into song sometime in the late 19th century with a popular tune of unknown origin. The lyrics depicted Jesse James as a man "who stole from the rich and gave to the poor;" was "a friend to the poor" who would "never rob a mother or a child" and was overall a pretty upright guy until "that dirty little coward (Bob Ford), he shot Mr. Howard (Jesse's alias) and laid poor Jesse in his grave." Versions of the song have been recorded dozens of times by singers ranging from Woody Guthrie and Pete Seeger to Johnny Cash and Bruce Springsteen.

The movies enhanced both the "victims of circumstance" and Robin Hood themes. The folks who run the James farm tourist site near Kearney, Missouri, compiled a list of 50 Jesse James films, and doubtless missed a few. They range from 1908's *The James Boys in Missouri* to *The Assassination of Jesse James* in 2007. The list includes two 1921 films in which Jesse's son Jesse Jr. portrays his father, and two late 1940s serials in which Jesse is played by Clayton Moore, better known for his long-running radio and television role as The Lone Ranger. The list also includes films in which Jesse meets The Three Stooges, Bob Hope and Frankenstein's daughter. All three are comedies, two of them intentionally so.

The most iconic of the Jesse James films, not to say it is particularly accurate, was 1939's *Jesse James*, starring Tyrone Power as Jesse and Henry Fonda as Frank. Also worth mentioning are 1957's *The True Story of Jesse James* (it isn't), starring Robert Wagner, and *The Great Northfield Minnesota Raid*, featuring Robert Duvall as a psychotic Jesse and Cliff Robertson as a dyspeptic Cole Younger. If the raid was great, the film was not. The Younger Brothers did get at least two films of their own, *Bad Men of Missouri* (1941) and *The Younger Brothers* (1949). Finally, 1980's *The Long Riders* is worth mentioning if for no other reasons than that it began as an off-Broadway musical and starred four sets of actor-brothers playing four sets of bandit-brothers.

And yes, there was a 1965-66 ABC television show. *The Legend of Jesse James* It starred Christopher Jones as Jesse and Allen Case as Frank. The show was well-named as being legendary in nature, as in seemingly every episode, the James Boys righted far more wrongs than they committed. They were knocked off the air after one season and 34 episodes by *The Lucy Show* and *Dr. Kildare*, but at least they were spared having to meet Frankenstein's daughter again.

Chapter 13 Notes

"Is that you" *Kansas City Star*, Feb. 17, 1903, p. 9.

"Be true to" George Huntington, *Robber and Hero*, p. 146.

What vexed him *Kansas City Star*, Feb. 17, 1903, p. 9.

The Minnesota newspapers, Mark Lee Gardner, *Shot All to Hell*, p. 178.

The necktie party Ibid., p. 211.

The newspaper was *Minneapolis Star Tribune*, Nov. 20, 1876, p. 1.

The sentences mollified *Chicago Tribune*, Nov. 21, 1876, p. 4.

Cole was initially, Homer Croy, *Cole Younger, Last of the Outlaws*, pp. 160-161.

"...It is false" *Hope (ND) Pioneer*, Aug. 20, 1886, p. 2.

"Good faith on" *St. Paul Globe*, July 14, 1897, p. 1.

"Twenty-five years" *Minneapolis Star-Tribune*, July 15, 1901, p. 1.

In late 1901, John Koblas, *The Great Cole Younger & Frank James Historical Wild West Show*, pp. 52-53.

The Minnesota Pardons Cole Younger, *Cole Younger by Himself*, p. 81.

Even their pursuers *St. Louis Globe-Democrat*, Dec. 5, 1876, p. 2.

At the James *St. Louis Globe-Democrat*, Nov. 26, 1876, p. 1.

More accurately they *(Nashville) Daily American*, Oct. 9, 1882, p. 5.

Frank arrived in Ibid.

Jesse rented a Ibid.

Other than an *The (Lawrence) Kansas Daily Tribune*, Oct. 9, 1879, p. 1.

"It is a shame" *Mexico (Mo.) Weekly Ledger*, Oct. 9, 1879, p. 3.

In 1880, Missourians *St. Louis Globe-Democrat*, Jan. 11, 1881, p. 10.

Fearful Ryan would *(Nashville) Daily American*, Oct. 9, 1882, p. 5.

The killings intensified *Chicago Tribune*, July 17, 1881, p. 4.

The robbery also deepened *Kansas City Star*, July 19, 1881, p. 1.

The chances of Ibid.

Announcement of the T.J. Stiles, *Jesse James: Last Rebel of the Civil War*, pp. 368-69.

Jesse made it Ibid.

That left two *(Nashville) Daily American*, Oct. 9, 1882, p. 5; *Chattanooga Daily Times*, April 11, 1882, p. 1.

"When he turned" *St. Joseph (Mo.) Weekly Gazette*, April 6, 1882, p. 1.

The legal system Ibid.

"I have no" Stiles, op. cit., p. 377.

Crittenden's stance was *St. Joseph (Mo.) Weekly Gazette*, April 6, 1882, p. 1

Jesse's mother Zerelda *Kansas City Times*, April 7, 1882, p. 1.

At one point Ibid.

Frank was tired *(Nashville) Daily American*, Oct. 9, 1882, p. 5.

Left unsaid was Ibid.

Throughout his career *Kansas City Times*, Sept. 29, 1872, p. 2; *Sedalia (Mo.) Democrat*, April 17, 1882.

After weeks of Gardner, op. cit., p. 273.

Frank was taken *St. Louis Globe-Democrat*, Feb. 9, 1883, p. 2.

Frank faced one William A. Settle, Jr., *Jesse James Was His Name*, p. 118.

But that changed *Knoxville (Tn.) Sentinel*, June 15, 1903, p. 2.

Sort of. He *St. Louis Post-Dispatch*, Nov. 10, 1901, p. 1.

The publicity boosted *Stark County (Oh.) Democrat*, Dec. 3, 1901, p. 1.

Frank frankly told *Decatur (Ill.) Daily Review*, Dec. 16, 1901, p. 1.

Occupying 30 train *Knoxville (Tn.) Sentinel*, June 15, 1903, p. 2.

On top of that *Columbia (Tn.) Herald*, June 12, 1903, p. 4.

"**We have severed"** *Chicago Inter Ocean*, Sept. 22, 1903, p. 5.

Frank's last interview Julian Street, "The Borderland," *Collier's Weekly*, Sept. 26, 1914, p. 24.

"Jesse James," the Carl Sandburg, *The American Songbag*, p. 420.

But as Sandburg *Los Angeles Times*, Oct. 20, 2015, p. 1; *Raleigh (N.C.) News & Observer*, Sept. 30, 2009, p. 14; from "Poor Pitiful Me," written by Warren Zevon.

CHAPTER 14

"Cody...you have fetched 'em!"

The world meets the Wild West

The colonel knew he should rally the troops. But first he needed to finish throwing up. The colonel in this case was Will Cody. The troops were about a hundred Lakota men, women and children who were pretty sure they were going to die. Of seasickness.

As Cody explained it in two or three of the seemingly innumerable versions of his memoirs, the Lakota believed, as did many Native American nations, that Indians attempting to cross "the Great Waters" would be struck with a terrible malady. It "would first prostrate the victim and then slowly consume his flesh, day after day," Cody wrote, "until at length the very skin itself would drop from his bones, leaving nothing but a skeleton." If you were a Lakota aboard the steamship *Nebraska* on April 1, 1887, chances were good you desperately pined for the landlocked version of Nebraska. It took all of Cody's persuasive powers to prevent a mass stampede down the gangplank just before the ship departed.

On board, Cody tried "to cheer them up and relieve their forebodings. But for two days, nearly the whole company was too sick for any other active service than feeding the fishes," he recalled, "in which I am not proud to say that I performed more than an ordinary share." By the third day, however, "we all began to mend so far that I called the Indians together in the main saloon and gave them a Sunday address." It seems to have worked, since none of the skin dropped off any of the Indians.

Cody and the Indians were on their way to England. Joining them were about 100 American cowboys and Mexican vaqueros, two sharp-shooting young women, 200 horses, 18 buffalo and an historically uncertain numbers of mules, elk, deer, Texas steers and donkeys. The assemblage formed Buffalo Bill's Wild West show. "One of the strangest cargoes that ever sailed from the United States," as one London newspaper put it, also included a gallery's worth of American artwork.

Both the art and the Cody conglomeration were to be part of an optimistically conceived but badly planned event called the American Exhibition. The brainchild of some English and American businessmen, the exhibition in London's West Brompton district was designed to promote U.S. agricultural and manufactured products. England yawned. "It is essentially a tradesmen's exhibition," sniffed *The Times* of London. "In no sense can it be held as representative of the industries of the States."

To broaden its appeal, the organizers decided to set up a gallery featuring American art, and two American-sized thrill rides. One was a huge slide down which riders plunged on wooden toboggans. The other was a "switchback railroad," the equivalent of a modern roller coaster. In case that wasn't enough to draw a crowd, they signed up Buffalo Bill. England perked up. "The Great Cow Boy show will draw far better than American industries, American fine arts or even American drinks," a Hampshire paper predicted.

For Cody and his business partner, the seasoned show business virtuoso Nate Salsbury, the exhibition held both promise and peril. If the Wild West show was a hit in London, it could open up other European countries for theatrical and financial conquest. If it flopped, however, if English audiences found war whoops and thundering buffalo boorish and boring, it could mean the show would limp home with a damaged aura in the eyes of domestic audiences as well.

It was a gamble of huge proportions, so Cody, Salsbury and their energetic publicist John Burke began collecting aces to pad their hands. Two came with no effort. In 1884, Cody received an unsolicited letter from the world's most well-liked American that would now come in very handy. "I have seen your Wild West show two days in succession, and have enjoyed it thoroughly," Mark Twain wrote. "Down to its smallest details, the show is genuine...your bucking horses were even more painfully real to me, as I rode one of those outrages once for nearly a quarter of a minute...it is often said on the other side of the water that none of the exhibitions which we send to England are purely and distinctly American. If you will take the Wild West show over there, you can remove that reproach."

An endorsement by Twain, who was quoted almost daily in the British press, was a very big deal. So was an endorsement from Henry Irving, then regarded as England's greatest actor. Irving saw the show in New York. On returning to England, he gushed to a reporter for London's top theatrical newspaper that "it impressed me immensely...you have real cowboys with bucking horses, real buffaloes...there are Indians who execute attacks on stage coaches which are driving at full speed ...the excitement is intense and I venture to predict that when it comes to London it will take the town by storm."

Working on the theory that the English were impressed by military men, publicist Burke began collecting personal endorsements from the U.S. Army's leading generals as to Cody's scouting and Indian-fighting prowess. Generals Wesley Merritt and Charles King were at Warbonnet Creek in 1876 when Cody shot it out with the Cheyenne warrior Yellow Hair and took the "first scalp for Custer." They obliged Burke's request for quotable blurbs with "he was cool and capable when surrounded by danger," and "no one has ever shown more bravery on the Western Plains ...". The English also liked military *titles,* but Cody had only been a non-ranked civilian scout. Nebraska Gov. John M. Thayer took care of that problem by giving Cody a colonel's commission in the Nebraska National Guard.

Now made even more real by a manufactured title, "Col. Cody" strolled aboard the *Nebraska* to take on the uncertainties of the Old World. Hundreds of well-wishers came down to the dock to see the ship off. The 36-member Cowboy Band struck up "The Girl I Left Behind Me," a favorite song of Cody's old outfit, the 5th Cavalry. "The upper deck was crowded with the tall figures of Indians," the *New York Times* reported, "who, clad in all their finery, seemed to wonder what on earth was going to happen and when...the cowboys, riders, shooters and Mexicans gave no troubles at all," although five stowaways were evicted just before the ship departed.

The ship's arrival was two days late because of rudder problems. The "feeding the fishes" induced by seasickness continued for some passengers for up to a week. Several of the animals died enroute, and were also fed to the fishes. Other than that, the voyage was uneventful. The company's reception when it arrived in England on April 15 augured well for the rest of the trip. English officials waived quarantine rules for the show's menagerie, despite recent outbreaks in the country of cattle-related diseases. A special train was waiting to take the company to the exhibition grounds. And reporters dispatched to verify the Indians were really Indians were satisfied. Although the ship was a bit ripe owing to the animals, a London *Daily News* scribe said, "the thing promised us is very real, and in Buffalo Bill's Wild West show the public has a unique treat in store."

Finishing touches were still being applied to the show's enormous arena, stables, buffalo corral and the company's living quarters. The $125,000 complex ($3.5 million in 2021) included a 20,000-seat open grandstand, 10,000 shaded seats and room for 10,000 standees. An artificial hill, complete with newly planted mature trees, was built for the Indian village. Cody and Salsbury were happy with the arena, unhappy with the unpredictable English weather and still worried about the show's prospects.

Their stomach butterflies multiplied when a note came from the Prince of Wales, announcing he had accepted an invitation from Cody and Salsbury to take in a dress rehearsal of the show a few days before the scheduled opening. The future King Edward VII was a short, stout, genial fellow. At the age of 46, he spent most of his time in ceremonial functions, or hunting, or fooling around with women who were not his wife, all the while waiting for his mother to die and pass on the crown. She seemed to be in no hurry. His mother was Queen Victoria, who in 1887 was marking her 50th year as ruler of the British Empire. In fact, all of England was abuzz with the celebration of Victoria's Golden Jubilee.

Cody liked the prince. He described him as "a plain-spoken, pleasant, kindly gentleman...I find less pride in him than I have experienced in third-rate civil officials elsewhere." Still, if the prince didn't like the show, the resulting negative publicity could be devastating. Fortunately, he loved it.

"...The (muddy) state of the arena and the nervous feeling inseparable from a first performance made me anything but comfortable," Cody wrote in one of his memoirs, "...(but) my fears were dispelled from the moment the Prince gave the signal, and the Indians, yelling like fiends, galloped out from the ambuscade and swept around the enclosure like a whirlwind. The effect was instantaneous and electric. The Prince rose from his seat and leaned eagerly over the front of the box, and the whole party seemed thrilled by the spectacle. 'Cody,' I said to myself, 'you have fetched 'em!' From that moment we were right—right from the word 'Go!'"

Buffalo Bill's Wild West show was a product of an evolutionary process that began on a night in mid-December 1872. That was when Will Cody stepped out on a Chicago theater stage and stumbled through a horrendous play, populated by a horde of white actors playing Indians and directed by a dime novel writer whose dramatic talents were even more lacking than his prose. Nearly paralyzed with stage fright, Cody forgot most of his lines, missed his cues, generally made a fool of himself—and was a smash hit.

For the next four years, Cody balanced his stage career with scouting for the U.S. Army and guiding various groups that wanted to visit the West and kill buffalo, find fossils or just look around. But disgusted with the Army's ineptitude in fighting Indians during the Sioux War and realizing he could make a lot more money on stage than being shot at, he formally ended his real-life western adventures in late September 1876. His primary dramatic vehicle through 1877 was *The Red Right Hand; or, Buffalo Bill's First Scalp for Custer*. It was based loosely—and I mean loosely—on Cody's actual killing and scalping of the Cheyenne warrior Yellow Hair during a July, 1876, skirmish in northwestern Nebraska.

But it didn't really matter what this play, or any of the other half-dozen plays that followed over the next decade, was about. Audiences came to see Buffalo Bill. If the faint traces of a plot remained similar from play to play, however, other elements did not. Cody began adding things to the stage dramas that would eventually end up as part of the foundation of his Wild West show.

During an 1877 tour of the West Coast, for example, he began experimenting with live animals performing on stage. In San Francisco, two horses proved too frightened to perform, but by the time the troupe reached Sacramento, they had settled down enough to play their roles. Most nights. That same year, he began recruiting real Indians to play the parts of, well, Indians. The Grant Administration had restricted most Native Americans to their assigned reservations. But under new President Rutherford B. Hayes, the Bureau of Indian Affairs loosened up enough to allow some Indians to perform with traveling shows. Cody personally knew very few Indians, so he relied on better-connected friends and associates to entice them into braving the footlights.

As bonafide Indians joined the cast, the plays' villains shifted away from "savage redskins" to renegade whites or Mormons, who with the possible exception of Roman Catholics were Gilded Age America's most widely hated religious group. If Indians did fight with Cody's character, it was usually due to a misunderstanding or them having been tricked into it by evil white men. And if there were any "bad" Indians in the play, they were most often played by white actors.

The overall amount of onstage violence also declined. After viewing a play whose cast included a mule named Jack Cass playing a mule character named Jerry, a Chicago reviewer noted that it was "shorn of much of the blood and thunder that characterized Cody's former plays." But he acknowledged that a few evil Mormon characters were killed whenever the plot bogged down. In place of the gore, Cody substituted bits that had little to do with the play, such as demonstrations of bullwhip cracking, or the Austin Brothers, trick-shot artists who plunked potatoes off each other's heads, snuffed out candles and shot cigars from people's hands. He spent freely on large and colorful advertising posters, and encouraged his increasingly more populous troupes to stroll around towns in their costumes before a show, especially the Indians.

Finally, Cody gradually learned that a season-to-season, seat-of-your-pants approach to show business didn't work well. He put together a company that employed professional actors and musicians and competent publicists, advance men and business managers. He also stopped taking on old Wild West pals like Texas Jack Omohundro, Wild Bill Hickok and Captain Jack Crawford to share the marquee. They were too unreliable, or too ambitious. There was room for only one star in a Buffalo Bill play.

Critics were divided as to the societal worth of Buffalo Bill stage productions. A Louisville, Kentucky, reviewer despaired at the futility of attacking what he called "simply a ten-cent novel put upon the stage...but it seems almost an idle task to say anything adversely about it, as those who enjoy such a piece are goodly in numbers, and nothing can keep them away." As for Cody, "he rides his white horse, shakes his long black curls, twirls his broad-brimmed hat, looks handsome and takes in the money and is happy. He is not required to do any acting."

A Little Rock. Arkansas, critic, on the other hand, stopped just short of deifying Cody: "All nations have plays and characters peculiar to themselves. The true, the original representation of America is wild plains and uninhabited forests. A hero of these scenes is purely American, and his name is Buffalo Bill...Mr. Cody is not only the hero of a drama written for himself, but he is the hero of a broad drama written by Nature and Fate."

Cody seldom paid attention to critics, good or bad. He made it clear his chief motivation was financial, not artistic. "I don't play on the stage or do anything else for fun of the thing," he said. "I work to make money." And he made money. The *New York Mirror*, a theater trade newspaper, reported with admirable precision that Cody's company netted $50,516.57 in the 1879-80 season and $51,819.40 the following year. That amounted to roughly $1.3 million annually in 2022 dollars.

If he made lots of money, however, he also spent it as if it might go out of style. Gordon W. Lillie, a Cody business partner who was better known as Pawnee Bill, once said that Cody "cared nothing for money except when he wanted it or needed to spend; then if he did not have it or could not borrow it, it made him sick; he would go to bed."

Cody bought into a sprawling Nebraska cattle ranch with Frank North, a pal from his Army scouting days. Later, he bought or built several houses in North Platte, Nebraska, for his family, as well as a 4,000-acre ranch for himself. He poured tens of thousands in legal fees into a lawsuit against a cousin in Cleveland. The dispute centered on 50 acres of prime central city property that Cody's grandfather had dementedly deeded away years before. The real estate had a potential value of millions, but Cody and his sisters ultimately lost the case.

He also spared no expense outfitting his Buffalo Bill public persona. A star-struck Kansas reporter breathlessly noted Cody's "heavy gold chain from which was suspended near the left vest pocket a huge gold horse-shoe set with diamonds. His scarf-pin is a solid gold representation of a buffalo head, with diamonds for eyes."

And he dropped more than a little buying drinks for the house—and himself. Excessive drinking was a problem. Plays were sometimes cancelled because the star was drunk, or else performed with a clearly plastered Buffalo Bill. Near the beginning of the 1882 season, a Janesville, Wisconsin, reviewer noted with delicate sarcasm that the play was marred because Cody "was laboring under a severe indisposition, superinduced by a too-free indulgence of intoxicants...Mr. Cody has a good company and a good orchestra, but he can't run a successful show unless he keeps sober."

Despite the handsome financial returns, Cody from time to time claimed he was nearing the end of his theatrical career. "I like raising cattle and horses better than the stage," he told an interviewer in the fall of 1881, "and will turn my attention to that branch of business after the next two years."

But the famed plainsman found ranching was just too much work. In the theatrical troupe's off-seasons, Cody returned to Nebraska to participate in the spring roundups at the ranch he co-owned with Frank North. But he candidly confessed in his memoirs "having been in the saddle all day and standing guard over the cattle all night, rain or shine, I could not possibly find out where the fun came in that North had promised me." For his part, North found his partner was not only lazy and easily distracted, but too excitable to have around the stock: He made the cattle nervous with his hard riding and tendency to suddenly start practicing his already excellent marksmanship. Coupled with Cody's disenchantment were heavy losses of horses and cattle to rustlers and the elements. Cody and North sold the ranch in 1882.

With the romance of ranching, or at least actually working on a ranch, gone, Cody continued his theatrical company through 1885. But he increasingly turned his attentions to a new kind of show business that would forever be associated with his name.

In his memoirs, Will Cody claimed that having found himself in 1882 "richer by several thousand dollars than I had ever been before," he conceived the idea "of organizing a large company of Indians, cowboys, Mexican vaqueros, famous riders and expert lasso throwers, with accessories of stage coach, emigrant wagons, bucking horses and a herd of buffaloes, with which to give a realistic entertainment of wild life in the plains."

Doubtless by curious coincidence, two of Cody's future partners would claim it was their idea. The first, a sharpshooting dentist named William F. "Doc" Carver, said he was already on the verge of launching a Wild West show when Cody visited Carver's Connecticut home and begged for a job. According to Carver, Cody at the time was down to his last $17. The second future partner, the show biz wiz Nate Salsbury, claimed he envisioned an outdoor spectacle built around horsemanship and other frontier feats while on a tour of Australia with his musical comedy troupe. Salsbury decided all he needed was a well-known Wild West figurehead like Buffalo Bill to pull it off.

While it's true Cody talked separately with both men about the idea in 1882, there are sizeable chunks of baloney in the origin versions of all three. In fact, the basic idea had been tried before. As early as 1843, the showman P.T. Barnum put together a production in Hoboken, New Jersey, that featured Indian dances and a small herd of young buffalo. At some point in the show the buffalo crashed through a fence and disappeared into an adjacent swamp. In 1872, Wild Bill Hickok headlined a "Grand Buffalo Hunt" near Niagara Falls in which Mexican vaqueros and Indians chased around three buffalo. A bear in the show provided the most excitement when it got loose and demolished a wagon that was selling sausages.

Whoever had the idea first, what eventuated in 1883 was a partnership between Cody and Doc Carver. Salsbury, who rightly considered himself the smartest of the three when it came to show business, declined to join. While he got along with Cody, Salsbury despised Carver as a frontier phony. Salsbury was right. Most of Carver's self-told stories of his life were bogus. He was <u>not</u> a feared Indian fighter who had run away from home as a youth and been raised by the Sioux, or a prodigious buffalo hunter, or a revered icon of the Plains tribes. But he was a real dentist. More importantly, he was a true marksman with an international reputation, and that was apparently good enough for Buffalo Bill.

The grand opening of the "Wild West: Hon. W.F. Cody and Dr. W.F. Carver's Rocky Mountain and Prairie Exhibition" took place in Omaha in mid-May, 1883. It was a smash success. The *Omaha Bee* reported a crowd of 8,000-plus witnessed "the only genuine exposition of wild western life ever put before the public...probably no scheme was ever started under more favorable auspices...".

The show had many of the key elements that would mark Buffalo Bill shows for the next three decades. There was an Indian pony race; a race between a mounted Indian and one on foot; shooting exhibitions by Carver, Cody and Capt. Adam Bogardus; bronc riding, and chasing buffalo and Texas steers around. The clear crowd favorite was "the Deadwood stagecoach attack," which featured Indians pursuing a coach pulled by six mules at top speed and a cowboy rescue party led by Cody and Carver that thundered in to save the day. The coach stunt was so popular, the crowd demanded an encore.

In terms of drawing large and enthusiastic crowds, the show was a success throughout the season, which ended in October. Cody and Carver, the *Hartford Courant* predicted after sold-out shows in Connecticut, "have in the 'Wild West' show a novelty that will line their pockets with gold...". But keeping gold in their pockets proved to be a big problem. Both Carver and Cody were inept money managers, and despite big box office receipts, they overspent on nearly everything. At the end of the season, they were lucky to break even. And that was only one of the problems.

Both of the owners drank like parched elephants. Pawnee Bill Lillie, who joined the show as an interpreter for the Indians, claimed "Cody was drunk every day for our first five weeks out." In addition to matching Cody drink for drink, Carver had little charisma and a vile temper. Frustrated at his poor shooting during one hangover-haunted show, Carver broke his rifle over his horse's head in front of a stunned audience. And Cody and Carver weren't the only ones in the show who enjoyed a cocktail or seven. It's said that of the 16 railroad cars needed to move the outfit, one of them was devoted almost entirely to liquor.

By far the worst event to befall Cody, however, was the sudden death of his 11-year-old daughter Orra while the show was in Chicago near the end of the season. Cody rushed home to Nebraska to console his wife. He then returned to have it out with Carver.

Even through his grief and alcoholic haze, Cody realized the show's long-term chances were dim with two fiscally irresponsible boozers at the helm. He probably had also grown weary of Carver's ill temper and posturing as a bonafide Western scout and Indian fighter. The two agreed to dissolve the partnership, and divided up the show's assets by flipping a coin. Luckily for Cody, he got the Deadwood coach.

While the partnership was dissolved, the enmity that developed between Cody and Carver lasted for decades. They fought in court over the trade rights to the term "Wild West" and a claim by Carver that Cody owed him $27,000. Carver got $10,000; Cody got the rights to the term, which proved almost impossible to protect from rival shows, including one started by Carver. The two also reportedly came close to fighting with guns on a St. Louis street before cooler heads prevailed.

With Carter's departure, Cody took on two new partners. One was Adam Bogardus, who, after Cody, became the show's top-billed performer. Bogardus was regarded as the world's best pigeon shooter—until he developed qualms about killing live birds. He then invented a machine that tossed clay discs in the air, and became the world's best clay pigeon shooter. (In addition to being more humane, clay was a lot cheaper than live birds.) A further attraction to Bogardus' act was the presence of his four young sons, all of them crack shots.

Nate Salsbury was the other new partner. His background was almost as colorful as Cody's. At 15, he enlisted in the Union Army as a drummer boy and saw action in several major battles. He was captured and confined for a time in the Confederacy's horrendous Andersonville Prison. After the war, he studied law but was lured away by the theater's siren call. Working his way up from the very bottom of the industry, he became one of America's top comedians. He formed a comedy troupe that toured internationally. He also wrote and produced *The Brook*, a hit play that not only ran for five years straight but is regarded by many theater historians as the quintessential archetype of modern musicals.

But Salsbury wasn't laughing when he got to St. Louis in April 1884 to help launch the Wild West show's new season. He found Cody "boiling drunk...surrounded by a lot of harpies called 'Old Timers' who were getting as drunk as he, at his expense." When Cody sobered up and read a blistering letter left by Salsbury, he responded with deep contrition.

"I solemnly promise you after this you will never see me under the influence of liquor," he wrote. "...I appreciate all you have done. Your judgement...is good and from this day on I will do my work to the letter. The drinking surely ends today and your Pard will be himself. And be on deck all the time." Cody would mostly live up to his promise, at least during the show's seasons. Although the two would routinely exasperate each other, they would remain partners until Salsbury's death in 1902.

The 1884 season began promisingly. The major addition to the 1883 show was a closing act that featured the good guys rescuing a pioneer family surrounded in their prairie cabin by Indians. Two weeks after opening in St. Louis, the show drew an astonishing 41,000 people to a single performance in Chicago. In New York, it packed the Polo Grounds for two weeks. Reviewers loved it. "The entertainment brings the life of the Wild West as it was to the view of all," one critic extolled. "It is a dime novel pictured by the heroes themselves."

The main consumers of dime novels—young boys—flocked to the shows. "I never knew there were so many small boys in New York until I went to see the show," a reporter marveled. "They were crowded in platoons around the outside of the fence of the Polo Grounds, swarmed the telegraph poles and adjoining trees and formed a veritable juvenile mob about the entrance."

The show's admission prices—50 cents for adults, 25 cents for kids—translated to about $14 and $7 respectively in 2022 currency. That was a prohibitive price for many kids, which is why they were consigned to the trees and telegraph poles to catch a glimpse. But Buffalo Bill had a soft spot for children and doled out hundreds of free tickets to them. He also let in the most inventive of the young con artists who tried to scam their way in. The approaches included a boy with a glass of water who told the ticket taker it was for a woman inside who had fainted, or the kid who donned an eyepatch and demanded entrance for a dime because he could only see half the show.

But the bright start of 1884 quickly turned into tragedy, blunders, disaster and bad weather of biblical proportions. Frank North, Cody's former ranch partner and the show's major liaison with its Indians, was thrown from his horse in Hartford, Connecticut, and trampled. He died the following year from his injuries.

After North was injured, Cody hired Pony Bob Haslam, one of the most famous riders for the Pony Express, who was now down on his luck. Haslam was charged with taking the show down the Mississippi River to New Orleans, where it would play as part of an international exposition, and book performances along the way. Haslam proved spectacularly inadequate. He hired an old boat with an incompetent captain and booked venues that were too small to be profitable. Cody, meanwhile, went to New Orleans to scout Haslam's choice for the show's performance there. What he found when he got there was a man crossing the site in a rowboat. Torrential rains—it would pour for a record 44 days in a row—had turned the arena into a lake.

Then more bad news arrived from 200 miles upriver. The show's boat had collided with another vessel and sank. Fortunately, it was in only four feet of water and no one died. Unfortunately, about $20,000 ($500,000 in 2022) worth of equipment and animals, including the buffalo, were lost. In despair, Cody wired Salsbury, who due to contractual obligations was in Denver with his comedy group. "OUTFIT AT BOTTOM OF RIVER," Cody reported. "WHAT DO YOU ADVISE?" Salsbury wired back "REORGANIZE AND OPEN ON YOUR DATE. HAVE WIRED YOU FUNDS."

Cody reorganized. In a week he rounded up enough of a show to open on time. But the unrelenting rains dampened attendance to pitiful levels. One performance took place before an audience of nine people. A demoralized Adam Bogardus quit the show and left the partnership. Total losses for the year reached a hefty $60,000 ($1.6 million in 2022.) The show was so broke that when a talented young woman circus sharpshooter asked for a job, she was told there was no money to hire additional acts. If she wanted to try out for Buffalo Bill's show, they told Annie Oakley, she would have to come back in a few months.

If 1884 was a nightmare for Will Cody, 1885 was a very pleasant dream. Cody's charisma and instincts and Salsbury's cool judgement combined to create a show that was greater than the sum of its parts. The individual acts combined to tell the story of America's indomitable quest to tame its seemingly untamable frontier. Wild animals were bested; Native Americas were vanquished; transportation lines were preserved and settlers' homes were saved. And it was all accomplished through the uncanny riding, roping and shooting skills of American men—and one woman.

The words "diminutive," "perky" and "confident" all defined Annie Oakley. She was just under five feet tall. She never walked into an arena—she skipped, pranced, danced, capered or tripped lightly, but never walked. And she never backed down from a challenge. On meeting the Prince and Princess of Wales, she thumbed her nose at royal protocol and shook hands first with the princess, and only then the prince. She later said it was out of sympathy for the princess having to suffer her husband's sometimes public extra-marital affairs.

On a dare, she once shot the ashes off a handheld cigarette. The hand was attached to the arm of the future Kaiser Wilhelm of Germany. When she was libeled by media mogul William Randolph Hearst's newspaper empire as a thief and cocaine addict, she filed law suits against 55 individual newspapers and spent thousands of dollars and untold hours and days testifying at each trial. She won 54 of them. And she is thought over her lifetime to have taught more than 15,000 women how to handle guns.

Born Phoebe Ann Mosely in Ohio in 1860, "Annie," as her sisters called her, was one of five children born to a twice-widowed mother. The family was so poor, Annie lived for a time in the equivalent of an orphanage, then was sent to live for two years with a foster family that treated her cruelly. She finally returned home, where her natural talent with a gun not only supplied the family with meat, but allowed her to sell surplus game to markets. She began to win shooting contests. At the age of 21, she bested professional shooter Frank Butler. At the age of 22, she married him. They remained nearly inseparable until their deaths, within a few weeks of each other, in 1926.

Oakley and Butler performed for various variety theaters, circuses and other traveling shows for a few years before being attracted to the Wild West show, in part after observing how well the company treated its animals. After being turned down in New Orleans by the Cody outfit in late 1884, Oakley was hired the following spring. She was not only hired; she was made the show's star. Butler, whose own shooting had faded due to vision problems, became her manager. Cody and Salsbury spent an eyebrow-raising $5,000 (about $138,000 in 2022) on promoting Oakley's prowess with firearms.

Her prowess was prodigious. In one challenge match, she broke 943 out of 1,000 thrown glass balls, shooting with a .22 caliber rifle. In another, she broke 4,772 of 5,000 using a shotgun. A routine stunt was to knock a cigarette out of her husband's mouth. And while other trick-shot artists cheated with rigged candles, apples and other targets, Annie Oakley was the real deal.

For almost every season from 1885 to 1901, when she retired because of injuries suffered in a train wreck, Oakley was the opening act for the Wild West show. She began the shows, publicist John Burke, explained, because the sight of a tiny, bouncy young woman entering the arena tended to soothe the nerves of women and children who might otherwise grow too apprehensive when the stampedes, stagecoach chases and settler's cabin attacks began.

Oakley wasn't the only new star attraction in 1885. After several years of trying, Cody was finally able to get federal officials to allow the Lakota leader Sitting Bull to join the show. After the Little Bighorn battle, Sitting Bull led his people to Canada. He eventually returned to the United States, spent two years as a prisoner of war (even though the war was long over), and then was restricted to a reservation that straddled the North Dakota/South Dakota border.

With Cody, the 54-year-old Bull was paid $50 a week ($1,400 in 2022), plus all the money he could make selling picture postcards of himself. He also sold his laboriously learned autograph, and items such as his "personal" tobacco pouches that he bought wholesale by the box. All in all, Sitting Bull made a fair piece of change in his one season with the show for doing nothing more than riding into the arena, often to hisses and boos from audiences still sore about Custer. But he was baffled by the poverty he saw among so many whites while others had so much, and that made him a soft touch for kids and down-and-outers who came around the show.

There was one unfortunate incident in Pittsburgh when a man who had lost a brother at the Little Bighorn tried to attack him. Sitting Bull defended himself by hitting the man in the face with a hammer, knocking out several teeth. But the Lakota leader was generally diplomatic for a guy who held most white people in contempt. In Boston he told an interviewer he had been treated very well by Long Hair (Cody) and White Chief (Salsbury). "When I return to my people, I shall tell them all about our friends among the White Men, and what I have seen."

One of Sitting Bull's conditions for doing the show was that he would get to meet the U.S. president, who in 1885 was Grover Cleveland, and explain how badly his people on the reservation were treated. He did visit the White House, but Cleveland brusquely dismissed him after a few minutes. Sitting Bull was irate. When officials tried to placate him by explaining people often waited months to talk to the Great White Father, he reportedly replied something translated as "White man heap damned fool!" There may not have been a connection, but he was not allowed by the Bureau of Indian Affairs to come back to Cody's show for another season.

The addition of Oakley and Sitting Bull, coupled with a tight, well-organized operation, meant the show did well at the box office. It played in 40 cities in America and Canada, before audiences totaling more than one million, and showed a net profit of around $100,000 ($2.8 million in 2022).

Salsbury and Cody decided the following year to risk tampering with their success. To eliminate the hefty expenses associated with moving from venue to venue, they planted the show for a full six months at a resort on New York's Staten Island. Several miles of railroad track were built to service the facilities, which resembled a sprawling military camp. A hundred electric lights were installed for evening performances. There were two shows each day, except Sundays. Seventeen daily ferries shuttled people from Manhattan and New Jersey.

The Wild West show ferries weren't the only hive of activity in New York Harbor in 1886. The Statue of Liberty, whose torch-bearing arm had been on display the Centennial Exposition in Philadelphia a decade earlier, was dedicated October 28, with a ceremony that reeked of Gilded Age hypocrisy. The featured speaker was President Cleveland, who had vociferously opposed any public funding for the statue. Despite being a symbol of "liberty and justice for all," the dedication was strictly a private affair. And although the monument was a depiction of Lady Liberty, the only two women allowed to attend were wives of French VIPs.

But the American public did get to look at the statue from afar, on its way to see Buffalo Bill. Most shows played to capacity crowds of 20,000. In one July week alone, more than 193,000 paid their 50-cent admissions (a quarter for kids.) Luminary visitors included P.T. Barnum, Mark Twain, General of the Army William T. Sherman and Thomas Edison. The *New York Times* predicted only slightly facetiously that Cody would soon "be able to buy himself a ranch as large as Rhode Island and spend his remaining days in luxurious idleness."

Even now, Salsbury and Cody weren't done pushing the envelope. In late November, they presented a different kind of spectacle, indoors, at Madison Square Garden. *The Drama of Civilization* was the story of America's pioneers. It incorporated many of the elements of the regular show but added a collection of gigantic—40 feet high and 150 feet long—curved paintings as moving backdrops. The scenery was staged so it had a 3D effect, making it appear that the riders and other performers were moving in and out of the mountains and valleys. Other effects included using steam-powered ventilators blowing thousands of dried leaves to simulate a cyclone.

Another twist was the addition of a new finale—"Custer's Last Stand." Cody played Custer. Adding verisimilitude was the fact that some of the Indians in the act had actually been at the Little Bighorn. Other than the Indians, however, the drama bore little resemblance to the real event.

The show was lauded by some critics, panned by others, and loved by the public. Total attendance during its three-month run was estimated at close to one million, and ticket demand was so great Salsbury took the then-unusual step of opening off-site sales offices in Brooklyn and New Jersey. Having completely triumphed in America, the entourage headed to England.

Buffalo Bill's Wild West show may have had its greatest cultural and historical impacts not in America, but in Europe. By the end of its year-long, three-city (London, Birmingham, Manchester) tour of England in 1887-88, the show gave more than 300 performances before 2.5 million spectators. It opened in Paris in March,1889, as part of an international exposition featuring the brand-new Eiffel Tower, then spent more than a year touring Italy, Spain, Germany and Austria. In fact, Cody biographer Louis S. Warren estimated the show performed for a cumulative nine years of its 30-year existence on foreign soil.

For millions of Europeans, Will Cody's show—and his Buffalo Bill persona—became the basis for their conception of what America was, or at least had been. The show, posited *The Times* of London, "represents in effectively realistic fashion, one very prominent phase of existing American life, some of it, indeed, rapidly passing away...We can easily imagine Wall Street for ourselves; we need to be shown the cowboys of Colorado."

The European appearances also allowed Cody to lay valid claim to the hoary but prestigious show-biz cliché of having "performed before the crowned heads of Europe." Even the reclusive Queen Victoria was persuaded to interrupt 26 years of mourning her late husband Albert and attend a private performance in 1887. Ensconced in a specially constructed box "richly draped with crimson velvet," the ruler of the British Empire summoned Cody and several cast members after the show "and expressed to him her entire satisfaction with all she had seen." She liked it so much, in fact, she had a second helping when the show returned in 1892.

Ten days after the queen's 1887 visit, her son, the Prince of Wales, came for his second look that season. This time he brought the kings of Denmark, Greece, Belgium and Saxony, all of whom took a ride together in the Deadwood coach as it was attacked by Indians and saved by cowboys. On departing, the prince asked Cody if had ever played before four kings. Cody replied with a bow "'I have, your Highness, but I never held such a royal flush as this against four kings.'" The prince laughed, and then had to explain the joke to the other royals, "who did not understand the American game of poker."

When it did return home, the show got bigger, and changed its name. Now "Buffalo Bill's Wild West and Congress of Rough Riders of the World," it employed a cast and crew of 640, with a truly international flavor—Germans, Russians, Argentines and Britishers to go with the Mexican vaqueros and American cowboys, cowgirls and Indians. In terms of success, it reached its American apogee in 1893, at yet another world's fair.

The World's Columbian Exposition opened in Chicago in May 1893. Designed to mark the 400th anniversary of Christopher Columbus' first voyage to the New World, it was a year late getting off the ground. The world was willing to wait. Over its six-month run, more than 27 million people passed through the gates of what became known as "The White City." The attractions ranged from life-sized replicas of Columbus' three ships to the "hoochy-coochy" gyrations of a belly dancer named "Little Egypt." George Ferris, a Pittsburgh civil engineer, presented fair-goers with an amusement ride that resembled a giant wheel and rotated passengers 264 feet into the air on a 20-minute, two-revolution ride. "Ferris wheels" caught on.

Although the expo covered 690 acres and had room for exhibits from 46 countries, it had no room for Buffalo Bill. Fair officials deemed the Wild West show was passe. It was also thought to not be sophisticated enough for the neoclassical splendor of the main grounds, and too big for the Midway with the rest of the carnival-type attractions. Undaunted, Salsbury leased 15 acres directly across from the exposition's main entrance and put up an arena with a grandstand large enough to hold an audience of 18,000.

It was a smash hit, with crowds averaging 25,000 per day to see two performances. Demand was so great, two more shows were added for Sundays. "The dash and vim of Buffalo Bill's horsemen at the Wild West exhibition...keep that place easily at the forefront of the World's Fair attractions," the *Chicago Tribune* noted. "The performance is kept up to the standard which was set when the performance was first given." By the close of the expo, the show had netted an impressive $1 million in six months, the equivalent of almost $30 million in 2022.

The Wild West would have some more good years. In fact, the 1890s would financially and artistically be its greatest decade. But its "dash and vim," slowly waned. Cody, who turned 50 in 1896, was no longer quite the splendid specimen of Wild West manhood he had been, although by mortal standards he still rode and shot superbly. The health of Nate Salsbury, the show's helmsman and chief problem-solver, deteriorated to the point that by 1894 he could no longer effectively manage the show.

In 1895, James Bailey, who was weaned in the circus business by Agnes Lake, Wild Bill Hickok's wife, and had partnered with P.T. Barnum, took over some of Salsbury's duties in return for one-third of the ownership. But Salsbury died in 1902, and Bailey in 1906. Because of debts Cody owed both men, Bailey's estate assumed Salsbury's ownership share. Bailey's heirs thus controlled two-thirds of the show but refused to assume any of its management duties. In desperation, Cody ran the show by himself for a couple of years, then merged it with a show run by an old associate, Pawnee Bill Lillie. The merger worked for a while.

But desperate for money and without Lillie's knowledge, Cody agreed to a deal in 1913 that effectively gave control of the show to two sleazy Denver newspaper executives. A slew of legal actions eventually led to the show's few assets being seized and sold at a bankruptcy auction. An American institution that had thrilled tens of millions over two continents died not with a bang, but a whimper.

Much of Will Cody's last 25 years was spent trying to extend his prominence in the national spotlight, protect his image and financially keep his head above water. A somewhat surprising attack on Cody's image surfaced in the late 1880s in the form of allegations he exploited and mistreated the Native Americans in his shows. It was surprising in that Cody had consistently and publicly empathized with Indians. "They have been very badly treated," he told an Arkansas newspaper in 1879. "There has never been a treaty but it has been broken" by whites. In 1885, he told Canadian reporters "in nine times out of ten, where there is trouble between white men and Indians, it will be found that the white man is responsible...Indians expect a man to keep his word."

Nonetheless, the Bureau of Indian Affairs (BIA) convened a hearing in the fall of 1890 to decide whether Indians should be allowed to further participate in shows such as Cody's. The Bureau's real concern was not about the Indians' treatment. After all, maltreatment was standard operating procedure at almost all of the reservations run by the BIA. The bureau's real concern was that the shows threatened the agency's complete control over the Indian nations as well asits efforts to coerce Indian assimilation into white culture.

But Indians who testified from Cody's show said they were better treated by Buffalo Bill and Nate Salsbury than they were by the federal government. One cast member displayed the $300 ($8,800 in 2022) he had saved to buy his children clothes for the winter. Another said his people had been raised on horseback and not as farmers, and the show "furnished us the same kind of work we were raised to; that is the reason we want to work for these men." Under pressure from congressional members who supported Cody, unfavorable press coverage of the hearings and the lack of any evidence Cody had mistreated the Indians in his show, the proposed ban was dropped.

A much more serious Indian-related issue sprang from a loose set of religious beliefs that began spreading among the Plains tribes in the mid to late 1880s. Adherents of the Ghost Dance believed a messiah would arise that would bring back the Indian dead, make the whites disappear and restore the natural ways of pre-Columbian life to America. This alarmed the inexperienced, uninformed and/or just plain slimy BIA officials, particularly at the Pine Ridge, South Dakota, reservation that housed the old Lakota leader Sitting Bull.

Aware that Cody and Sitting Bull were friendly, General Nelson Miles asked Cody to make a risky trip in late 1890 to "secure the person of Sitting Bull" and deliver him to federal troops. Cody agreed to try. But before he could get there, Sitting Bull was killed by members of his own tribe serving as reservation police, in a battle that also saw the deaths of a dozen police and followers of the Lakota leader.

Two weeks later, an effort by the 7th Cavalry, George Custer's old outfit, to confiscate rifles from a Lakota band at Wounded Knee Creek turned into a massacre of about 190 Indians, most of them women and children. In the wake of the tragedy, Lakota leaders of the Ghost Dance movement were rounded up and imprisoned at a fort near Chicago. In an effort to defuse further trouble, General Miles asked Cody to enlist the prisoners for his next show in Europe. Cody complied, which helped restore his reputation as a square dealer with Indians and helped end the Ghost Dance "uprising." America's reprehensible treatment of Native Americans, however, continued unabated.

Another public controversy for the aging scout was much closer to home. Will and Louisa Cody had never been anyone's idea of a perfect couple. Since marrying just after the Civil War's end, they seldom lived together, or even spoke to each other. There were incessant quarrels over finances. On the rare times he was "home" in North Platte, Will stayed at the ranch and Louisa stayed at the Cody home in town. After years of considering it, Will finally demanded a divorce in 1905. Louisa refused to grant it. He took her to court, and the trial in Cheyenne, Wyoming, was front-page news across the country. "The indications are that Col. Cody's hair-breadth escapes from buffaloes and Indians will be considered tame in comparison with his experiences in divorce court," the *Chicago Tribune* gleefully predicted.

The charges and countercharges were highly entertaining to all but the combatants. Will contended Louisa was an incessant nag who "has subjected me to intolerable indignities (and) caused me to leave home for peace of mind." He also charged her with scheming to corner family funds for herself, and on one occasion trying to poison him.

Louisa countered that Will drank too much, dallied with other women (including Queen Victoria, which was highly improbable), neglected his children and provided so poorly for the family she had to take in sewing to make ends meet. She also explained the poisoning incident was an accident and a result of her slipping him a love potion to arouse his ardor. The judge took a month to reach a decision. After ordering that the names of the women Cody was accused of dallying with be stricken from the record (including Queen Victoria's), the judge rejected Will's divorce petition and ordered that he pay Louisa's court costs. The two finally reconciled in 1910 and remained married for the rest of Will's life.

In view of his long struggles to get along with his wife, it should be noted that Will Cody was fairly outspoken when it came to women's rights, particularly for a Gilded Age man. Like many westerners, he supported women's suffrage decades before the 19th Amendment granted adult American females the right to vote. In 1913, even as the show was swirling down the financial drain, he loaned one of the show's covered wagons to a big suffragette parade in New York City. In addition, five of the show's cowgirls rode in the parade, and five of the Indians rode as their guards. But Cody went a step further than just supporting suffragism. "Let them (women) do any kind of work they see fit," he said in 1899, "and if they do it as well as men, give them the same pay." America is still waiting on that one.

Lack of marital bliss was only one of Cody's problems in the last years of his life. Another was money, or the lack thereof. In addition to his share of Wild West show profits, Cody was paid well for allowing the visage of Buffalo Bill to appear in ads for dozens of products that included Winchester rifles, Stetson hats, Quaker oats and Mennen's borated talcum powder.

But Cody's handsome income almost unerringly found its way into bad investments. One was in a drink called Panamilt. Derived from grains, its inventors assured Cody that because it contained no caffeine, it would be wildly popular with Mormons as a coffee substitute. It wasn't. Another was a patent medicine supposedly based on an Iroquois herbal remedy. White Beaver's Cough Cream was guaranteed to cure most ailments of the respiratory system. It didn't. With a partner, he sank thousands into building a canal on the Nebraska prairie that was supposed to irrigate 12,000 acres and entice a community of Mormons to buy 80-acre tracts. The canal only wetted 4,000 acres, and the Mormons didn't show. And in terms of total dollars lost, the champion bad investment may have been an Arizona silver mine, whose operators mined Cody's pockets of an estimated $500,000 ($14.8 million in 2022).

Then there was creating a town. In the mid-1890s, a group of speculators led by a George T. Beck got the idea to build an irrigation system on federal land in the Big Horn Basin of Northwest Wyoming. Under a congressional act approved in 1894, private parties could claim hundreds of thousands of acres of public land with the condition that they provide it with enough water to make it farmable. Beck and his partners, who soon included Will Cody, planned to move water to the land from the sulphureous, and thus aptly named, Stinking Water River through a canal system.

Their Shoshone Irrigation Company succeeded in renaming the river to something more attractive—the Shoshone. But the U.S. Post Office blocked the company from also calling their planned town Shoshone because there was already a settlement nearby with that name. So they called it Cody, after their most famous investor.

The investors, particularly Cody, poured money into the project. Cody opened a newspaper in the tiny town and eventually built an ornate hotel he named after his daughter Irma, But the company failed to attract enough settlers or investors. By 1904, they ceded their rights to the land back to the federal government, which eventually completed an irrigation project that included two sizeable dams, one of them named Buffalo Bill. The human Buffalo Bill, meanwhile, was forced to sell off his holdings in and around his namesake town, including the hotel.

Despite failing health, Will Cody never gave up performing. In 1913, he formed a moving picture company that produced "authentic" re-creations of events such as his fight with Yellow Hair. In addition to Cody playing himself, the eight one-reel films featured some of the Indians from his Wild West shows as well as 600 troops of the 12th U.S. Cavalry, supplied by his old friend General Miles. Like other Cody ventures, however, the film business flopped.

A year before his death, he went to work for a traveling show that paid him $100 a day to lead a parade, sometimes on a horse and sometimes in a car, depending on how he was feeling.

Whatever his means of transport, he appeared in every show of the season. He had a private rail car, a valet, and the name "Buffalo Bill" appeared prominently in the show's advertising. "Now that my health is good," he wrote his sister Julia, "I must get to making big money."

But his health wasn't good. His heart, liver and other organs were failing. On Jan. 9, 1917, he made his own funeral arrangements. On January 10, he died at the Denver home of his sister. He was a month short of his 71st birthday.

Buffalo Bill's ability to draw a crowd didn't end with his death. Cody had hoped to be buried on Cedar Mountain, which overlooks the town of Cody. But his widow and one of the sleazeball Denver newspaper executives who had ripped him off in the Wild West show's final days conspired to have him interred in a monument on Lookout Mountain, which is in the city of Golden, Colorado, and overlooks Denver. Why isn't clear, although the prevailing rumor was the newspaper creep offered to pay for everything if the body stayed in Colorado, and Louisa, who was concerned about the state of Cody's finances, agreed. As it turned out, she was left with an estate worth the 2021 equivalent of about $2.1 million. Will Cody might have been surprised he was still worth that much.

He probably would not have been surprised that in death he was lionized. His body lay in state in the Colorado capitol to allow thousands to pass by and pay their respects. Condolence telegrams arrived from the German Kaiser, the British king and the American president. "He was the last link in the chain of historic personalities of his kind that figure in American history," said John Burke, who had served as Cody's chief image builder for more than a quarter of a century. "…"His tours of Europe left his name and personality indelibly stamped as a typical American in all the lands he visited."

There was little, however, that was typical about William F. Cody. Even among legendary Wild West figures, he stands out. Bat Masterson, Wyatt Earp and Wild Bill Hickok were well-known figures at the time of their deaths. But none of them was really legendary until years of biographical puffery, movies, television and merchandising elevated them to iconic status. George Custer and Jesse James were closer to the legend level when they died, and were initially aided by favorable post-mortem publicity. But the passage of time darkened their reputations, and even if they are now legendary, they are regarded by very few as heroic.

But Will Cody was truly a legend in his own time. By the time of his death, hundreds of dime novels—200 by the author Prentiss Ingraham alone—had helped to overwhelm the real-life frontiersman and replace him, or at least pair him, in the public eye with the larger-than-life Buffalo Bill. The contemporary dual persona of the man was the perfect Wild West legend, the essential blend of fact and fiction that epitomized his time and place.

As it turned out, Cody didn't need—or get—any help from movies like 1944's mawkish *Buffalo Bill,* starring Joel McCrea, or 1976's crappy-on-every-level *Buffalo Bill and the Indians* with Paul Newman as Cody. And he wasn't boosted by the plethora of 1950s and 60s television shows. Only one of them, *Buffalo Bill Jr.*, bore his name, and it was about a fictional orphan who was only named after Cody and had nothing to do with the historical figure.

Baby boomers who hear the name Bat Masterson most likely form a mental picture of actor Gene Barry from the 1950s television show. Younger Americans might hear the name Wyatt Earp and picture Kurt Russell or Kevin Costner from the 1990s films. But the best representation of Buffalo Bill might just be himself, in the 21st century form of a holographic image that greets visitors to one wing of the splendid Buffalo Bill Center of the West in Cody, Wyoming.

"If in following me through some of the exciting scenes of the Old West your interest is rewarded," the image says, "I shall feel richly repaid."

Chapter 14 Notes

As Cody explained William F. Cody, *Story of the Wild West and Campfire Chats,* pp. 704-05.

On board, Cody Ibid.

Cody and the *Lloyd's Weekly Newspaper*, April 10, 1887, p. 7.

Both the art *The Times* (London), May 10, 1887, p. 10.

To broaden its *Hampshire (UK) Telegraph and Naval Chronicle*, April 2, 1877, p. 11.

It was a Louis S. Warren, *Buffalo Bill's America*, pp. 294-95.

An endorsement by Cody, op. cit., p. 713.

Working on the Joy S. Kasson, *Buffalo Bill's Wild West*, p. 74.

Now made even *New York Times*, April 1, 1887, p. 8.

Other than being *The Daily News* (London) April 16, 1887, p. 6.

Cody liked the Cody, op. cit., pp. 727-728.

"...The state of" Ibid.

There was also *Chicago Tribune*, Sept. 18, 1880, p. 10.

Critics remained divided *Louisville (Ky.) Courier-Journal*, March 15, 1881, p. 1.

A Little Rock *Daily Arkansas Gazette* (Little Rock) Dec. 2, 1879, p. 6.

If he made Sandra K. Sagala, *Buffalo Bill on Stage*, p. 161.

He also spared *Leavenworth (Ks.) Times*, Oct. 9, 1881, p. 5.

And he dropped *Janesville (Wisc.) Daily Gazette*, Sept. 1, 1882, p. 4.

Despite the handsome *Leavenworth (Ks.) Times*, Oct. 9, 1881, p. 5.

But the famed Robert Carter, *Buffalo Bill, the Man Behind the Legend*, p. 219.

In his memoirs, Cody, op. cit., p. 693.

The grand opening *Omaha (Neb.) Bee,* May 21, 1883, p. 8.

In terms of *Hartford (Ct.) Courant*, July 26, 1883, p. 3.

Both of the Carter, op. cit., p. 251.

"I solemnly promise" Kasson, op. cit., p. 52.

The 1884 season *New Orleans Times-Picayune*, Dec. 14, 1884, p. 6.

The main consumers *Brooklyn Daily Eagle*, June 22, 1884, p. 3.

There was one *Boston Globe*, July 31, 1885, p. 5.

One of Sitting Bull's *Chicago Inter Ocean*, July 2, 1885, p. 3.

But Salsbury and *New York Times*, June 27, 1886, p. 6.

Although Buffalo Bill's Warren, op. cit., p. 297.

For millions of *The (London) Times*, May 10, 1887, p. 10; Nov. 1, 1887, p. 9.

It also laid *London Morning Post*, May 12, 1887, p. 5.

Ten days after *San Francisco Chronicle*, June 21, 1887, p. 1.

It was a *Chicago Tribune*, June 18, 1893, p. 26.

Another public controversy Chicago Tribune, Feb. 17, 1905, p. 1.

A somewhat surprising Daily Arkansas Gazette (Little Rock), Dec. 3, 1879, p. 8; Warren, op. cit., p. 195.

Despite his long Carter, op. cit., p. 389.

They poured money Cody, Wyoming is as of this writing a tidy town of about 10,000 that is home to the Cody Stampede, an annual rodeo that is one of America's largest. It also hosts hundreds of thousands of tourists each year who use it as a base to visit Yellowstone National Park, the East entrance of which is about 50 miles west. The Irma hotel is still operating.

A year before Ibid., p. 442.

Buffalo Bill's ability In 1948, the American Legion post in Cody offered $10,000 ($111,000 in 2021) to anyone who could bring Buffalo Bill's body "home." The American Legion post in Denver retaliated by posting armed guards around the grave. Both gestures were meaningless, since the monument's caretakers had poured 20 tons of concrete over Cody's remains. They are still there.

He probably would *Washington Post*, Jan. 11, 1917, p. 5.

Keepers of the Flame

It's a brisk and brilliantly blue-skyed January morning in the Texas Panhandle town of Mobeetie, and I am the only living person in the graveyard. Somewhere near here, precisely 144 years ago to the day, the beautiful saloon girl Mollie Brennan saved a young Bat Masterson's life. She did this by throwing herself in front of him during his gunfight with U.S. Army Corporal Melvin A. King. At least that's what it says on the granite headstone over which I'm standing. The headstone belongs to Mollie, and is in the Old Mobeetie Cemetery.

In Mollie's day, the town was known as Sweetwater, a wilderness oasis of gambling, whiskey and saloon girls for hundreds of buffalo hunters. Now it's called Mobeetie (which is widely believed to be Comanche for "buffalo dung"), a hamlet of about 100 inhabitants. There are no gambling joints or saloons or saloon girls in Mobeetie anymore– or much of anything else. There isn't even a Taco Bell or Subway within 25 miles, which I'm pretty sure in 2020 is against the law in the United States. But at least there are still several hundred buffalo nearby. They are in a feedlot, waiting to be turned into bison burgers. They stand quietly in corrals full of what the Comanche might call "mobeetie."

A month or two after my visit to Molly's grave, a former secondary school history teacher is speaking to a small group in a retirement community near Phoenix. His 90-minute presentation is entitled "The Unquiet Shades of Little Bighorn." Along with his shorts, golf shirt and tennis shoes, the speaker is wearing a straw hat. The hat, he explains, is to illustrate the kind of head covering many 7th Cavalry soldiers may have been wearing at the time of the epic battle. It was very hot the day of the fight, and the hats were cooler than the army-issue cavalry caps.

His lecture is informal, sprinkled with historical tidbits that evoke a steady stream of "wow," "interesting," and similar comments from his small audience. "We're going to the (Little Bighorn) monument in June,' a woman tells me as the group disperses. "This has gotten me more excited about it. I'm going to get that book he mentioned." She doesn't elaborate on precisely which of the several books he mentioned she is going to get. But she appears to be enthused.

Now it is shortly after Christmas, and I am in front of my television, watching a just-released movie starring Tom Hanks and called *News of the World*. It's a Western. Hanks plays Capt. Jefferson Kidd, a former Confederate Army officer whose world has been shattered by the war. Moving through isolated hamlets in the Southwest, he makes his living by reading newspapers to people who have little contact with the outside world. "Maybe," he says, "just for tonight, we can escape our troubles and hear of the great changes that are happening out there." He is also handy with a revolver, and there are Indians and some bad white guys and an orphaned girl who speaks no English and was raised as an Indian. It's like a Buffalo Bill play, only with newspapers and Tom Hanks.

What all this should tell you is that in 21st century America, the Wild West is still alive, and located wherever you look hard enough for it.

From time to time in our history, we've shifted the geographic boundaries of what we consider the Wild West (or frontier if you prefer.) Set in the 18th century, James Fenimore Cooper's five-novel series, the Leatherstocking Tales, defined America's frontier as "the interminable forests of the west...one vast expanse of woods...dotted by the glittering surfaces of lakes, and intersected by the waving lines of rivers." In other words, everything west of Albany, New York.

That changed bigtime in 1803. Faced with an offer he couldn't refuse, President Thomas Jefferson temporarily ignored the U.S. Constitution and bought 828,000 square miles of North America from the French for a price equaling about $428 a square mile in 2022 dollars. (He got the required congressional authorization after the deal, so it's still ours.) We picked up another 500,000 square miles after the war with Mexico formally ended in early 1848. In return for ceding one-third of its entire real estate holdings, Mexico got the 2022 equivalent of about $1,200 per square mile. That was better than the French did, but then again Mexico lost the war and didn't have a choice about selling or not. In any event, the Wild West now stopped at the Pacific Ocean.

But in 1893, a 32-year-old University of Wisconsin history professor contended the Wild West had stopped, period. At the very same time Will Cody was re-creating scenes from a Wild West that both was and never was at his show across from the Columbian Exposition in Chicago, Frederick Jackson Turner was a few miles away, reading a paper to the ninth annual meeting of the American Historical Association. The paper was entitled "The Significance of the Frontier in American History."

Boiled down, Turner's argument was that America's national identity was shaped and matured as it moved west. Old ways of doing things, imported mainly from Europe, were dropped in favor of pragmatic approaches that better fit frontier conditions, whether it was irrigating farmland, fencing livestock or removing cactus thorns. But, he added, the American frontier was for all intents and purposes closed by 1893. As evidence, he pointed out the U.S. Census bureau in 1890 had decided America's "unsettled area" could no longer be defined as a specific region because there were at least scattered settlements of white people all across the map.

"Up to our day," Turner read, "American history has been in large degree the history of the colonization of the West...since the days when the fleet of Columbus sailed into the waters of the New World, America has been another name for opportunity...and now, four centuries from the discovery of America, at the end of a hundred years of life under the Constitution, the Frontier has gone, and with its going has closed the first period of American history."

Almost precisely 67 years after Turner's address in Chicago, a Boston-bred politician accepted the Democratic Party's presidential nomination in Los Angeles and announced America was starting over. "I stand tonight facing west on what was once the last frontier," John F. Kennedy said. "From the land that stretches 3,000 miles behind me, the pioneers of old gave up their safety, their comfort and sometimes their lives to build a new world here in the West...(but) the problems are not all solved and the battles are not all won, and we stand today on the edge of a new frontier...".

But to my mind both Turner and Kennedy had limited visions of what constitutes the American Frontier.It's not just a geographic area, an historical period or a set of obstacles to overcome. It's a truth, based on a sometimes-shifting combination of fact and myth.

The cultural historian Richard Slotkin suggests that myths are basically stories told and retold until they become symbols of how we as a society think and behave. For example, the Battle of the Little Bighorn has been recounted so persistently in various forms that if I tell you my favorite football team played "like the cavalry at Custer's last stand," you'd have a pretty good idea what I was talking about. Similarly, if you tell me you are "getting out of Dodge," I've seen enough episodes of *Gunsmoke* to know you are making a hasty and almost certainly prudent exit from a precarious situation.

Legendary figures, and the legends that surround them, have the same role. If you stand up to a bullying boss like you were "Wyatt Earp at the OK Corral," or get treated by a salesman "like he was Jesse James," we know enough about what these figures represent in American culture to get the reference. It doesn't matter in this case that both Earp and James killed people in cold blood or committed other crimes from time to time. It's their image, not their reality, that makes them important. They may be legends because of a single act—the aforementioned OK Corral gunfight, for instance. It may be because they looked the parts they played—Buffalo Bill and Wild Bill come to mind. Or it may be the outlaw in each of us that gets to live vicariously through the daring of the James Boys and Younger

Brothers, without having to pull any triggers.

And sometimes it's a combination of factors that makes the legend. Let's say there was a fellow who fought valiantly in the Civil War for the Union and was rewarded with rapid promotions. After the war, he stayed in the army at a reduced rank and lobbied hard for the chance to go west and fight Indians. He even wrote a book about his experiences. And let's say he was something of a hard-ass when it came to driving his men, and led them into a trap in which they were heavily outnumbered. Finally, let's say that despite receiving a head wound and a broken leg, he held out with his men for more than a week, subsisting on rotting horse meat until a relief force showed up and saved them.

Sounded like George Armstrong Custer until that last sentence, didn't it? It was actually a guy named Major George "Sandy" Forsyth. The fight is known as the Battle of Beecher Island. It happened in 1868 on a tributary of the Arikaree River in eastern Colorado. It pitted 50 volunteer scouts against anywhere from 200 to 600 Cheyenne and Sioux. All but six of the scouts survived. So why have most Americans never heard of George Forsyth and almost every American knows who George Custer was? Well, Forsyth didn't wear buckskins, didn't have long flowing blonde locks, didn't hobnob with newspaper editors and Washington politicians, didn't blow his own horn at every opportunity, didn't have a wife who made him into a demi-god after he died—and he didn't achieve martyrdom by losing.

Most of all, George Forsyth failed to grab the media's attention. Wild West figures who became legends were aided in almost all cases by two 19th century developments. One was the rapid advancement of photography, which made it easier for people outside the frontier to accept them as real. At the same time, the explosion of cheap, mass-produced books and magazines helped make them larger than life, with each dime novel or breathless article topping its predecessor with even bigger feats of daring. Gilded Age Americans were just as inclined to believe what they read, if they read it often enough and in enough different places, as 21st century Americans are to believe what they see online if they see it on multiple websites.

In the 20th century, print was supplanted by movies and television in elevating Wild West legends, or relegating them to also-ran status. John Wesley Hardin killed or wounded at least 17 men—allegedly including one fellow whose snoring annoyed him—did a long stretch in prison, became a lawyer and was killed in a saloon while playing a dice game. Hollywood devoted one film to him. Billy the Kid killed eight men and has more than 50 movies to his credit. In the legends racket, it certainly helps to have a catchy nickname.

In the first decades of the 21st century, there is impressive evidence that the Wild West is enjoying a resurgence of interest in popular culture. Hollywood, for example, seems to have rediscovered the Western film genre. According to Comscore, a web-based media analysis company, the film industry cranked out 49 Western-themed movies between 2010 and 2019, more than double the number in the previous decade. "The Western is as American as apple pie," a ViacomCBS executive told the *Wall Street Journal* in March 2021.

Slices of Western pie, in the form of antiques and collectibles, are also fetching a pretty penny. The Winchester rifle used by John Wayne in the films *True Grit* and *Rooster Cogburn* sold for $88,500 at a January 2021 auction ($88,500 in 2022 dollars.) And a 10-guage shotgun, represented to be the very firearm Wyatt Earp used to blast Curly Bill Brocious during the Vendetta Ride of 1882, went for a hefty $375,000 at a Dallas auction in February 2020, even though there is doubt among some historians that Earp ever shot Brocious with any kind of weapon.

It's going on 150 years since this country celebrated its 100th birthday, and the Americans who made things happen then might be delighted, or appalled, at how it turned out. Alexander Graham Bell might be overjoyed at the sight of his invention's descendant emerging from a shirt pocket, stuffed with more information than was contained in all the libraries in the world in his lifetime. Eli Lilly might retch at the voracious greed of the pharmaceutical industry he helped create. P.T. Barnum might be president of the United States.

But I'd bet the Wild West legends who were born or nurtured in 1876 could find someplace to feel at home, because America's Wild West is still alive and well. Some of the places might even look familiar.

It is a warm and quiet Sunday morning in Dodge City, Kansas, and I am sitting at a poker table with Doc Holliday. Doc is staring at an empty chair opposite him, while reaching with his right hand for a revolver on his left hip, tucked partially beneath his coat. He has a cold, unblinking look in his eyes, quite possibly because he is made of bronze. So are the poker table and the chairs in which Doc and I are seated. Behind us is the town's newly renovated Boot Hill Museum. In front of us, a freight train is passing slowly on the tracks paralleling the street we're sitting next to, which is the town's main thoroughfare. The street is named Wyatt Earp Boulevard.

A few blocks away, Wyatt himself stands larger than life, holding a long-barreled pistol in his right hand while pivoting to see something that has caught his attention just behind him. A glob of bird poop ignominiously decorates his left shoulder. Such is the fate of bronze statues.

Even so, Dodge likes metal likenesses of Wild West icons. In addition to Holliday and Earp, there is the bronze likeness of a big Texas Longhorn known as El Capitan. By the end of 2021, Bat Masterson, complete with cane and derby hat, and leaning on a saloon bar, was scheduled to be unveiled. And directly in front of the Dodge Visitors Center is a 6'7" statue of actor James Arness (matching his actual height), reprising his iconic role as Dodge's fictional U.S. marshal Matt Dillon on *Gunsmoke*, the longest-running Western in television history.

It says volumes about the inextricable blend of Wild West fact and fiction that a statue of a television character greets visitors to what is almost certainly America's most famous genuine cowtown. And this is still very much a cowtown. The two biggest employers in Dodge as of 2021 were the National Beef and Cargill Meat Solutions meatpacking plants. Just over the hill from this city of about 28,000, there is a spot where you can look down on feedlots full of hundreds, if not thousands, of cattle awaiting their dates with destiny. Or McDonald's.

When it comes to playing up its Wild West past, Dodge doesn't stop at bronze statues, nor is it shy about mixing fact with fabulism. The "Dodge City Trail of Fame" is a mélange of sidewalk medallions, informational storyboards, historic buildings and pole-mounted art banners. For the most part, they celebrate places, people and events in Dodge's past, such as Hamilton "Ham" Bell. Mr. Bell lived in Dodge for 73 of his 94 years, 36 of them as a lawman, and ran businesses that ranged from a livery stable to the town's first auto dealership. But there are also some head-scratchers on the trail, such as a medallion that bears the name of Henry Fonda. The only connection I can deduce is that Fonda once portrayed Wyatt Earp in a film—set in Tombstone, Arizona.

Dodge hasn't always been as enthusiastic about embracing its past. In 1885, the cattle drives from Texas were stopped for fear of splenic fever spreading to domestic stock. Within a decade, the former "Wickedest Little City in America" had embraced prohibition. "...The city is now a paragon of virtue, sobriety and industry," a local newspaper crowed in 1899. In actuality what the city became was just another sleepy, windy, dusty town, 335 miles from Kansas City, 380 miles from Denver, and light years from anyone's idea of a tourist destination.

But in 1932, longtime local dentist O.H. Simpson decided to entertain delegates to a regional Rotary Club convention. He did so by placing plaster death masks and boots on some of the graves in the "Boot Hill" cemetery that served as Dodge's quick-and-easy burial ground from 1872 to 1878. Other townsfolk erected a billboard identifying the site as "Dodge City's Famous Boot Hill, Grounds of the Six-Shooting Bad Men." A small curio shop opened, and a tourist attraction was born.

Then Hollywood came along. In 1939, Warner Brothers released *Dodge City*, starring Errol Flynn and Olivia De Havilland.("West of Chicago there was no law," the movie's advertising posters declared, "west of Dodge, no god.") An enterprising delegation of Dodge citizens convinced the studio to premiere the film, which turned out to be a huge box-office hit, in its namesake town. The premiere drew an immense crowd to the small town and garnered nationwide press attention for Dodge.

Suddenly this Wild West stuff looked financially pretty interesting. After World War II, a small museum was opened. In the mid-1950s, television did the movies one better. On Sept. 6, 1955, *The Life and Legend of Wyatt Earp* debuted on ABC. Four nights later, CBS countered with *Gunsmoke.* Both shows were set in Dodge (although not filmed there), simultaneously making it TV's safest city, with Wyatt Earp *and* Matt Dillon patrolling the streets,and America's most dangerous city, with at least one person, and usually more, being shot every week.

A wooden replica of Dodge's Front Street as it appeared in 1876 was opened in 1958, in ceremonies presided over by actor Hugh O'Brian, television's Wyatt Earp. The first of what became an annual 10-day "Dodge City Days" fete began in 1997. And in May 2020, the town's Boot Hill Museum opened a sparkling $6 million, 13,000 square-foot addition that provided more space for the museum's 28,000-plus artifacts and 45,000 photos.

"I think we have a leg up on many places," a ticket-taker at the museum told me, "since so much of what we have here is the real thing."

While Dodge is still a cowtown, Deadwood is most decidedly no longer a mining town, unless mining tourists counts. Cutting down trees and extracting minerals from the earth as the basis for the local economy gave way in the early 1990s to selling Wild Bill keychains and enticing visitors to feed the town's 4,600-plus slot machines. If there is one characteristic Deadwood has developed through its century and a half of existence, it's flexibility.

It had to be flexible to survive. From its beginnings in 1876, Deadwood has struggled through fires, floods, blizzards, more fires, and the routing of a major highway that missed the town by 14 miles. Through it all, Deadwoodians ambled along to a decidedly different drumbeat than the rest of the state of South Dakota, or the rest of America for that matter.

Despite being illegal, gambling joints openly flourished until 1947, when reluctant local law enforcement officials acquiesced to the demands of state agencies and shut them down.

Up until the morning of May 21, 1980, one could walk three blocks from the elementary school down Main Street, enter one's choice of a white, beige, purple or green door, stroll up 26 steps and visit one of Deadwood's quartet of openly operating brothels. "As long as people keep their noses clean," the chief of police explained to a bemused out-of-town reporter in February, 1980, "we don't bother them." That changed when federal and state law enforcement raided the establishments on the aforementioned May morning and got a permanent injunction shutting them down.

By the mid-1980s, the town was literally falling apart. Many of the older buildings were unusable and boarded up. Streets were so filled with potholes that city officials pondered the idea of replacing paved roads with gravel ones to save money. But in 1988, Deadwood convinced the rest of the state to amend the South Dakota constitution and legalize gambling in the town of about 1,300 permanent residents. Having already become the first U.S. city to be designated a national historic site in its entirety, Deadwood became just the third American locale, after Nevada and Atlantic City, New Jersey, to have legalized casino gambling in the 20th century.

The financial windfall to the town was beyond anyone's wildest dreams. Deadwood officials expected to net from $100,000 to $500,000 in the first full year of gambling operations. The take was $6.2 million. By 2019, Deadwood's share (the state also gets a percentage) over the first three decades of gambling was $194 million. The money paid for a raft of civic improvements, and the lure of the town's two dozen-plus casinos attracted an estimated $350 million in private investments in hotels, restaurants and a convention center.

If gambling wasn't enough of an inducement to visit, the town received another promotional boost in 2004 with the debut of an HBO mini-series. *Deadwood* was disturbingly violent, jarringly profane and outrageously entertaining. Following the show's first season, the Deadwood Chamber of

Commerce reported a 350 percent increase in brochure requests, a doubling of phone calls seeking information and more than 42 million visits to its website. "The show is giving us visibility nationwide," Mayor Francis Toscano said. "(And) any publicity is better than no publicity."

There can of course be too much of a good thing, and in attracting two million tourists each year, Deadwood's Wild West aura is sometimes obscured by a Disneylandish onslaught of tour buses, staged street shootouts and Calamity Jane curly fries. But there are undeniable nuggets to be found as well.

One of those nuggets perches above the town, on a pine tree-studded hilltop. The Mt. Moriah Cemetery is so pretty it makes you wish you didn't have to be dead to stay there on a long-term basis. Besides Wild Bill Hickok and Calamity Jane Canary, its residents include Seth Bullock, the town's first marshal and a prominent businessman who gained international recognition through his depiction as a leading character in the HBO series. Another occupant is Dora DuFran, a well-known Black Hills madam who was buried with her pet parrot, Fred. The latter departed after he choked on a wax cherry he snatched from a woman's hat. Dora died of a heart attack, although not at the same time as Fred.

Another Deadwood gem is the Adams Museum. Established in 1930 as a catch-all for eclectic and oddball items—a fitting idea for Deadwood—the museum evolved into a thoughtful encyclopedia of the town's past. Items range from an impressive and locally excavated fossilized plesiosaur to leather straps that bound the wrists of three desperadoes who were hanged in the 1890s.

Best of all, the museum deftly balances historical fact with the recognition that legends and lies have played a key role in shaping the town's image. A placard entitled "Living with Legends" lists several Deadwood denizens who became worldwide celebrities, then adds: "*These characters were not universally revered in their day. Some were known only in Deadwood. A few were even despised. But for more than a century, the mass media has given each a role, not only in the city's promotional efforts, but in the global imagination of the American West."*

And Deadwood is still tickling the imagination. In the summer of 2020, the town's latest attraction opened. It's a $15 tour, in an historical sense, of one of the Main Street brothels that was closed in 1980. You must be 16 or older, and there are no senior discounts.

While finding a place to park in Deadwood can be a headache, it is never a problem at the Warbonnet Battlefield historic site. Finding the site itself can be a major pain, but you needn't worry about the parking. The monument—and that is stretching the generally accepted use of the term—is where Buffalo Bill Cody fought and killed the Cheyenne warrior Yellow Hair in July, 1876, and claimed the "first scalp for Custer."

It's tucked into the sparsely populated northwest corner of Nebraska, surrounded by arid plains and rolling hills given over to cattle grazing and crisscrossed with a tangled maze of numbingly identical rutted dirt roads. The site is administered by the U.S. Forest Service, which is pretty funny when you think about it, since the nearest forest would appear to be at least two time zones away.

Because the monument is surrounded by land leased to private ranches, it's enclosed with barbed wire, apparently to keep cattle out. There doesn't appear to be much that cattle could damage. At the top of a small but steep hill is a narrow 7-foot-tall pyramid of rocks embedded in concrete. A bronze plaque notes that this is the site where *"Seven Companies of the Fifth U.S. Cavalry under Col. Wesley Merritt intercepted 800 Cheyennes and Sioux enroute to join Indians in the North, July 17, 1876."*

About 100 yards south of the hill, almost obscured by weeds and surrounded by a waist-high wrought-iron fence, is a second rocks-and-concrete marker about half the height of the one on the hill. It bears a plaque that reads *"On this spot, W.F. Cody, Buffalo Bill, Killed Yellow Hair or Hand, the Cheyenne leader who with a party of warriors dashed down the ravine to waylay two soldiers coming from the West, July 17, 1876."*

That's it—unless you can stop complaining long enough about the long hot drive to let your imagination kick in. Then maybe, just maybe, you can hear the sound of trumpet calls and shouts in the distance, or the muffled thuds of horses' hooves that are supposed to haunt the site, along with eerie green lights that illuminate the field on nights around the anniversary of the skirmish.

The story of how the plaques got here is almost as interesting as the site itself, and much less dusty. It seems that in 1930, a group of Wyoming men who were striving to memorialize important historic locales in the West enlisted the help of two guys who had actually been at the Warbonnet fight. One was Gen. Charles King, who was a captain with the 5th in 1876 and went on to become a distinguished officer and author. The other was Christian Madsen, who was a trooper, and went on to become a famous Oklahoma lawman. Both men visited the area and looked it over. After some disagreement as to the precise locations of events, the 86-year-old King deferred to the 79-year-old Madsen, and they decided this was close enough.

On Sept. 6, 1934, the two markers were dedicated in a ceremony that a local newspaper said commemorated "the epic period of Northwest Nebraska's settlement." Such as it was. The hilltop marker was financed by a group of local citizens and veterans. The smaller marker was paid for by the widow of Johnny Baker, the sharpshooting "Cowboy Kid" who had starred in Buffalo Bill's Wild West shows and whom Will Cody regarded as a son. "Few people in this vicinity were informed of the erection (of the monuments)" or the historic site's location, a local paper noted. After nearly a century, it seems to have stayed that way.

Those who prefer their battlefields a bit more defined might head about 375 miles northwest, to the Little Bighorn Battlefield National Monument, in southeastern Montana. In a sense, it's the site of two battles, fought more than a century apart. The first was a brutal, bloody fight for survival. The second was a bloodless but still-fierce struggle to balance history. For the first fight, see Chapter 4. For the second, read on.

The monument covers an area of sere, rolling hills, separated by ruts and ravines that give way to greener pastures and cottonwood thickets near the placid stream on the valley floor. It began life in 1879, three years after the battle, as a national cemetery. By 1978, when the cemetery was declared full, it hosted slightly more than 5,000 soldiers who fought in almost every U.S. military conflict, from the Spanish-American War to Vietnam.

In 1881, a 12-foot-high, 18-ton granite memorial was erected and inscribed with the names of the officers, enlisted men and white civilians who died during the battle between the 7th Cavalry and the Plains tribes. While George Custer and the 7th's officers had already been moved to other cemeteries, the remains of the enlisted men were dug up from their original graves and reburied at the base of the monument. The memorial is at the top of Last Stand Hill. Just below it is a field of 52 simple white markers, surrounded by a waist-high fence. The markers designate where the bodies of Custer and the men with him were found. Only Custer's marker, roughly in the center of the group, bears a name.

About five miles away from the obelisk are a series of bluffs where the pummeled vestiges of the 7th's survivors, under major Marcus Reno and Captain Frederick Benteen, fought desperately to escape Custer's fate. There is a 45-minute stroll on a paved walkway around the bluffs' perimeter, with 18 stops. A cellphone guide and/or excellent booklet by the Western National Park Association explains elements of the battle, complete with observations left behind by fighters from both sides.

Then there is the site's newest addition—and what might be viewed as a monument to the "Second Battle of the Little Bighorn." Completed in 2003, the memorial, near the 7th Cavalry obelisk, consists of a stone wall that semi-circles a 12-foot-high, 35-foot-long bronze wire sculpture of three Indian warriors on horseback. The sculpture, in the words of one writer, "looks like a line drawing in the sky." The side of the wall facing the sculpture bears five inscribed panels, each representing one of the three Indian nations that fought Custer—the Cheyenne, Lakota and Arapaho—and the two that scouted for the 7th, the Crow and Arikara.

At the roots of the installation is a struggle that began less than 50 years after Custer's demise. In 1925, the daughter of Lame White Man, a Cheyenne warrior who died in the battle, asked federal officials to place a marker honoring her father at the battlefield. She was ignored. In the decades that followed, Native American individuals and groups periodically—and fruitlessly—requested that as rather significant participants in the battle, i.e., the winners, they be represented at the monument.

In June 1988, a group of 40 Indian activists placed a steel plaque at the base of the 7th Cavalry obelisk. The plaque read *"In honor of our Indian patriots who fought and defeated the U.S. Cavalry in order to save our women and children from mass murder. In doing so, preserving our rights to our Homeland, Treaties and Sovereignty."* American Indian Movement spokesman Russell Means said the plaque was also meant to protest the presence of the cavalry memorial, contending it was tantamount to a memorial for Nazi troopers being placed in Jerusalem.

Park officials removed the plaque, but the action pricked some consciences in Congress. In 1991, Rep. Ron Marlenee, R-Montana, and Rep. Ben Nighthorse Campbell, R-Colorado, introduced a bill that not only called for construction of an Indian-centric memorial at the monument, but for renaming the monument itself. What had originally been christened as the Custer Battlefield National Monument, they argued, should be the Little Bighorn Battlefield National Monument. Campbell, the only Native American member of Congress, argued that A) no other national battlefields were named after individuals; B) renaming the site would go a long way toward healing the wounds still festering from America's shameful treatment of Indians, and C) the Indians won.

Many Custerphiles were apoplectic. They contended the name change would somehow distort history, was an obsequious bow to political correctness, and could confuse potential visitors who might not be able to find the monument under a new name. Seriously, that's what they argued. As to the Indian memorial, the director of the Custer Battlefield Historical and Museum Association said "I see no more need for putting an Indian memorial there than I see the need for building a monument to the Japanese at Pearl Harbor or the Mexicans at the Alamo."

Despite such, uh, well-reasoned objections, Congress overwhelmingly approved both the name change and Indian memorial and President George W. Bush signed it into law in late 1991. Having done the right thing, however, was apparently such a strange experience for federal officials they neglected to include any money to finance a new memorial. It took another 11 years for $2.3 million to be allotted for the work. In the meantime, park officials began adding red granite markers to denote where Indian warriors were believed to have fallen during the battle. In 1999, 74 years after his daughter first asked, Lame White Man got his battlefield marker.

Finally, on June 25, 2003, on the 127th anniversary of the battle's start, more than 4,000 people gathered to see the formal unveiling of the Indian memorial. "We unite today to write the chapter unfinished," said Crow Tribal Chairman Carl Venne. "The circle has not been complete until today."

But completing circles that link the past with the present and future isn't limited to monuments. It applies to people too.

Frank Spence sits back in his chair, sips his lemonade, and talks about his great-grandfather, the robber and killer. "When I was growing up, he was just not spoken of," Spence says. "He abandoned his family; he did bad things. It's not something to brag about."

It's a Wednesday morning at the Wild Horse West Bar & Grill, on a flat stretch of Sonoran Desert about 20 miles north of downtown Phoenix. I'm meeting Spence mainly to talk about his hobby. But given the subject of this book, talking about his ancestor seems unavoidable.

Great-grandpa was a Cowboy, and not the get-along-little-dogie kind. In early 1880s Arizona, Pete Spence was part of a loosely organized gang that rustled cattle, robbed stagecoaches and tangled in and around Tombstone with the Earp Brothers and Doc Holliday. Another of the Cowboys was Frank Stilwell, the man Wyatt Earp gunned down at the Tucson railroad station in 1882. "Great-grandfather was partners with Frank Stilwell," Spence says. "They did everything together, some legal and some not legal. They had a saloon in Bisbee, they had a timber business selling timber to the mines, they had a livery in Charleston, and they robbed stage coaches."

One of the other things Spence and Stilwell were suspected of having done together was murdering Morgan Earp. Wyatt partially avenged his brother in Tucson by killing Stilwell, and then went looking for Spence at a wood camp Spence owned. Spence wasn't there, having cleverly taken refuge in the Tombstone jail by turning himself in. So Wyatt killed another man at the camp that he suspected of also being in on the killing of Morgan. Spence was charged with Morgan Earp's murder, mainly on evidence offered by his wife. The charges were dropped after the judge decided she couldn't testify against her own husband.

But great-grandpa Spence had correctly deduced Wyatt Earp wasn't concerning himself with the legal system in hunting down his brother's killers. "When all the killing started (by Wyatt and his Vendetta Ride posse)," Frank Spence explains, "my great-grandfather decided that was not too smart a thing to be involved in, so he moved to Silver City (New Mexico), after he abandoned my great-grandmother." Somewhat improbably, Pete Spence became a lawman in New Mexico, before reverting to character. After pistol-whipping a prisoner to death, Spence went to prison, was pardoned after 18 months and died a goat rancher at the age of 62.

At the time of our conversation, Frank Spence is 70. In his working days, he was a highly successful commercial general contractor, so successful that he retired at 58. Then he became a U.S. Customs and Border Protection officer for a while before retiring again. And then he threw his considerable energy into a hobby at which he became proficient enough to be ranked among the world's best. His hobby is dressing like his great-grandfather did and shooting pistols, rifles and shotguns that would have been familiar to Wyatt Earp or Wild Bill Hickok.

It's called Cowboy Action Shooting. Its origin can be traced to a couch in Orange County, California, on a rainy afternoon in 1981. The couch was occupied by Harper Creigh, a former U.S. marine who owned a highly successful architectural and topographical model firm, loved to shoot and at the moment was bored stiff. Idly watching an old Western on television, Creigh got the idea to get together some buddies, dress up like Wild West figures, get some antique firearms or replicas of antique firearms, and have some kind of shooting contest.

The eventual result was the Single Action Shooting Society (SASS), which as of 2021 had more than 100,000 members in all 50 states and 18 foreign countries. The basic tenets are simple: dress up as a Wild West character, come up with an alias that is unique and "printable before a wide audience," and figure out what kind of shooting events you might like to compete in.

Frank Spence's character is a working cowboy named Frank Stilwell. His favorite event is "duelist style," which means shooting pistols with each hand, then using rifles and shotguns in competition that is judged on speed, accuracy, safety, technique and being a good sport—what SASS calls the "Spirit of the Game." Spence is very good at the game. He has won state championships in Texas, New Mexico, Arizona and Nevada and finished third twice in the world championships in his 60-and-over category.

"The SASS tent covers those who like dressing up, who like the competition, who like the shooting or just like the spectacle," he says. "There are people who have shot in other kinds of competitions, but SASS is much more friendly and much less cutthroat. Shooters will actually lend their backup firearms to competitors who are having trouble with their own. I've seen it again and again; it just attracts those kinds of people."

It must, because Spence offers to take me to nearby range and try my luck with his twin Ruger New Model .38 special revolvers with 4-5/8th inch barrels. They look vaguely like the old Mattel Fanner 50s my folks gave me when I was 7, which were the last guns of any kind I have owned. Most SASS members use modern replicas of 19th century firearms. "The real antiques are too valuable," Spence says. "We run 'em hard, so these are all exact replicas. You wouldn't take a $5,000 gun out there and run it hard. I'll shoot 60,000 rounds per year, in practice and competition."

At the range, Spence patiently shows me how to load the cartridges into the barrel's chambers, half-cocking the hammer and making sure one is left empty so the hammer doesn't accidentally come down on a loaded chamber. Holding the gun in my right hand, supported around the wrist by my left hand, I pull the hammer back with my left thumb, and squeeze the trigger with my right hand's appropriately named trigger finger.

The result is a satisfying ping as the bullet hits a round metal target maybe 25 feet away. I repeat the process perhaps 80 times over the next half hour, sometimes hitting the various targets and sometimes terrorizing the surrounding dirt and vegetation. A cow wanders into a dry streambed between the shooting tables and the targets and is clearly unimpressed. "If he keeps coming," one of the range masters laconically notes, "maybe we'll have lunch."

Spence occasionally takes a turn, shooting with both hands and getting off 10 accurate shots in the time it takes me to fire once or twice. The gun is lighter than I expected, the kickback negligible. Spence says it's because the cartridges are lightly loaded with powder, since there's no need to ensure the targets are permanently injured.

Another fellow SASS shootist who is there to take a lesson from a world champion, wanders over to say hello. He is Bill Hallinan, a self-described "recovering attorney" from nearby Scottsdale. At 75, Hallinan, whose alias is "Lefty Law," says his passion is still golf. But hunting buddies convinced him to give Cowboy Shooting a try. "I've competed three or four times," he says. "I'm not very good, but I really like getting into the character. What kid who grew up in the 40s and 50s didn't want to be a cowboy?"

A few weeks later, I attend the "Winter Range," which is another name for the National Championship of Cowboy Action Shooting, at a state-owned range near where the foothills give way to the McDowell Mountains north of Phoenix. It's perfect shooting weather: blue skies dabbed by wispy white clouds, just the hint of a breeze, temperatures in the low 70s.

Perhaps a thousand people roam the grounds, many if not most outfitted in replica regalia, from Annie Oakleys to Butch Cassidys. There are gamblers, dancehall girls, drovers and desperadoes. Earplugs and eye protection are the only giveaways that someone has not just stepped from the streets of Laredo instead of getting out of the RV from Toledo.

The air is filled with pops and pings. The former comes from the low-load pistol, rifle and shotgun ammunition that is constantly being fired somewhere on one of the dozen-plus contest venues. The latter comes from most of the shots hitting metal squares or circles that serve as targets. At the cowboy matches, shooters empty their two six-guns, then race to adjacent stands to fire repeating rifles and double-barreled shotguns. The shooting takes place behind various facades of hotels, forts, trains and saloons. The targets are considerably closer to the stands than the distances portrayed between dueling gunfighters in the movies, and therefore much closer to the reality of almost all actual Wild West gunfights. After each round, the shooters empty their firearms under the eyes of an observer at the loading tables to ensure no one is walking around with a loaded gun.

The SASS crowd is only part of the Winter Range event. The 5,000-member Cowboy Fast Draw Association is also well represented. Starting in Deadwood in 2002, the CFDA takes a different approach to reliving the Wild West. In these matches, six competitors assume a crouched position, knees bent and torsos arched backward as if they were dodging a punch. When a light illuminates in the center of a 24-inch disc in front of them, they yank the single-action .45 caliber six-guns from holsters strapped low across their waists and fire wax bullets. A hit on the disc records the time—to a thousandth of a second—it takes for the bullet to get from gun to target. Holsters and guns have restrictions that seek to keep them as close to the 19th century as possible. No Hollywood stunt fast-draw holsters or specially modified guns are allowed.

The targets are 15 feet to 21 feet away. If that sounds pretty close, try this: Put your hand at your hip, draw it to your waist, move your thumb as if retracting a pistol hammer, and squeeze your index finger as if pulling a trigger. Do it in a half-second or less, and you might want to strap on a Colt Peacemaker and mosey on down to the range.

One fellow, who has been at it almost 18 years and is, well, realllly fast, told me he had a six-month slump once "during which I couldn't hit the sky." He finally figured out that one of the heels on his boots had worn down. "That's all it takes to throw you off, just that little bit." It takes a fast draw champion about 3/10ths of a second to draw, fire and hit the target. Assuming you are normal, it takes you about that long to blink.

All of this fun doesn't come cheap, and takes hours of practice, which goes a long way to explaining why it seems to mainly be a hobby for older folks. But not everyone here is of pension age. Page Karsten, aka "Cowgirl Up," has been shooting since she was seven, which was all of eight years ago. Dressed in an outfit that hearkens to a sort of "saloon girl on her way to church" theme, she has just skunked an opponent in a fast-draw competition, putting up some enviable speeds. Of course at maybe 5'1" tall on a stretched-out day, she doesn't have as far to bend as some others.

Page is from Rancho Cucamonga in California. She got into the fast-draw life because her dad was involved, "and he wanted to make it into a father-daughter thing, and I tried it and really liked it." It also sparked an interest in the Old West. "I like watching Western movies and television...I guess mostly I like the drama. It seems like life was not as crazy back then. And the clothes were cool."

In a gentle but cold and steady rain on a Wednesday morning in September, three dozen people gather before the cemetery monument of a hometown hero. The town is Northfield, Minnesota, a community of about 20,000 maybe a 45-minute drive south of the Minneapolis-St. Paul megaplex.

The hero is Joseph Lee Heywood, who died 144 years and two days ago.

Heywood was the bookkeeper for the First National Bank of Northfield, and was filling in as cashier on Sept. 7, 1876, when the James-Younger gang showed up. He was shot and killed by Frank James after refusing to open the bank's vault, which contained the town's treasury, the cash reserves of a local college and a substantial share of the life savings of Northfield's citizenry.

In normal years, a memorial service at Heywood's grave—which is in a cemetery down the street from the bank and across from the local high school—kicks off the annual "Defeat of Jesse James Days" festival. Northfield has celebrated it every year since 1946. The festival usually includes a carnival, arts and crafts exhibits, live music, refreshments from the town's distillery, cidery and two breweries, and a pretty lively reenactment of the robbery, complete with horses, period costumes and replica firearms.

But this is no normal year. Restrictions and precautions imposed by the Covid-19 pandemic mean the festival has been reduced to this face-masked and socially distanced outdoor graveside ceremony, and some "virtual events" online. "We're naturally disappointed," Mayor Pro Tem Clarice Grabau tells me, "but we're pretty resourceful. We'll do the best we can with what we have come up with and hope next year is back to normal."

Nestled on both sides of the small but scenic Cannon River, Northfield has a neat and cozy feel, aided and abetted by the ambiance of two colleges, Carleton and St. Olaf, a handsome greenbelt adjoining the river and a downtown core whose tidy streets are enhanced by hanging baskets of flowers. Petunias, I think.

Unlike Dodge City or Deadwood, Northfield isn't a treasure chest of Wild West experiences, nor a mecca for fans of the American Frontier. In fact, if it weren't for the seven minutes of pandemonium surrounding the 1876 bank robbery, it would probably be best known as the birthplace of Malt O'Meal breakfast cereal.

But it does have the very bank where the robbery took place, meticulously restored to the way it looked in 1876. The adjoining museum artfully lays out its exhibits in a tick-tock succession that allows visitors to follow the fateful day's events as they unfolded. The exhibits are relatively modest, but honestly presented. There's the single-shot Civil War-era rifle that medical student Henry Wheeler used to kill bandit Clell Miller, and the pistol Wheeler carried the rest of his life as protection against potential revenge from Miller's family. There are several photos of Miller's corpse, alongside that of fellow outlaw Bill Chadwell, who was also killed during the robbery. And there is the bank ledger for the day following the robbery, showing the loss of a paltry $26.70, thanks to Heywood.

Back at the cemetery, a genial, bespectacled fellow who has lived in Northfield for about seven years and is president and CEO of the local hospital is giving a short speech. The point of the ceremony, says Steve Underdahl, is to honor a man who put the well-being of his community before his own safety.

In 1876, Underdahl points out, there was no FDIC insurance, no government or social safety net. If the gang had left with the town's money, there was no replacing it. So Heywood refused to hand it over, and died because of it. The sacrifice of a bank clerk in 1876, he continues, is comparable to the sacrifices being made during the current Covid-19 crisis by people in jobs that we ordinarily don't think of as particularly heroic or dangerous: grocery store clerks, fast food workers, nurses' aides, care home employees.

"Most of the time," he concludes, "when we get through a crisis, we come out of it because these regular folks make the difference. It's always regular folks that save the world."

He's right of course. Legends, Wild West or otherwise, can entertain us, inspire us, educate us and bind us together as communities, nations and cultures. But it's the regular folks—who thus inspired, entertained educated and bound together—go out and save the world. And that's precisely why we need from time to time to transform some regular folks, with all their flaws and failings, into legends.

Chapter 15 Notes

"Up to our" Frederick Jackson Turner, *The Frontier in American History*, p. 1; pp. 37-38.

Almost precisely 67 *Tampa (Fla.) Tribune*, July 16, 1960, p. 4.

In the first *Wall Street Journal*, March 6, 2021.

Dodge hasn't always *Dodge City Globe*, Aug. 3, 1899, p. 1.

It had to *Sioux Falls (SD) Argus-Leader*, Feb. 4, 1980, p. 2.

If gambling wasn't *Mansfield (Oh.) News-Journal*, March 6, 2005, p. 23.

On Sept. 6 *Northwest Nebraska News*, Sept. 6., 1934, p. 1; *Crawford (Neb.) Tribune*, Sept. 14, 1934, p. 6.

Then there is *Rapid City (SD) Journal*, May 18, 2003, p. A9.

Many Custerphiles were *Detroit Free Press*, April 21, 1991, p. 15.

Finally, on June 25, *Billings (Mt.) Gazette*, June 26, 2003, p, 12A.

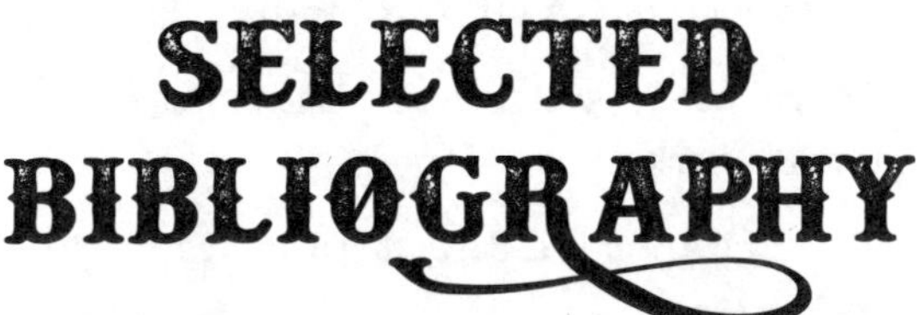

SELECTED BIBLIOGRAPHY

1876 and the Gilded Age:

Axelrod, Alan. *The Gilded Age: 1876-1912, Overture to the American Century.* New York: Sterling Publishing, 2017.

Barnum, Phineas T. *Life of P.T. Barnum, Written by Himself, Including His Golden Rules for Money-Making.* Buffalo: The Courier Company, Printers, 1888.

Bergamini, John D. *The Hundredth Year: The United States in 1876.* New York: G.P. Putnam's Sons, 1976.

Boyer, Paul S. (ed.) *The Oxford Companion to United States History.* Oxford (UK): Oxford University Press, 2001.

Brogan, Hugh. *The Penguin History of the United States of America.* London (UK): Penguin Books, 1985.

Brown, Dee. *The Year of the Century: 1876.* New York: Charles Scribner's Sons, 1966.

Carter, Hodding. The Angry Scar: The Story of Reconstruction. New York: Doubleday & Company, 1959.

Cashman, Sean Dennis. *America in the Gilded Age: From the Death of Abraham Lincoln to the Rise of Theodore Roosevelt* (3rd ed.). New York: New York University Press, 1993.

Chernow, Ron. *Grant.* New York: Penguin Press, 2017.

Cornell, William Mason. *The Life of Samuel Jones Tilden, Governor of the State of New York.* Boston: Lee & Shepard, 1876.

Craughwell, Thomas J. *Stealing Lincoln's Body.* Cambridge (Ma.): Belknap Press, 2007.

Devol, George H. *Forty Years a Gambler on the Mississippi.* New York: Home Book Co., 1894.

Enss, Chris. "First the West, Then the Rest of the Nation." *Western Writers of*

America Roundup Magazine, Vol. XXVII, No. 4 (April, 2020), pp. 8-11.

Furnas, J.C. *The Americans: A Social History of the United States, 1587–1914.* New York: G.P. Putnam's Sons, 1969.

Harris, Neal. *Humbug: The Art of P.T. Barnum.* Boston: Little, Brown and Company, 1973.

Hayes, Rutherford B. *Diary and Letters of Rutherford B. Hayes, 19th President of the United States* (Five Volumes). Columbus (OH): Ohio State Archeological and Historical Society, 1922.

Hilton, Suzanne. *The Way It Was—1876.* Philadelphia: Westminster Press, 1975.

Johnson, Paul. *A History of the American People.* New York: Harper Collins Publishers, 1999.

Kahn, E.J. Jr. *All in a Century: The First 100 Years of Eli Lilly and Company.* Indianapolis: Eli Lilly and Company, 2007.

Kunhardt, Phillip P. Jr, Phillip P. Kunhardt III, Peter W. Kunhardt. *P.T. Barnum: America's Greatest Showman.* New York: Alfred P. Knopf, 1995.

Lepore, Jill. *These Truths: A History of the United States.* New York: W.W. Norton & Co., 2018.

Levine, Peter. *A.G. Spalding and the Rise of Base Ball: The Promise of American Sport.* New York: Oxford University Press, 1985.

Morris, Roy Jr. *Fraud of the Century: Rutherford B. Hayes, Samuel Tilden, and the Stolen Election of 1876.* New York: Simon & Schuster, 2003.

Moulton, Candy. "We Won't Back Down." *True West Magazine*, Vol. 67, No. 6 (July/August 2020), pp. 44-46.

Powers, Ron. *Mark Twain: A Life.* New York: Free Press, 2005.

Rowell, John W. *Yankee Artillerymen: Through the Civil War with Eli Lilly's Indiana Battery.* Knoxville (Tn.): University of Tennessee Press, 1975.

Rugoff, Milton. *America's Gilded Age: Intimate Portraits from an Era of Extravagance and Change, 1850-1890.* New York: Henry Holt and Company, 1989.

Sandhurst, Phillip. *The Great Centennial Exhibition, Critically Described and Illustrated.* Philadelphia: P.W. Ziegler & Co., 1876.

Schlereth, Thomas J. *Victorian America: Transformation in Everyday Life.* New

York: Harper Collins Publishers, 1991.

Skrabac, Quentin R. Jr. *H.J. Heinz: A Biography*. Jefferson N.C.: McFarland & Co., 2009.

Sullivan, Wilson. *New England Men of Letters*, New York: Macmillan and Co., 1972.

Thorn, John. *Base Ball in the Garden of Eden: The Secret History of the Early Game.* New York: Simon & Schuster, 2011.

Twain, Mark and Charles Dudley Warner, *The Gilded Age: A Tale of Today*. New York: Nelson Doubleday Inc., 1983. (Reprint of 1873 original edition.)

Vidal, Gore. *1876: A Novel.* New York: Ballantine Books, 1976.

Weymouth, Lally. *America in 1876: The Way We Were.* New York: Vintage Books, 1976.

Wiegand, Steve. *U.S. History for Dummies* (4th ed.) Hoboken, N.J.: Wiley & Sons, 2019.

The West:

-- *The Wild West.* New York: Time-Life Books, 1993.

Abbott, E.C., and Helena H. Smith. *We Pointed Them North.* Chicago: R.R. Donnelley & Sons, 1991.

Brown, Dee. *The American West.* New York: Touchstone Press, 1994.

Bunnell, David Hugh. *Good Friday on the Rez.* New York: St. Martin's Press, 2017.

Cunningham, Eugene. *Triggernometry: A Gallery of Gunfighters.* Norman Ok.: University of Oklahoma Press, 1996.

Dykstra, Robert R. *The Cattle Towns.* Lincoln, Neb.: University of Nebraska Press, 1968.

Foy, Eddie and Alvin F. Barlow. *Clowning Through Life.* New York: E.F. Dutton & Co., 1928.

Frates, Kent F. "The Hero or Goat of Beecher Island." *True West magazine,* Vol. 68, No. 5 (June 2021), pp. 46-49.

Goetzmann, William H. and William N. Goetzmann. *The West of the Imagination.* New York: W.W. Norton & Company, 1986.

Hyslop, Stephen G. *The Old West.* Washington D.C.: National Geographic, 2015.

Isenberg, Andrew C. *The Destruction of the Bison: An Environmental History, 1750-1920.* Cambridge UK: Cambridge University Press, 2001.

Hornaday, William T. *The Extermination of the American Bison.* Washington D.C.: Federal Printing Office, 1889.

Kyle, Chris (with William Doyle). *American Gun: A History of the U.S. in Ten Firearms.* New York: William Morrow, 2013.

Miller, Nyle H. and Joseph W. Snell. *Why the West Was Wild: A Contemporary Look at the Antics of Some Highly Publicized Cowtown Personalities.* Norman Ok.: University of Oklahoma Press, 1963.

Moulton, Candy. *The Writer's Guide to Everyday Life in the Wild West from 1840-1900.* Cincinnati: Writer's Digest Books, 1999.

O'Brien, Dan. *Buffalo for the Broken Heart: Restoring Life to a Black Hills Ranch.* New York: Random House, 2001.

O'Brien, Dan. *Great Plains Bison.* Lincoln, Neb.: University of Nebraska Press, 2017.

Parks, Rita. *The Western Hero in Film and Television.* Ann Arbor, Mich.: UMI Research Press, 1982.

Parsons, Chuck, and Norman Wayne Brown. *A Lawless Breed: John Wesley Hardin, Texas Reconstruction and Violence in the Wild West.* Denton Tx.: University of North Texas Press, 2013.

Rosa, Joseph G. *The Gunfighter: Man or Myth?* Norman, Ok.: University of Oklahoma Press, 1989.

Rosa, Joseph G. *Age of the Gunfighter: Men and Weapons of the Frontier, 1840-1900.* Norman, Ok.: University of Oklahoma Press, 2002.

Schoenberger, Dale T. *The Gunfighters.* Caldwell, Idaho: The Caxton Printers, 1976.

Sennett, Ted. *Great Hollywood Westerns.* New York: Henry N. Adams Inc., 1990.

Slotkin, Richard. *The Fatal Environment: The Myth of the Frontier in the Age of Industrialization, 1800-1890.* New York: Athenium Books, 1985.

Slotkin, Richard. *Gunfighter Nation: The Myth of the Frontier in Twentieth-Century America.* Norman, Ok.: University of Oklahoma Press, 1998.

Smits, David D. "The Frontier Army and the Destruction of the Buffalo,

1865-1883." *Western History Quarterly*, Vol. 25, No. 3 (Autumn 1994), pp. 312-338.

Sutton, Fred E. and A.B. MacDonald. *Hands Up!* Indianapolis: Bobbs-Merrill Co., 1926

Trachtman, Paul. *The Gunfighters.* Alexandria Va.: Time-Life Books, 1974.

Turner, Frederick Jackson. *The Frontier in American History.* New York: Henry Holt and Company, 1921.

Wheeler, Keith. *The Townsmen.* New York: Time-Life Books, 1975.

Winkler, Adam. *Gunfight: The Battle over the Right to Bear Arms in America.* New York: W.W. Norton & Co., 2013.

Wister, Owen. *The Virginian: A Horseman of the Plains.* New York: Bantam Books, 1985. (Reprint of 1901 original edition.)

Bat Masterson/Sweetwater Texas:

Cobb, Irvin S. *Exit Laughing.* Ann Arbor (Mich.): Gryphon Books, 1971.

DeArment, Robert K. *Bat Masterson: The Man and the Legend.* Norman Ok.: University of Oklahoma Press, 1979.

DeArment, Robert K. *Gunfighter in Gotham: Bat Masterson's New York City Years.* Norman Ok.: University of Oklahoma Press, 2009.

DeMattos, Jack. *Masterson and Roosevelt.* College Station (Tx.): Creative Publishing Co., 1984.

Dixon, Olive K. *Life of "Billy" Dixon.* Austin Tx.: State House Press, 1987.

Harris, Sallie B. *Hidetown in the Texas Panhandle: 100 Years in Wheeler County and Panhandle of Texas.* Hereford Tx: Pioneer Book Publishers, Inc., 1968.

Hening H.B. (ed). *George Curry, 1861-1947: An Autobiography.* Albuquerque New Mexico: University of New Mexico Press, 1986.

Lewis, Alfred Henry. *The Sunset Trail.* New York: A.L. Burt Company, 1905.

Little, Edward Campbell. "The Battle of Adobe Walls." *Pearson's Magazine,* January 1908, pp. 74-85.

Manz, William H. "Benjamin Cardozo Meets Gunslinger Bat Masterson." Albany, NY: *New York State Bar Assn. Journal,* Vol. 76, No. 6 (July/August 2004), pp. 9-17.

Masterson, William Barclay. *Famous Gunfighters of the Western Frontier.* Mineola NY: Dover Publications, 2009.

O'Connor, Richard. *Bat Masterson.* Garden City, NY: Doubleday and Co., 1957.

Sheffy, Lester Fields. *The Life and Times of Timothy Dwight Hobart, 1855-1935.* Canyon Tx.: Panhandle-Plains Historical Society, 1950.

Thompson, George G. *Bat Masterson: The Dodge City Years.* Fort Hays Ks.: Fort Hays State University Masters Thesis, Spring, 1939.

Wyatt Earp/Dodge City:

Barra, Allen. *Inventing Wyatt Earp: His Life and Many Legends.* Lincoln (Neb.): University of Nebraska Press, 2008.

Bell, Bob Boze. *The Illustrated Life & Times of Wyatt Earp* (4th ed.). Peoria (Az.): Tri Star-Boze, 2000.

Bell, Bob Boze. "Wyatt Earp in Hollywood." *True West Magazine*, Vol. 62, No. 10 (October 2015), pp. 20-30.

Boessenecker, John. *Ride the Devil's Herd: Wyatt Earp's Epic Battle Against the West's Biggest Outlaw Gang.* Toronto (Canada): Hanover Square Press, 2020.

Boyer, Glen (ed.). *I Married Wyatt Earp: The Recollections of Josephine Sarah Marcus Earp.* Tucson, Az.: University of Arizona Press, 1981.

Burns, Walter Noble. *Tombstone, An Iliad of the Southwest.* New York: Grosset & Dunlap, 1927.

Clavin, Tom. *Dodge City: Wyatt Earp, Bat Masterson and the Wickedest Town in the American West.* New York: St. Martin's Press, 2017.

Clavin, Tom. *Tombstone: The Earp Brothers, Doc Holliday, and the Vendetta Ride from Hell.* New York: St. Martin's Press, 2020

Dworkin, Mark J. *American Mythmaker: Walter Noble Burns and the Legends of Billy the Kid, Wyatt Earp and Joaquin Murrieta.* Norman Ok.: University of Oklahoma Press, 2015.

Guinn, Jeff. The *Last Gunfight: The Real Story of the Shootout at the O.K. Corral—and How it Changed the American West.* New York: Simon & Schuster, 2011.

Isenberg, Andrew C. *Wyatt Earp: A Vigilante Life.* New York: Hill and Wang, 2013.

Lake, Stuart. *Wyatt Earp, Frontier Marshal* (reprint of 1931 original.) New York: Pocket Books, 1994.

Markley, Bill. *Wyatt Earp and Bat Masterson: Lawmen of the Legendary West.* Helena Mt.: TwoDot Publishing, 2019.

Palenske, Garner A. *Wyatt Earp in San Diego: Life After Tombstone.* Santa Ana Ca.: Graphic Publishers, 2011.

Stephens, John Richard (ed.). *Wyatt Earp Speaks!* New York: Fall River Press, 2015.

Tefertiller, Casey. *Wyatt Earp: The Man Behind the Legend.* New York: MJF Books, 1997.

Vestal, Stanley. *Dodge City: Queen of Cowtowns.* Lincoln Neb.: University of Nebraska Press, 1998.

Walsh, Raoul. *Each Man in His Time.* New York: Farrar, Straus and Giroux, 1974.

Wright, Robert H. *Dodge City, The Cowboy Capital and the Great Southwest.* Wichita Ks.: The Wichita Eagle Press, 1913.

Young, Roy B., Gary L. Roberts and Casey Tefertiller. *A Wyatt Earp Anthology: Long May His Story Be Told.* Denton, Tx.: University of North Texas Press, 2019.

George Armstrong Custer/ Little Big Horn:

Brown, Dee. *Bury My Heart at Wounded Knee: An Indian History of the American West.* New York: Holt, Rinehart & Winston, 1970.

Connell, Evan S. *Son of the Morning Star: Custer and the Little Bighorn.* New York: Harper & Row, 1984.

Custer, Elizabeth B. *"Boots and Saddles," or Life in Dakota with General Custer.* New York: Harper & Brothers, 1885.

Custer, Elizabeth B. *Following the Guidon.* New York: Harper and Brothers Publishers, 1899.

Custer, George A. *My Life on the Plains* (reprint of original 1874 ed.). New York: Promontory Press, 1995.

Donovan, James. *A Terrible Glory: Custer and the Little Bighorn.* New York: Back Bay Books, 2008.

Elliott, Michael A. *Custerology: The Enduring Legacy of the Indian Wars and George Armstrong Custer*. Chicago: The University of Chicago Press, 2007.

Gray, John S. *Centennial Campaign: The Sioux War of 1876*. Norman, Ok.: University of Oklahoma Press, 1976.

Hatch, Thom. *The Last Days of George Armstrong Custer*. New York: St. Martin's Press, 2015.

Hunt, Frazier, and Robert Hunt (ed.) *I Fought with Custer: The Story of Sergeant Windolph, Last Survivor of the Battle of the Little Big Horn*. Lincoln, Neb.: University of Nebraska Press, 1987.

Kazanjian, Howard, and Chris Enss. *None Wounded, None Missing, All Dead: The Story of Elizabeth Bacon Custer*. Guilford Ct.: TwoDot Publishing, 2011.

Leckie, Shirley. *Elizabeth Bacon Custer and the Making of a Myth*. Norman, Ok.: University of Oklahoma Press, 1993.

Liddic, Bruce R. (ed.) *I Buried Custer: The Diary of Pvt. Thomas Coleman, 7th U.S. Cavalry*. College Station (Tx.): Creative Publishing, 1979.

McMurtry, Larry. *Custer*. New York: Simon & Schuster, 2012.

Merington, Marguerite (ed.) *The Custer Story: The Life and Intimate Letters of General Custer and His Wife Elizabeth*. New York: Devin-Adair Co., 1940.

Philbrick, Nathaniel. *The Last Stand: Custer, Sitting Bull and the Battle of the Little Bighorn*. New York: Viking Press, 2010.

Powers, Thomas. *The Killing of Crazy Horse*. New York: Alfred P. Knopf, 2010.

Utley, Robert M. *Custer: Cavalier in Buckskin*. Norman, Ok.: University of Oklahoma Press, 2001.

Utley, Robert M. *The Lance and the Shield: The Life and Times of Sitting Bull*. New York: Henry Holt & Co., 1993.

Utley, Robert M. and Wilcomb E. Washburn. *The American Heritage History of the Indian Wars*. New York: American Heritage/Bonanza Books, 1977.

Van de Water, Frederic F. *Glory Hunter: A Life of General Custer*. Lincoln Neb.: University of Nebraska Press, 1934.

Welch, James, and Paul Stekler. *Killing Custer: The Battle of the Little Bighorn and the Fate of the Plains Indians*. New York: Penguin Books, 1995.

Whittaker, Frederick. *A Complete Life of Gen. George A. Custer*. New York: Sheldon & Company, 1876.

Buffalo Bill Cody/Warbonnet Creek:

Bricklin, Julia. *The Notorious Life of Ned Buntline: A Tale of Murder, Betrayal, and the Creation of Buffalo Bill.* Guilford, Ct.: TwoDot, 2020.

Carter, Robert A. *Buffalo Bill Cody: The Man Behind the Legend.* New York: John Wiley & Sons, Inc., 2000.

Cody, William F. *Buffalo Bill's Life Story: An Autobiography.* New York: Farrar and Rinehart, 1920.

Cody, William F. *Life of the Hon. William F. Cody, Known as Buffalo Bill the Famous Hunter, Scout and Guide: An Autobiography.* Hartford, Ct.: American Publishing Co., 1879.

Cody, William F. *Story of the Wild West and Campfire Chats.* Philadelphia: Historical Publishing Co., 1888.

Cody, William F., *True Tales of the Plains.* New York: Empire Books Co., 1908.

Cody, William F. and William Lightfoot Visscher, *Life and Adventures of Buffalo Bill, Col. William F. Cody.* Chicago: John A. Stanton, publishers, 1917.

Davies, General Henry E. *Ten Days on the Plains.* New York: private publication, 1871.

Hall, Roger A. *Performing the Wild Frontier, 1870-1906.* Cambridge, UK: Cambridge University Press, 2001.

Hedren, Paul L. "The Contradictory Legacies of Buffalo Bill's First Scalp for Custer." *Montana: The Magazine of Western History,* Vol. 55, No. 1 (Spring 2005), pp. 16-35.

Hedren, Paul L. *First Scalp for Custer: The Skirmish at Warbonnet Creek.* Lincoln Neb.: University of Nebraska Press, 1980.

Kasson, Joy S. *Buffalo Bill's Wild West: Celebrity, Memory and Popular History.* New York: Hill and Wang, 2000.

King, Charles. *Campaigning with Crook and Stories of Army Life.* New York: Harper & Brothers, 1890.

Miles, Nelson A. *Personal Recollections and Observations of General Nelson A. Miles.* Chicago: The Werner Company, 1897.

Monaghan, Jay. *The Great Rascal: The Life and Adventures of Ned Buntline.* Boston: Little Brown & Co., 1952.

Peotto, Thomas. *Dark Mimesis: A Cultural History of the Scalping Paradigm.* Vancouver, B.C.: University of British Columbia doctoral thesis, January 2018.

Russell, Don. *The Lives and Legends of Buffalo Bill.* Norman Ok.: University of Oklahoma Press, 1979.

Sagala, Sandra K. *Buffalo Bill on Stage.* Albuquerque NM: University of New Mexico Press, 2008.

Sell, Henry Blackman and Victor Weybright. *Buffalo Bill and the Wild West.* Basin, Wy.: Big Horn Books, 1979.

Sheridan, Philip H. *Personal Memoirs of Phillip Henry Sheridan, General, United States Army (Vol. II).* New York: D. Appleton and Company, 1902.

Warren, Louis S. *Buffalo Bill's America: William Cody and the Wild West Show.* New York: Alfred A. Knopf, 2005.

Wetmore, Helen Cody. *Buffalo Bill, Last of the Great Scouts.* Stamford Ct.: Longmeadow Press, 1994. (unabridged reprint of the 1899 original edition.)

Wild Bill Hickok/Deadwood:

Bell, Bob Boze. *The Illustrated Life & Times of Wild Bill Hickok.* Cave Creek (Az.): Two Roads West, 2018.

Buel, J.W. *Life and Marvelous Adventures of Wild Bill, the Scout (reprint).* London: American Cowboy Books, 2017.

Clavin, Tom. *Wild Bill: The True Story of the American Frontier's First Gunfighter.* New York: St. Martin's Press, 2019.

Connelley, William Elsey. *Wild Bill and His Era: The Life and Adventures of James Butler Hickok* (2nd ed.).New York: Cooper Square Publishers, 1972.

Dexter, Pete. *Deadwood: A Novel.* New York: Vintage Books, 2005

Griffith, T.D. (ed.) *Deadwood: The Best Writings on the Most Notorious Town in the West.* Guilford, Ct.: TwoDot Publishing, 2010.

Jones, Karen R, *Calamity: The Many Lives of Calamity Jane.* New Haven (Ct.): Yale University Press, 2020.

McLaird, James D. "Calamity Jane, the Life and Legend." *South Dakota History,* Vol. 24, No. 1 (Fall/Winter 1994), pp. 1-19.

McLaird, James D. "'I Know...Because I Was There:' Leander P. Richardson

Reports the Black Hills Gold Rush." *South Dakota History*, Vol. 34, Nos. 3 and 4, Fall/Winter 2001, pp. 239-268.

Nichols, George Ward. "Wild Bill." *Harper's New Monthly Magazine*, Vol. 34, No. 201, February, 1867, pp. 273-286.

Parker, Watson. *Deadwood: The Golden Years.* Lincoln, Neb.: University of Nebraska Press, 1981.

Richardson, Leander P. "A Trip to the Black Hills." *Scribner's Monthly*, Vol. XIII, No. 6 (April 1877), pp. 748-756.

Richardson, Leander P. "Last Days of a Plainsman." *True West Magazine*, Vol. 13, No. 2 (November-December 1965), pp. 22-23; 44-45.

Rosa, Joseph G. "George Ward Nichols and the Legend of Wild Bill Hickok." *Arizona and the West*, Vol. 19, No. 2 (Summer 1977), pp. 135-162.

Rosa, Joseph G. *They Called Him Wild Bill: The Life and Adventures of James Butler Hickok* (2nd ed.). Norman, OK.: University of Oklahoma Press, 1974.

Rosa, Joseph G. *Wild Bill Hickok, Gunfighter: An Account of Hickok's Gunfights.* Norman, Ok.: University of Oklahoma Press, 2001.

Rosa, Joseph G. *Wild Bill Hickok, the Man and his Myth.* Lawrence, Ks.: University Press of Kansas, 1996.

Wilstach, Frank J. *Wild Bill Hickok, Prince of the Pistoleers.* New York: Doubleday, 1926.

Woodard, Aaron. *The Revenger: The Life and Times of Wild Bill Hickok.* Guilford, Ct.: TwoDot Publishing, 2018.

James-Younger Gang/Northfield:

Croy, Homer. *Cole Younger: Last of the Great Outlaws.* Lincoln, Neb: University of Nebraska Press, 1999.

Edwards, John Newman. "A Terrible Quintette." A reprint of a special supplement originally published in the *St. Louis Dispatch*, Nov. 22, 1873. Manchester, UK: Hurstwood Enterprises Ltd., 2002.

Gardner, Mark Lee. *Shot All to Hell: Jesse James, the Northfield Raid, and the Wild West's Greatest Escape.* New York: William Morrow, 2014.

Goodrich, Thomas. *Black Flag: Guerilla Warfare on the Western Border, 1861-1865.* Bloomington, Ind.: Indiana University Press, 1995.

Huntington, George. *Robber and Hero: The Story of the Northfield Bank Raid.* Northfield, Mn.: Northfield Historical Society Press, 1994.

James, Jesse Jr. *Jesse James, My Father: The First and Only True Story of His Adventures Ever Written.* Cleveland: Buckeye Publishing Co., 1899.

Koblas, John. *The Great Cole Younger & Frank James Historical Wild West Show.* St. Cloud, Mn.: North Star Press, 2002.

Muehlberger, James P. *The Lost Cause: The Trials of Frank and Jesse James.* Yardley, Pa.: Westholme Publishing, 2013.

Settle, William A. Jr. *Jesse James Was His Name; or, Fact and Fiction Concerning the Careers of the Notorious James Brothers of Missouri.* Lincoln, Ne.: Bison Books, 1977.

Stiles, T.J. *Jesse James: Last Rebel of the Civil War.* New York: Vintage Books, 2003.

Triplett, Frank. Jesse James: *The Life, Times, and Treacherous Death of the Most Infamous Outlaw of All Time.* New York: Skyhorse Publishing, 2013 reprint of 1882 original.

Yeatman, Ted. P. *Frank and Jesse James: The Story Behind the Legend.* Naperville, Il.: Cumberland House Publishing, 2000.

Younger, Cole. *The Story of Cole Younger, by Himself.* CreateSpace Independent Publishing Platform (public domain reprint), 2017.

INDEX

ACKNOWLEDGMENTS

First of all, I'd like to thank me. This was a lot more work than I thought it would be, and my motivation in becoming a journalist and author in the first place was to avoid work. But it's done. And as my old pop used to say, "if it's done, it's good."

Much more deserving of thanks is my wife Cecilia, who once again put up with months of me whining, pouting, fretting, swearing and droning on and on about trivia while grinding out another book. Gracias, Ceil, and I promise, only eight or ten more...

Thanks also to Rob Gunnison, Bobbie Metzger, Steve Capps and Steven and Sue Boudreau for agreeing to read the manuscript chapter by painful chapter; catching goofs; making (mostly) good suggestions, and offering encouragement.These folks have been my friends for a cumulative total of slightly less than 250 years, and they should be profusely thanked just for that, let alone their help on the book. Plus, none of them look a day over 90.

I owe a huge debt of gratitude to Bruce Bortz and Bancroft Books. Bruce is not only thoughtful, imaginative and thorough, he's one of the precious few publishers left in America who care about the worth of a story for its own sake. Similar appreciation is due Tracy Copes, for her most excellent cover design and handsome layout of the rest of the book.

Thanks to Warren Stricker and Millie Vanover of the Research Center at the Panhandle-Plains Historical Museum in Canyon, Texas. Thanks also to Mike Watts at the U.S. Forest Service office in Chadron, Nebraska; Sam Hanna at the Buffalo Bill Center of the West; and the folks at the convention and visitors bureaus in Deadwood and Dodge City. The staffs at the Arizona, Missouri, Kansas and Northfield, Minnesota historical societies were generous with their time and knowledge, as were the folks at Carleton College's Gould Library.

And at the risk of leaving important people out, thanks to just some of the biographers of Wild West figures who inspired me to take a whack at it myself: Robert K. DeArment on Bat Masterson; Casey Tefertiller and Andrew Isenberg on Wyatt Earp; Robert M. Utley and James Donovan on George Custer; Louis S. Warren and Don Russell on Buffalo Bill; Joseph G. Rosa on Wild Bill, and Mark Lee Gardner, T.J. Stiles and Ted P. Yeatman on the James-Younger Gang.

Finally, thanks Granddad.

ABOUT THE AUTHOR

Steve Wiegand is an award-winning journalist and history writer. His 35-year journalism career was spent at the at the *San Diego Evening Tribune*, where he was chief political writer; *San Francisco Chronicle*, where he was state capitol bureau chief; and *Sacramento Bee*, where he was a special projects writer and politics columnist.

He is the author, co-author or contributing author of nine books, including *The Dancer, the Dreamers and the Queen of Romania*; *U.S. History for Dummies*; the *Mental Floss History of the World; The American Revolution for Dummies* and *Lessons from the Great Depression for Dummies.*

He lives in Arizona, where he enjoys playing poker and the harmonica, although usually not at the same time.